Acknowledgments

The author would like to acknowledge the contribution of Glenn S. Coffey, JD, Ph.D. from the University of North Florida to the creation of this guide. Always, his encouragement and support act as an unparalleled foundation.

In addition, the author would like to thank Lisa Bruno, representative from Fastcase, for providing a cost-efficient and reliable source of case law information.

Lisa Anne Zilney, Ph.D.
Southern Illinois University

Guide to Criminal Procedure
for Illinois

Lisa Anne Zilney
Southern Illinois University

THOMSON
WADSWORTH

Australia • Canada • Mexico • Singapore • Spain • United Kingdom • United States

Executive Editor: Sabra Horne
Development Editor: Julie Sakaue
Assistant Editor: Jana Davis
Editorial Assistant: Elise Smith
Marketing Manager: Terra Schultz
Marketing Assistant: Annabelle Yang

Project Manager, Editorial Production: Megan E. Hansen
Print Buyer: Doreen Suruki
Permissions Editor: Sarah Harkrader
Cover Designer: Yvo Riezebos
Cover Image: Donovan Reese/Getty Images
Text and Cover Printer: Thomson West

For more information about our products,
contact us at:
Thomson Learning Academic Resource Center
1-800-423-0563

For permission to use material from this text or product,
submit a request online at
http://www.thomsonrights.com.

Any additional questions about permissions
can be submitted by email to
thomsonrights@thomson.com.

Library of Congress Control Number: 2004112622

ISBN: 0-534-64346-9

Thomson Wadsworth
10 Davis Drive
Belmont, CA 94002-3098
USA

Asia
Thomson Learning
5 Shenton Way #01-01
UIC Building
Singapore 068808

Australia/New Zealand
Thomson Learning
102 Dodds Street
Southbank, Victoria 3006
Australia

Canada
Nelson
1120 Birchmount Road
Toronto, Ontario M1K 5G4
Canada

Europe/Middle East/South Africa
Thomson Learning
High Holborn House
50/51 Bedford Row
London WC1R 4LR
United Kingdom

Latin America
Thomson Learning
Seneca, 53
Colonia Polanco
11560 Mexico D.F.
Mexico

Spain/Portugal
Paraninfo
Calle/Magallanes, 25
28015 Madrid, Spain

Introduction

There are two interesting sections of the Illinois Constitution that do not fit nicely within the confines of the overall discussion of criminal procedure in Illinois. Thus, each will be provided here and should serve as a guide of the underlying principles of the Constitution when reviewing this guide:

> Every person shall find a certain remedy in the laws for all injuries and wrongs which he receives to his person, privacy, property or reputation. He shall obtain justice by law freely, completely, and promptly (Article One, Section Twelve, Illinois Constitution).

> A frequent recurrence to the fundamental principles of civil government is necessary to preserve the blessings of liberty. These blessings cannot endure unless the people recognize their corresponding individual obligations and responsibilities (Article One, Section Twenty-Three, Illinois Constitution).

OVERVIEW

This guide elaborates criminal procedure in the state of Illinois. As such, this guide provides:

(1)   Detailed examination of the Illinois Constitution;

(2)   An elaboration of the Illinois Revised Statutes; and

(3)   Illinois cases to develop further an understanding of criminal procedures and its applications.

CONCEPTUAL FRAMEWORK OF THIS TEXT

Each chapter in this guide is organized in the same format and is designed to parallel issues examined in your text. This guide assumes that you have read materials on criminal procedure and understand the basic principles. Each chapter is organized into sections and each section comprises the following:

(1)   An overview of the main issues addressed in this particular area of criminal procedure. This overview will include relevant sections of the Illinois Constitution as well as a delineation of the applicable Illinois Revised Statutes; and

(2)   One or two cases from the Illinois courts that address specifically the main issues of each section. Each case is prefaced by a brief introduction to alert you to the main criminal procedure addressed by the court. Following each case are several reading comprehension questions to assess your basic knowledge of the case and the facts presented, as well as critical thinking questions designed to further develop your comprehensive of the procedures and their application.

This guide should prove a useful supplement to general criminal procedure and provide you with a more in-depth understanding of the workings of criminal procedure in Illinois.

Table of Contents

Chapter One

Criminal Procedure: The Big Picture

In a constitutional democracy such as the United States, crime control is a balance between the search for truth and a commitment to fairness that limits governmental power. This power is limited by the U.S. Constitution and state constitutions and is interpreted by the U.S. Supreme Court. Historically and presently, balancing result and process creates tension as individual liberties sometimes interfere with community security. Thus, there is a continual shift between government power and individual rights, process and result. What results is a shift in balance between formal and informal criminal procedures, and so long as the general principles put forth in the U.S. Constitution are maintained, the Illinois Constitution may act to expand these individual freedoms. In the quest for truth and fairness, procedure is continually reinterpreted in the state and federal court system.

Because we address here the larger picture, rather than a view from the state level, we will focus primarily on the role of the Constitution. This chapter will review:

(1)   The balance between order and liberty; and

(2)   Laws, discretion, due process, and precedent.

SECTION 1: THE BALANCE

OVERVIEW

In our critical examination of criminal procedure and the government's power over crime control, we must keep in mind that the United States is a constitutional democracy wherein neither a single individual nor a majority of the citizens have power over us as individuals. A balance must continually be struck between community security, which ensures the safety of all community members, and individual autonomy, where individuals have the right of control over themselves and their actions so long as these actions do not compromise the security of the larger community. The balance between government power and individual control is one that is very flexible, changes over time and with historical circumstance, and one that falls within a zone as opposed to a point on a continuum. Thus, the courts move within this balance between order and liberty.

In a constitutional democracy, crime control also depends on the balance between result and process. The result side of this balance involves a search for the truth, consisting of the apprehension, conviction, and punishment of guilty individuals, and the freeing of innocent people caught in the criminal justice system. The process side of the balance involves a commitment to fairness that limits the power of the government and is outlined in the U.S. Constitution and in every state constitution. The Constitution acts as a set of general principles that are interpreted in the final analysis by the U.S. Supreme Court.

Balancing result and process has historically and continues to create tension as individual liberties may interfere with the protection of community security. Thus, on occasion a guilty party will go free in order to ensure that government control stays within its bounds. In a constitutional democracy however, the priority is not crime control, but fair process, except in situations involving extreme emergencies such as war wherein the Bill of Rights can be disregarded. This was evident and continues to be evident during the government's war on drugs and the current war on terrorism which we be discussed later. The foundation of ensuring fairness in procedure is the exclusionary rule which forces the court to throw out evidence of a defendant's guilt if the methods by which the evidence were obtained were in violation of the U.S. or state Constitutions. The exclusionary rule is used only in the United States and while it is at the root of criminal procedure as will be seen in many cases, it is also extremely controversial. No system, historically or currently, has succeeded in balancing perfectly the tension between government power and individual rights.

In the United States, the Constitution became an infamous effort to embed in law a balance between government power and individual liberty. Anti-Federalists however, feared relying on such a general protection, and thus added the Bill of Rights as an amendment to further protect the liberty of individuals against the potential abuses of government power. Each state's Bill of Rights has similar or identical provisions to those in the U.S. Bill of Rights, and it is the role of the state courts to interpret and apply these constitutional provisions as will be illustrated through the examination of cases throughout this guide.

Enhanced government power prior to the 1960s eventually led to the due process revolution which moved the balance back to process and individual rights. Critics argued this created a criminal justice system that was soft on crime and the pendulum began to swing back to result in the early 1970s nationwide. One cannot simply explain the movement between process and result as occurring from the personal beliefs of individual judges. Instead, judges are to defer to the will of the citizenry as expressed by elected officials in a historic principle called judicial restraint. Increasingly judges have accomplished this by deferring to elected branches of government.

CASE

The cases below are consolidated in the wake of People v. Blue, 189 Ill. 2d 99, 138-39 (2000), wherein a unanimous court held that the cumulative effect of prosecutorial misconduct and trial error had deprived the defendant of a fundamentally fair trial and thus warranted reversal notwithstanding overwhelming evidence of defendant's guilt. As you read, keep in mind the balance that must be maintained between process and result.

JUSTICE RARICK delivered the opinion of the court: In Blue, this court recognized that a pervasive pattern of error, engendered in the main by prosecutorial misconduct, had divested defendant of his right to a fair, orderly, and impartial trial, a substantial right that inures to a criminal defendant whether guilty or innocent. In Blue, where the trial was permeated by the presentation of emotionally charged evidence, and the prosecutors "encouraged the jury to return a verdict grounded in emotion, and not a rational deliberation of the facts" (Blue, 189 Ill. 2d at 139), the members of this court, acting "as guardians of constitutional rights and the integrity of the criminal justice system" (Blue, 189 Ill. 2d at 139), reversed and remanded for a new trial. Disposition of the instant cases requires that we further delineate the dimensions of Blue, applying the principles and standards of review utilized in that case.

Consolidated for purposes of appeal are the cases of People v. Cowley, No. 90693, and People v. Parker, No. 90706.

Defendants Cowley and Parker were codefendants of Murray Blue, and their trials involved the same prosecutors. Cowley's case was severed from Blue's and the two were tried simultaneously, but with separate juries. Parker's jury trial took place several months later. Ultimately, Parker and Cowley were each convicted of first degree murder and two counts of attempted murder. In addition, Cowley was convicted of two counts of aggravated battery with a firearm and possession of a controlled substance with intent to deliver; Parker was convicted of two counts of possession of a controlled substance with intent to deliver. The appellate court reversed the convictions of both defendants, relying upon our decision in Blue. In Cowley, the appellate court noted the errors this court had identified in Blue, and the bases of this court's disposition in that case, concluding, "Our supreme court reviewed the exact record before us, and we are bound by its findings of error." Cowley, 317 Ill. App. 3d 834, 842. In Parker, the court similarly stated: "Because the supreme court reviewed a similar record and found error as to identical evidence and similar tactics as evidenced in this record, and found that Blue did not receive a fair trial despite overwhelming evidence of his guilt, we are bound by the findings of the supreme court that the errors were so fundamental to the integrity of the judicial process and of such magnitude that the accused here was denied a fair trial. Accordingly, this defendant's convictions should be reversed as he was denied a fair trial." Parker, 317 Ill. App. 3d at 850.

The records in Parker and Cowley are indeed similar to that of Blue; they are not identical. Defendant Johnson was tried before a jury and convicted of first degree murder and three counts of aggravated discharge of a firearm. The appellate court reversed and remanded, stating: "The defendant claims he was the victim of prosecutorial excess during his murder trial before a jury. He was. He was inaccurately described at trial as a convicted narcotics salesman and a convicted felon. In addition, his failure to testify was argued by inference and his lawyer was referred to as `a professional criminal defense lawyer.' We conclude that serious trial errors, taken in combination, were not harmless beyond a reasonable doubt." Johnson, 317 Ill. App. 3d 666, 667-

68. Thus, the common threads that bind these cases for purposes of appeal are alleged patterns of prosecutorial misconduct and related trial error, the utilization of cumulative-error analysis, and reliance upon this court's opinion in Blue.

The State raises multiple issues, only some of which are actually germane to our disposition of these consolidated cases. Among these are the following arguments. The State contends, "under due process analysis there was no cumulative error that justified the reversal of DeAngelo Johnson's convictions." With respect to defendants Cowley and Parker, the State argues that the appellate court misapplied Blue, as there was "no pervasive pattern of prosecutorial misconduct" in either case and the juries were called upon to return verdicts "based on a dispassionate evaluation of the facts and the complex rules of accountability rather than emotion and sympathy for the victim."

Initially, we note that a pattern of intentional prosecutorial misconduct may so seriously undermine the integrity of judicial proceedings as to support reversal under the plain error doctrine. Indeed, concern over the cumulative effect of errors that "created a pervasive pattern of unfair prejudice," much of it attributable to misconduct of the prosecutors, is what drove this court's analysis in Blue. This court recognized in Blue the "synergistic effect" that multiple errors of this kind can have in a trial. Blue represents an important step this court has taken to stem prosecutorial misconduct, a problem that courts across the country have, for the most part, been unable or unwilling to control. Within this milieu, and against the precedential backdrop of Blue, we now turn our attention to the facts of these consolidated cases. We begin with the cases of Blue's codefendants, Clyde Cowley and Jimmie Parker.

These cases involve two shootings at different times and different locations: the shooting of Victor Young (the first shooting) and, later the same day, the contemporaneous shooting of Officers Daniel Doffyn and Milan Bubalo (the second shooting). The evidence suggests that Young was shot because he sold drugs for a rival street gang and, perhaps, because Blue believed Young had discussed Blue's activities with the police. The officers were later shot as they tried to apprehend Blue, Cowley and Parker as they fled from Blue's apartment. Young testified that, on the day he was shot, he had exchanged words with Blue, who was at the time visible in the first-floor window of an apartment building in Chicago. When Blue produced a gun, Young began to run and was felled by gunshot wounds to the hip or buttocks. From the ground, Young looked behind him and saw Blue run out of the apartment building, accompanied by Cowley and Parker. Parker was holding a weapon and, at Blue's direction, also shot at Young. Young testified that he saw Blue, Cowley and Parker run through a vacant lot. A few minutes later, Young observed a black Lincoln Continental drive north. Young knew the car belonged to Blue. Blue, Cowley, and Parker fled to Blue's apartment which is located across the street from Chicago's 15th District police station. Because Blue had forgotten his keys, he had to break the glass of his front window to gain entry. That resulted in a neighbor's report of a burglary in progress.

Officer Elois Jackson testified that she was at the 15th District police station when she heard a report over her police radio of a burglary in progress. Jackson told the dispatcher she could respond to the call. She and several other police officers proceeded to the apartment building across the street, the location given in the report. Officer Jackson testified that, as she approached the building, she saw Officers Bubalo and Doffyn walking to the front of the building. She entered a gangway at the south side of the building, leading toward its rear. As she reached the far end of the gangway, she was approached by two black males. One carried a gun with his hands extended in front of him. The other male appeared to be unarmed. Jackson keyed in her radio that she had an emergency, pointed her gun at the men, and yelled at them to get on the ground. The unarmed man, later identified as Parker, raised his hands in the air, but did not immediately go to the ground. The other man turned and started to run away. Eventually, Parker followed Jackson's command to get to the ground. As he did so, Jackson heard gunfire. Jackson remained behind the wall of the gangway, with her gun trained on Parker, until other officers arrived.

Officer Bubalo testified that he and Officer Doffyn were in the parking lot of the police station when they learned of the suspected burglary across the street. They went to investigate the reported burglary. Bubalo testified that he went inside the building followed by Doffyn. Officer Bubalo further testified that Doffyn ran down the steps from the first-floor landing and out of the building. According to Bubalo, Doffyn never drew his service weapon at any time. When Bubalo reached the backyard of the building, he saw Doffyn struggling with a black male. Doffyn had the man, whom Bubalo identified in court as Cowley, and Cowley was trying to break free. Almost immediately, Bubalo heard several gunshots fired in quick succession. Both Doffyn and Cowley fell to the ground, with Doffyn lying face down on top of Cowley. Bubalo testified that, just as Doffyn and Cowley dropped, Bubalo himself sustained a gunshot wound to his left hip. As he fell to the ground, Bubalo saw Blue running toward him. Blue fired a gun at Bubalo and Bubalo returned fire. Bubalo fired a total of five shots; one struck Blue in the back of the head. This shot caused Blue to fall face forward to the ground. After Blue fell, Bubalo radioed for help, disarmed Blue, and crawled to the aid of Doffyn and Cowley. Bubalo underwent surgery the next day for a total replacement of his left hip. Officer Doffyn died from a gunshot wound to his head.

Police officers searched the first-floor apartment with the broken front window. Not knowing whether there were other offenders inside, they entered and searched the apartment. No one was inside. In the living room, they found several bags of marijuana on a table and a jacket with .38-caliber bullets in its pocket. In the bedroom, they found plastic bags containing rock cocaine and folded tin packets containing heroin. Also in the bedroom were $5,385 in cash, a scale and a razor blade. An open box of nine-millimeter cartridges lay on the bed. They did not see any mail, receipts, bills or other papers connecting Cowley or Parker to the apartment. A drinking glass on the living room table had Cowley's fingerprint on it. In addition to the foregoing evidence, each defendant gave a statement that was ultimately admitted at his trial. Cowley gave both an oral statement to a police officer, shortly after the shooting, and a subsequent written statement to an assistant State's Attorney at the hospital. Cowley told the assistant State's Attorney that on the afternoon of March 8, 1995, Blue, Parker and Charlie "Chow Mein" pulled up in Blue's car and told Cowley they had to take care of business with Puff, a rival drug dealer infringing on their territory. Blue gave Cowley a loaded .38-caliber gun to protect himself and "watch the others' backs." The four men then went to a building to wait for Puff and his workers. They intended to kill Puff or one of his workers to teach them a lesson. Before Puff or any of his workers arrived, Charlie left the building. Shortly thereafter, Parker saw Charlie talking to Victor Young. Young had sold drugs for Blue in the past, but at the time of the incident was selling drugs for someone else and had been known to "stick up" Blue's workers. Although Young did not work for Puff,

Blue said, "Let's shoot him," and started shooting. As Blue, Parker and Cowley left the building to run to Blue's car, Parker also fired at Young. Cowley still had the .38-caliber gun when they left the scene of the first shooting.

In both Parker's and Cowley's cases, the State utilized an exhibit and evidence which, in Blue, this court held warranted reversal when considered in conjunction with the prosecutors' improper closing argument and testifying objections. More to the point, the prosecutors obtained admission and display of Officer Doffyn's blood- and brain-splattered uniform, they presented the emotionally charged testimony of Officer Doffyn's father, much of which was irrelevant and obviously intended to appeal to the jury's emotions, and they succeeded in compounding these errors by the introduction of transparently inflammatory testimony that served only to highlight the ceremonies and oath associated with Officer Doffyn's service and duties as a police officer, matters irrelevant to defendants' guilt or innocence. During each defendant's trial, the bloodied and brain-splattered uniform of Daniel Doffyn was displayed on a life-size, headless mannequin, which was later taken into the jury room during deliberations. The uniform consisted of Doffyn's shirts, police jacket and bulletproof vest. The clothing was torn as a result of medical treatment rendered to Officer Doffyn.

In Blue, this court found "the potential prejudice of the uniform outweighed its probative value." That pattern was to continue throughout Blue's trial, and it is impossible not to notice it in the trials of Cowley and Parker as well. In the trial of these cases, as in Blue, the testimony of Officer Doffyn's father, Roger Doffyn, was presented by the State. This court in Blue noted that the State had apparently elicited a portion of Mr. Doffyn's testimony to: "highlight the poignancy of the family's loss and to suggest to the jury that the family's pain could be alleviated by a guilty verdict. Moreover, the knowledge of these facts surely heightened the impact of the State's emotional closing argument on the jury."

In the trial of these cases, as in Blue, the prosecutors presented the testimony of Commander Joseph Delopez of the Chicago police department. In Cowley's case, Delopez testified in person; in Parker's trial, the testimony was offered by way of stipulation. As part of Delopez's testimony, the oath of office sworn by Officer Doffyn was read to the jury. Delopez was also permitted to testify that Doffyn's police badge was retired and is now displayed in the "honored star case" at Chicago police department headquarters. This court in Blue held that the testimony was irrelevant to the issue of guilt or innocence and speculated whether the evidence was elicited "by design" to intensify the State's "nakedly prejudicial" closing argument which followed. This court's comments in Blue obviously apply to the instant cases as well.

We find no meaningful differences between these three instances of error identified in Blue and their occurrence and impact in the trials of Cowley and Parker. As the State notes, one kind of error identified in the evidentiary portion of Blue's trial is not present in either Parker's or Cowley's case. The juries in these cases were not exposed to the prosecutors' "testifying objections" during the cross-examination of Etoya Nelson. In a bit of wishful advocacy, the State suggests that this violation of the advocate-witness rule was the "most egregious error" identified in Blue. While the prosecutors' conduct in this respect was undoubtedly unprofessional and improper, and certainly contributed to this court's decision in Blue, the error does not bear the weight the State attributes to it. Indeed, the predominant feature of this court's cumulative error analysis in Blue concerned the prosecutors' relentless appeal to the jurors' passions and emotions, culminating in a "nakedly prejudicial" closing argument.

We now consider the State's closing arguments in these cases, and we begin with the State's closing argument in Parker's trial. There is no mistaking that much of the argument was aimed at directly at the sympathies of the jury or was intended to evoke outrage. Though the prosecutor did not explicitly ask the jury to send a message of support to law enforcement, the jury could not have missed the import of his argument, which was clear from the outset:

"In March of 1995, Daniel Doffyn was a 40 year old rookie police officer. And you have learned, ladies and gentlemen, over the course of the last few days that on March 8, 1995, he was more than just a 40 year old rookie police officer. You have learned, ladies and gentlemen, that he was a hero. He risked his life in the backyard at 750 North Lorel as did his partner, Milan Bubalo[,] to serve and to protect the people who lived in the 15th District. And you have also learned, ladies and gentlemen, that in March of 1995, this guy sitting right over here was a gun tooting, drug dealing cop killer. And while Dan Doffyn's duty and oath was to serve and protect, Jimmie Parker's duties was to maim, kill and destroy." The prosecutor's theme and emotional appeal continued as he discussed the events immediately preceding the shooting of Officer Doffyn: "Dan Doffyn is now struggling with Clyde Cowley as Milan Bubalo told you. And Dan Doffyn was just doing his job. And as he struggled with Dan, with Clyde, Dan Doffyn, who looked like this when he was sworn in to be a police officer for us, to serve us, and to protect us, later looked like this with his head shaved at the Cook County Hospital where they looked at that horrible gunshot wound to his skull. And that shiny bright uniform is covered in blood and brain matter. And a 40 year old hero falls to the ground. And within hours he's dead."

We must consider the foregoing remarks in conjunction with others in the prosecutor's well-orchestrated argument-companion comments which were clearly intended to do service to the same theme and achieve the same end of arousing the jury's passion and outrage. Although these isolated comments might otherwise occupy the margins of proper argument as exhortations to fearlessly administer justice, an overview of the prosecutor's argument reveals their dichotomous presentation was likely calculated to avoid the appearance of urging the jurors to use their verdict to send a message of support to the police, a tactic that this court deemed improper in Blue. Referring to Parker, Cowley and Blue explicitly, and unidentified others implicitly, the prosecutor in this case stated: "They think they run this society. Ladies and gentlemen, we are going to ask that you respond affirmatively that they do not. We as a society do not have to live in their twisted world. We do not have to accept their values. We don't have to allow that to happen in our community. We don't have to allow these guys blasting sawed off shotguns at other human beings. We as a people can stand together and say, no, you're not going to do it here. And if you do, you have the-you will be held responsible for your actions."

To the extent that the concept of general deterrence is employed in our criminal justice system, it is generally associated with punishment and imposition of sentence. The broader problems of crime in society should not be the focus of a jury considering the guilt or innocence of an individual defendant, lest the remediation of society's problems distract jurors from the awesome responsibility with which they are charged. We are aware that courts have, in the past, both sanctioned and condemned prosecutors' exhortations to "send a message" that crime in general will not be tolerated.

The prosecutor also mischaracterized evidence and the applicable law, and suggested that the defense was deceptive in its dealings with the jurors. The prosecutor repeatedly stated that defendants had "celebrated" by drinking beer upon their return to Blue's apartment after the first shooting. There was no evidence that Parker, by drinking beer after the first shooting, was "celebrating death." This is simply another instance of the prosecutor's tactic of attempting to stir outrage in the jury. At one point in his argument, when he was discussing the law of accountability, the prosecutor incorrectly advised the jury that Parker's state of mind was irrelevant to guilt or innocence, then, after an objection was overruled, suggested that the defense was engaging in deception or trying to confuse the jury. Unless predicated on evidence that defense counsel behaved unethically, it is improper for a prosecutor to accuse defense counsel of attempting to create reasonable doubt by confusion, misrepresentation, or deception. Later in rebuttal argument, the prosecutor again implied (ironically) that the defense was interested in something other than a result grounded on the applicable law. Although instances of identified error in the prosecutor's closing argument at Parker's trial are already legion, we note, in conclusion, two final examples of irrelevant argument obviously intended to inflame the passions of jurors. In two instances, early in his closing argument, the prosecutor made reference to a school's proximity to the location where the defendants parked upon their return to Blue's apartment. The proximity of the school to Blue's apartment was irrelevant to any issue properly before the jury. Finally, as in Blue, the prosecutor interjected references to Officer Doffyn's family that, given their context, can only be construed as strained attempts to invoke the jury's sympathy and thus influence its decision.

As in Blue, we see in this case cumulative error and a pervasive pattern of unfair prejudice that denied defendant a fair trial and cast doubt upon the reliability of the judicial process. We note that the prejudice in this case, as in Blue, was engendered in the main by prosecutorial misconduct. As in Blue, the coalescence of improper, emotion-laden evidence, and inflammatory argument obviously designed to exploit that evidence, created a synergism of parallel errors. As in Blue, a new trial is necessary in this case to preserve and protect the integrity of the judicial process, as "the trial court allowed the guilty verdict to rest on considerations other than the evidence alone." Thus, we affirm the judgment of the appellate court in cause No. 90706.

We now turn our attention to Clyde Cowley's case. Many of the errors we have noticed in Blue's and Parker's trials occurred in Cowley's trial as well. Therefore, our discussion of the legal principles applicable thereto applies with equal force to disposition of the State's appeal in cause No. 90693. Of course, Cowley was tried simultaneously with Blue; therefore, with the exception of the prosecutors' violation of the advocate-witness rule, the identical evidentiary errors identified in Blue were also present in Cowley's trial. Specifically, Cowley's trial was tainted by the display of Doffyn's bloodstained, brain-splattered uniform and the irrelevant, inflammatory portions of testimony given by Roger Doffyn and Commander Joseph Delopez. There are also striking parallels in the prosecutors' closing arguments in the three trials. The prosecutor included the same irrelevant reference to the nearby grammar school. We see in the prosecutor's closing argument the same exhortation to "send a message" to the community. Finally, as he did in Parker's closing argument, the prosecutor in Cowley's case ended his argument by casting the jury's decision as a choice between good and evil.

We have discussed the legal principles applicable to comments of this kind, and we need not reiterate them here. Suffice it to say that these remarks are improper. Their prejudice is enhanced by the parallel evidence the State adduced in this case. Although we acknowledge that much of the middle portion of the State's argument was properly based upon relevant evidence and represents a studied and laudable discussion of principles of accountability, we believe that the coalescence of the factors we have discussed in this opinion requires a new trial and affirmance of the appellate court's judgment, as a means of preserving the integrity of the judicial process. Thus, we affirm the judgment of the appellate court in cause No. 90693.

Before turning our attention to DeAngelo Johnson's case, we feel compelled to reiterate that prosecutorial misconduct, such as that which permeated the trials of Blue, Parker, and Cowley, undermines the very foundations of our criminal justice system. Our system of justice requires that a defendant's guilt or innocence be determined based upon relevant evidence and legal principles, upon the application of reason and deliberation by a jury, not the expression of misdirected emotion or outrage by a mob. Though perhaps not as egregious as the prosecutors' misconduct in these cases, we are seeing such behavior with an "alarming" frequency, which "causes legitimate public concerns regarding the fairness and integrity" of criminal trials. Misconduct on the part of prosecutors cannot be allowed to continue unchecked. To call it "error" is to mischaracterize it, as it represents nothing less than an attempt to subvert a defendant's fundamental right to a fair trial. Multiple instances of this kind of conduct in the course of a criminal trial threaten the trustworthiness and reputation of the judicial process, and this court will take corrective action to preserve the integrity of the process. We mean it as no hollow warning when we say that prosecutors risk reversal of otherwise proper convictions when they engage in conduct of this kind.

We note that our decision in Blue does signal our intolerance of pervasive prosecutorial misconduct that deliberately undermines the process by which we determine a defendant's guilt or innocence.

REVIEW SECTION

READING COMPREHENSION

Articulate the claims of prosecutorial misconduct discussed in each case.

What reasoning was employed by the Supreme Court of Illinois to warrant reversal and remand further proceedings?

THINKING CRITICALLY

Do you believe the Supreme Court of Illinois leaned more toward process or result in deciding this case? Articulate your position.

SECTION 2: LAWS, DISCRETION, DUE PROCESS, AND PRECEDENT

OVERVIEW

As the balance shifts between process and result, so does the balance between formal and informal criminal procedures. Formal criminal procedure is concerned with the rules as written in the Constitution, laws, judicial precedents, and other written sources. Conversely, informal criminal procedure or discretionary decision making is concerned with unwritten rules made by professionals based on training and experience. Informal criminal procedure is how the system works on a day-to-day basis with each step creating a decision for a professional in the criminal justice system. The only limit to discretionary decision making is that it cannot violate the general principles put forth in the U.S. Constitution.

Discretionary decision making is extremely important in softening written rules, yet fairness and predictability require the certainty and protection provided by such rules. In essence, informal criminal procedures are used to counter balance actions that technically violate a written rule but were not intended by the legislature to be illegal. It is impossible to predict the myriad of ramifications of each statute enacted. Thus, discretion and written law work together to promote a balance between process and result intended to capture the spirit of legislation.

Discretion however, is not entirely discretionary. The objective basis requirement ensures that the government employ facts to support each restraint on individual liberty. In addition, as the limit to be imposed on individuals increases, so does the fact basis required for support. The law may only deprive an individual of life, liberty, privacy, and property according to fair procedures, known as hearing before condemnation. Such judicial review, or review by the court of the actions of other branches of government to ensure such actions comply with the Constitution, is essential to the legal system. This review occurs at all stages of the criminal justice system and is known as due process.

According to Article One, Section Two of the Illinois Constitution, due process entails:

> No person shall be deprived of life, liberty or property without due process of law.

In order to maximize fairness and predictability, judges are bound by *stare decisis*. This requires judges to adhere to the precedent of either their own court or superior courts within their jurisdiction. While courts do alter precedent they do so reluctantly and by indicating that a prior decision does not apply to the facts of the case in question. Once a lower court has determined a finding, the defendant can appeal a conviction by requesting a higher court to review the action. Most requests to review decisions of lower courts made to the U.S. Supreme Court are based on writs of certiorari which involves review of a case with important constitutional issues. These Constitutional issues are of main concern in a Supreme Court review, rather than individual guilt or innocence.

CASE

In *Illinois v. Washington,* the question is whether due process is implicated in a claim of innocence based upon new evidence so as to permit the claim to be raised in a petition under the Post-Conviction Hearing Act (725 ILCS 5/122-1). The Supreme Court of Illinois holds that it is.

PEOPLE V. WASHINGTON
Supreme Court of Illinois
665 N.E.2d 1330 (1996)

Justice FREEMAN delivered the opinion of the court.

In 1982, Kurtis Washington was sentenced to 25 years in prison for murdering Tony Hightie. Hightie had been murdered outside his home in Chicago shortly after 9 p.m. on May 9, 1980. Washington was implicated in the crime by Donna McClure, Hightie's girlfriend, and Ronald Tapes. McClure and Tapes witnessed the murder. At trial, they said that they had been sitting in a parked car near Hightie's home when they were approached by a man. The man said that he was looking for someone named Will. When McClure and Tapes proved no help, the man approached Hightie just as he left his home. Hightie had been wearing a jacket and hat that belonged to Tapes' brother who was named William. McClure and Tapes said that after a few words with Hightie, the man shot him. The man, McClure and Tapes said, was Washington. Washington's defense was that he had been at a grocery store at the time of Hightie's murder. The store cashier, a person who had accompanied Washington, and Washington's mother all testified to that fact.

The appellate court affirmed the conviction and sentence on direct review (No. 1-82-1868 (unpublished order under Supreme Court Rule 23)). In 1990, Washington filed a post-conviction petition, alleging nine grounds of error, six of which asserted ineffective assistance of trial counsel. One of the grounds was that Washington's trial counsel, a private attorney who also served as Washington's appellate counsel, failed to investigate evidence that someone other than Washington murdered Hightie. The claim was supported with an affidavit of Jacqueline Martin dated March 3, 1990. Evidence was permitted on that as well as the other ineffective-assistance claims. The trial judge held an in camera hearing in which he considered Martin's testimony. Underlying the claim at issue in this appeal is the substance of that testimony.

Martin told how Hightie had been shot after having been mistaken for someone else. Martin, who was 16 years old at the time, told how she had been present when Marcus Halsey, then her boyfriend, and Frank Caston had left Halsey's house to revenge an earlier beating of Halsey's brother. She, Halsey, Caston, and Caston's girlfriend drove in a car to an alley in a neighborhood in Chicago. She later learned that it happened to be the neighborhood where Hightie lived. Martin told how, after Halsey and Caston left the car, she had heard two gunshots, and, when the two returned, she had heard Halsey say "it was the wrong guy." Halsey and Caston later changed clothes, discarding in another alley what they had earlier worn. Martin said that they drove to the home of one of Halsey's sisters, where she stayed the rest of the night. Halsey was questioned by police the next morning. Martin accompanied him to the police station, as did Caston's girlfriend. At the station, Martin found in her pocket bullets that Halsey had handed to her the night before. She said that she threw the bullets away. Martin said that after the police questioning, Halsey had threatened to kill her if she told anyone what had happened. Halsey's threats continued, Martin said, and so she eventually stopped going to Halsey's house. Some months later, Halsey's brother confronted her as she was walking near a park and forcibly took her to Halsey. She said that she was kept against her will at Halsey's house for three weeks to a month. She eventually escaped with the help of an unnamed acquaintance whom she happened to see while looking out a window. Martin said that she went immediately to her mother's house. That same day she left for Mississippi. She stayed there for six years. Martin told how at the time of the hearing she still feared Halsey. In view of Martin's in camera testimony, Washington successfully sought to amend his post-conviction petition to add a tenth claim based upon the newly discovered evidence.

The trial judge denied relief under the first nine claims Washington asserted, including the ineffectiveness claim which was supported by Martin's affidavit and testimony. Regarding that claim, the judge referred to testimony given by Washington's defense counsel that, in preparation for trial, he had tried to contact Martin. Counsel had also testified that he believed Washington had a strong alibi defense and his strategy was to focus on that rather than to try to prove that someone other than Washington murdered Hightie. However, the trial judge granted a new trial on the ground that Martin's testimony was new evidence which, if believed, would have "had some significant impact" upon the jury. The State appealed. Washington cross-appealed, contesting the denial of relief on the petition's other nine claims. The appellate court affirmed the grant of relief as to the newly discovered evidence claim without addressing the others. We granted the State's petition for leave to appeal. Meanwhile, Washington, who had been released on an appeal bond, was charged with, pleaded guilty to, and was sentenced to probation for an unrelated offense. We revoked his appeal bond. Though Washington had failed to appear after the bond revocation, his counsel again filed a cross-appeal contesting the denial of relief under the petition's other claims. The State moved to strike the cross-appeal under the fugitive dismissal doctrine. We granted that motion, leaving for this appeal only consideration of Washington's newly discovered evidence claim.

The claim Washington raised is a "free-standing" claim of innocence; unlike the ineffective-assistance claim supported by Martin's testimony, the newly discovered evidence is not being used to supplement an assertion of a constitutional violation with respect to his trial. The issue is not whether the evidence at trial was insufficient to convict Washington beyond a reasonable doubt. The appellate court rejected that challenge on direct appeal. The issue is whether Washington's claim of newly discovered evidence can be raised in a petition under the Post-Conviction Hearing Act to entitle Washington to a new trial. Post-conviction relief is Washington's remaining hope for a judicial remedy, the time limitations of other avenues offering relief for such a claim having lapsed.

To decide the issue, we must see if either a federal or Illinois constitutional right is implicated in such a freestanding claim of innocence, since Post-Conviction Hearing Act relief is limited to constitutional claims. Washington argues that his claim implicates due process protections. The beginning point for addressing that argument is Herrera v. Collins, 506 U.S. 390, 113 S.Ct. 853, 122 L.Ed.2d 203 (1993), where the Supreme Court rejected the contention as a federal constitutional matter. In light of our own constitution's due process guaranty, we must also assess Washington's argument as a matter of Illinois constitutional jurisprudence. Rollins v. Ellwood, 141 Ill.2d 244, 275, 152 Ill.Dec. 384, 565 N.E.2d 1302 (1990).

Due Process Under the Illinois Constitution. The possibility remains that Washington's claim may be cognizable under the Illinois Constitution's due process protection. That protection is stated as it is in the fourteenth amendment: no person "shall be deprived of life, liberty or property without due process of law." The Record of Proceedings of the Constitutional Convention does not reveal anything as to what the drafters intended for the Illinois protection different from the federal counterpart. Nevertheless, in People v. McCauley, 163 Ill.2d 414, 440, 206 Ill.Dec. 671, 645 N.E.2d 923 (1994), we noted that we labor under no self-imposed constraint to follow federal precedent in lockstep in defining Illinois' due process protection. We found historical support to say that, as a state matter, due process should protect against deliberate attempts to deny legal counsel.

As for Washington's claim here, there are decisions in which this court has perfunctorily evaluated new evidence claims in cases brought under the Post-Conviction Hearing Act. But neither this court nor the appellate court has ever expressly identified the constitutional right implicated in a freestanding claim of innocence based upon new evidence. It is because that issue is raised here for the first time that the State sought leave to appeal under Supreme Court Rule 317(a) (134 Ill.2d R. 317(a) (allowing appeals as of right when questions under the federal or Illinois Constitutions are raised for the first time in and as a result of the action of the appellate court)). Again, Post-Conviction Hearing Act relief is impossible if no constitutional right is implicated in the claim asserted.

Perhaps the closest this court has come to determining that our constitution's due process clause could be a means to recognize a newly discovered evidence claim for post-conviction purposes was in People v. Cornille, 95 [171 Ill.2d 487] Ill.2d 497, 69 Ill.Dec. 945, 448 N.E.2d 857 (1983). Here we must determine: Should additional process be afforded in Illinois when newly discovered evidence indicates that a convicted person is actually innocent? We believe so as a matter of both procedural and substantive due process. In terms of procedural due process, we believe that to ignore such a claim would be fundamentally unfair. Imprisonment of the innocent would also be so conscience shocking as to trigger operation of substantive due process. We have no difficulty seeing why substantive due process as a matter of Illinois constitutional law offers the grounds for such a conclusion. The Supreme Court rejected substantive due process as means to recognize freestanding innocence claims because of the idea that a person convicted in a constitutionally fair trial must be viewed as guilty. That made it impossible for such a person to claim that he, an innocent person, was unfairly convicted. We think that the Court overlooked that a "truly persuasive demonstration of innocence" would, in hindsight, undermine the legal construct precluding a substantive due process analysis. The stronger the claim--the more likely

13

it is that a convicted person is actually innocent--the weaker is the legal construct dictating that the person be viewed as guilty. A "truly persuasive demonstration of innocence" would effectively reduce the idea to legal fiction. At the point where the construct falls apart, application of substantive due process principles is invited. We believe that no person convicted of a crime should be deprived of life or liberty given compelling evidence of actual innocence. Given the limited avenues that our legislature has so far seen fit to provide for raising freestanding claims of innocence, that idea--but for the possibility of executive clemency--would go ignored in cases like this one. We therefore hold as a matter of Illinois constitutional jurisprudence that a claim of newly discovered evidence showing a defendant to be actually innocent of the crime for which he was convicted is cognizable as a matter of due process. That holding aligns Illinois with other jurisdictions likewise recognizing, primarily as a matter of state habeas corpus jurisprudence, a basis to raise such claims under the rubric of due process. That only means, of course, that there is footing in the Illinois Constitution for asserting freestanding innocence claims based upon newly discovered evidence under the Post-Conviction Hearing Act. Procedurally, such claims should be resolved as any other brought under the Act. Substantively, relief has been held to require that the supporting evidence be new, material, noncumulative and, most importantly, of such conclusive character as would probably change the result on retrial. As for this case, we find neither reason to disagree with the appellate court that those concerns were satisfied nor need to elaborate upon that conclusion. The judgment of the appellate court is affirmed.

Justice MILLER, dissenting:

I do not agree with the majority's conclusion that a freestanding claim of newly discovered evidence of innocence constitutes a basis for relief under the Post-Conviction Hearing Act in a noncapital case. Accordingly, I dissent. The defendant seeks to establish his right to a new trial under the Post-Conviction Hearing Act by alleging newly discovered evidence of his innocence of the murder for which he was convicted 14 years ago, in 1982. To be eligible for post-conviction relief, a defendant must establish a constitutional violation in the proceedings that resulted in his conviction. The majority correctly concludes that the defendant's claim of actual innocence does not implicate any federal constitutional rights. The majority finds, however, that the same claim implicates the due process guarantee of the Illinois Constitution and thus may be pursued under our state's Post-Conviction Hearing Act.

The majority fails to explain, as an initial matter, why the due process clause of the Illinois Constitution should be interpreted differently from the due process clause of the United States Constitution. Invoking the flawed decision People v. McCauley, 163 Ill.2d 414, 206 Ill.Dec. 671, 645 N.E.2d 923 (1994), the majority simply declares that we are under no obligation to construe provisions of the Illinois Constitution in lockstep with the United States Supreme Court's interpretation of corresponding provisions of the United States Constitution. Before adopting an interpretation that varies from one given by the United States Supreme Court, however, we should seek some legitimate, objective ground for distinguishing the language of the state constitution from that of the United States Constitution. In the present case, the majority acknowledges that the language of the federal and state due process guarantees is identical and, further, that there is nothing in the debates of the 1970 state constitutional convention that

14

suggests that the drafters intended the Illinois provision to mean something different from its federal counterpart. The majority nonetheless concludes that the due process clause of the Illinois Constitution requires a different and more expansive meaning than the same language commands under the federal constitution, and that notions of procedural and substantive due process separately sustain the defendant's action here. Neither ground is persuasive.

Illinois law affords convicted defendants a number of opportunities to raise allegations of newly discovered evidence of innocence; the availability of these forms of relief refutes the majority's conclusion that procedural due process compels a post-conviction remedy for the same claim. First, a defendant may present such evidence in a motion for a new trial, filed within 30 days of the verdict or finding of guilty. If the defendant discovers the evidence too late to satisfy the preceding time limit, relief may be available under section 2-1401 of the Code of Civil Procedure. While at one time it was the rule that claims of newly discovered evidence could not be raised in a petition under section 72 of the Civil Practice Act, which was the statutory predecessor to section 2-1401, more recent cases have recognized that such claims may be prosecuted under section 2-1401. Notably, the two-year time limit for bringing actions under section 2-1401 corresponds to the two-year limit imposed by Rule 33 of the Federal Rules of Criminal Procedure, which provides the sole means for bringing claims of newly discovered evidence of innocence by convicted defendants in the federal system.

Because Illinois law provides convicted defendants with sufficient means by which to raise claims of actual innocence, I do not agree with the majority that considerations of procedural due process mandate an additional remedy under the Post-Conviction Hearing Act. As an alternative basis for today's holding, the majority concludes that principles of substantive due process also compel recognition of the defendant's claim. This further rationale is equally unpersuasive, however. A defendant seeking to assert a claim of actual innocence in a post-conviction petition has, by definition, been convicted of the charge following a trial or a guilty plea. A defendant who cannot obtain relief in a motion for new trial or in a petition under section 2-1401 of the Code of Civil Procedure does not lack all recourse. In Illinois, a convicted defendant who wishes to raise a claim of newly discovered evidence outside the preceding time limits may submit a petition for executive clemency. Clemency "is the historic remedy for preventing miscarriages of justice where judicial process has been exhausted." The availability of this additional avenue of relief should not be ignored.

Finally, I would note that the out-of-state authorities cited by the majority in support of today's decision are fundamentally different from the case at bar. The present appeal arises from a petition filed under our state's Post-Conviction Hearing Act by a defendant who was sentenced to imprisonment for his offense. The cases cited by the majority either involve capital defendants or were maintained under statutes that do not expressly require a constitutional violation as a predicate for relief. Because this defendant was not sentenced to death for the underlying conviction, we need not determine here whether a different rule should apply to capital defendants. The state statutes in the two other cases cited by the majority did not require allegations of constitutional violations, unlike the Illinois provision at issue here.

A number of questions remain in the wake of the majority's holding in this case. It is difficult to reconcile the result in the present appeal with our decision People v. Brown, 169 Ill.2d 94, 214 Ill.Dec. 257, 660 N.E.2d 964 (1995), which recently reaffirmed the rule that an allegation of perjury does not raise a constitutional claim in the absence of knowledge of the false testimony by the prosecution. In addition, today's decision, unless otherwise limited, paradoxically will make relief more readily available when the claim of newly discovered evidence of innocence is raised in a post-conviction petition than when it is raised in a motion for a new trial. In a motion for a new trial, a defendant must show diligence in obtaining the new evidence in addition to demonstrating its conclusive character. Under today's decision, however, a defendant who raises the same claim in a post-conviction petition may apparently obtain relief by establishing the material, noncumulative, and conclusive character of the new evidence, without regard to his diligence in obtaining it.

In sum, unlike the majority, I do not believe that the Illinois Constitution provides greater due process protection in this context than does the United States Constitution, and thus I do not agree that the present defendant's claim represents a ground for post-conviction relief.

Dissenting Opinion Upon Denial of Rehearing, Chief Justice BILANDIC, dissenting:

I do not agree with the majority's recognition of this newly found constitutional right for the reasons stated in Justice Miller's dissent. I write separately today, however, to focus on an equally important issue that has been overlooked by my colleagues: What standard for relief should apply to a post-conviction petitioner raising a freestanding claim of actual innocence based on newly discovered evidence?

Without any analysis, the majority applies the standard applicable to a defendant's post-trial motion for a new trial. The majority then awards the defendant a new trial in which he can present his newly discovered evidence, the testimony of Jacqueline Martin. This standard is not appropriate for analyzing post-conviction petitioners' claims of actual innocence for many reasons. The standard (1) does not comport with the rationale underlying the majority's recognition of this due process right; (2) wrongly cloaks the already-convicted defendant with a new presumption of innocence; (3) gives no consideration to the need for finality in criminal proceedings; and (4) inappropriately requires a new trial, which may take place decades after the crime and original trial. Also, the standard is not consistent with that applied in other jurisdictions.

Given the many serious problems with the majority's standard, it is not surprising that other jurisdictions have explicitly rejected it. This court should not have adopted it either. I urge my fellow justices to rectify this grave error as quickly as possible.

REVIEW SECTION

READING COMPREHENSION

According to the Supreme Court of Illinois, how were the respondents' due process rights violated?

THINKING CRITICALLY

Do you believe there was a violation of due process in this case that legitimated a new trial under the Post-Conviction Hearing Act?

Discuss your opinion regarding the Justices' interpretation of the Illinois Constitution in comparison with the U.S. Constitution. Do you agree with the majority or dissent?

CONCLUSION

Crime control is the balance struck between the search for truth and a commitment to fairness which serves to limit governmental power through the U.S. and state's constitutions as interpreted by the U.S. Supreme Court. To maximize both individual liberties and community security, there must be a balance between process and result. What occurs is a balancing of formal and informal criminal procedures, designed to maintain the general principles of the U.S. Constitution and the Illinois Constitution. While sections of the Illinois Constitution will be elaborated throughout this guide, Article I, The Bill of Rights is provided in full text in the appendix. This chapter addressed the balance between order and liberty, as well as laws, discretion, due process, and precedent. The reinterpretation of how truth and fairness are guaranteed rests in the hands of the court system.

Chapter Two

The Constitution and Criminal Procedure

Criminal procedure comes from a variety of sources and is continually reinterpreted in court decisions. As there is a balance between process and result, there also exists a balance between laws which are specifics passed by legislatures, and constitutions which are principles to guide the populace. A main source of criminal procedure provisions is the Bill of Rights which provides rights to individuals at the local, state, and federal levels. This chapter details the exchange between the U.S. Constitution and the U.S. Supreme Court, with specific emphasis on due process and equal protection of laws. As such, the focus of this chapter remains at the federal level to elaborate the importance of the Constitution. Elements therein will be elaborated with specific reference to Illinois throughout the remainder of this guide.

This chapter will review:

(1)   The sources of criminal procedure;

(2)   Due process; and

(3)   Equal protection of the law.

SECTION 1: SOURCES OF CRIMINAL PROCEDURE

OVERVIEW

In examining the differences between laws and constitutions, it should be noted that laws are detailed and changing rules passed by state or federal legislatures, and constitutions are general and involve a relatively permanent set of principles. Constitutions are the highest forms of law and are vested with political authority. Theoretically, the Illinois Constitution, reflects the will and values of the people of the state and can only be changed by the people, thereby binding the government. The rules or criminal procedures that must be followed at all stages of the criminal justice system can be found in constitutions, court decisions, statutes, and administrative rules.

Most criminal procedure provisions are found in the Bill of Rights. Indeed, of the 28 provisions in the Bill of Rights, 12 are guarantees to individuals suspected, charged, or convicted of crimes. Since the 1960s, these guarantees have been applied to state and local, as well as federal governments. Within the Constitution there are two criminal procedure provisions: habeas corpus and guarantee of a trial by jury.

Habeas corpus is intended to review the constitutionality of the petitioner's imprisonment and is a noncriminal or civil proceeding. According to Article One, Section Nine of the Illinois Constitution:

The privilege of the writ of habeas corpus shall not be suspended except in cases of rebellion or invasion when the public safety may require it.

The second criminal procedure guaranteed by Article One, Section Thirteen of the Illinois Constitution is trial by jury:

The right of trial by jury as heretofore enjoyed shall remain inviolate.

According to the supremacy clause, Article VI of the U.S. Constitution, this is the final authority that binds criminal procedure. The courts however have established the principle of judicial review which gives the U.S. Supreme Court, as opposed to the Congress or the President, final responsibility for interpretation of the meaning of the Constitution. While all levels of the court system can interpret the Constitution, the Supreme Court makes final interpretations that bind lower courts, executives, legislatures, and all criminal justice officials. This power is somewhat limited by two factors. First, on a day-to-day basis local courts and police administer the interpretations as the Supreme Court is at the top of a very large criminal justice system pyramid. Second, because very few cases ever reach the Supreme Court, much interpretation is conducted at the level of the U.S. Court of Appeals, U.S. District Courts, and state courts.

You want to keep in mind that because of supervisory power to manage lower federal courts, the control of the U.S. Supreme Court is stronger over federal courts than state courts. The U.S. Supreme Court can control criminal procedures at the state level only if such actions are in violation of the U.S. Constitution. In Illinois for example, the Supreme Court has jurisdiction over cases wherein the death penalty is imposed, cases that pass upon the validity of a state or federal statute or construe a provision of the state or federal constitution, and in district court cases wherein there is conflict with another court, writs or orders by a district court of appeal that require immediate resolution.

As mentioned previously, state constitutions guarantee parallel rights to those outlined in the U.S. Constitution and Bill of Rights, as well as guarantee rights that may not be guaranteed in these other provisions. While the U.S. Constitution sets the minimum standards required by the states, each state in their Constitution is free to raise this minimum. The final authority in cases based on the Illinois Constitution are the Illinois state courts, as the U.S. Supreme Court cannot interpret state constitutions and statutes so long as it complies with the U.S. Constitution.

Remember that criminal procedures can be found not only in constitutions, court decisions, and statutes, but also in administrative rules. During the beginning of the 20th century in response to dissatisfaction with justice administration, the *Federal Rules of Criminal Procedure* was created. This set of rules was authorized by Congress and involved practitioners and scholars detailing rules to put the spirit of the U.S. Constitution into daily criminal justice system procedure. At the state level, the rules that put the spirit of the Illinois Constitution into daily criminal justice system procedure are elaborated in the *Illinois Compiled Statutes (ILCS)*. Because these rules do not elaborate the period prior to arrest, the *Model Code of Pre-Arraignment Procedure* was established in the 1970s. Although this document is not law, it is frequently cited by the courts in decisions. The ILCS is a recent compilation of the Illinois statutory law which took effect in 1993, and thus deserves some elaboration here.

When Illinois became a state in 1818, the legislature began passing laws that were organized in 1845 into *Revised Statutes*. This volume related to criminal jurisprudence and outlined all the statutory law in a single printed volume. The statutes were further revised into the *1874 Revised Statutes*, and have not been amended until ILCS took effect on January 1st, 1993. The statutory law of other states has been organized either by legislatures or private publishers. Given the historical and legislative context of the state of Illinois, the ILCS was devised inductively. Keep in mind that the ILCS is organized and numbered using acts and sections. This guide will refer primarily to Act 725, entitled "Criminal Procedure," formerly the *Code of Criminal Procedure of 1963*.

SECTION 2: DUE PROCESS

OVERVIEW

When the Confederacy was defeated during the Civil war and slavery was abolished, guarantees of state's rights and equal protection became extremely important. The Fourteenth Amendment guarantees:

> No state shall . . . deprive any citizen of life, liberty, or property
> without due process of law.

This sentiment is mirrored in Article One, Section Two of the Illinois Constitution as provided in the first chapter. The Illinois elaborates this right somewhat in Article One, Section One:

> All men are by nature free and independent and have certain
> inherent and inalienable rights among which are life, liberty and
> the pursuit of happiness. To secure these rights and the protection
> of property, governments are instituted among men, deriving their
> just powers from the consent of the governed.

Remember that the 1960s due process revolution resulted in the expansion of individual rights. This was accomplished as more individuals were included in constitutional protections and states and the federal government became compelled to extend these guarantees to the most vulnerable classes. The concept of due process is vague and thus subject to varied interpretations by the U.S. Supreme Court, though at minimum guarantees fair procedures when deciding cases.

While the underlying goal was to protect individuals from excessive government power, the U.S. Supreme Court was unwilling to apply the Fourteenth Amendment to state criminal proceedings until the 1930s, arguing it was a local matter and should not be in the hands of the federal government. Once the First World War began however, suspicions of excessive and arbitrary government were reinvigorated and the U.S. Supreme Court applied for the first time the due process clause of the Fourteenth Amendment to state criminal procedures in *Brown v.*

Mississippi (297 U.S. 278 1936). The due process clause requires that "state action, whether through one agency or another, shall be consistent with the fundamental principles of liberty and justice which lie at the base of all our civil and political institutions."

Brown v. Mississippi (297 U.S. 278 1936) and *Powell v. Alabama* (287 U.S. 45 1932) were paramount in establishing the fundamental fairness doctrine of due process. This doctrine provides that due process commands states to notify defendants of charges, and provide a full fact hearing prior to conviction and punishment. In Illinois, this is elaborated as "a person arrested with or without a warrant shall be taken without unnecessary delay before the nearest and most accessible judge . . . and the judge shall inform the defendant of the charge against him and shall provide him with a copy of the charge" (725 ILCS 5/109-1)

In sum, the fundamental fairness doctrine commands the states to provide a fair trial. This doctrine focused on general fairness defined at the state level, and while due process may include some specific guarantees of the Bill of Rights, this is neither a requirement nor intentional. From the 1930s until the 1950s, majority of the court continued to reject the notion that the Bill of Rights applied to criminal procedure at the state level, though came to recognize during the latter part of this period that the Bill of Rights does impose limits at this level. The controversy was: what are these limits?

The court began to reject the fundamental fairness doctrine in favor of interpreting the Fourteenth Amendment using the incorporation doctrine. The incorporation doctrine applied the provisions of the Bill of Rights to state criminal procedures, and this was the position of majority of the court by the 1960s. The incorporation doctrine focused on specific procedures as outlined in the Bill of Rights and applied at the state level. When the Court adopted this doctrine, contention remained regarding whether all or a select portion of the provisions of the Fourteenth Amendment should be included in due process. In cases decided by the Courts in the 1960s, all provisions of the Fourteenth Amendment were included except indictment by grand jury. The U.S. Supreme Court suggested that these rights were to apply at the state level exactly as in federal proceedings. The result was not only a shift in reasoning for intervention at the state level, but also an expanded role in the ways in which day-to-day criminal justice is implemented. Nevertheless, much local experimentation is still permitted, as in the case of testimony via closed circuit television.

CASE

In *People v. Schmitt,* a jury convicted the defendant of aggravated criminal sexual assault and criminal sexual assault. The constitutional argument at issue in this case is found in Article One, Section Eight of the Illinois Constitution and reads as follows:

> In criminal prosecutions, the accused shall have the right to appear
> and defend in person and by counsel . . .

At trial, the victim, defendant's nine-year-old son, C.S., testified via closed circuit television, as permitted by section 106A-3 of the Code of Criminal Procedure of 1963. On appeal, the defendant challenges the constitutionality of this procedure, raises a denial of due process claim, various evidentiary issues, and urges an amendment to the sentencing order to clarify discrepancies in the entries. Please be aware that some of the case description is graphic due to the nature of the offense.

PEOPLE V. SCHMITT
U.S. Supreme Court, Appeal from the Supreme Court of Florida
Appellate Court of Illinois, Fourth District.
562 N.E.2d 377, 204 Ill.App.3d 820 (1990)

C.S.'s parents were divorced when he was five years old. His mother has legal custody but C.S. visited his father, the defendant, every weekend at the house where defendant and the defendant's mother lived. C.S. testified that, on occasion, the defendant asked him to lie down on a couch. The defendant would then remove C.S.'s pants and underwear and lick his penis. C.S. told his grandmother, Dorothy Post, defendant also licked his rectum. C.S. stopped visiting the defendant in July 1988 after Post observed C.S. licking the buttocks of one of his cousins. When she confronted him with the behavior, C.S. denied licking his cousin. Post then asked, "Who did that, [C.S.]? Did you get that from Mindy or Tim?" C.S. testified he told her he got it from Tim, his father. Post testified C.S. told her he learned the behavior from his dad.

The defendant was charged by information with aggravated criminal sexual assault and criminal sexual assault. He subsequently filed several motions in *limine*, including a motion to prohibit the State from calling an expert witness to testify about rape-trauma syndrome. At the hearing on this motion, the prosecutor represented to the court that C.S. had been traumatized by the abuse and had become hostile and angry, and suffered nightmares and bed-wetting. Subsequently, the State filed a motion to videotape C.S.'s testimony pursuant to section 106A-2 of the Code. The State argued the procedure was necessary to protect C.S. from further trauma: "I think at his age he doesn't have the ability to put in perspective the seriousness of the sexual acts or the fact that his first sexual experience may have well been a homosexual experience with his father. To ask this child to get in front of 12 people, 14 people with alternates, and describe this type of sexual relations with his father I think is going beyond what we could ever appropriately accomplish in a court of justice."

Judge Cashman denied the motion, after determining the statute was unconstitutional (People v. Bastien (1989), 129 Ill.2d 64, 133 Ill.Dec. 459, 541 N.E.2d 670). The State then filed a motion to allow C.S.'s testimony via closed-circuit television. The State argued the procedure was in C.S.'s best interest. The defendant objected to the motion, claiming the procedure would violate his rights under the confrontation clause. He also argued the State failed to show the procedure was necessary. Judge Welch presided at this motion hearing and overruled the defendant's objections. Judge Welch specifically found the closed-circuit television procedure was in C.S.'s best interest. At trial, C.S. was the first witness and testified by closed-circuit television. The prosecutor, defense counsel, defendant, Judge Welch, C.S., and C.S.'s mother were in the judge's chambers during C.S.'s testimony, which was broadcast into the courtroom for the jury. There were two television monitors in the courtroom. A clear, color picture and clear sound were transmitted instantaneously from the judge's chambers to the courtroom. The defendant was not screened from C.S.'s sight. The camera focused on C.S.'s upper body and face.

Before leaving the courtroom to go to chambers, Judge Welch explained to the jury that C.S. would testify by closed-circuit television from chambers. He told the jury who would be in the room with C.S. during his testimony and who would remain in the courtroom. He also explained how the equipment functioned and instructed the jury to adjust the television monitors in the courtroom if necessary. The bailiff remained in the courtroom and was to notify the court immediately if there were equipment problems in the courtroom. The defendant also testified at trial and denied ever licking C.S.'s penis. He hypothesized that C.S. made the statements to avoid punishment for licking his cousin. The jury convicted the defendant on both counts and the circuit court sentenced him to nine years' imprisonment.

The first issue is whether the circuit court violated the defendant's right of confrontation under the sixth amendment of the United States Constitution and under article I, section 8 of the Illinois Constitution when it permitted C.S. to testify via closed-circuit television. The defendant argues his constitutional right of confrontation was violated because the jury was not present in the room with C.S. while he testified and because the State failed to show the procedure was necessary. The right of confrontation is unique to the defendant and functions to guarantee the defendant a face-to-face meeting with witnesses appearing before the trier of fact. This right of confrontation: (1) insures that the witness will give his statements under oath--thus impressing him with the seriousness of the matter and guarding against the lie by the possibility of a penalty for perjury; (2) forces the witness to submit to cross-examination; (3) permits the jury that is to decide the defendant's fate to observe the demeanor of the witness in making his statement, thus aiding the jury in assessing his credibility.

This case does not present a confrontation problem. The statute specifically includes the defendant and his attorney in the room where the child is testifying. The trial court here followed the provisions of the statute, and the defendant and his attorney were in the judge's chambers while C.S. testified. The defendant was thus afforded face-to-face confrontation with C.S. and an opportunity to cross-examine the child. The defendant's attorney cross-examined C.S., who testified under oath and indicated he understood the importance of telling the truth. The defendant in this case was given full opportunity to probe and expose infirmities in C.S.'s testimony. C.S. was not forgetful, confused, or evasive. Instead, his testimony was clear, convincing, unrehearsed, and reliable. The final function of the confrontation right is allowing the jury to observe the witness' demeanor. The jury here had adequate opportunity to assess the child's demeanor while he testified, though the jury was not in the room with C.S. The television camera provided a clear view of C.S.'s upper body, face, and facial expressions and the picture was transmitted in color. The camera angle may have afforded the jury a closer view of C.S. than would have been possible from the witness stand in the courtroom.

We reject the defendant's arguments that the jury could not sufficiently assess C.S.'s demeanor because his entire body was not shown. Likewise, we reject the defendant's argument that there was error because the camera failed to show the entire room and those present. As stated heretofore, defendant was present during C.S.'s testimony, to cross-examine, to expose infirmities, and to call to the attention of the jury, as fact finder, reasons to give "scant weight" to the same. We find no error or unfairness, particularly in view of Judge Welch's comments to the jury in which he listed those persons who would be in chambers during C.S.'s testimony. The defendant also contends the State failed to show the closed-circuit-television procedure was necessary in this case. The statutory standard is not necessity but "the best interest of the child." Judge Welch specifically found the closed-circuit television procedure was in C.S.'s best interest. The record supports this finding and thus there was no abuse of discretion.

Further, the statute does not require a hearing to determine whether the best interest of the child would be served by allowing him to testify via closed-circuit television. The defendant would have this court require such a hearing. The legislature did not impose such a requirement and therefore we decline to do so. Had the legislature intended to require a hearing, it would have so provided. In this case the representations of the prosecutor to the court, that closed-circuit television was in C.S.'s best interest, provided a sufficient basis for the finding by the court.

The defendant urges application of the recent United States Supreme Court decision <u>Maryland v. Craig</u> (1990), 497 U.S. 836, 110 S.Ct. 3157, 111 L.Ed.2d 666. The Craig decision is distinguishable on several grounds and thus inapplicable to this case. The defendant in Craig owned and operated a prekindergarten and kindergarten center. She was accused and convicted of sexually abusing six-year-old B.E. The State moved to allow B.E. to testify via closed-circuit television and introduced expert testimony that B.E. would suffer 'serious emotional distress such that she could not reasonably communicate,' if required to testify in the courtroom. The defendant challenged the constitutionality of the statute alleging it denied her the right of confrontation. Unlike the Illinois statute, the Maryland statute excluded the defendant from the room where the child testified and required the defendant to observe the proceedings by closed-circuit television. Thus the Craig case involved confrontation clause issues. The Court concluded Maryland's closed-circuit television procedure preserved the requisites of the confrontation clause.

As discussed earlier, the Illinois statute requires only a finding that the closed-circuit television procedure would be in the child's "best interest." The trial court here made an individualized finding that C.S.'s best interest would be served by allowing him to testify by closed-circuit television. Thus, Craig is also distinguishable as to the statutory showing required to invoke the closed-circuit television procedure. The circuit court in this case complied with the statutory requirements for using closed-circuit television. Only those persons enumerated in the statute were permitted in the judge's chambers while C.S. testified and his testimony was transmitted to the jury in the courtroom. C.S. testified under oath in the physical presence of the defendant and the defendant's attorney cross-examined the child. The defendant was not denied his rights under the confrontation clause when C.S. testified via closed-circuit television.

The defendant contends the closed-circuit television procedure denied him due process. We disagree. The statute which allowed C.S. to testify by closed-circuit television was constitutional and followed meticulously by Judge Welch. There was no denial of due process. The defendant next objects to the admission of Post's testimony that C.S. told her the defendant licked C.S.'s

24

rectum, because he was charged only with having licked the child's penis. The defendant claims this testimony violated section 115-10 of the Code. Prior to admitting corroborative-complaint testimony, the circuit court held a hearing pursuant to section 115-10(b)(1). At this hearing, Post testified C.S. told her he was being touched by his dad in that he was licked on his penis and his butt. Defense counsel argued section 115-10 only permits witnesses to corroborate that a complaint was made, but no details of the complaint. After hearing Post's testimony, the trial judge concluded identification of the perpetrator was unnecessary, and ruled Post could testify. The judge reiterated this latter aspect of the ruling before hearing the State's offer on the police officer's corroborative-complaint testimony. Defense counsel made no objection to Post testifying that C.S. complained of being licked on the butt. In proceedings before the jury, the prosecutor asked Post whether C.S. identified where on his body he had been licked, and Post answered, "on his penis and on his rectum." Several questions later, defense counsel renewed an objection lodged earlier and moved for a mistrial because Post "violated the Court's previous order restraining the testimony that can be given," basically objecting because Post testified C.S. identified defendant as the person who committed the acts in question. The court overruled the objection, stating identification was not the issue.

Raising the issue for the first time on appeal, defendant argues Post's testimony that he licked C.S.'s rectum was evidence of a crime with which he was not charged. He maintains the testimony should not have been admitted as it was highly prejudicial and biased the jury against him. Generally, evidence of collateral crimes is inadmissible if relevant only to show a defendant's propensity to commit a crime. The State argues defendant has waived this issue. We agree--first, by failure to raise this objection below and by specific objection on other grounds; second, by cross-examining on this point; and, third, by failure to include it in his motion for a new trial. Defendant urges application of the plain error exception to the waiver rule. However, this exception "will be applied only when substantial rights of the defendant are affected or the evidence in the case is closely balanced." This is not such a case.

On the merits, there was no error in admission of this testimony. Section 115-10, as amended, permits admission of such details of the child's complaint, including identification, even if not on an element of the crime charged, and absent testimony by the child as to that particular detail. Here, the court held a proper section 115-10 hearing outside the presence of the jury in order to determine that the time, content, and circumstances of the statement provided sufficient safeguards of reliability to permit admission of the evidence as an exception to the hearsay rule; the court made the requisite statutory determination; and the court gave the cautionary instruction required by the statute.

The defendant also argues his conviction should be overturned because the cumulative effect of the errors alleged to have occurred during trial deprived him of a fair trial. We disagree. There were no errors depriving him of a fair trial, individually or cumulatively. Even if there were errors, they were harmless and do not warrant vacating the conviction. Finally, the defendant contends, and the State agrees, this case should be remanded for correction of the sentencing order. The defendant was charged with both aggravated criminal sexual assault and criminal sexual assault. Both charges involved a single act, the defendant placing his mouth on C.S.'s penis. The jury returned guilty verdicts on both counts. The court sentenced the defendant to nine years' imprisonment for aggravated criminal sexual assault but did not impose a sentence for the criminal sexual assault conviction. One sentencing order and the notice of appeal state defendant was convicted of two counts of aggravated criminal sexual assault. A later sentencing order shows defendant was convicted of both aggravated criminal sexual assault and criminal sexual assault. We agree with the parties that the cause should be remanded to clarify the record to reflect a judgment entered on the verdict of guilty to one count of aggravated criminal sexual assault. Affirmed as modified, and cause remanded.

REVIEW SECTION

READING COMPREHENSION

Detail the facts of this case.

Detail the constitutional issue of concern and the determination of the court on this issue.

THINKING CRITICALLY

Does testimony by closed-circuit television violate the rights of the accused to a fair trial and due process?

SECTION 3: EQUAL PROTECTION OF THE LAW

OVERVIEW

Equality before the law is deeply embedded in a constitutional democracy and has been since 1868 in the Fourteenth Amendment. In Illinois, equality before the law on the basis of sex is guaranteed in Article One, Section Eighteen of the Illinois Constitution:

> The equal protection of the laws shall not be denied or abridged on account of sex by the State or its units of local government and school districts.

Further, equal protection on the basis of religion is elaborated in Article One, Section Three, and equal protection on the basis of handicap in Article One, Section Nineteen of the Illinois Constitution. You will note that specific elaboration of equal protection based on race/ethnicity is absent. While this does not translate to equal treatment for each individual by criminal justice officials, it does mean that investigation, apprehension, conviction, and punishment cannot occur for reasons that are considered unacceptable. In bringing a claim that equal protection was denied, claimants must prove discriminatory effect, and discriminatory purpose which means that specific officials intended to discriminate based on illegal criteria against the claimant in question. If discriminatory effect and discriminatory purpose are proved, the claimant must also disprove the presumption of regularity. Thus, the claimant must disprove the presumption that actions by the government are lawful in the absence of clear evidence to indicate otherwise. As you can imagine, this is extremely difficult to accomplish.

CASE

Chavez v. Illinois State Police is a case that centers around the plaintiffs' claim that the Illinois State Police stop, detain, and search African-American and Hispanic motorists solely on the basis of their race. Magistrate Judge Edward A. Bobrick's Report and Recommendation addressing the defendants' motion for partial summary judgment is provided.

CHAVEZ V. ILLINOIS STATE POLICE
United States District Court, N.D. Illinois, Eastern Division
27 F.Supp. 2d 1053 (1998)

The magistrate judge recommended that the defendants' motion be granted as to the equal protection claims of plaintiffs Peso Chavez and Gregory Lee, all plaintiffs' freedom of movement claims, and the claims against defendants Kenneth Hall, Lonnie Inlow, Kathleen Sauter and Michael Snyders, but denied as to Chavez' Fourth Amendment claims. He also recommended that the defendants' motion for summary judgment as to plaintiff Joseph Gomez' claims and the plaintiffs' motion to strike certain paragraphs of the defendants' Local Rule 12(m) statements be denied. The plaintiffs object to all portions of the R & R adverse to them.

The following objections to additional reports and recommendations are also before the court: (1) the plaintiffs' objections regarding their motion to compel enforcement of subpoenas directed to the Office of the Secretary of State; (2) the plaintiffs' objections regarding their motion to modify discovery subpoena; (3) the plaintiffs' objections regarding their motion to file affidavits in opposition to the defendants' motion to strike and dismiss their claims for equitable relief and supplemental state law claims; (4) the plaintiffs' and defendants' objections regarding the defendants' motion to strike and dismiss the plaintiffs' claims for equitable relief and supplemental state law claims; (5) the plaintiffs' objections regarding their motion to certify a plaintiff class; and (6) the defendants' objections regarding the March 16, 1998 report and recommendation addressing Gregory Lee. In addition, the following motions are also before the court: (1) the plaintiffs' motion to continue the stay with respect to the defendants' summary judgment motion; (2) the plaintiffs' motion to stay additional pending matters; and (3) the plaintiffs' motion to withdraw and substitute the declaration of Martin Shapiro and associated filings.

The court previously accepted the magistrate judge's R & R and noted that a statement of reasons would follow. The court subsequently stayed proceedings in this case so that the plaintiffs could resolve certain issues with respect to their statistical evidence. As these matters have been resolved, the court now explains its reasoning with respect to the R & R and modifies it only insofar as it now finds that Gillette, Graham, and Cessna are entitled to qualified immunity to the extent that the plaintiffs seek to impose liability on them based on Thomas' admittedly (for summary judgment purposes) improper stop of Chavez. In addition, the court finds that Gillette and Cessna are entitled to qualified immunity based on their participation in the search of Chavez' vehicle. Thus, Gillette and Cessna's motion for summary judgment as to Chavez' Fourth Amendment stop and search claims and Graham's motion for summary judgment as to Chavez' Fourth Amendment stop claim are granted. The court also overrules all of the objections to the magistrate judge's reports and recommendations. Finally, the court denies the plaintiffs' motion to continue the stay with respect to the defendants' summary judgment motion, the plaintiffs' motion to stay additional pending matters, and the plaintiffs' motion for leave to withdraw and substitute the declaration of Martin Shapiro and associated filings.

This court adopts the factual background in the magistrate judge's R & R, which was based on the parties' Local Rule 12 submissions. To briefly summarize, the plaintiffs claim, on behalf of themselves and similarly-situated individuals, that the Illinois State Police have a practice of stopping, detaining, and searching African-American and Hispanic motorists based on their race and without legally sufficient cause or justification. The plaintiffs' claims do not, however, begin with allegations of discrimination against African-American or Hispanic motorists. Instead, they arise from the stop, search, and arrest of a white motorist, George Koutsakis. See People v. Koutsakis, 272 Ill.App.3d 159, 208 Ill.Dec. 549, 649 N.E.2d 605 (Ill.App.3d Dist. 1995). In November, 1992, a state trooper stopped Koutsakis for exceeding the posted speed limit on Interstate 80 by four miles. Koutsakis denied that he was speeding. While the trooper wrote Koutsakis a warning ticket, a second trooper arrived with a drug-sniffing dog. The dog "alerted" and the police discovered 250 pounds of marijuana in the ensuing search of Koutsakis' vehicle.

Attorney Nancy Hollander represented Koutsakis in the criminal proceedings against him. She suspected that state troopers were stopping motorists based on skin tone or travel patterns, and thus decided to see if she could establish that the stop of Koutsakis was pretextual. To investigate this hunch, she hired plaintiff Peso Chavez, a private investigator and New Mexico resident, to recreate the circumstances leading to Koutsakis' stop and arrest. Accordingly, Chavez emulated the circumstances surrounding Koutsakis' stop and arrest by renting a red car with California license plates and placing open maps, fast food wrappers, a cellular phone, and a gym bag in his rental car. He then headed out to Interstate 80 for a test drive, with the full intent of being stopped. On his first day out — February 17, 1993 — Chavez, followed by Katherine Austin from the Public Defenders' Office, saw state troopers on Interstate 80 three times but was not stopped.

The next morning, Chavez and Austin set out again, traveled to the western edge of Bureau County, Illinois, and began driving east on Interstate 80. State Trooper Larry Thomas was parked on the east-bound shoulder of Interstate 80 at mile post 53. When Chavez' vehicle passed him, he decided to follow it. Thomas followed Chavez for 24 miles, or almost one half hour, although he could not explain why he decided to do so. It is undisputed that Chavez traveled at no more than 60 miles per hour, although the speed limit was 65. According to Thomas, he stopped Chavez at about mile post 77 for failing to signal a lane change. Chavez, like Koutsakis, denied that he committed any traffic violation. Attorney Austin, who was following Chavez, also denied that Chavez had committed any traffic violation. Similarly, State Trooper Dan Gillette, who was parked at a turn-around in the median at mile post 77 and was facing and monitoring eastbound traffic, observed no violation. Instead, according to Gillette, he heard Thomas' radio traffic indicating the stop before he saw Chavez' and Thomas' vehicles pass him. Thomas and Chavez pulled over east of the area where Gillette was located, and Gillette pulled out of the turn-around and joined them. Thomas requested and received Chavez' driver's license and issued a warning ticket based on Chavez' alleged failure to signal. In his report on the incident, Thomas listed Chavez' race as "white," despite the fact that the report contained a listing for "Hispanic." Chavez, Thomas, and Gillette disagree as to the events that ensued, although everyone agrees that the entire stop took between 35 and 55 minutes.

Trooper Thomas' Version - Trooper Thomas noticed that Chavez' vehicle had California license plates and a rental company registry, and that a small suitcase, discarded fast food bags, and a map were in the car. He also saw Chavez' hands shake, and thought Chavez was nervous. Thomas testified there is nothing unusual about an individual's hands shaking or nervousness during a traffic stop, or the presence of a small suitcase, fast food bags, and a map. By the time Thomas had gone back to his car, Gillette had arrived and told Thomas he was going to talk to Chavez. While back at his car, Thomas ran a check on Chavez' driver's license and ran a criminal history, although he cannot remember the results. Thomas does not know why Gillette wanted to talk to Chavez. Other portions of Thomas's testimony are inconsistent, although the inconsistencies do not rise to the level of a disputed issue of material fact. Thomas testified that he returned to Chavez' car, issued a warning ticket, and told Chavez he was free to go. He also testified, however, that he continued to talk to Chavez and unsuccessfully requested permission to search Chavez' vehicle.

After Thomas issued the warning ticket, Trooper Graham arrived in a canine unit with his police dog. Thomas asked Chavez if he would consent to a canine "walk-around" but did not recall Chavez' response. Thomas' field report indicates that Chavez consented. Graham then conducted a walk-around and the dog alerted, thereby indicating that drugs were in Chavez' vehicle. In response to the alert, Gillette, Graham, and Trooper Cessna, who by now had arrived on the scene, searched Chavez' car while Chavez waited in Thomas' car. The officers did not find any contraband.

Sergeant Gillette's Version - Gillette testified that Thomas was speaking with Chavez when he arrived at the scene. After Thomas finished his conversation, Gillette sat in Thomas' car with Thomas. Gillette said that Thomas told him there was something funny about Chavez, that he smelled air freshener in the car and that he had seen no luggage. Gillette suggested Thomas run a criminal history and Gillette then went over to Chavez' vehicle. Gillette asked Chavez where he was going and Chavez responded that he was going to Chicago for the day. Gillette testified that, at this point, Chavez' eyes "went up into the right, which is a clear sign of deception." Gillette said that Chavez did not know what he was going to do or who he was going to see in Chicago. Gillette also said that Chavez did not know what he did for a living. Gillette thought that Chavez did not know what he did for a living because Chavez did not know what he was going to be doing in Chicago. Gillette also testified that he saw a road atlas and fast food wrappers in the car, and thought the car was too clean to have come from Albuquerque. In addition, Gillette testified both that there was no luggage in Chavez' car and that there was one piece of luggage in the car.

Gillette then returned to Thomas' vehicle. Thomas told Gillette that the criminal check was negative. In response, Gillette told Thomas that he thought something was wrong with Chavez' vehicle because there were too many "indicators." Thereafter, Thomas asked Chavez for permission to search his car. Chavez refused, and the canine unit arrived. Based on the indicators, Gillette felt there was sufficient reason to detain Chavez for a canine walk-around. Gillette testified Chavez did not consent to the walk-around, although Thomas' field report said that he had consented. Gillette also testified that, although the dog alerted, no drugs were found in Chavez' vehicle.

Peso Chavez' Version - Chavez testified that his goal on the day of the traffic stop and search was to be pulled over. He denied, however, that he violated any traffic laws before he was pulled over. Chavez testified that Thomas told him that he might have missed Chavez signaling his lane change. The defendants say that Thomas offered Chavez a general apology during the search. According to Chavez, after Thomas issued the warning ticket, he did not tell Chavez that he was free to go. Instead, Chavez felt that he was not free to leave at any point during the encounter. Chavez testified that Thomas did not so much ask him to consent to a search of the vehicle, as tell him he wanted to search it. Chavez admits that he became nervous during the encounter, fearing that, if the search was unsuccessful, the troopers would become frustrated and plant evidence. He also testified that the troopers' attitude during the search was that there simply had to be drugs in Chavez' vehicle and they were going to find them. Chavez does not claim that the troopers made any racially based remarks during the encounter, and Chavez' report to Hollander included no references to race or racial motivation.

As noted by the magistrate judge, the vast majority of evidence before the court pertains to Chavez. The plaintiffs have, however, developed some facts relating to plaintiffs Gregory Lee and Joseph Gomez. Gregory Lee, whom the court assumes is African-American, testified that he was stopped, searched, and detained three times in a single year, and that each stop was unjustified. The plaintiffs claim that during one of these stops, the state trooper referred to Lee using the phrase "you people," although there is no corroborating evidence of this in the record. The plaintiffs admit that Lee cannot identify any similarly situated white motorist who was treated differently. Joseph Gomez was stopped by Illinois state troopers on March 24, 1994, and again in early 1995. He joined this case in May of 1996.

According to the plaintiffs, defendants Kathleen Sauter, Lonnie Inlow, and Kenneth Hall supervised state trooper districts in Illinois where the plaintiffs claim violations took place. In turn, defendant Michael Snyders was involved in "Operation Valkyrie," a drug interdiction program. It is undisputed that these defendants did not personally supervise any of the troopers who allegedly violated the plaintiffs' rights. The plaintiffs also seek to hold Snyder liable for training state troopers to consider race as a factor in determining who to stop, search, and detain on Illinois highways. The defendants disagree with this characterization of Snyders' training sessions.

The plaintiffs originally supported their claims with statistics and an analysis of those statistics prepared by their expert, Martin Shapiro. Shapiro based his opinion on materials prepared by Temple University's Center for Public Policy, which had analyzed the electronic data provided by the defendants to prepare it for Shapiro's analysis. Shapiro compared the percentage of whites, African-Americans and Hispanics in Illinois with the percentage of those races specified in Illinois State Police field reports. Shapiro also considered the 1990 Nationwide Personal Transportation Survey. In Shapiro's opinion, the statistics regarding the race of the population and drivers in Illinois versus the race of drivers reflected in the field reports did not correlate and the variance was too wide to occur by chance.

The plaintiffs subsequently discovered — after the objections to the R & R had been fully briefed — that Temple University's Center for Public Policy had presented Shapiro with incomplete or incorrect data. Accordingly, the plaintiffs sought to stay consideration of the defendants' motion for partial summary judgment so they could obtain a new analysis of the data. The court granted the motion to stay, reasoning that, if the statistics did not in fact support the plaintiffs' equal protection claim, that claim would not be properly before the court. In other words, if the revised analysis correlated with the racial breakdown of Illinois drivers, the plaintiffs would almost certainly have to withdraw their equal protection claim. Given this possibility and the concomitant standing problem that would result if the statistics did not support the plaintiffs' claims, the court declined to reach the merits of one of the central issues in this case — equal protection — when the viability of that issue was so uncertain. Thus, the court stayed consideration of the objections and allowed the plaintiffs to investigate and correct its statistical evidence.

As things turned out, however, the new and revised statistics are more favorable to the plaintiffs. They thus seek to withdraw and substitute a corresponding new and revised declaration from Shapiro, as well as all corresponding portions of their response to the motion for partial summary judgment. The defendants oppose the motion, contending that the proposed substitutions will simply cause additional delay. The court need not reach the numerous arguments raised by the plaintiffs regarding the revised Shapiro declaration because, as discussed in detail below, statistical evidence cannot be used to satisfy the Equal Protection Clause's similarly situated requirement. This means that the main utility of the revised Shapiro declaration is that it allows the court to reach the merits of the plaintiffs' equal protection claims. Of course, this is a pyrrhic victory in light of the court's ruling regarding the plaintiffs' equal protection claim. It also necessarily means that consideration of the revised analysis would not affect the court's disposition of the equal protection claims. For these reasons, the plaintiffs' motion to withdraw and substitute the revised Shapiro declaration and corresponding materials is denied.

The defendants seek summary judgment on portions of the plaintiffs' complaint, arguing that: (1) Chavez and Lee's equal protection claims must fail because Chavez and Lee have not established that they were treated differently than similarly situated white motorists; (2) summary judgment on Chavez' Fourth Amendment detention and search claims is warranted because the state troopers acted with probable cause; (3) the plaintiffs' freedom of movement claims have no constitutional basis; (4) they are entitled to qualified immunity on the plaintiffs' freedom of movement and Fourth Amendment claims; (5) summary judgment on the plaintiffs' claims against supervisory individuals is warranted as those defendants were not personally involved in the allegedly wrongful conduct; and (6) Jose Gomez' claims are barred by the statute of limitations. Specifically, the magistrate judge recommended that the motion for summary judgment on Peso Chavez and Gregory Lee's equal protection claims, the plaintiffs' freedom of movement claims, and the plaintiffs' claims against Kenneth Hall, Lonnie Inlow, Kathleen Sauter and Michael Snyders based on supervisory liability be granted, and that the motion for summary judgment on Chavez' Fourth Amendment claims and Joseph Gomez' claims be denied.

The plaintiffs and the defendants each have objected to portions of the R & R adverse to the respective parties. Accordingly, the court will review the portions of the R & R addressing dispositive matters to which the parties have objected *de novo*. With respect to the remaining parts of the R & R addressing dispositive matters, the court notes that a district court may review any issue presented *de novo*, even if no party has objected. With respect to portions of the R & R addressing nondispositive matters, the court reviews for clear error. With these principles in mind, the court turns to the R & R and the parties' objections.

The magistrate judge recommended that the court grant the defendants' motion for summary judgment on Chavez and Lee's equal protection claims, based on the plaintiffs' failure to identify similarly situated white motorists who were treated differently from the plaintiffs. The magistrate judge also held that the plaintiffs' statistical evidence was insufficient to meet this burden, and that, even if it was not, the statistical evidence was flawed. The plaintiffs object, contending that the magistrate judge incorrectly required them to prove their claims of discrimination, and provide names of similarly situated white motorists who were not stopped in order to survive summary judgment. They also argue that their expert's analysis of statistics regarding Illinois state trooper stops is sufficient to enable them to withstand summary judgment. Finally, they argue that U.S. v. Armstrong, 517 U.S. 456, 465-67, 116 S.Ct. 1480, 1487, 134 L.Ed.2d 687 (1996), is inapplicable, and even if it does apply, it does not require them to show that similarly situated white motorists were treated differently than African-American and Hispanic motorists.

To establish a *prima facie* violation of the Equal Protection Clause, the plaintiffs must show that they: (1) are members of a class; (2) who are similarly situated to members of another class; and (3) were treated differently from members of that other class. The plaintiffs must also show purposeful and intentional acts of discrimination based on their membership in a class, as opposed to discrimination on an individual basis. In addition, they must show that the challenged conduct had a discriminatory effect and was motivated by a discriminatory purpose. This means that, in a race case, plaintiffs must show that similarly situated individuals of a different race were not subjected to the challenged conduct. Statistical evidence showing that all defendants prosecuted during a certain year were African-American fails to satisfy this requirement.

The plaintiffs argue that Armstrong does not apply to this case because Armstrong is a selective prosecution case. The court disagrees. Armstrong is applicable because the Supreme Court specifically based its holding on equal protection principles. Armstrong is also particularly helpful to the court in this case because it addressed the precise arguments raised by the plaintiffs here that: (1) there is no absolute requirement that they show a failure to prosecute similarly situated individuals; and (2) statistics demonstrating that all persons subject to the allegedly wrongful conduct were of a certain race satisfy the "similarly situated" requirement. The Supreme Court specifically rejected these arguments, and reaffirmed the requirement that an equal protection plaintiff in a selective prosecution case identify individuals of other races that could have been prosecuted for the same offense, but were not. Armstrong also held that a study showing that all persons prosecuted were black did not meet the similarly situated requirement, explaining that the "required threshold" for equal protection claims is "a credible showing of different treatment of similarly situated persons."

The plaintiffs' arguments are based on the same flawed premise which was asserted and rejected by the Supreme Court in Armstrong. Thus, the plaintiffs' contention that they need not identify white motorists treated differently than the plaintiffs must fail. In addition, the plaintiffs' attempt to distinguish Armstrong by arguing that a prosecutor's decision as to whom to charge is different from a state trooper's decision as to whom to stop is unavailing. Regardless of the degree of judicial deference given to either decision, the central inquiry in each case is whether any plaintiff was treated differently than a similarly situated person of a different race. The answer to this question lies not in the deference given to the decision-maker in the respective situations, but in whether the decision(s) made resulted in impermissible treatment of similarly situated persons. Accordingly, the plaintiffs' attempt to distinguish Armstrong based on the fact that a state trooper, as opposed to a prosecutor, decided which motorists to stop must fail.

The plaintiffs have pointed to only one white motorist who is genuinely similarly situated to Chavez — George Koutsakis. Chavez was paid to recreate the circumstances surrounding Koutsakis' stop, search, and arrest as closely as possible. Chavez did this. He was then stopped and subjected to a search of his vehicle, just like Koutsakis. Simply put, the Illinois state troopers treated Chavez exactly like the white motorist emulated. Chavez' stop and search thus fails to show that he was treated any differently than a similarly situated white motorist. The plaintiffs contend that attorney Katherine Austin, who was following Chavez when he was stopped but who was not stopped herself, is a similarly situated white motorist who was treated differently than Chavez. However, the record shows that Chavez is similarly situated to Koutsakis rather than Austin. Chavez and Koutsakis are both male, drove the same color cars with California license plates, had the same items visible in their cars, and denied that they violated traffic laws yet received warning tickets. In contrast, the record does not reveal any commonalities between Chavez and Austin, other than the fact that they both were driving on the same stretch of Interstate 80. This lone commonality fails to establish that Austin was similarly situated to Chavez. The court also notes that the record is devoid of any evidence regarding other specific white motorists who recreated the circumstances surrounding the stops of the allegedly mistreated minority motorists.

In their objections addressing Gregory Lee's equal protection claims, the plaintiffs do not take exception to the magistrate judge's finding that Lee failed to present evidence regarding specific similarly situated white motorists who were treated differently. Instead, they focus on the alleged use of the phrase "you people" by the state trooper who stopped Lee. According to Lee, the police singled him out, stopped him, and searched him due to his race. His claim is thus analogous to a selective prosecution claim based on the equal protection clause. Claims of selective prosecution are judged under ordinary equal protection standards. To make a *prima facie* case for selective prosecution, the claimant must establish both that he was singled out for prosecution to the exclusion of others similarly situated, and that the allegedly selective decision to prosecute the claimant was based upon an impermissible ground. Lee attempts to avoid this test by arguing that he did not raise a selective prosecution claim. Specifically, Lee contends that, in order to prevail on his § 1983 equal protection claim, he must show that the police "purposefully discriminated against him because of his identification with a particular (presumably historically disadvantaged) group." Lee's characterization of his argument as an equal protection claim, as opposed to a selective prosecution claim, does not save the day as the same standards govern selective prosecution and equal protection claims.

Lee has not pointed to a white motorist who was treated differently. Instead, he asks the court to infer that he was treated differently from white motorists solely because the trooper who stopped him made a racist remark. The court acknowledges that Lee, unlike the police, cannot control which motorists are stopped and thus cannot control the data available to him. Nevertheless, the fact remains that Lee's claims are based solely on alleged mistreatment of him, not the dual elements of mistreatment of him and proper treatment of similarly situated white motorists. The equal protection clause includes a comparative element, but Lee has not offered any facts relating to this element. Thus, while the court in no way condones the alleged use of the phrase "you people," it concludes that Lee's equal protection claim cannot withstand summary judgment because the absence of a similarly situated white motorist is fatal to Lee's equal protection claim.

The plaintiffs' statistical evidence in support of their equal protection argument consists of the analysis of their expert, Martin Shapiro. Regardless of which version of Shapiro's declaration the court considers, the plaintiffs' theory is the same. Specifically, the plaintiffs contend that Shapiro's analysis, which compares the percentage of whites, African-Americans and Hispanics in Illinois with the percentage of those races specified in Illinois State Police field reports and the 1990 Nationwide Personal Transportation Survey, shows that the numbers in the field reports are materially different from the numbers in the general population and the transportation survey. The plaintiffs set forth numerous challenges to the magistrate judge's analysis of their statistics. The court need not specifically address these arguments or consider whether the new statistics suffer from the same infirmities as the original statistics because, as noted above, statistical evidence in equal protection cases is insufficient to show that similarly situated persons of varying races are treated differently.

The plaintiffs contend that non-statistical evidence also supports their claims of discriminatory treatment. They point to the following evidence: (1) Illinois state police permit consideration of race as a factor in deciding which motorists to stop; (2) Illinois state troopers admit they use race as "one of the indicators" in determining whether to search a vehicle for contraband; (3) Illinois state police training manuals emphasize the alleged predominance of Hispanics as drug couriers; (4) testimony of African-American motorists recounting allegedly discriminatory law enforcement by the Illinois State Police; and (5) Illinois state police refuse to open a case when a citizen complains that he was stopped due to race. The plaintiffs contend that this evidence allows their claims to survive summary judgment because it demonstrates a material issue of disputed fact as to the defendants' motivation. The plaintiffs also argue that their evidence allows the court to infer that the defendants acted with discriminatory intent.

These arguments suffer from the same inadequacies as the arguments relating to Lee's equal protection claim. Again, even taking the above evidence as true, plaintiffs are unable to prevail on their equal protection claim because they have failed to point to a white motorist who was treated differently. This is critical, as the Supreme Court requires the plaintiffs to show that similarly situated individuals of a different race were not subjected to the challenged conduct. As with Lee, the absence of allegations regarding the comparative element of the equal protection clause dooms the plaintiffs' equal protection claims. Accordingly, the plaintiffs' objections to this portion of the R & R are overruled, and the defendants' motion for summary judgment on the plaintiffs' equal protection claims is granted.

The officers' apparent violation of Chavez' Fourth Amendment rights, based on their admission for purposes of this motion that Chavez did not commit a traffic violation, does not end the court's inquiry. Specifically, Gillette, Graham, and Cessna are still entitled to summary judgment if they can demonstrate that they are protected by qualified immunity. In their objections, Gillette, Graham, and Cessna argue that they had a right to rely on the information provided to them by Thomas. Although they do not specify what information Thomas provided to each officer, the essence of their position is that they were entitled to rely on a presumption that Thomas' stop of Chavez was justified. The magistrate judge recommended denial of all of the defendants' qualified immunity claims relating to Chavez, reasoning that Chavez had a clearly established right to be free of an unreasonable search. He also noted that it was clearly established that the police officers need probable cause to stop and detain a motorist and search for narcotics. He then concluded that, because Thomas' stop of Chavez was unreasonable from its inception, all of the officers subsequently involved in the stop were precluded from asserting a qualified immunity defense. Government officials performing discretionary functions generally are shielded from liability for civil damages unless their conduct violates clearly established statutory or constitutional rights of which a reasonable person would have known. A right is clearly established when its contours are sufficiently clear so that a reasonable official would realize that what he is doing violates that right. Qualified immunity is available if the official could reasonably have believed that his or her actions were lawful, even if the official ultimately turns out to have been mistaken.

As noted above, Gillette, Graham, and Cessna argue that they relied on unspecified information provided by Thomas as to the rationale for the stop and thus are entitled to qualified immunity. The court parts company with the magistrate judge as it does not agree that the facts in this case do not support a finding of qualified immunity with respect to Gillette, Graham, and Cessna to the extent that the plaintiffs seek to impose liability based on Thomas' stop of Chavez. The key inquiry with respect to qualified immunity is whether a reasonable officer could have believed that probable cause existed in light of clearly established law and the information possessed by the officer. To evaluate the officers' qualified immunity claim, the court must examine their specific knowledge of the facts from the perspective of a reasonable officer. Here, the only specific fact known by the officers is that another officer had previously stopped Chavez. Police officers are entitled to rely on information provided by other officers. This begs the question: did Thomas actually provide any information to Gillette, Graham, or Cessna? The defendants do not point to any specific information provided by Thomas, other than the fact that the officers knew that Thomas had previously stopped Chavez. Despite the plaintiffs' arguments, Gillette, Graham, and Cessna were entitled to rely on the presumption that Thomas had stopped Chavez based on an actual traffic violation. This means that Gillette, Graham, and Cessna are entitled to qualified immunity to the extent that the plaintiffs seek to impose liability on them based on Thomas' admittedly (for summary judgment purposes) improper stop of Chavez. With this in mind, the court turns to the next issue — whether Gillette, Graham, and Cessna's conduct at the scene was reasonably related to their presumption regarding the existence of a valid justification for the stop in the first instance.

A vehicle may be searched without a warrant if there is probable cause to believe that the car contains contraband. Chavez observes that he was not, in fact, concealing drugs in his car, and contests the qualifications of the canine who alerted to his vehicle. Nevertheless, it is uncontested that Gillette identified indicators that suggested drug activity. These indicators included California license plates, open maps, fast food wrappers, and air freshener. Indeed, Chavez admits that he intentionally emulated Koutsakis, a known drug courier, and that he was nervous during his encounter with the police. The search was also based, at least in part, on the fact that the canine handled by Graham, alerted, thereby indicating (albeit erroneously) the presence of drugs in Chavez' vehicle. Working from the premise that Gillette, Graham, and Cessna were entitled to believe that Thomas had properly stopped Chavez, the court is unwilling to conclude that Gillette and Cessna's search and their conduct during that search violated any clearly established constitutional right, as they were entitled to rely on the assumption that the stop was valid. In addition, it was not unreasonable for these officers to rely on the dog's alert as the basis for their ultimately fruitless search of Chavez' vehicle as they could not be expected to know of the issues relating to the dog's reliability. Accordingly, the undisputed facts demonstrate that Gillette and Cessna could reasonably have believed that their actions with respect to Chavez were lawful. Thus, they are entitled to qualified immunity, even though the underlying basis of the stop concededly did not occur. The court thus declines to accept the magistrate judge's R & R as to Gillette and Cessna's qualified immunity defense. Instead, the court finds that Gillette and Cessna are entitled to summary judgment on Chavez' Fourth Amendment claims based on qualified immunity.

The magistrate judge recommended that the defendants' motion to strike plaintiffs' claims for equitable relief be granted and that the defendants' motion to dismiss plaintiffs' state law claims be denied. Both sides have objected to the portions of the R & R which are adverse to them. Specifically, the plaintiffs claim that the magistrate judge based his recommendation with respect to the claims for equitable relief on an incorrect assumption that his recommendation on the defendants' motion for partial summary judgment, if sustained, would require this result. With respect to the recommendation regarding their motion to dismiss the plaintiffs' state law claims, the defendants contend that this court lacks jurisdiction and that the Illinois Court of Claims is the only court that may properly adjudicate these claims.

On February 9, 1996, the court granted the defendants' motion to dismiss the plaintiffs' claims for equitable relief based on lack of standing. Two amendments of the complaint later, the defendants moved to strike the plaintiffs' claims for equitable relief, the magistrate judge agreed that this was warranted, and the plaintiffs objected to that portion of the R & R. The plaintiffs seek an injunction against the defendants' alleged practice of stopping, detaining, and searching motorists based on race. The magistrate judge recommended dismissal of this request for injunctive relief, due to his recommendation with respect to the defendants' motion for partial summary judgment. The plaintiffs object, arguing that the magistrate judge's recommendation regarding equitable relief was based on an erroneous belief that a recommendation of partial summary judgment was enough to doom the claims for injunctive relief. According to the plaintiffs, the remaining pending claims form an adequate basis for their request for injunctive relief. The plaintiffs thus conclude that dismissal of the request for injunctive relief is incorrect. The plaintiffs also object to the magistrate judge's ruling denying their motion for leave to submit additional authority with respect to their motion.

The plaintiffs indeed have several claims pending as the defendants have only obtained partial summary judgment. The critical fact, however, is that the claim which forms the basis of the plaintiffs' request for class certification — equal protection — is not viable for the reasons discussed above. The question thus is whether the plaintiffs' pending claims can support their request for equitable relief. The answer to this question is "no," as the plaintiffs lack standing to obtain an injunction on their own behalf and the absence of an order certifying a class means that injunctive relief on behalf of the putative class would be improper.

The court agrees with the magistrate judge's conclusion that the court may properly consider matters outside the complaint when determining whether standing exists. The plaintiffs' standing to pursue their equitable claims, however, has not changed since the court's February 9, 1996 order denying the plaintiffs' motion for equitable relief. As the court previously noted, City of Los Angeles v. Lyons, 461 U.S. 95, 103 S.Ct. 1660, 75 L.Ed.2d 675 (1983), mandates that: "[t]he plaintiff must show that he `has sustained or is immediately in danger of sustaining some direct injury' as a result of the challenged official conduct and the injury or threat of injury must be both `real and immediate,' not `conjectural or hypothetical.'" Past "exposure to illegal conduct does not in itself show a present case or controversy regarding injunctive relief ... if unaccompanied by any continuing, present adverse effects." Moreover, past wrongs do not necessarily add up to the "real and immediate threat of future injury" necessary to satisfy the case or controversy requirement of Article III.

Before the court considers whether the plaintiffs have standing to pursue their request for equitable relief, it must determine what materials are properly before the court. The court concludes, in its discretion, that the parties' submissions do not, and will not, include any additional materials, as requested in the plaintiffs' objections to the magistrate judge's order denying the plaintiffs' leave to file affidavits in opposition to the defendants' motion to strike the plaintiffs' state law claims. This is because the court believes that the magistrate judge's order addressing this nondispositive motion was eminently reasonable in light of the procedural posture of this case, the timing of the plaintiffs' request, and the impact of the motion on the defendants. Accordingly, the plaintiffs' objections to the magistrate judge's order addressing the plaintiffs' motion for leave to file additional affidavits are overrruled.

With this in mind, the court turns to the motion to dismiss the plaintiffs' equitable claims. After careful consideration of the parties' submissions, the court concludes that the plaintiffs have failed to establish that injunctive relief based on the individual plaintiffs' claims is proper. Accordingly, the court grants the defendants' motion to strike the plaintiffs' request for equitable relief based on their individual claims without prejudice. The plaintiffs may renew this request if warranted by further proceedings with respect to the claims which survive the defendants' motion for partial summary judgment. To the extent that the plaintiffs seek injunctive relief on behalf of the putative class, the absence of an order certifying a class dooms any such request.

The plaintiffs' amended complaint includes three supplemental state law claims pursuant to 28 U.S.C. § 1367. Specifically, the plaintiffs claim that the defendants: (1) subjected them to unlawful searches and seizures in violation of Article I, § 6 of the Illinois Constitution; (2) violated their equal protection rights under Article I, § 2 of the Illinois Constitution; and (3) are liable for false imprisonment. The magistrate judge concluded that federal jurisdiction over these claims was proper and rejected the defendants' argument that the Illinois Court of Claims had to adjudicate them. The defendants object, contending that the Illinois Court of Claims has exclusive jurisdiction. In resolving this question, the court is bound by state rules of immunity. Under Illinois law, and specifically, the Court of Claims Act, the Illinois Court of Claims has "exclusive jurisdiction to hear and determine ... all claims against the State for damages in cases sounding in tort, if a like cause of action would lie against a private person or corporation in a civil suit ...." 705 ILCS § 505/8(d). According to the defendants, when an Illinois state trooper purportedly violates a state law claim by breaching a duty imposed solely as a virtue of his or her state employment, the Illinois Court of Claims has exclusive jurisdiction. Unsurprisingly, the plaintiffs disagree, contending that actions against state employees in their personal capacities are not suits against the state. They also assert that suits seeking damages for alleged constitutional violations are generally personal capacity suits.

The magistrate judge recommended that the defendants' motion to strike the plaintiffs' state law claim be denied, noting that only certain suits against state employees are suits against the state and thereby fall within the exclusive jurisdiction of the Illinois Court of Claims. The magistrate judge also noted that it is presumed that a state or its department does not violate the laws or constitution of that state and that, if such a violation does occur, it is solely an action of the servant or the agent of the state.

The Illinois Supreme Court has adopted a three-prong test to determine whether an action is against the State (and thus is within the exclusive jurisdiction of the Illinois Court of Claims) Healy v. Vaupel, 133 Ill.2d at 309, 140 Ill.Dec. 368, 549 N.E.2d at 1247. Specifically, an action is against the State if: (1) the plaintiff does not claim that the State's agent or employee acted beyond the scope of his authority; (2) the duty allegedly breached was not owed to the public generally independent of the fact of State employment; and (3) the alleged actions involved matters ordinarily within the agent or employee's normal and official State functions. Alternatively, an action is also deemed to be an action against the State if judgment in the plaintiff's favor could control the actions of the State or subject it to liability. Neither party has focused on the dispositive point with respect to sovereign immunity, which is that, according to the Illinois Supreme Court, the Court of Claims does not have exclusive jurisdiction if the plaintiff asserts that the state employee acted in violation of statutory or constitutional law. Thus, the defendants' arguments are irrelevant. For these reasons, the court agrees with the magistrate judge that federal jurisdiction over the plaintiffs' state law claims is proper and overrules the defendants' objections to the corresponding portion of the R & R addressing that issue.

The defendants' motion for partial summary judgment is granted in part and denied in part. Specifically, the defendants are entitled to summary judgment with respect to: (1) plaintiff Peso Chavez and plaintiff Gregory Lee's equal protection claims; (2) all plaintiffs' freedom of movement claims; (3) the claims against defendants Kenneth Hall, Lonnie Inlow, Kathleen Sauter and Michael Snyders; (4) Chavez' Fourth Amendment stop and search claims against Gillette and Cessna; and (5) Chavez' Fourth Amendment stop claim against Graham. The defendants' motion for summary judgment with respect to Chavez' Fourth Amendment search claim against Graham and the claims of plaintiff Joseph Gomez is denied. The following objections to additional reports and recommendations are overruled: (1) the plaintiffs' objections regarding their motion to strike certain paragraphs of the defendants' Local Rule 12(m) statements; (2) the plaintiffs' objections regarding their motion to modify discovery subpoena; (3) the plaintiffs' objections regarding their motion to file affidavits in opposition to the defendants' motion to strike and dismiss their claims for equitable relief and supplemental state law claims; (4) the plaintiffs' and defendants' objections regarding the defendants' motion to strike and dismiss the plaintiffs' claims for equitable relief and supplemental state law claims; (5) the plaintiffs' objections regarding their motion to certify a plaintiff class; and (6) the defendants' objections regarding the March 16, 1998 report and recommendation addressing Gregory Lee. The plaintiffs' objections regarding their motion to compel enforcement of subpoenas directed to the Office of the Secretary of State are overruled without prejudice to renewal by no later than 10 days after the date of this order. Finally, the court denies the plaintiffs' motion to continue the stay with respect to the defendants' summary judgment motion, the plaintiffs' motion to stay additional pending matters, and the plaintiffs' motion to withdraw and substitute the declaration of Martin Shapiro and associated filings.

REVIEW SECTION

READING COMPREHENSION

Detail the plaintiffs' complaints in this case.

Detail the relevance of *U.S. v. Armstrong* (1996) in this case.

What is the three-prong test elaborated by the Illinois Supreme Court to determine whether an action is against the state?

THINKING CRITICALLY

Why is the claim for equal protection not viable in this case? Do you agree or disagree?

CONCLUSION

State law provides the specifics passed by legislatures, and the Illinois Constitution is the principle used to guide citizens. This chapter outlined the difficulty of leading moral crusades in this country, through an elaboration of the sources of criminal procedure. It is the role of the courts to, in an attempt to balance process and result, interpret and reinterpret criminal procedure. Where however, should issues of morality be decided – in the courts or in the legislature? This chapter detailed the exchange between the U.S. Constitution and the U.S. Supreme Court, with specific emphasis on due process and equal protection of laws.

Chapter Three

Searches and Seizures

As a guiding principle, Article One, Section Six of the Illinois Constitution reads as follows regarding searches and seizures:

> The people shall have the right to be secure in their persons, houses, papers and other possessions against unreasonable searches, seizures, invasions of privacy or interceptions of communications by eavesdropping devices or other means. No warrant shall issue without probable cause, supported by affidavit particularly describing the place to be searched and the persons or things seized.

This is premised on the notion that while crime control depends on police gathering of information, this information frequently results from reluctant sources, and authorities must use only legal methods to obtain facts. To control crime, government officials rely on searches and seizures, interrogation, and identification procedures, all of which are involuntary. Thus, the state has created guidelines to ensure both the rights of individuals and fact-finding by police officials.

This chapter will review:

(1)   Searches and seizures;

(2)   The "expectation of privacy;"

(3)   Plain view, hearing, smell, and touch; and

(4)   Seizures.

SECTION 1: SEARCHES AND SEIZURES

OVERVIEW

Article One, Section Six of the Illinois Constitution comprises the main elements of the Fourth Amendment which was created to ensure the government follow the law in obtaining evidence. Initially warrants were used against seditious libels to control criticism of the government, and agents had the power to search anyone, at anytime, in any location. Opposition to the blanket power of such a general warrant was written into the Constitution in the Fourth Amendment. A reasonableness limit was established to protect one's liberty or right of movement, and one's privacy from government intrusion.

To determine whether or not the government has complied with the Fourth Amendment involves analysis of three questions that will be elaborated over several chapters:

(1)   Was the action by the government a search or a seizure?

(2)   If considered a search or a seizure, was it an unreasonable search or seizure?

(3)   If considered an unreasonable search or seizure, should the evidence obtained during the unreasonable search be excluded from consideration?

Further, actions taken by the government that may be considered Fourth Amendment searches or seizures take place in three stages that will also be elaborated over several chapters:

(1)   Encounters between citizens and government officials in public places;

(2)   Encounters between citizens and government officials after transportation to the police station; and

(3)   Encounters occurring after conviction between prisoners and jail/prison officials.

Not all encounters by government officials are considered searches and/or seizures, though keep in mind that as the level of government intrusion increases, the objective basis or facts and circumstances required to justify the action also increase. As you read cases involving motions to suppress evidence illegally seized, keep in mind the following partial text from 725 ILCS 5/114-12:

> (a) A Defendant aggrieved by an unlawful search and seizure may move the court for the return of property and to suppress as evidence anything so obtained on the ground that: (1) The search and seizure without a warrant was illegal; or (2) The search and seizure with a warrant was illegal because the warrant is insufficient on its face; the evidence seized is not that described in the warrant; there was not probable case for the issuance of the warrant; or, the warrant was illegally executed.

CASE

In *People v. Lampitok,* the defendant was arrested and charged with five offenses based on evidence found in his motel room by three probation officers. The officers went to the motel to verify whether defendant's fiancée had violated her probation order. Upon their arrival, defendant informed the officers that Bircher was not present but that she had been staying there. Despite defendant's objection, the officers conducted a warrantless search of the room pursuant to a search condition of Bircher's probation order and seized several items as evidence. Lampitok was later arrested and charged based on this evidence. After making several factual findings, the circuit court allowed the defendant's pretrial motion to quash arrest and suppress evidence. A divided appellate court affirmed. The Supreme Court of Illinois granted the State's petition for leave to appeal to address whether a search of defendant's motel room in which a probationer subject to a search condition was staying was reasonable under the fourth amendment.

PEOPLE V. LAMPITOK
Supreme Court of Illinois
Docket No. 93699-Agenda 2-May 2003.

Because we are reviewing the circuit court's ruling on a pretrial motion, the record before us is limited. In July 2000, defendant and Bircher were engaged to be married and were living with Bircher's cousin, Bobby Craig, Bircher's daughter, and two other roommates in an apartment on Madison Street in Charleston. Bircher reported this apartment as her place of residence as required by her probation order. Defendant and Bircher had been living in this apartment for approximately one month when Craig asked them to leave because the landlord was coming to inspect the apartment. Craig was listed on the lease, and the lease prohibited him from having roommates. At the motion hearing, Bircher testified that "Craig asked us to leave for a couple of days so they could do the inspection and then we were allowed to go back." Bircher also testified that she had clothes at this apartment, and her mailing address was in Charleston. She did not notify her probation officer about being at the motel because she had not moved. She acknowledged that under her probation order, which she had signed, her residence could be searched at any time.

On July 12, 2000, the first night away from the Charleston apartment, Bircher stayed with her cousin, Lori, in Mattoon, and defendant stayed at the U.S. Grant Motel in Mattoon. Defendant registered for the motel room while Bircher stayed in the car; defendant paid for the room for the nights of July 12 and 13. Bircher did not have a key to the room. Bircher and her daughter stayed in the room with defendant the night of July 13, and Bircher brought clothing with her. Bircher obtained a Salvation Army voucher to pay for the motel room for the night of July 14. Bircher testified that they intended to return to the Charleston apartment on the morning of July 15.

Probation Officer Steve Kelly also testified at the hearing. Bircher's probation officer, Mitch Goodwin, had attempted a routine home visit at Bircher's Charleston apartment on the morning of July 14. Kelly testified that Goodwin told him that "he made contact with two relatives and they stated that she no longer lived there, she was staying with Mr. Lampitok at the U.S. Grant Motel in Mattoon." Kelly, Goodwin, and fellow probation officer Vicki Starwalt discussed the situation. The three officers decided to go to the motel primarily to verify whether Bircher violated her probation order by changing residences without prior notification and also to verify whether Bircher was in further violation by residing in the presence of weapons or drugs. Kelly had previous personal encounters with defendant during which he suspected that defendant had been under the influence of drugs. During these encounters, defendant acknowledged that Bircher was on probation. Kelly admitted that at that time they had no information that defendant was involved in any illegal activity.

The officers arrived at the motel around 1:15 p.m. Goodwin and Kelly stopped at the motel office to ask what room Bircher was staying in, and they were directed to room 14. Goodwin knocked repeatedly on the door; the officers could hear movement in the room. Eventually, defendant answered the door. Goodwin asked whether Bircher was there, and defendant responded that she was not. Kelly also testified that "Officer Goodwin asked him if Kitty was staying there with him and he said yes." After additional conversation not disclosed in the record, Kelly informed defendant that they were going to enter the room. Defendant refused and attempted to close the door. Because Kelly was in the doorway with his foot in the door jam, defendant was unable to close the door. The officers entered, and nothing illegal was in plain view. Bircher was in fact absent, but she had left her two-year-old daughter in defendant's care. The officers did not have a warrant to search the motel room. As the officers began to search the room, defendant fled. Starwalt attended to the young girl. Kelly discovered a soft makeup bag containing a pistol and ammunition between the mattress and box springs of the bed. He also found a sword and a knife on the floor underneath this portion of the bed. Goodwin discovered a syringe and a plastic baggy with a white powder, later determined to be a controlled substance. Kelly speculated that Goodwin discovered this evidence in a duffel bag in the closet, but he was not certain because he was busy searching at the time.

Certain conditions of Bircher's probation order are relevant to this case: (1) That the Defendant shall not violate any criminal statute of any jurisdiction. (6) That the Defendant shall keep her Probation Officer advised of her place of residence and employment at all times, advising the Probation Officer prior to any change of residence or employment. (8) That the Defendant shall not possess a firearm or other dangerous weapon. (11) That the Defendant shall submit to a search of her person, residence, or automobile at any time as directed by her Probation Officer to verify compliance with the conditions of this Probation Order. Bircher's two-year probation period began April 6, 1999, so she clearly was on probation at the time of the July 14, 2000, search.

On the basis of the evidence seized from the motel room, defendant was arrested and charged with unlawful possession of a weapon by a felon, unlawful possession of firearm ammunition by a felon, unlawful possession of a hypodermic syringe, unlawful possession of a controlled substance, and armed violence. The circuit court made numerous findings when allowing defendant's motion to quash arrest and suppress evidence. The court stated that "a warrantless search was conducted without defendant's consent. The Probationer, Kitty Bircher, was not present. The defendant has standing to object to same. He was the registered tenant of the room searched with an expectation of privacy." The court found that paragraph 11 of Bircher's probation order was not authorized by section 5-6-3 of the Unified Code of Corrections. The court further condemned the search given the lack of applicable "regulations, guidelines, standards or procedures" comparable to those present in Griffin v. Wisconsin, 483 U.S. 868, 97 L. Ed. 2d 709, 107 S. Ct. 3164 (1987), and the lack of "reasonable grounds to believe that contraband was present or that the Probationer or the defendant had committed a criminal offense." The court also found that the motel room was not Bircher's residence.

A divided appellate court affirmed. The appellate court agreed with the circuit court that defendant was the registered tenant of the room and that he had an expectation of privacy in the room. The order did not review the finding that the room was not Bircher's residence because it did not consider that fact to be dispositive in its analysis. The order noted that although section 5-6-3(b) of the Code does not list submission to a probation search as a possible condition, it "may be" permissible under the section's general authorization of "other reasonable conditions relating to the nature of the offense or the rehabilitation of the defendant." However, Bircher's probation order required her to "submit to a search as directed by her Probation Officer." Because she was not present at the time of the search, she could not be directed by her probation officer to submit to the search. Thus, the search was not authorized by the probation order. In addition, defendant was not a probationer, the officers had no information that defendant was involved in criminal activity, and he did not consent to the search, making the search constitutionally unreasonable as to him.

The special concurrence noted that the relevant issue was whether the officers reasonably believed that the motel room was Bircher's residence rather than whether it was her actual residence. The record contained sufficient facts to find that the officers reasonably believed the room was Bircher's residence so that she was in violation of her requirement to notify them of a change in residence. The concurrence disagreed with the majority order's finding that defendant did not have a reduced expectation of privacy because he cohabited with a probationer. However, the concurrence agreed that the search did not comply with the probation order's specification that it be "directed by her Probation Officer," which required either Bircher's presence or notice of the search. Because the search was also warrantless, the evidence was properly suppressed on this basis. The dissent agreed with the special concurrence that the officers had a reasonable belief that the motel room was Bircher's residence and that defendant had a reduced expectation of privacy. However, the dissent did not agree that the probation order required Bircher's presence at the search because the probationer could always evade probation conditions by not answering the door or having another falsely claim she was gone.

The complexity of this issue and the inclusion of three separate appellate opinions in this order create an unusual disposition. The concurring and dissenting justices agree on the resolution of some issues so that they become the holding of the appellate court even though they are not found in the principal order. Specifically, these two justices agree that the officers had a reasonable belief that the motel room was Bircher's residence and that defendant had a reduced expectation of privacy. Two justices found that the language of Bircher's probation order required her to be present during a search so that she could initially submit to that search directed by her probation officer, the basis on which the court affirmed suppression of the evidence. Thus, although fourth amendment principles are discussed, the appellate court's affirmance of the suppression of the evidence is based on noncompliance with the terms of the probation order. In reviewing this appellate decision, we examine whether the search was unconstitutional so that the evidence it uncovered was properly suppressed. This fourth amendment analysis has several components: (A) a discussion of relevant case law, demonstrating that the search must be reasonable at its inception and in its scope under the totality of the circumstances; (B) a determination of what level of individualized suspicion is required for the probation search to be justified at its inception; (C) an evaluation of what level of individualized suspicion the officers had that Bircher was in violation of her probation order; (D) an examination of whether the scope of the search exceeded the initial justification for the search; and (E) an analysis of whether Bircher's acceptance of the search condition in her probation order constituted prospective consent to all searches, waiving fourth amendment protection.

The burden of proof is on the defendant at a hearing on a motion to suppress evidence. If the defendant makes a *prima facie* case that the evidence was obtained through an illegal search, then the State can counter with its own evidence. At the hearing, defendant contended that evidence was seized pursuant to an unconstitutional search; he offered testimony to support that the search of his motel room was nonconsensual, warrantless, and suspicionless and that the probationer, Bircher, was not present during the search. The State responded that this search was proper because the search was conducted pursuant to the search condition in Bircher's probation order and was conducted in compliance with fourth amendment principles. Generally, a circuit court's ruling on a motion to suppress evidence presents a mixed question of law and fact. The reviewing court upholds the factual findings and witness credibility determinations of the circuit court unless they are against the manifest weight of the evidence. If the reviewing court accepts the factual findings, it reviews *de novo* whether suppression is appropriate under those facts. In the present case, our conclusions do not depend upon factual findings by the circuit court that are disputed by the parties, so we conduct *de novo* review.

In his motion to quash arrest and suppress evidence, defendant challenged the search on both federal and state constitutional grounds. Defendant provides no specific argument that the Illinois Constitution should provide broader protection than that of the fourth amendment in this situation. Thus, we follow United States Supreme Court decisions on fourth amendment issues in this case. Pursuant to the exclusionary rule, courts are precluded from admitting evidence that is gathered by government officers in violation of the fourth amendment. The rule is not designed to redress the invasion of privacy experienced by the search victim. Instead, the exclusionary rule is a judicially created remedy that protects fourth amendment rights by deterring future unlawful police conduct. The exclusionary rule may be invoked by the victim of the unlawful search when the State seeks to introduce the evidence uncovered by the search in a criminal prosecution. The fourth amendment of the United States Constitution requires searches and seizures to be reasonable, "measured in objective terms by examining the totality of the circumstances." A defendant can claim fourth amendment protection if he or she has a "legitimate expectation of privacy" in the area or item searched. A legitimate expectation of privacy must be "one that society is prepared to recognize as reasonable" rather than a mere subjective expectation. We have held that hotel or motel guests generally are accorded the same fourth amendment protection in their rooms as residents in their private homes. A person's right to retreat into his or her home without unreasonable governmental interference is a core fourth amendment principle. A person's expectation of privacy is affected by living with another person, a point which typically arises in third-party consent cases. The law recognizes that a cohabitant possesses common authority over the premises such that he or she can consent to a search of the common area, meaning property of which there is "joint access or control for most purposes." Nonetheless, because cohabitation does not completely remove a person's expectation of privacy, defendant can claim fourth amendment protection in the motel room. Law enforcement officers are not entitled to enter, much less search, a person's home without a warrant absent exigent circumstances. Under the fourth amendment, entry into a motel room is the equivalent of entering into a defendant's home. The State does not assert that exigent circumstances existed in this case.

Further analysis is needed to determine whether the officers were entitled to search the motel room for evidence that Bircher had violated her probation order. In the usual case, the fourth amendment requires the government to obtain a warrant supported by probable cause before conducting a search. The Court has noted, however, that "there are exceptions to the warrant requirement. When faced with special law enforcement needs, diminished expectations of privacy, minimal intrusions, or the like, the Court has found that certain general, or individual circumstances may render a warrantless search or seizure reasonable."

In Illinois, Section 5-6-3 of the Code addresses conditions of probation. Subsection (a) specifies eight required probation conditions; subsection (b) provides numerous examples of conditions that the court in its discretion may require, "in addition to other reasonable conditions relating to the nature of the offense or the rehabilitation of the defendant as determined for each defendant." Neither subsection lists a search condition, so this provision does not impose a particular standard of suspicion to support a search. We decline to follow the State's suggestion that the requirement that other discretionary probation conditions be "reasonable" itself imposes a "reasonable grounds" requirement specifically upon probation searches. In addition, the Illinois Administrative Code contains no regulation of probation searches.

We apply the totality-of-the-circumstances test to the facts of this case to determine whether this search was reasonable at its inception and in its scope under the fourth amendment. When evaluating the propriety of this search pursuant to Bircher's search condition, we balance the level of intrusion on personal privacy against the degree of need for the search to promote legitimate government interests. The State of Illinois certainly has a legitimate interest in promoting its probation system effectively. We recognize that our probation system serves the purposes of rehabilitating probationers while punishing them and protecting the public from crime. We agree that supervising the administration of the probation system is a "special need" of the state beyond the typical needs of law enforcement that justifies a greater governmental intrusion on privacy than would be constitutional as to an ordinary citizen. In addition, imposing the traditional warrant and probable-cause requirements would unduly interfere with the effective administration of the Illinois probation system. The probation officer, given his or her personal experience with the probationer, is better able to determine the level of supervision required than a neutral magistrate, and the process of obtaining a warrant would delay the officer's ability to respond to evidence of misconduct by the probationer. Similarly, requiring probable cause would facilitate the probationer's evasion of probation conditions through concealment of misconduct. We acknowledge that the importance of the Illinois probation system may justify a warrantless search of a probationer upon a lesser degree of suspicion than probable cause.

A probationer has a reduced expectation of privacy compared to ordinary citizens because he or she is a criminal offender. Specifically, section 5-6-3 of the Code authorizes the imposition of reasonable probation conditions, which legitimately limit a probationer's liberty. Because Bircher agreed to a more limited probation search condition, her expectation of privacy was not as diminished, and more individualized suspicion was required by the fourth amendment. However, we conclude that a probation search of Bircher upon no individualized suspicion would be constitutionally unreasonable. In addition, although Bircher has a reduced expectation of privacy as a probationer subject to a search condition, the search of the motel room remains a significant intrusion on her privacy. Again, whether or not room 14 was Bircher's actual residence at the time of the search, we regard fourth amendment protection for guests in motel rooms the same as for residents in their private homes. The primacy of fourth amendment protection against intrusions into a person's home further encourages us to require some level of individualized suspicion prior to a probation search of a probationer's residence.

After balancing these privacy and government interest considerations under the circumstances of this case, we find that the officers were constitutionally authorized to search the motel room only if they had reasonable suspicion of a probation violation by Bircher. Even though neither Bircher's probation order nor Illinois regulations imposed a reasonable suspicion requirement, the search can be valid under the fourth amendment if the officers actually had reasonable suspicion of a probation violation supporting the probation search. Even though the Supreme Court has not yet directly addressed this issue, we note that the clear majority of federal courts of appeals also require reasonable suspicion to support a probation search. In addition, none of the cases in which the Court has permitted warrantless searches without individualized suspicion involved a search of the home. "Exceptions to the requirement of individualized suspicion are generally appropriate only where the privacy interests implicated by a search are minimal and where other safeguards are available to assure that the individual's reasonable expectation of privacy is not subject to the discretion of the official in the field" (Delaware v. Prouse, 440 U.S. 648, 654-55 (1979). In contrast, a search of a person's home, whether consisting of one room or an entire house, cannot be characterized as a minor invasion of privacy. The clear trend in the federal courts of appeals and the rarity of the Court's allowance of warrantless, suspicionless searches provide additional support for our conclusion that a probation search of the residence of a probationer subject to a search condition like Bircher's complies with the fourth amendment reasonableness requirement only if the searching officers had reasonable suspicion of a probation violation.

Next, we evaluate whether the officers had reasonable suspicion that Bircher had violated her probation order so that the search was justified at its inception under the fourth amendment. Reasonable suspicion exists when "articulable facts which, taken together with the rational inferences from those facts, warrant a reasonably prudent officer" to investigate further. Reasonable suspicion is a less stringent standard than probable cause, but it requires more than a mere hunch on the part of the officer. An officer's good-faith, subjective belief that he or she has sufficient suspicion to justify the intrusion alone is inadequate to satisfy the objective reasonable suspicion standard. In the present case, the officers decided to go to the motel on July 14 because Bircher's relatives told Officer Goodwin that Bircher was no longer living at the Charleston apartment and that she was staying with defendant at a specific Mattoon motel. If this constituted a change in residence, Bircher had violated the probation condition requiring her to give her probation officer notice of such a change. The officers were told at the motel's front desk that Bircher was staying in room 14. Upon answering the door to room 14, defendant admitted that Bircher was staying there.

Officer Kelly identified an additional purpose to going to the motel: to check for the presence of weapons and/or drugs because she was staying with defendant. However, Kelly admitted at the motion hearing that he "had no specific information from anyone that Mr. Lampitok was doing anything illegal." Instead, any notion that defendant could bring Bircher in contact with weapons or drugs appears to be based on a prior encounter. Kelly and defendant were at a scene where drugs and a syringe were present and arrests were made. Defendant was not arrested during this incident, but Kelly speculated that defendant appeared to be "under the influence of something." On this basis, defendant's "reputation preceded him." No testimony at the hearing otherwise potentially linked defendant or Bircher with drugs or weapons, and Bircher's conviction leading to her sentence of probation was for felony forgery rather than for a drug- or weapon-related offense. The State aptly summarizes this evidence as: (1) Bircher never informed her probation officer that she left the Charleston apartment, and (2) she was living with a suspected drug user.

The information the officers possessed that Bircher might be in the presence of drugs or weapons was less substantial than knowledge of criminal history. The record indicates that one officer had a subjective perception that defendant was a drug user; there is no indication in the record that defendant was ever arrested for or convicted of a drug-related offense. Absolutely no evidence links Bircher directly with drugs or weapons. We conclude that the officers did not have reasonable suspicion that Bircher violated her probation order by possessing weapons or drugs merely because she cohabited with defendant, a suspected drug user. Individualized suspicion must be based at least in part on facts indicating possible present criminal activity. The additional fact that defendant delayed opening the motel room door for an unspecified time period is insufficient to show that the officers had reasonable suspicion that Bircher possessed weapons or drugs. Thus, a search by the officers of room 14 for the sole purpose of discovering drugs and weapons was unreasonable in violation of the fourth amendment under the facts of this case.

A closer question is presented by whether officers had reasonable suspicion that Bircher was in violation of her probation order by changing residences without notifying her probation officer in advance. In evaluating whether reasonable suspicion exists, the court should consider the quality and content of information known to officers as well as the reliability of the source of the information. Certain factors can support a finding of reasonable suspicion, including corroboration of the tip through observation by officers, inclusion of details in the tip, explanation of the basis of knowledge of the tip by the informant, and little passage of time between receiving tip and acting upon it by officers. Other factors can belie such a finding, including anonymity of the tipster, and absence of track record of supplying reliable information by known tipster. However, deficiency or uncertainty in the reliability of the informant can be compensated for by a strong level of detail and corroboration of the content of the tip, and vice versa. The officers received information from three sources that Bircher was staying at the motel rather than her listed Charleston apartment. Though not anonymous, they had no track record of providing reliable information. In addition, Craig had an incentive to lie because he was violating his lease by allowing Bircher and defendant to reside there. However, as relatives and roommates, they had explained the source of their knowledge. In addition, the relatives gave the specific name of the motel at which Bircher was staying, which was corroborated before the search took place by the motel clerk and defendant himself, neither of whom had an incentive to answer as they did. The officers certainly had a reasonable suspicion prior to the search that Bircher was staying at the motel. However, at issue is whether Bircher had changed her residence from the Charleston apartment to room 14 because she would have been in violation of her probation order only if she had changed residences without giving prior notice to her probation officer. Thus, the officers needed to have reasonable suspicion that room 14 had become Bircher's residence. Kelly admitted at the suppression hearing that he did not have independent knowledge about the reliability of these relatives. The record does not indicate whether Goodwin knew that these relatives were also Bircher's roommates or that under his lease Craig had reason to convey an impression that he had no roommates given the imminent inspection by his landlord. We conclude that the officers reasonably decided to investigate further whether Bircher had in fact changed her residence because the statement that she had moved came from Bircher's relatives present at the Charleston apartment. Thus, we find that the officers had reasonable suspicion that Bircher had changed residences without providing prior notification, in violation of her probation order. At the inception of the search, the officers were constitutionally justified in searching room 14 to verify whether Bircher had in fact changed residences in violation of her probation order but not to look for weapons and drugs.

Our fourth amendment inquiry does not end here, however. Under Terry, we must determine whether the search "was reasonably related in scope to the circumstances which justified the interference in the first place." We already have found that the officers were not entitled to search for weapons or drugs under the facts of this case; they were entitled only to verify that Bircher was residing in room 14. We find that the officers were only authorized to check whether Bircher was in fact in room 14 despite defendant's statement to the contrary. Searching for Bircher herself was the constitutional limit to a probation search premised on reasonable suspicion that Bircher had changed residences without notifying her probation officer. The record, however, discloses that none of the evidence used to charge defendant was found in plain view. Clearly the search between the mattress and box springs of the bed, for example, was conducted to check for weapons and drugs rather than to confirm Bircher's residence in the room. Thus, we find that the circuit court properly suppressed all the evidence found in room 14 because it was discovered beyond the constitutionally reasonable scope of the probation search.

We address a final fourth amendment issue raised by the State. The State asserts that Bircher's acceptance of the conditions of her probation constituted prospective consent that waived fourth amendment protection. None of the probation conditions explicitly express a waiver of fourth amendment rights. Each of the 20 conditions of Bircher's probation, including the search condition, begin with the phrase "That the Defendant" shall do or refrain from doing certain things. The inclusion of this phrase is significant because it shows that compliance by Bircher is dependent on her conduct. In other words, the search condition did not directly empower her probation officer to conduct searches to verify compliance; it required action by Bircher, that she "shall submit" to a search. The term "shall" is often the focus of scrutiny during statutory interpretation. We note the primary definition of "shall" is, "has a duty to; more broadly, is required to." In other words, by accepting the probation order, Bircher accepted a duty to submit to a probation search when directed to do so by her probation officer. Creating such a duty implies a requirement of further action by Bircher rather than a prospective consent toward possible future, unspecified searches. We are informed about the meaning of "submit" by examining the usage of this term elsewhere in the probation order. The term "submit" appears only in one other condition (20). It is reasonable to conclude that "submit" was used similarly in the search condition, that upon the request of the probation officer she would either have to agree to permit the search or face possible probation revocation. These probation conditions were mandatory limits upon the liberty of Bircher. However, their mandatory nature did not remove the element of choice from Bircher's life. During the period of her probation, Bircher repeatedly was faced with the decision of whether to comply with these conditions or whether to face revocation of her probation and possible incarceration, just as all citizens are subject to the requirements and proscriptions of civil and criminal laws and regulations. We find that the plain language of this probation search condition affirmatively required Bircher's probation officer to ask her to consent—or submit—to a particular search prior to conducting it; agreeing to the probation order did not constitute a prospective consent to all probation searches that waived fourth amendment protection.

The circuit court properly suppressed the evidence found in room 14 because the search that uncovered it was constitutionally unreasonable in its scope. The judgment of the appellate court is affirmed.

REVIEW SECTION

READING COMPREHENSION

Detail the facts of the case and the role of the traditional warrant and probable cause requirements.

THINKING CRITICALLY

Agree or disagree with the following statement by the Illinois Supreme Court in this case: "Imposing the traditional warrant and probable cause requirements would unduly interfere with the effective administration of the Illinois probation system."

SECTION 2: EXPECTATION OF PRIVACY

OVERVIEW

Until 1967 the trespass doctrine was implemented by the U.S. Supreme Court to define searches. This doctrine deemed a 'search' by officers any physical invasion of a 'constitutionally protected area,' which included persons, houses, papers, and effects as named in the Fourth Amendment. In 1967 in *Katz v. United States*, the privacy doctrine became law. This doctrine interpreted the Fourth Amendment to protect persons as opposed to places, whenever a citizen has an expectation of privacy recognized by the larger society. What was not so clearly elaborated was when an individual has a reasonable expectation of privacy, and what constitutes a plain-view search by government officials. While in theory the privacy doctrine shifted the balance in favor of the citizenry, courts almost always weigh the balance in favor of the government. Established by the privacy doctrine was a test to determine whether a government action can be considered a search. First, the subjective privacy prong addresses whether the citizen had an actual individual expectation of privacy. Second, the objective privacy prong addresses whether the subjective expectation of privacy is one that would be considered reasonable by society.

Fourth Amendment protection extends to persons, houses, papers, and effects, however places considered unprotected such as open fields, public places, and abandoned property are not guaranteed. What are the guidelines however in defining an unprotected place? With regard to open fields, included are privately owned lands that are not within the area immediately surrounding one's home. To determine this, the court considers the distance from the home, the presence/absence of a fence, the purpose of the area in question, and the measures taken by a citizen to protect this area from public view. A public place is considered publicly owned areas and private places that are open to the public. Abandoned property includes both physical abandonment as well as an intention to surrender the expectation of privacy. The court has adopted a totality-of-circumstance test to differentiate a place with an expectation of privacy from a place considered unprotected and thus not addressed by the Fourth Amendment.

CASE

In *People v. Pitman,* the defendant was indicted in circuit court on one count of unlawful manufacture of cannabis, in that he knowingly manufactured more than 500 grams but not more than 2,000 grams of a substance containing cannabis. He filed a motion to suppress evidence and quash arrest. Defendant moved to suppress, *inter alia*, marijuana plants seized following a search of a farm occupied by defendant. At the close of a hearing, the circuit court granted defendant's motion to suppress. The State brought an interlocutory appeal to the appellate court. The appellate court, with one justice dissenting, reversed the circuit court's suppression order and remanded the cause to the circuit court for further proceedings. The Supreme Court of Illinois has allowed the defendant's petition for leave to appeal and reverses the judgment of the appellate court, affirms the suppression order of the circuit court, and remands the cause to the circuit court for further proceedings.

PEOPLE V. PITMAN
Supreme Court of Illinois
Docket No. 95783 — Agenda 2 — March 2004.

Mary Pitman owned a 93-acre farm in Macoupin County. Pitman is defendant's mother and Sherry White's aunt; White is defendant's cousin. The farm contained two residences, a farmhouse and a trailer. In July 1999, White lived in the farmhouse; defendant, his girlfriend Amy Curtis, and their two children lived in the trailer. On Friday, July 16, or Saturday, July 17, 1999, White drove behind a person she believed to be a police officer. She followed him to his home. Unbeknownst to White, the officer was Alan Bondy, the chief of police. White knocked on his front door and they spoke on his porch. According to White: "I knocked on the door and told him I had a question to ask him, because I was living at a farm and keeping the upkeep, and someone else that was living on the same farm, but down the road, was growing marijuana, and I was wanting to know if I would get into any trouble, or if the person that owned the land would get their farm taken away, and if there was a couple that lived there, and if they would get their kids taken away." According to White, Bondy responded: "He said, `It wouldn't be the Pitman farm out there, would it?' I didn't say nothing, and I could tell he could tell by the look on my face. But I said, `Well, if you know if it's the Pitman farm, why don't you go out there and bust him?' He said he knew Shane Pitman had been growing marijuana for a while, and they was after the bigger guys, that they weren't going to bother him." At the end of their conversation, according to White: "he told me that I wouldn't get in no trouble, I more or less just took it that that would be it. I turned around and left and went home back to the farm." Their entire conversation lasted under a minute. White testified that she did not describe the location of the plants. She did not give Bondy permission to come onto the premises to search. She did not ask Bondy to have defendant arrested and the plants removed. Between that day and July 20, White was never contacted by anyone from the Illinois State Police. No law enforcement officer ever asked her anything about the plants. She never gave anyone permission to come onto the premises.

Alan Bondy testified as follows. White knocked on his front door and he answered. According to Bondy: "She introduced herself as Sherry White, said she was renting a farm from her Aunt Mary out east of town." Further: "She was concerned over cannabis being grown on the property and was curious whether she would get in trouble or the owner of the property, being her Aunt Mary, would be subject to lose the property because of the cannabis being grown." Bondy asked White if defendant was growing the marijuana, and White responded "yes." White asked Bondy that if he knew that defendant was growing the marijuana, why did Bondy not go out to the farm and arrest defendant? Bondy told White that the farm was located outside of his jurisdiction. Further, according to Bondy, White gave him details as to where the marijuana was growing on the premises: "She said that she had found 13 Dixie cups with starter plants in them, she had found a patch of plants growing behind the barn, behind the house that she lived in. The barn was behind the house that she stayed in, and it was growing behind the barn, and there was another patch across the creek that was growing, on the other side of a hill or somewhere." White informed Bondy that "Shane was cultivating, he was taking care of the plants, and that's what made her nervous." However, White was somewhat relieved when Bondy offered his opinion that the farm was not in jeopardy because White came forward with this information, and because Mary Pitman had no knowledge of defendant's activity. Bondy told White that he would have to relay the information to the proper authorities. He told White that "the Drug Task Force would be out there and do an investigation, and they would contact her." The entire conversation lasted "not more than 5 to 10 minutes."

According to Bondy, the extent of his involvement was that he took a statement from White and relayed that information to the Illinois State Police. Bondy telephoned the Task Force and left a message. The following week, Dale Reels returned Bondy's call, and Bondy gave Reels the information. Dale Reels was a patrolman with the Carlinville police department, assigned to the South Central Illinois Drug Task Force, which was a unit of the Illinois State Police. At approximately 1 p.m. on Monday July, 19, 1999, Officer Reels telephoned Bondy. Reels had known defendant for a few months because defendant had been a confidential informant for the Drug Task Force. The next day, Tuesday, July 20, 1999, Officer Reels drove to the Pitman farm. During his testimony, Reels was asked whether there was "ample time for you to go obtain a search warrant for the premises on the basis that there is cannabis growing there," to which he answered, "There would have been time, yes." Officer Reels arrived at the Pitman farm at approximately 2:25 p.m. With him was Macoupin County deputy sheriff Ron Lewis, also assigned to the Drug Task Force. Neither Reels nor Lewis had spoken with White prior to that time. They went to the premises to interview White.

The 93-acre farm was located along a road that ran north and south. The farm was on the west side of the road; the farmhouse faced the road to the east. A driveway off of the road was located on the north side of the house. On one side of the driveway was a sign that read "Private Property" and on the other side a sign that read "No Trespassing." Defendant's trailer was located "at least a football field's length" north of the house. The trailer had its own driveway off of the road. Reels and Lewis had previously been to defendant's trailer when defendant had been an informant. The testimony conflicts at this point. According to Reels and Lewis, they went to the front door of the house, knocked, and called, "Anybody home?" Hearing no answer, they went to the back door and knocked. Upon hearing no answer, they walked toward the barn located behind the house. However, Amy Curtis, defendant's girlfriend, testified that on the afternoon of July 20, 1999, she was driving past the farm when she saw an automobile parked in the driveway. From previous encounters, she recognized the automobile as an unmarked police car. She pulled into the driveway behind the police car and exited her car. She saw one man on the front porch at the door and another sitting in the police car. According to Curtis: "I asked him Can I help you? And he said I am looking for Sherry White." Curtis responded that White was at work, but would return home between 3 and 3:30 p.m. Curtis then returned to her car, backed out of the driveway, and drove up the road to her trailer. She saw the police car back out of the driveway and drive away from the house. Reels and Lewis were each asked whether a woman drove to the house and asked them why they were there. Each responded that he could not remember. Also, neither Reels nor Lewis could remember seeing the "Private Property" and "No Trespassing" signs posted on the driveway.

According to Reels and Lewis, after they received no answer at the back door of the house, they walked away from the house and toward the barn. That building was one of several outbuildings west of the house. The barn was located approximately 50 yards directly behind the house. The barn had large doors on the east and west sides. The south side of the barn did not have a wall;

rather, it had a canopy off of it that covered a feedlot. The east doors of the barn were open. Reels and Lewis entered the east side of the barn. Once inside, they first saw rolls of carpet and loose straw. The officers next observed marijuana plants growing in the feedlot on the south side of the barn. Some of the plants were planted in five-gallon buckets and some were planted in the ground. These mature plants were at least four feet tall; many were taller than six feet. The plants were interspersed with thick horseweeds. In addition to these mature plants, Reels and Lewis observed small marijuana plants in Dixie cups, known as starter plants, located outside along the southwest side of the barn. Reels and Lewis testified that they did not see the marijuana plants from any road, from the driveway, or even at the open doorway on the east side of the barn. Rather, they could see the plants only after they entered the barn.

Reels and Lewis returned to their car and left the farm; they were on the premises for no longer than five minutes. Approximately two hours later, they returned with a third officer, Joe Konnecker. The three officers set up surveillance at several points around the barn. At approximately 5 p.m., defendant appeared and entered the barn. The officers then took defendant into custody and seized the marijuana plants. According to Reels and Lewis, after defendant was taken into custody, White made her presence known to the officers, invited them into the farmhouse, and made a handwritten statement. White testified that she wrote the statement only after the officers threatened her with a felony charge. The officers left defendant at the farm. On December 3, 1999, defendant was indicted on one count of unlawful manufacture of cannabis and arrested on January 18, 2000.

Defendant moved to quash his arrest and to suppress, *inter alia*, the seized marijuana plants. At the close of the suppression hearing, the trial court granted defendant's motion. The circuit court found that White never consented to the officers' entry onto the property. Accordingly, the circuit court concluded that "the search was improper because it was done as part of a trespass." The circuit court suppressed the marijuana plants. On appeal, the appellate court, with one justice dissenting, reversed the circuit court's suppression order. The appellate court held that defendant did not have a legitimate expectation of privacy in the barn area because: (1) the area was outside of the curtilage of defendant's trailer and the farmhouse, and (2) the barn was abandoned. Accordingly, the appellate court concluded that the officers' entry into the barn did not violate defendant's constitutional rights. In light of that conclusion, the appellate court did not address whether White consented to the search. The appellate court remanded the cause to the circuit court for further proceedings. We allowed defendant's petition for leave to appeal. Additional pertinent facts will be discussed in the context of the issues raised on appeal.

Defendant contends that the appellate court erred in reversing the circuit court's order granting his motion to suppress. In reviewing a circuit court's ruling on a motion to suppress, mixed questions of law and fact are presented. Findings of historical fact made by the circuit court will be upheld on review unless such findings are against the manifest weight of the evidence. This deferential standard of review is grounded in the reality that the circuit court is in a superior position to determine and weigh the credibility of the witnesses, observe the witnesses' demeanor, and resolve conflicts in their testimony. However, a reviewing court remains free to undertake its own assessment of the facts in relation to the issues presented and may draw its own conclusions when deciding what relief should be granted. Accordingly, we review *de novo* the ultimate question of whether the evidence should be suppressed. This standard of review supplants what had been the traditional standard of review for suppression orders. This court formerly stated that a trial court's ruling on a motion to suppress would not be disturbed on appeal unless that ruling was manifestly erroneous, but *de novo* review was appropriate where neither the facts nor the credibility of witnesses was questioned.

This court has interpreted the search and seizure provision found in section 6 in a manner that is consistent with the fourth amendment jurisprudence of the United States Supreme Court. Warrantless searches are generally considered unreasonable unless they fall within a few specific exceptions. It is now fundamentally recognized that the Fourth Amendment protects people, not places. But the extent to which the Fourth Amendment protects people may depend upon where those people are. Accordingly, to claim the protection of the fourth amendment, a defendant must demonstrate that he or she personally has an expectation of privacy in the place searched and that his or her expectation is reasonable. Defendant initially contends that the State waived for appellate review the issue of whether the barn was within the curtilage of the farmhouse or the trailer. Defendant posits that the State's sole theory at the suppression hearing was White's implicit consent to the search, and that the State never raised the issue of curtilage. In the appellate court, according to defendant, the State argued that defendant lacked standing to challenge the legality of the search of the barn and the resulting seizure of the marijuana plants. We cannot accept defendant's waiver argument. In the circuit court, the State filed a motion to reconsider the suppression order. The State contended that defendant did not have a legitimate expectation of privacy in the barn because, *inter alia*, he lived a significant distance from the barn and it was not part of the curtilage of his mobile home. We agree with the State that it sufficiently raised the argument that defendant did not have a reasonable expectation of privacy in the barn. Further, in light of the record, it was appropriate for the appellate court to characterize the State's argument as an argument that the searched area did not fall within the curtilage of defendant's residence.

Turning to the merits, a person does not have a legitimate expectation of privacy for actions conducted outside in fields, except in the area immediately surrounding the home. Thus, fourth amendment protection extends to a home's curtilage, i.e., the land immediately surrounding and associated with the home. Conversely, no legitimate expectation of privacy attaches to land outside of the home's curtilage, i.e., open fields. In determining whether a particular area falls within a home's curtilage, a court asks whether the area harbors the intimate activities commonly associated with the sanctity of a person's home and the privacies of life. The extent of the curtilage is determined by factors that bear upon whether an individual reasonably may expect that the area in question should be treated as the home itself. These factors include: (1) the proximity of the area claimed to be the home's curtilage; (2) whether the area is included within an enclosure surrounding the home; (3) the nature of the uses to which the area is put; and (4) the steps taken by the resident to protect the area from observation by people passing by.

The appellate court applied these factors as follows: As to the first factor, the barn is located between 40 and 60 yards from the farmhouse, the closest residence even under defendant's analysis. Such a substantial distance does not support an inference that the barn should be treated as an adjunct of the house. Second, the barn was not within an enclosure surrounding the farmhouse or the trailer. The open nature of the land between the barn and the two residences negates an expectation of privacy in the barn area. Third, the barn was no longer used for agricultural purposes and was only used by Mary Pitman to store rolls of carpet. Last, nothing prohibited observation of the barn area from those standing in the open field. Mary Pitman testified a `no trespassing' sign and `private property' sign were posted at the entrance to the driveway. However, as the Supreme Court has noted it is not generally true that `no trespassing' signs effectively bar the public from viewing open fields in rural areas. Accordingly, the curtilage of both the trailer and the farmhouse did not extend to the barn area. We agree with the appellate court.

Abandonment. The appellate court answered this question in the negative, reasoning as follows: "The record contains no facts that defendant utilized the barn itself. With the doors unlocked and wide open as well as an open side, the barn was not secured. The barn was essentially abandoned. Generally, no expectation of privacy exists in property that has been abandoned. Thus, defendant had no expectation of privacy in the barn. Accordingly, the officers' entry into the barn and search of the barn area did not violate defendant's constitutional rights. In light of our finding that defendant's constitutional rights were not violated by the police officers' search, we need not address whether White consented to the search." We disagree with this reasoning.

The controlling principles are settled: Abandoned property is not subject to Fourth Amendment protection because Fourth Amendment protection only extends to places and items for which a person has a reasonable expectation of privacy, and no person can have a reasonable expectation of privacy in an item that he has abandoned. To demonstrate abandonment, the government must establish by a preponderance of the evidence that the defendant's voluntary words or conduct would lead a reasonable person in the searching officer's position to believe that the defendant relinquished his property interests in the item searched or seized. We look at the totality of the circumstances, but pay particular attention to explicit denials of ownership and to any physical relinquishment of the property. The record in the present case is devoid of any evidence that defendant relinquished his expectation of privacy in the barn. The appellate court's conclusion to the contrary was erroneous.

Thus, the question remains whether defendant had a legitimate expectation of privacy in the barn. We conclude that he had. Several factors should be examined to determine whether a defendant possesses a reasonable expectation of privacy: (1) ownership of the property searched; (2) whether the defendant was legitimately present in the area searched; (3) whether defendant has a possessory interest in the area or property seized; (4) prior use of the area searched or property seized; (5) the ability to control or exclude others from the use of the property; and (6) whether the defendant himself had a subjective expectation of privacy in the property.

The circuit court's findings of fact, with the entire record, support the conclusion that defendant had a legitimate expectation of privacy in the barn. Although defendant did not own the farm, and specifically the barn, defendant clearly had a possessory interest in the entire farm and had the ability to control or exclude others from the use of the property. The record shows that Mary Pitman conferred on defendant the legal authority to take care of the farm. The illegal nature of defendant's activities did not make defendant's expectation of privacy unreasonable. Further, defendant need not have taken affirmative steps to proclaim his expectation of privacy. The fact that the public could have discovered the plants by trespassing on the farm fails to legitimize an otherwise invalid search. A defendant simply must outwardly behave as a typical occupant of the space in which the defendant claims an interest, avoiding anything that might publicly undermine his or her expectation of privacy. We hold that defendant had a legitimate expectation of privacy in the barn. Since Reels and Lewis searched defendant's barn without a warrant, the search is deemed unreasonable under the fourth amendment unless the search falls within a specific exception.

A well-settled, specific exception to the fourth amendment's warrant requirement is a search conducted pursuant to consent. This consent may be obtained not only from the individual whose property is searched, but also from a third party who possesses common authority over the premises. Such authority is based on mutual use of the property by persons generally having joint access or control for most purposes. Therefore, it is reasonable to recognize that any of the cohabitants has the right to permit the inspection in his or her own right, and that the others have assumed the risk that one of their number might permit a common area to be searched. Further, a warrantless search based on the consent of a person having apparent, though not actual, authority to give such consent is lawful if, at the time of the search, the police reasonably believe that person to have common authority over the place or item to be searched. In the suppression order, the circuit court focused on the issue of whether White consented to the search. The only information the police officers had here is that a lady by the name of White came in, told Bondy something, and asked Bondy to have the police contact her. From there on, the rest of the things that the officers did was over and above and beyond the information that they had. They had nobody's consent at that time. The State contends, as an additional reason to affirm the appellate court, that White expressly, or at least impliedly, consented to the search of the barn. The State contends that the circuit court's finding to the contrary was against the manifest weight of the evidence. We uphold the circuit court's finding of no consent. Whether consent has been given is a question of fact to be determined initially in the circuit court. Because a court of review is not in a position to observe witnesses as they testify, it is not within the province of a court of review to assess the credibility of witnesses. When the evidence on the issue of consent is conflicting, this court will uphold the circuit court's finding unless it is clearly unreasonable. After reviewing the evidence presented at the suppression hearing, we cannot say that the circuit court's finding of no consent was unreasonable.

For the foregoing reasons, the judgment of the appellate court is reversed; the order of the circuit court which granted defendant's motion to suppress, is affirmed; and the cause is remanded to the circuit court for further proceedings. Appellate court judgment reversed; circuit court order affirmed; cause remanded.

JUSTICE THOMAS, dissenting: I agree with the majority's conclusions that the barn was in the open fields, outside of the curtilage, and that Sherry White did not consent to the search. I disagree, however, with the majority's conclusion that defendant had a reasonable expectation of privacy in the barn. The majority's analysis on this issue is at odds with all of the state and federal cases that have considered searches of barns or outbuildings located on farm property lying outside of the curtilage of a farmhouse. I therefore dissent.

Initially, I note that defendant's motion to suppress did not allege that he had a reasonable expectation of privacy in the barn. Nor did defendant specifically raise this issue in the trial court. Instead, defendant only alleged and argued that (1) police entered the premises without the consent of the owner or tenant; (2) police were trespassing when they came onto the property; and (3) there was no exigent circumstances to justify a warrantless search. The burden of proof is on the defendant at a hearing on a motion to suppress. Only if the defendant makes out a *prima facie* case that the evidence was obtained through an illegal search does the burden shift to the State to counter with its own evidence. Before a defendant can complain of a violation of the fourth amendment, he has to make a showing that he has a reasonable expectation of privacy in the place or thing being searched and that his expectation is reasonable. Here, defendant did not make out a *prima facie* case showing that he had a reasonable expectation of privacy in the barn. Indeed, defendant did not even allege that he had a reasonable expectation of privacy in the barn in his motion to suppress. I would therefore find that, at the very least, any insufficiency in the record should be resolved in favor of the State. I would also find that the State correctly argued in its motion to reconsider that defendant had failed to meet the threshold requirement of showing that he had a legitimate expectation of privacy in the area searched.

On the merits, the majority in effect holds that a person who has a possessory interest in any kind of man-made structure lying outside of the curtilage of a farmhouse also has a reasonable expectation of privacy in the structure. The question of whether defendant had a reasonable expectation of privacy in the area searched or the items seized must be resolved in view of the totality of the circumstances of the particular case. The relevant facts and circumstances here show that defendant did not have a reasonable expectation of privacy in the barn. First, it was undisputed that defendant did not own the barn-Mary Pitman owned it. Second, defendant was not present at the barn at the time it was searched and the marijuana plants were discovered. Third, it does appear that defendant had a possessory interest in the area searched. However, a possessory interest, standing alone, is insufficient to establish a reasonable expectation of privacy. Fourth, there is no evidence that defendant made any prior use of the property searched. Arguably, it could be said that defendant incidentally used the barn in connection with his cultivation of the marijuana plants outside the barn. However, an expectation of privacy based on illegal activity is not one that society is prepared to recognize as legitimate. Fifth, there was no evidence presented that defendant had a right to exclude others from the barn. I do not believe that these facts establish that he had a right to exclude others from the barn. Furthermore, even if defendant had both a possessory interest in the property and the right to exclude others, this would not be sufficient in itself to show a reasonable expectation of privacy. As I will explain more fully below, courts that have decided whether a defendant enjoyed a reasonable expectation of privacy in a barn outside the curtilage have looked to whether the barn was being put to a business use on behalf of the farm and whether defendant took any reasonable steps to effect privacy, such as closing and locking the barn doors. Finally, given the wide-open nature of the barn and defendant's lack of use, it is clear defendant himself had no subjective expectation of privacy in the area searched. Defendant was not even effectively using the barn as a cover for his illegal activity, as he grew marijuana outside of the barn.

It is clear that no federal court would hold, as the majority does, that a possessory interest, plus the right to exclude others, automatically creates a reasonable expectation of privacy in a wide-open, three-sided barn lying in open fields. Presumably, the majority would find a reasonable expectation of privacy in any structure, no matter how dilapidated and open to view, as long as the possessor has a right to exclude others. This is a conclusion that finds no precedent in fourth amendment law. For the foregoing reasons, I would affirm the judgment of the appellate court. I believe it was correct when it determined that defendant had no reasonable expectation of privacy. Accordingly, I respectfully dissent.

REVIEW SECTION

READING COMPREHENSION

Detail the facts of this case.

What are the specific conditions that make a warrantless search reasonable?

How is abandonment established?

THINKING CRITICALLY

Elaborate the issue of an "expectation of privacy" and the rationale behind this protection.

Use the opinion of the majority and the dissent to articulate your position on this case.

SECTION 3: PLAIN VIEW, HEARING, SMELL, AND TOUCH

OVERVIEW

When government officials discover evidence using their ordinary senses (seeing, touching, smelling and hearing), these are not considered Fourth Amendment searches. Three conditions must be met however in order to comply with the plain-view doctrine:

(1)   Officers are in a location in which they have a legal right to occupy;

(2)   Officers do not use the assistance of advanced technology to improve upon ordinary senses; and

(3)   The discovery of the evidence by the office is by chance.

The difficulty in applying the plain-view doctrine surrounds the issue of what is considered advanced technology.

CASE

In *People v Pakula,* defendants were indicted by a grand jury for the offense of possession of more than 500 grams of a substance containing cannabis. The cannabis was seized by the police from the defendants' back yard where it was growing. Prior to trial, the defendants moved to suppress the cannabis. The trial court granted defendants' motion to suppress ruling that even though the cannabis was plainly observable from outside the premises of the defendants' home and yard, and the police could discern that it was cannabis from a location where they had a right to be, the seizure was illegal. The trial judge found that there was no consent given by the defendants for the seizure of the evidence, and in the opinion of the trial court, no exigent circumstances were present and no reason existed for the police not to get a search warrant. The state has appealed from the order suppressing the evidence seized. The issue presented for review is: whether the seizure of the cannabis growing in defendant's back yard was unreasonable, consistent with the Fourth Amendment to the Constitution of the United States and its prohibition against unreasonable intrusion into a person's privacy.

PEOPLE V. PAKULA
89 Ill.App.3d 789, 411 N.E.2d 1385 (1980)

The facts surrounding the seizure of the evidence were presented at the hearing on the motion to suppress by the police officers who were involved and the defendant Annette Pakula. Officer Stahl testified that on the night before the arrest of the defendants and the seizure of the cannabis, another police officer, agent Drew Peterson, received a call from the police dispatcher regarding a report of cannabis growing in the backyard. At approximately 11:30 A.M. of the following morning officer Stahl and agents Peterson and Sullivan drove to verify the address and location. They then proceeded one block north to observe the defendants' back yard and to see if cannabis was growing there. Officer Stahl reported that they could see what appeared to be cannabis growing in defendants' back yard from their vantage point standing on the sidewalk. The defendants' entire back yard was surrounded by a steel chain link fence through which the officers could see. After observing the cannabis growing from a block away they decided to get a closer look and they then entered upon the private property of an adjoining landowner. From this closer observation point the police observed three large cannabis plants growing with the tomato plants in the garden. After making these observations all three then proceeded to the Police Department to get uniformed policemen to aid them in approaching the house and to seize the cannabis. No one remained behind to prevent possible destruction of the cannabis. At least thirty minutes elapsed before the police returned to the Pakula residence with two uniformed police officers. Agent Peterson then went to the front door with the uniformed officers. After knocking on the door he allegedly informed Annette Pakula about the cannabis growing in her back yard. Mrs. Pakula was not then arrested. The officers entered the Pakula fenced back yard and seized the cannabis growing in the garden as well as searching and seizing some smaller cannabis seedling plants found growing in a container on a patio. Only after the seizure was Mrs. Pakula arrested and several days after that her husband Steven Pakula was arrested. Officer Stahl admitted that no search warrant had been obtained, and that they had returned to the residence intending to seize the cannabis. Agent Peterson fully corroborated the version related by Officer Stahl's testimony.

Annette Pakula testified in her own behalf. She admitted that she was present when the seizure was made, but stated that she had not given the officers consent to enter her back yard or to seize anything. The State's first argument is that the seizure was valid under the open fields doctrine. Under the theory of the open fields doctrine incriminating evidence in plain view in an open field is not the subject of constitutionally protected privacy. Illinois has recognized the validity of the open fields doctrine in plain view search and seizure cases.

In response to the State's argument that the cannabis was in plain view in an open field the defendants claim that the fenced back yard was within the curtilage of his residence. In our view, the determination of the issue presented to us, the legality of the seizure, should not turn exclusively upon the ancient property law concept of curtilage. The Pakula back yard was completely enclosed by a fence and was not accessible to the general public. The officers gained entry to seize the cannabis by opening and going through the closed gate after Annette Pakula refused to consent to their warrantless entry. The Pakula's dog instinctively barked and confronted the police as intruders and had to be restrained. The facts of the present case establish that the defendants expected their back yard to be private and free from outside intrusion. Under the circumstances we believe this expectation of privacy was reasonable and one that society is prepared to recognize.

The seizure in this case was without a warrant. Searches and seizures conducted outside the judicial process, without prior approval by judge or magistrate, are per se unreasonable under the Fourth Amendment subject only to a few specifically established and well-delineated exceptions. Those few exceptions are search by consent, search incident to arrest, and search based on probable cause where there are exigent circumstances which make it impractical to obtain a warrant. While the record quite clearly proscribes any argument that the seizure was consensual, the state does argue that the seizure was incident to the arrest of Annette Pakula and therefore within an exception to the warrant requirement. We reject the State's argument. The arrest of Annette Pakula did occur in temporal proximity to the seizure of the cannabis. However, both Officer Stahl and Agent Peterson were very definite in their testimony that she was not arrested until after the seizure. This fact is undisputed and destroys the State's argument. The final exception available to the State to justify the warrantless seizure in the instant case is a search and seizure based upon probable cause, resulting from plain view where there are exigent circumstances which make it impractical to obtain a warrant. The trial court specifically found that no exigent circumstances were present. His finding is very strongly supported by the evidence. No claim of exigent circumstances has been made. We agree with the trial judge when he stated, "I can see no reason why the police couldn't have gotten a warrant had they desired without doing jeopardy. I think they could have gotten a warrant without endangering the contraband that they finally seized." The burden of proof is on the State to establish that all the elements of the plain view exception to the warrant requirement are present, including the existence of exigent circumstances. The State failed to meet its burden in this case.

It has been suggested that viewing the contraband in plain view itself justifies the warrantless seizure of the evidence. To the contrary plain view alone is never enough to justify the warrantless seizure of evidence. Stated differently the warrantless intrusion into the defendants' privacy is not justifiable merely by a pre-intrusion plain view observation. Under the facts of the present case we cannot conceive of any cognizable inconvenience to the State in obtaining either a search or arrest warrant. The case before us is one of an admittedly planned warrantless seizure which cannot be justified on plain view grounds. The trial court correctly found that no exigent circumstances existed to justify the warrantless seizure of evidence in the case at bar. The warrantless seizure of the cannabis was unreasonable and violative of defendants' Fourth Amendment rights. The trial court properly granted the motion to suppress the cannabis seized. For the reasons stated the judgment of the Circuit Court is affirmed.

REVIEW SECTION

READING COMPREHENSION

Detail the events precipitating the seizure of drugs from the defendant's backyard.

Elaborate why the plain-view doctrine was rejected by the court in this case.

SECTION 4: SEIZURES

OVERVIEW

According to the Fourth Amendment, a seizure occurs when an officer removes an individual's right to leave or stay in a particular location. In an actual-seizure stop an officer prevents one from leaving, and in a show-of-authority stop an individual submits to the encounter because they do not feel free to depart. Should the police use intimidation or coercion in the questioning of an individual, a show-of-authority stop becomes a seizure. Keep in mind however, that the same result does not occur from police using either psychological pressure or invoking a sense of moral duty.

CASE

In *People v McArthur,* police officers with probable cause to believe that there was hidden marijuana, prevented the defendant from entering his home unaccompanied by an officer for about two hours while they obtained a search warrant. Once they did so, the officers found drug paraphernalia and marijuana, and arrested McArthur. He was subsequently charged with misdemeanor possession of those items. He moved to suppress the evidence on the ground that it was the fruit of an unlawful police seizure, namely, the refusal to let him reenter his home unaccompanied. The Illinois trial court granted the motion, and the State Appellate Court affirmed. Given the nature of the intrusion and the law enforcement interest at stake, this court holds that the brief seizure of the premises was permissible under the Fourth Amendment.

PEOPLE V. MCARTHUR
U.S. Supreme Court
531 U.S. 326 (2001)

Although, in the ordinary case, personal property seizures are unreasonable unless accomplished pursuant to a warrant, there are exceptions to this rule involving special law enforcement needs, diminished expectations of privacy, minimal intrusions, and the like. The circumstances here involve a plausible claim of specially pressing or urgent law enforcement need. Moreover, the restraint at issue was tailored to that need, being limited in time and scope, and avoiding significant intrusion into the home itself. Consequently, rather than employing a per se rule of unreasonableness, the Court must balance the privacy-related and law enforcement-related concerns to determine if the intrusion here was reasonable. In light of the following circumstances, considered in combination, the Court concludes that the restriction was reasonable, and hence lawful. First, the police had probable cause to believe that McArthur's home contained evidence of a crime and unlawful drugs. Second, they had good reason to fear that, unless restrained, he would destroy the drugs before they could return with a warrant. Third, they made reasonable efforts to reconcile their law enforcement needs with the demands of personal privacy by avoiding a warrantless entry or arrest and preventing McArthur only from entering his home unaccompanied. Fourth, they imposed the restraint for a limited period, which was no longer than reasonably necessary for them, acting with diligence, to obtain the warrant.

The conclusion that the restriction was lawful finds significant support in this Court's case law and in no case has this Court held unlawful a temporary seizure that was supported by probable cause and was designed to prevent the loss of evidence while the police diligently obtained a warrant in a reasonable period. The Court is not persuaded by the countervailing considerations raised by the parties or lower courts: that the police proceeded without probable cause; that, because McArthur was on his porch, the police order that he stay outside his home amounted to an impermissible "constructive eviction"; and that an officer, with McArthur's consent, stepped inside the home's doorway to observe McArthur when McArthur reentered the home on two or three occasions. 304 Ill. App. 3d 395, 713 N. E. 2d 93, reversed and remanded.

On April 2, 1997, Tera McArthur asked two police officers to accompany her to the trailer where she lived with her husband, Charles, so that they could keep the peace while she removed her belongings. The two officers, Assistant Chief John Love and Officer Richard Skidis, arrived with Tera at the trailer at about 3:15 p.m. Tera went inside, where Charles was present. The officers remained outside. When Tera emerged after collecting her possessions, she spoke to Chief Love, who was then on the porch. She suggested he check the trailer because "Chuck had dope in there." She added (in Love's words) that she had seen Chuck "slid[e] some dope underneath the couch." Love knocked on the trailer door, told Charles what Tera had said, and asked for permission to search the trailer, which Charles denied. Love then sent Officer Skidis with Tera to get a search warrant. Love told Charles, who by this time was also on the porch, that he could not reenter the trailer unless a police officer accompanied him. Charles subsequently reentered the trailer two or three times (to get cigarettes and to make phone calls), and each time Love stood just inside the door to observe what Charles did.

Officer Skidis obtained the warrant by about 5 p.m. He returned to the trailer and, along with other officers, searched it. The officers found under the sofa a marijuana pipe, a box for marijuana (called a "one-hitter" box), and a small amount of marijuana. They then arrested Charles. Illinois subsequently charged Charles McArthur with unlawfully possessing drug paraphernalia and marijuana (less than 2.5 grams), both misdemeanors. McArthur moved to suppress the pipe, box, and marijuana on the ground that they were the fruit of an unlawful police seizure, namely, the refusal to let him reenter the trailer unaccompanied, which would have permitted him, he said, to "have destroyed the marijuana." The trial court granted McArthur's suppression motion. The Appellate Court of Illinois affirmed and the Illinois Supreme Court denied the State's petition for leave to appeal. We granted certiorari to determine whether the Fourth Amendment prohibits the kind of temporary seizure at issue here.

This Court has interpreted the Fourth Amendment as establishing rules and presumptions designed to control conduct of law enforcement officers that may significantly intrude upon privacy interests. Sometimes those rules require warrants. We nonetheless have made it clear that there are exceptions to the warrant requirement. When faced with special law enforcement needs, diminished expectations of privacy, minimal intrusions, or the like, the Court has found that certain general, or individual, circumstances may render a warrantless search or seizure reasonable. In the circumstances of the case before us, we cannot say that the warrantless seizure was per se unreasonable. It involves a plausible claim of specially pressing or urgent law enforcement need. We conclude that the restriction at issue was reasonable, and hence lawful, in light of the following circumstances, which we consider in combination.

First, the police had probable cause to believe that McArthur's trailer home contained evidence of a crime and contraband, namely, unlawful drugs. The police had had an opportunity to speak with Tera McArthur and make at least a very rough assessment of her reliability. They knew she had had a firsthand opportunity to observe her husband's behavior, in particular with respect to the drugs at issue. And they thought, with good reason, that her report to them reflected that opportunity. Second, the police had good reason to fear that, unless restrained, McArthur would destroy the drugs before they could return with a warrant. Third, the police made reasonable efforts to reconcile their law enforcement needs with the demands of personal privacy. They neither searched the trailer nor arrested McArthur before obtaining a warrant. Rather, they imposed a significantly less restrictive restraint, preventing McArthur only from entering the trailer unaccompanied. They left his home and his belongings intact--until a neutral Magistrate, finding probable cause, issued a warrant. Fourth, the police imposed the restraint for a limited period of time, namely, two hours. As far as the record reveals, this time period was no longer than reasonably necessary for the police, acting with diligence, to obtain the warrant. Given the nature of the intrusion and the law enforcement interest at stake, this brief seizure of the premises was permissible.

We have found no case in which this Court has held unlawful a temporary seizure that was supported by probable cause and was designed to prevent the loss of evidence while the police diligently obtained a warrant in a reasonable period of time. Nor are we persuaded by the countervailing considerations that the parties or lower courts have raised. McArthur argues that the police proceeded without probable cause. But McArthur has waived this argument. And, in any event, it is without merit. The Appellate Court of Illinois concluded that the police could not order McArthur to stay outside his home because McArthur's porch, where he stood at the time, was part of his home; hence the order "amounted to a constructive eviction" of McArthur from his residence. This Court has held, however, that a person standing in the doorway of a house is in a public place, and hence subject to arrest without a warrant permitting entry of the home. Regardless, we do not believe the difference to which the Appellate Court points--porch versus, e.g., front walk--could make a significant difference here as to the reasonableness of the police restraint; and that, from the Fourth Amendment's perspective, is what matters.

The Appellate Court also found negatively significant the fact that Chief Love, with McArthur's consent, stepped inside the trailer's doorway to observe McArthur when McArthur reentered the trailer on two or three occasions. McArthur, however, reentered simply for his own convenience, to make phone calls and to obtain cigarettes. Under these circumstances, the reasonableness of the greater restriction (preventing reentry) implies the reasonableness of the lesser (permitting reentry conditioned on observation).

In sum, the police officers in this case had probable cause to believe that a home contained contraband, which was evidence of a crime. They reasonably believed that the home's resident, if left free of any restraint, would destroy that evidence. And they imposed a restraint that was both limited and tailored reasonably to secure law enforcement needs while protecting privacy interests. In our view, the restraint met the Fourth Amendment's demands. The judgment of the Illinois Appellate Court is reversed, and the case is remanded for further proceedings not inconsistent with this opinion. It is so ordered.

Justice Stevens, dissenting. The Illinois General Assembly has decided that the possession of less than 2.5 grams of marijuana is a class C misdemeanor. In so classifying the offense, the legislature made a concerted policy judgment that the possession of small amounts of marijuana for personal use does not constitute a particularly significant public policy concern. While it is true that this offense--like feeding livestock on a public highway or offering a movie for rent without clearly displaying its rating --may warrant a jail sentence of up to 30 days, the detection and prosecution of possessors of small quantities of this substance is by no means a law enforcement priority in the State of Illinois. Because the governmental interest implicated by the particular criminal prohibition at issue in this case is so slight, this is a poor vehicle for probing the boundaries of the government's power to limit an individual's possessory interest in his or her home pending the arrival of a search warrant. Given my preference, I would, therefore, dismiss the writ of certiorari as improvidently granted.

Compelled by the vote of my colleagues to reach the merits, I would affirm. As the majority explains, the essential inquiry in this case involves a balancing of the "privacy-related and law enforcement-related concerns to determine if the intrusion was reasonable." Under the specific facts of this case, I believe the majority gets the balance wrong. Each of the Illinois jurists who participated in the decision of this case placed a higher value on the sanctity of the ordinary citizen's home than on the prosecution of this petty offense. They correctly viewed that interest as one meriting the most serious constitutional protection. I would affirm.

REVIEW SECTION

READING COMPREHENSION

Detail the facts of this case.

Elaborate why the restriction in this case was reasonable according to the court.

THINKING CRITICALLY

Do you agree or disagree with the balance of privacy-related and law enforcement-related concerns regarding the intrusion in this case? Keep in mind that the offense was a misdemeanor.

Articulate your finding in this case using the majority and dissenting opinions.

CONCLUSION

The Fourth Amendment of the U.S. Constitution and Article One, Section Six of the Illinois Constitution are designed to ensure that government officials conform to the law when obtaining evidence. While crime control obviously depends on police gathering of information from often reluctant sources, authorities are bound by law when obtaining evidence. To control crime and balance the rights of individuals, the state has created guidelines as outlined in constitutions and interpreted by the courts. This chapter reviewed searches and seizures; the "expectation of privacy;" and plain view, hearing, smell, and touch. These are a few of the issues that deal directly with placing a reasonable limit on government officials and establishing the protection of liberty and privacy from government intrusion of the citizenry.

Chapter Four

Stop and Frisk

According to the Fourth Amendment to the U.S. Constitution and Article One, Section Six of the Illinois Constitution, a seizure occurs when a government official removes an individual's right to leave or stay in a specific location. Officers do not violate the Fourth Amendment when they approach individuals in a public place and request responses to questions, or request to search an individual. "Stop and frisk" was brought to the American colonies by the English and was not challenged in the U.S. until the 1960s.

As outlined by 725 ILCS 5/107-14, temporary questioning without arrest involves the following:

> A peace officer, after having identified himself as a peace officer, may stop any person in a public place for a reasonable period of time when the officer reasonably infers from the circumstances that the person is committing, is about to commit or has committed an offense as defined in Section 102-15 of this Code, and may demand the name and address of the person and an explanation of his actions. Such detention and temporary questioning will be conducted in the vicinity of where the person has stopped.

Further, as elaborated in 725 ILCS 5/108-1.01, a search during temporary questioning involves:

> When a peace officer has stopped a person for temporary questioning pursuant to Section 107-14 of this Code and reasonably suspects that he or another is in danger of attack, he may search the person for weapons. If the officer discovers a weapon, he may take it until the completion of the questioning, at which time he shall either return the weapon, if lawfully possessed, or arrest the person so questioned.

This chapter will review:

(1)   Stops, frisks, and the Fourth Amendment;

(2)   Stops and the Fourth Amendment;

(3)   Special situation stops; and

(4)   Frisks and the Fourth Amendment.

SECTION 1: STOPS, FRISKS, AND THE FOURTH AMENDMENT

OVERVIEW

In sum, a Fourth Amendment stop involves a brief detention for the purposes of investigation by law enforcement. A Four Amendment frisk involves a once-over-lightly pat-down of a suspect to protect officers from potential harm. As discussed earlier, the greater the invasion upon the individual, the greater the objective basis required for support on the part of government officials. Indeed, officers need relatively few suspicious facts to support a stop and frisk as it represent the beginning of the criminal justice process and is thus considered more visible, but less intrusive than other measures. What is important to consider as you read this chapter is the visibility of stop and frisks. Because a stop and frisk occurs where many other individuals can view its occurrence, this transparency of police control has an impact on public perception of police power. Most individuals have probably witnessed a stop and frisk of another individual, if you have not been subjected to one yourself. Recall this experience and reflect on how this incident shaped your perception of police power in this community. Reflect on how this perception may be intensified if you reside in a low-income or minority neighborhood where police presence is greater, thus increasing the transparency of police power even further.

To determine whether or not the government has complied with the Fourth Amendment involves analysis of three questions that we began discussion of in Chapter Three:

(1)   Was the action by the government a stop and frisk?

(2)   If considered a stop and frisk, was it unreasonable?

(3)   If considered an unreasonable stop and frisk, should the evidence obtained be excluded from consideration?

As in the case of search and seizure outlined in the previous chapter, if the action can not be considered a stop and frisk, the Fourth Amendment and Article One, Section Six of the Illinois Constitution do not apply.

There are two clauses in both the Fourth Amendment of the U.S. Constitution and Section Six of the Illinois Constitution that are included in this analysis. The first is the reasonableness clause which in Article One, Section Six of the Illinois Constitution reads:

> The people shall have the right to be secure in their persons, houses, papers and other possessions against unreasonable searches, seizures, invasions of privacy or interceptions of communications by eavesdropping devices or other means.

The second is the warrant clause which in Article One, Section Six of the Illinois Constitution reads:

No warrant shall issue without probable cause, supported by
affidavit particularly describing the place to be searched and the
persons or things to be seized.

Prior to the 1960s, the U.S. Supreme Court viewed the warrant and reasonableness clauses and
firmly connected in what was called the conventional Fourth Amendment approach. After 1960,
the court shifted to a reasonableness Fourth Amendment approach which suggested that the two
clauses are separate. What this meant in practice was that searches and seizures that occur
without a warrant can still be considered reasonable by the courts. In light of this, when does
Section Six of the Illinois Constitution require warrants? And, what does 'unreasonable' really
mean?

While a search and seizure can be based on warrants and probable cause, most must pass the
reasonableness test. The government must prove to the court that the need to either search or
seize outweighed any invasion of liberty and privacy of the individual. In addition, the
government must prove that there were enough facts to support the search or seizure. To answer
the reasonableness question, the courts use a totality of circumstances approach to analyze each
case individually. Needless to say, in creating law enforcement strategies this complicates things
immeasurably. Because the courts have been attempting to sort out what is and is not reasonable
since the 1960s, and still are not entirely clear, it should come as no surprise that this chapter is
extensive in both case example and discussion. The lack of clarity from the courts extends to all
lower courts which are bound to follow these decisions, as well as to state legislatures who
attempt to incorporate court decisions into criminal procedure guidelines. In each case what
remains the same is that the need to control crime must outweigh the invasion that occurs of
individual rights.

CASE

In *People v Flowers,* the defendant was charged in the circuit court with one count of possession
of a controlled substance. The circuit court granted defendant's motion to suppress evidence that
was seized from him during a police stop and frisk. The circuit court ruled that the frisk was
illegal because the officer did not have a reasonable belief that defendant was armed and
dangerous. The State appealed to the appellate court and the appellate court reversed the
suppression order. The Supreme Court of Illinois granted the defendant's petition for leave to
appeal and reverse the appellate court.

PEOPLE V. FLOWERS
Supreme Court of Illinois
688 N.E.2d 626, 179 Ill.2d 257 (Ill., 1997)

The only witness to testify at the suppression hearing was Officer Stephen Wilson of the
Danville police department. Officer Wilson testified that the police department had received a
telephone call at 1:22 a.m. on July 12, 1995, from an anonymous caller who reported seeing a
black male wearing a white T-shirt and riding a bicycle go to the rear of a house for sale. The
caller reported hearing what sounded like glass breaking at that time. Officer Wilson, along with

two fellow officers, responded to the report. Officer Wilson testified that there were two houses that had "for sale" signs and they checked both houses for signs of damage or illegal entry and found them to be secure. They saw no broken windows in either house. At 1:39 a.m., Officer Wilson was still on the block when he saw defendant, a black male, riding a bicycle. Officer Wilson activated the police lights on his car and effectuated a stop of defendant because defendant matched the description given by the earlier caller.

Shortly after he stopped defendant, Officer Wilson was joined by a fellow officer. Officer Wilson asked defendant if he had been in the area earlier and defendant responded that he had been. In response to further questions, defendant stated that he had been at his girlfriend's house and was now returning to his home. Defendant gave the officer his address and that of his girlfriend. Defendant had a bag on the front of his bicycle. Officer Wilson asked defendant what was in the bag and defendant told him it contained clothing. Defendant gave the officer consent to search the bag. The search revealed that the bag contained clothing. Officer Wilson then patted the defendant down for weapons. Officer Wilson asked defendant "what he had on his person." In response, defendant took some items, including nail files and a piece of tissue paper, out of his pockets and showed them to the officer. Defendant was straddling his bicycle during the frisk. Officer Wilson testified that he felt a "tube-like item" in defendant's pocket, which he believed to be a crack pipe. He asked defendant if it was a crack pipe and defendant responded that it was. Officer Wilson then continued the frisk which revealed a plastic bag containing a small amount of a substance the officer believed to be cocaine. Officer Wilson testified that he frisked defendant "for my safety as well as his." However, when asked whether he had any particular reason to believe that defendant had a weapon, Officer Wilson responded: "No. I do that as a common thing in my job, to pat people down for my safety as well as theirs."

At the conclusion of the suppression hearing, the trial court ruled that the stop of defendant was valid under 725 ILCS 5/107-14 and Terry v. Ohio, 392 U.S. 1, 88 S.Ct. 1868, 20 L.Ed.2d 889 (1968). The trial court found, however, that the frisk was invalid. The trial court therefore granted defendant's motion to suppress the evidence obtained as a result of the frisk. The State filed a certificate of impairment and appealed to the appellate court. The appellate court reversed the suppression order, finding that the frisk was valid. The appellate court noted that Officer Wilson was investigating a "possible burglary" and that defendant "fit the description of the suspect." The court also noted that the officer had testified that he routinely frisked suspects for his safety and the safety of the suspects. The court then reasoned that, in this society, Officer Wilson's caution was warranted.

The sole issue presented in this appeal is the validity of Officer Wilson's frisk of defendant. The trial court determined that the frisk was invalid and that the evidence obtained as a result must be suppressed. We find that the trial court's ruling was not manifestly erroneous and must therefore be upheld. Reasonableness under the fourth amendment generally requires a warrant supported by probable cause. A limited exception to the traditional requirement was recognized by the Supreme Court in Terry v. Ohio, 392 U.S. 1, 88 S.Ct. 1868, 20 L.Ed.2d 889 (1968). In Terry, the Court held that a police officer, under appropriate circumstances, could briefly detain a person for investigatory purposes and, if necessary for safety, conduct a limited protective search for weapons. Under the Terry exception, a police officer may briefly stop a person for temporary questioning if the officer reasonably believes that the person has committed, or is about to commit, a crime. If the officer reasonably believes that the person stopped is armed and dangerous, the officer may subject the person to a limited search for weapons, commonly referred to as a frisk. Defendant does not challenge the propriety of Officer Wilson's stopping him for questioning. We therefore make no comment on the validity of the stop. Defendant challenges the legality of Officer Wilson's frisk of defendant's person. Whether an investigatory stop is valid is a separate question from whether a search for weapons is valid. Rather, in order to validly conduct a weapons frisk under Terry and section 108-1.01, the officer must have reason to believe that the individual whose suspicious behavior he is investigating at close range is armed and presently dangerous to the officer or to others. The sole justification for the search allowed by the Terry exception is the protection of the police officer and others in the vicinity, not to gather evidence. The scope of the search is therefore strictly limited to a search for weapons.

The validity of a frisk conducted during a valid investigatory stop is assessed by an objective standard. The question is whether a reasonably prudent person in the circumstances would be warranted in the belief that his safety or that of others was in danger. The officer conducting the frisk must be able to point to specific, articulable facts which, when taken together with natural inferences, reasonably warrant the intrusion. These facts need not meet probable cause standards, but must constitute more than a mere hunch. Although the standard is an objective one, the officer's subjective belief regarding the safety of the situation is one of the factors that may be considered in determining whether a weapons frisk was valid under Terry.

In this case, the circuit court heard the evidence presented at the suppression hearing and ruled that the frisk of defendant was invalid because there was no indication whatsoever that defendant presented a danger to the officers. A trial court's ruling on a motion to suppress will not be overturned unless it is manifestly erroneous. The record in this case amply supports the trial court's ruling. The State does not dispute that the only possible justification for searching defendant in this case is the Terry exception. The evidence presented at the suppression hearing, however, failed to establish any facts which would support a reasonable belief that defendant was armed and dangerous. First, Officer Wilson expressly testified that he had no reason to believe that defendant had a weapon. Although the officer's subjective belief is not dispositive of the validity of the frisk, it is probative of that determination. This is particularly true where, as here, the officer candidly admits that he had no reason to believe that the defendant was armed.

Officer Wilson's subjective assessment aside, there were no objective circumstances which would support a reasonable belief that defendant was armed and dangerous. Officer Wilson testified that he was responding to a report, by an anonymous caller, of a possible burglary or break-in of a residence. The caller's only basis for believing a burglary had taken place was hearing what sounded like glass breaking. When the officers investigated, however, they found that the residences in question were secure and observed no broken windows. Defendant was not observed by the officers until approximately 15 minutes later. Thus, at the time defendant was stopped, Officer Wilson and the other officers had already investigated and found no evidence that the possible crime reported by the anonymous caller had been committed or attempted.

Further, there was no evidence that defendant attempted to avoid Officer Wilson when he approached or engaged in any other evasive or suspicious behavior. To the contrary, defendant was completely cooperative with the police officers. Defendant provided the officers with the information they requested, including a plausible explanation for why he was in the area. Defendant answered truthfully when asked about the contents of his bag and gave the officer consent to search the bag. The contents of the bag--clothing--revealed no evidence of any criminal activity on defendant's part. Defendant even showed Officer Wilson the contents of his pockets in response to the officer's questioning. Moreover, Officer Wilson was not alone when he frisked defendant but was joined by another officer shortly after he stopped defendant. Under these circumstances, the trial court was correct in concluding that there was no indication that defendant presented a threat to the officers' safety. There was therefore no justification for frisking defendant.

Most problematic about the frisk in this case is Officer Wilson's asserted reason for frisking defendant. Officer Wilson's testimony indicated that he frisked defendant, not because of any particularized suspicion that defendant was armed, but simply because it was his routine to frisk persons stopped for investigatory questioning. The appellate court found that Officer Wilson's routine of frisking detainees for "safety" reasons validated the frisk of defendant. Both Officer Wilson's testimony and the appellate court's acceptance of that testimony reflect a misapprehension of the scope and purpose of the Terry exception. First, the officer's testimony reveals an erroneous belief that a weapons frisk is always appropriate following an investigatory stop. This court has repeatedly recognized that the right to frisk does not automatically follow from a valid stop. A weapons frisk is valid only when the officer has reason to believe that a particular individual is armed and dangerous. More importantly, the officer's testimony reveals a misapprehension of the narrow scope of the Terry exception. The Supreme Court has repeatedly emphasized that the "stop and frisk" allowed by Terry is an exception to the general probable cause requirement and, as such, must be narrowly applied. The Court also recognized, however, that it could not blind itself to the need for police officers to protect themselves while investigating suspicious activity. The Court in Terry therefore struck a balance between the individual's "cherished" right to be free from an invasion of personal security and law enforcement officers' need to protect themselves by allowing a narrowly drawn authority to permit a reasonable search for weapons for the protection of the police officer. The limited exception recognized in Terry thus clearly does not permit police officers to engage in a practice of routinely frisking individuals, without concern for whether a particular person poses a danger. Here, Officer Wilson's testimony indicated that he conducts no individualized consideration of whether any particular suspect is armed, but simply applies a general rule that all persons he stops on suspicion of criminal activity should be frisked for "safety" reasons. Such a generalized approach to the power to frisk granted by Terry is improper.

This court's decision People v. Galvin, 127 Ill.2d 153, 129 Ill.Dec. 72, 535 N.E.2d 837 (1989), supports our holding here. In Galvin, the trial court granted the defendant's motion to suppress evidence obtained during a weapons frisk. The police officer who conducted the frisk testified at the suppression hearing that he had been participating in a police surveillance on September 14, 1986, in a residential area where a number of burglaries had recently taken place. The officer had been given some information about possible suspects in the burglaries. On the night of one of the prior burglaries, an anonymous witness had observed a black male, who appeared to be hiding something under his jacket, walk from an alley and get into a brown Oldsmobile in which another black male was waiting. The witness wrote down the license plate number of the car and gave it to a neighbor who passed it on to the police. During the police surveillance on September 14, the testifying officer observed the defendant slowly driving a brown Oldsmobile with that license plate number through the area. The defendant and another man, both of whom were black, exited the vehicle and walked into the backyard of an unlighted house. They were not seen again until 40 minutes later, when they returned to the car. The officer had run a license plate search and discovered that the car belonged to the defendant, who, the officer knew, had previously been arrested for burglary and theft. Another officer saw one of the men put an unknown object into his pocket. The officers continued to observe the men as they drove the Oldsmobile around the area, stopping in several locations. The officers followed the men for approximately two to three miles as they drove out of the area and, joined by two other police cars, effectuated a stop of the defendant's vehicle. A total of five officers were present at the scene of the stop. The defendant had exited the car and was cooperating with the officers when the testifying officer frisked the defendant. The frisk revealed a rifle ammunition magazine with live ammunition in the defendant's pocket. The officer who conducted the frisk testified that he did not believe that the defendant was armed or dangerous. The trial court granted the defendant's motion to suppress the evidence obtained as a result of the frisk.

This court upheld the suppression of the evidence in Galvin. The court found that the investigatory stop of the defendant was valid under Terry and section 107-14 of the Code. The frisk, however, was found to be invalid. The Galvin court considered all the circumstances surrounding the frisk, noting in particular that multiple, armed officers were present at the scene, the defendant was cooperative and the officer who conducted the frisk did not believe that the defendant was armed. The court found that, under these circumstances, the trial court was not manifestly erroneous in determining that there were no facts which would support a reasonable belief that the defendant presented a threat to the officers' safety. Notably, the Galvin court rejected the contention that the frisk was valid simply because the officer responded affirmatively when asked by the prosecution whether he conducted the frisk to "protect his own safety." The court noted that the officer never pointed to any specific facts which made it reasonable to believe that his safety was in danger.

In this case, there is even less evidence that defendant was armed and dangerous. The State contends that reasonable justification existed for the search because defendant was a possible burglary suspect. This position is not persuasive. First, by the time Officer Wilson stopped defendant, he and his fellow officers had already investigated the report and found no evidence that a burglary had been committed or attempted. There is thus no basis in the record for characterizing defendant, at that point, as a possible burglary suspect. Moreover, even if defendant could properly be characterized as a possible burglary suspect at the time he was stopped, the State's reliance on this factor alone is contradictory to this court's holding in Galvin. In Galvin, this court specifically rejected the State's argument that a frisk for weapons is justified every time a burglary suspect is stopped. The court declined to adopt a legal presumption that every burglary suspect is armed and dangerous, so as to justify a search for weapons under the Terry exception. Rather, the Galvin court emphasized that the reasonableness of every search must be judged by the particular facts and circumstances surrounding it.

In sum, the record in this case provides no basis for overturning the trial court's ruling granting defendant's motion to suppress. Officer Wilson testified that he had no reason to believe that defendant was armed and dangerous and there were no objective facts which indicated that defendant was armed and dangerous. The trial court's ruling was not manifestly erroneous. The appellate court's judgment reversing the trial court is therefore reversed and the circuit court order is affirmed. Appellate court judgment reversed; circuit court judgment affirmed.

REVIEW SECTION

READING COMPREHENSION

Detail the facts of this case, including an elaboration of when a stop and frisk is considered reasonable by the courts.

THINKING CRITICALLY

Agree or disagree with the narrow application of the Terry rule used by the courts. What are possible consequences of a broader Terry application?

SECTION 2: STOPS AND THE FOURTH AMENDMENT

OVERVIEW

When examining encounters between individuals and police, there are three types:

(1)   Voluntary encounters are those not involving any sort of police force or coercion and thus the Fourth Amendment does not apply;

(2)   Stops are brief but involuntary seizures that occur in public places, and which require reasonable suspicion according to the Fourth Amendment; and

(3)   Arrests are involuntary detentions that usually occur in a police station, last an extended period of time, and require probable cause according to the Fourth Amendment.

As we discuss stops in this section, keep in mind that a 'reasonable' stop must include an objective basis that adds up to reasonable suspicion by the officer, and that the scope of the stop must be both short and occur at the initial scene. What is reasonable suspicion as required in a stop and how does it differ from probable cause as required in an arrest? Reasonable suspicion involves examination of the totality of the facts that lead an officer to suspect a crime may be occurring. To build reasonable suspicion, government officials may rely on either direct information or hearsay information. In contrast, probable cause involves an examination of the totality of the facts that lead an officer to believe that a crime is occurring. These distinctions are extremely important to keep in mind as you read the cases in this and the following chapter. The question that should remain in the forefront of your mind is: Did the officer <u>suspect</u> or <u>believe</u> that a crime <u>may be</u> or <u>is</u> occurring.

CASE

In *People v Thompson,* a faulty brake light provided a pretext to stop the defendants' van. The defective light cloaked the stop's real purpose which was confirmation by the police of uncorroborated information from an anonymous telephone call.

PEOPLE V. THOMPSON
670 N.E.2d 1129, 283 Ill.App.3d 796 (Ill.App. 5 Dist., 1996)

Patrol officers searched for defendants' van after a radio dispatch from headquarters that conveyed information received from an unidentified caller. The officers were told that defendants were headed to Carbondale from Carterville with alcohol and guns in their van. Officers located and followed the van because of the dispatched information. The van was initially discovered on a heading that contradicted the caller's predicted route of travel. In addition, the caller had not clearly informed of criminal conduct. The manner in which the alcohol and guns were being transported was not spelled out. The Carbondale police possessed uncorroborated and partially discredited information about defendants. The reliability of the information could be measured only by stopping the defendants, searching the van, and finding alcohol and guns. The police followed the van because of their desire to conduct such a search. They were aware, however, of the legal value of the information they possessed. Consequently, they did not stop the defendants until they detected a traffic violation. They waited for a valid excuse to stop the van.

The police effected a traffic stop for driving with a defective right rear brake light. The stop was not motivated by a desire to enforce the rules of the road. The traffic stop matured into a series of nonconsensual searches. As a result of those searches, police found and seized two pistols and a bag of marijuana. Defendants were charged with drug and weapons violations. The trial court suppressed the contraband based on the pretextual nature of the stop. The State appeals. We must first decide whether the fourth amendment prohibits pretextual traffic stops. In <u>People v. Guerrieri, 194 Ill.App.3d 497, 141 Ill.Dec. 580, 551 N.E.2d 767 (1990)</u>, this court defined the standard for testing the legitimacy of a traffic stop motivated by reasons other than enforcement of the Illinois Vehicle Code. We stated: "The proper inquiry is whether a reasonable officer would have made the seizure in the absence of an illegitimate motive." This standard for testing the constitutional reasonableness of traffic stops is no longer viable. It has been recently repudiated by the <u>Supreme Court. Whren v. United States, 517 U.S. ----, 116 S.Ct. 1769, 135 L.Ed.2d 89 (1996)</u>.

In a unanimous decision, the United States Supreme Court silenced the argument that traffic offenders may challenge probable cause stops generated by hidden reasons unrelated to enforcing the rules of the road. Ulterior motives do not invalidate police conduct that is justifiable on the basis of probable cause to believe that a violation of the law has occurred. The constitutional reasonableness of a traffic stop does not depend on the actual motivations of the police officers involved. The defendants operated a van without a working brake light. When this defect was noticed, the police possessed probable cause to believe a traffic law of this state was being violated. Even though the traffic offense masked other reasons for the stop unsupported by probable cause, ulterior motives cannot make otherwise lawful conduct illegal. The pretextual nature of the stop did not invalidate it. The police had probable cause for the stop. The inquiry ends there.

The trial court's order of suppression rested upon our view of fourth amendment protection in a pretextual traffic stop setting. Our view was wrong. The pretextual nature of the stop was an unsound reason upon which to bar the use of evidence. Clearly, the stop shrouded a desire to search. It was, in truth, no more than a means to reach such an end. Nevertheless, the stop was based on probable cause and, therefore, enjoyed constitutional footing. Conduct that conforms with the Constitution, regardless of the motivation, cannot taint the evidence produced. Only conduct that offends the Constitution need be deterred by suppression of its yield. The trial court found that but for the anonymous tip, unsupported by probable cause, the stop would not have occurred. It found that the stop was a mere pretext to conduct an exploratory search. The defendants were illegally stopped and this illegality formed the basis of the suppression order. Therefore, the trial court did not have to focus on reasons tendered to support how and why the traffic stop evolved into a series of searches.

The validity of a traffic stop does not automatically afford a reasonable basis to fulfill an underlying ambition to conduct a search. Our determination that the initial stop was valid but pretextual does not resolve the legitimacy of the challenged search. Rather, it requires our examination of the record to determine the reasonableness of actions taken after the traffic stop. The State argues that circumstances after the stop warranted a protective search. The protective search, if valid, produced evidence that provided probable cause to arrest. The arrest, supported by probable cause, allowed incidental search of the van. Although we address this argument in anticipation of its submission to the trial court on remand, we decline the invitation to declare the search valid. Any determination on the legality of the search, on the record presented, would require us to decide issues of credibility.

The hearing on the motion to suppress involved a significant amount of undisputed testimony. The focal point of the search, however, is marked by a sharp contrast in the evidence. The salient circumstances tendered to justify the search diverge in unresolved conflict between the testimony of defendant Mary Thompson and Sergeant Dan Stearns of the Carbondale Police Department. The facts and circumstances of the search are presented to us as follows.

In the early afternoon of Sunday, August 28, 1994, the Thompson van, with Larry, Mary, and their 10-year-old son aboard, traveled a path to the Carbondale AutoZone store. The Thompsons wanted to buy a light bulb for their van. The Carbondale police warned the defendants the day before that the van had a defective right rear brake light. The warning was accompanied by a significant delay while a German shepherd and Carbondale officers conducted a search of their van. Sergeant Dan Stearns (Stearns) conducted a watch meeting with patrolmen on Sunday morning. He told the watch of "rumors" about the Thompsons. He warned patrolmen that the

Thompson van might harbor drugs and guns. At approximately noon, via dispatch, Stearns learned of an anonymous call to the department. According to Stearns, the dispatch reported the transport of alcohol and guns in the Thompson van. Another officer at the scene, patrolman Wilmore, contradicted Stearns' version of the dispatch. Patrolman Wilmore claimed the dispatch reported transport of drugs and guns. Stearns spotted the van shortly after receiving the radio dispatch. He followed it to the AutoZone parking lot. Larry Thompson exited the van and started to enter the store. Before he could enter, Stearns stopped him. Stearns again advised that the van had an inoperable brake light. Then he attended to the real purpose for the confrontation.

Standing on the parking lot, Stearns related the nature of the anonymous call and told Larry that the van needed to be searched. Larry immediately disavowed the truth of the caller's claim and added that he never drank alcoholic beverages. Stearns responded by conducting a search of Larry's person. Larry had no weapons on him. He was allowed to enter the store. Stearns was in close proximity to Larry throughout this encounter. Stearns was never asked whether he detected any odor of alcohol. During the encounter on the parking lot, two more Carbondale squad cars arrived in response to Stearns' summons for backup. The squad cars encircled the van. After Stearns allowed Larry to leave, he walked around the van to Mary Thompson, who was seated in the front passenger's seat. Only two of the other three officers at the scene testified at the hearing. Patrolman Wilmore testified that the radio dispatch warned that defendants' van potentially harbored drugs and guns. Patrolman Baxter testified that Stearns had alerted the watch to "rumors" about the van. Both officers testified that when they arrived at the scene of the parked van, they knew that other members of their department had searched it less than 24 hours earlier with negative results.

The crucial encounter between Mary Thompson and Sergeant Stearns is in dispute. The evidence consists of two decidedly different versions of the same event. According to Sergeant Stearns, he left the area of his conversation with Larry Thompson to follow up on the anonymous tip. He approached Mary Thompson, apprised her of the purported information, and told her he needed to search the van. As he told her of his need to search, he saw Mary stuffing something into a duffel bag between her legs. He saw on the console two Hardee's cups containing an "amber colored" liquid. He also saw the blade of a machete knife under the duffel bag. Stearns could not recall whether he ordered Mary out of the van or whether she exited on her own. In either event, Stearns did not use physical force to remove her from the van. Stearns advised Mary as she was exiting the van that he needed to search her bag. Mary had the bag on her arm and was still trying to stuff something into it. Stearns grabbed the bag, Mary held on, and a struggle ensued. Patrolman Baxter then grabbed Mary, which enabled Stearns to remove the bag from her arm. Stearns searched the bag and found a gun and marijuana. Mary was then arrested.

According to Mary Thompson, two large plastic cups labeled Hardee's were housed in the van's console between the bucket seats. The cups contained iced tea. The machete knife was on the floorboard of the van where it was placed the day before. The Carbondale police had stopped the Thompsons the day before for operating the van on a faulty brake light. Assisted by a German shepherd, they searched the entire van, seized the knife, but returned it in an unsheathed condition before allowing them to leave. Mary remained in the van with the Thompsons' 10-year-old son while Larry left to enter the store. She saw and heard Stearns' encounter with her husband. When her husband entered the store, Stearns approached her side of the van and opened the door. She was told that the van needed to be searched. Stearns asked for consent to search, which she refused. Stearns then grabbed her arm and pulled her out of the van. He pulled the duffel bag off of her arm and searched it. Thereafter, Stearns had patrolman Edwards handcuff her and take her to his squad car. Mary did not attempt to stuff anything into her bag. Patrolman Wilmore was outside his squad car, standing near the rear of the van during the encounter between Dan Stearns and Mary Thompson. He saw Mary pushing Stearns away. He saw her resisting Stearns' efforts to search. Wilmore did not see Mary stuffing anything into the bag. According to Mary Thompson, patrolman Edwards handcuffed her after the bag was searched. Patrolman Edwards did not testify. The Thompsons' son did not testify. Both were potentially in position to observe the disputed events.

The State's argument assumes the truth of Stearn's testimony. It ignores the testimony of patrolman Wilmore that the dispatch tracked the rumors discussed earlier that day at the watch meeting. It assumes that an anonymous caller tipped off the transport of alcohol in the van, rather than drugs. Based on Stearns' testimony, the State tenders the following argument. Stearns' approach of Mary Thompson allowed him to corroborate the anonymous tip by observation of the iced tea. The iced tea's amber color led him to suspect that it was beer. Thus, observation of the iced tea gave Stearns reason to credit the caller's prediction that alcohol could be found in the van. If the prediction about alcohol was true, the prediction about guns from the same source could be true as well. The State argues that an articulable suspicion formed. This suspicion, coupled with Mary's furtive conduct toward a duffel bag that rested atop a machete knife, justified a protective search of the bag. The State concludes that Stearns reasonably believed, based on specific and articulable facts that Mary Thompson posed a danger to him.

In addition to the testimony of patrolman Wilmore, the State's argument ignores the possibility that Stearns opened the door, announced a need to search the van, and then asked permission to do so. It ignores the possibility that, having failed to obtain consent, Stearns pulled Mary from the van and searched her purse, without any furtive conduct on her part. To accept the State's argument, we are required to usurp a function of the trial court to which we routinely defer. Therefore, it is appropriate to remand and allow the trial court to determine what actually happened. Because this legal issue was not the focus of the original hearing, the trial court should reopen the evidence to afford both parties an opportunity to present further testimony. We are mindful of a finding in the original suppression order that touched on the absence of testimony justifying a reasonable belief that the officers were in danger. Stearns did not state that his observations and responses were tied to safety considerations. Indeed, on several occasions he testified that his actions after the stop were motivated by a desire to confirm the anonymous tip rather than by a need to conduct a protective search. Nevertheless, if his testimony is accepted, it gives rise to an inference from which the State may legitimately argue that a protective search was warranted. If we are reading the trial court's view too narrowly, if its finding is based upon a broader view of the circumstances and testimony as a whole, the trial court should state its bases for rejecting the State's argument. It should enunciate clearly why it finds that Sergeant Stearns lacked a reasonable belief that his safety was in peril.

The standard to be applied is well established. The Constitution permits police to take certain precautions for their own protection. If an officer reasonably believes that circumstances after a traffic stop pose a danger, the law allows a limited right to search in the absence of probable cause. Reasonableness requires analysis of all the circumstances to arrive at a proper balance between public interest and personal privacy and allows leeway for officers to act on less than probable cause when specific and articulable facts raise safety concerns. Reasonableness does not, however, surrender personal security to arbitrary interference by police officers. This case presents a number of exceptional circumstances, uncommon to other cases where traffic stops evolved into reasonable protective searches. We emphasize that a proper analysis of a protective search necessitates an assessment of the reasonableness in all the circumstances involved.

One circumstance sets this case apart from other cases that have validated protective searches made in the course of traffic stops. This was a pretextual stop. We know that the officers stopped the van motivated by a desire to search it. The officers recognized that their information did not afford a reasonable basis to arrest or search. They therefore refrained from stopping the van until they detected a traffic offense. Thereafter, their actions were calculated to develop a legal reason to support a search. The officers' subjective intent in a pretextual setting cannot make otherwise lawful conduct illegal. It cannot invalidate the stop. A pretextual stop, by definition, harbors an underlying ambition to exceed its original scope. Once a traffic stop's pretextual nature is established, as it was in this case, we know that the true objective is to find a legal excuse to accomplish a warrantless search. This goal exposes to careful scrutiny disputes over ensuing events. The Carbondale police might have executed the pretextual stop under circumstances more favorable to the argument that officer safety justified the search. The general conditions surrounding the stop do not favor the use of safety concerns as a justification for the officers' desired agenda.

There is one additional circumstance atypical to most protective searches made in the course of traffic stops. The officer released the traffic offender. He allowed the offender to leave the scene of the stop. He then focused on the passenger seated in the van, not because of any violation of the law or safety concern, but because of his unreliable anonymous information about the van. Stearns' own testimony assigns his information about the van as the sole motivation for approaching Mary Thompson. Stearns' testimony also belies a reaction to the observations he made on approach to the van. He did not immediately remove Mary Thompson from the van and frisk her. Rather, he explained the telephone call and expressed a need to search the van because of it. Although these circumstances all enter into analysis of the reasonableness of the search, they do not necessarily outweigh one circumstance focal to the question. Stearns may not have been concerned over safety in the initial phase of his encounter with Mary Thompson. In fact, there was very little upon which a concern could be based. A woman rummaging through her handbag while seated in a vehicle awaiting her husband is not necessarily an activity expected to strike fear in the heart of a police sergeant surrounded by three backup officers. However, Stearns' claim that Mary Thompson continued to reach into the bag as she exited the van is a circumstance capable of causing legitimate safety concerns. Such an act, coupled with her demeanor over another search of the van, could rightfully target the handbag for a precautionary search. The Constitution would not restrain Stearns from preempting her potential retrieval of a weapon from the bag under such circumstance.

Stearns may well have developed a reasonable belief that Mary Thompson posed a threat to officer safety because of her persistent access to the contents of her handbag. This belief may well have been justified despite other circumstances that mitigated against it. Mary Thompson claims that she did not engage in such activity. In fact, she claims that Sergeant Stearns asked for her permission to search and pulled her from the van when he did not receive it. Obviously, this factual dispute needs to be resolved. Ultimately, the question turns on what Sergeant Stearns reasonably believed. The reasonableness of his belief must be weighed in light of all of the circumstances presented. If he reasonably believed that he was in potential peril, the law allows a limited protective search to assure against it. Such a determination, however, necessitates resolution of certain facts that were left unsettled after the original hearing.

Accordingly, we reverse and remand this case to the trial court for further proceedings consistent with this opinion. Reversed and remanded.

REVIEW SECTION

READING COMPREHENSION

Detail the scenario in which Thompson got arrested.

Discuss the differences between reasonable suspicion and probable cause as related to the facts of this case.

THINKING CRITICALLY

Do you agree or disagree that pretextual traffic stops should be a permissible way to stop potential suspects and conduct an exploratory search?

SECTION 3: SPECIAL SITUATION STOPS

OVERVIEW

We know already that reasonable suspicion is required for a stop, and probable cause is required for arrest, and that voluntary encounters are indeed just that and therefore not addressed by the Fourth Amendment or Article One, Section Six of the Illinois Constitution. The lines begin to blur however in the discussion of special situation stops. The courts have delineated that under some special situations it is reasonable to move or detain individuals based on no articulable facts at all. These circumstances include but are not limited to: the movement of passengers out of stopped vehicles for the safety of the officer; detention of individuals entering the United States by way of an international border; and detaining a number of individuals in a particular place such as in a roadblock. Is it constitutional to, based on no individualized suspicion at all, move or detain individuals?

CASE

In *People v Bartley,* the defendant was stopped at a police checkpoint roadblock. Officers at the checkpoint observed the defendant and arrested him for driving under the influence of intoxicating liquor. The trial court granted the defendant's motions to suppress his arrest and the related evidence. The State certified that the suppression order substantially impairs its ability to prosecute the defendant, and filed a notice of appeal.

PEOPLE V. BARTLEY
125 Ill.App.3d 575, 466 N.E.2d 346 (Ill.App. 3 Dist., 1984)

Just prior to midnight on Saturday, December 18, 1982, officers from the McDonough County Sheriff's Department, Macomb City Police, Illinois State Police and Illinois Secretary of State Police set up a checkpoint on a five lane street in Macomb. The checkpoint was located at a point between the city's only all-night restaurant and the central business district. The checkpoint operated for approximately two hours. Following the hearing on the defendant's motion to suppress, the trial court found that the purpose for establishing the instant checkpoint was to apprehend DUI violators. The court concluded that the State's interest in apprehending DUI violators did not outweigh the intrusion caused by a checkpoint stop of citizens. The court held that the roadblock arrest violated the Fourth Amendment and therefore suppressed the evidence resulting from the defendant's arrest. Based on the record, there can be little doubt that the roadblock was established for the purpose of apprehending drunk drivers. Therefore, the sole question on appeal is whether such roadblocks are constitutionally permissible.

A checkpoint or roadblock stop constitutes a seizure within the meaning of the Fourth Amendment. In United States v. Martinez-Fuerte (1976), 428 U.S. 543, 96 S.Ct. 3074, 49 L.Ed.2d 1116, the Supreme Court declared that vehicle stops at a fixed checkpoint are consistent with the Fourth Amendment and do not require a warrant. A checkpoint stop involved minimal intrusion. The objective intrusion, which the court defined as the stop, questioning and visual inspection of the vehicles' occupants, was the same in checkpoint and roving patrol stops. However, subjective intrusion, defined as concern, surprise or alarm generated in the minds of lawful travelers, was much less in the case of checkpoint stops which were conducted at fixed locations with ample warning as to what a motorist was to expect. Also, checkpoint stops were considered less intrusive because officers had no discretion as to which cars would be inspected. The regularized manner in which the checkpoint operated was neither arbitrary, random nor capricious. Based on the minimal intrusion involved, limited police discretion, the important government interest at stake and the unavailability of effective alternatives, the court approved warrantless checkpoint stops.

The constitutionality of a roadblock designed to detain all traffic in order to screen out intoxicated drivers is an issue of first impression in Illinois. This balancing test involves three considerations: (1) the gravity of public concern served by the seizure; (2) the degree to which the seizure advances the public interest and; (3) the severity of the interference with individual liberty. Regarding the first factor, it is beyond dispute that drunk drivers are a grave menace to the public and that stronger measures are needed to cope with the problem. However, we must bear in mind that in cases where the Supreme Court has either expressly or impliedly sanctioned checkpoint stops, the criminal activity targeted was of such a nature that there was no other less intrusive but equally effective means of detecting violators. In contrast, the foremost method of detecting drunk drivers has been by observing driving behavior. An intoxicated motorist can be easily discerned by a trained officer without having to stop all traffic at a roadblock. Another less intrusive means of deterring drunk drivers is through the enactment of stiffer penalties. We find that the State has failed to demonstrate the superiority of a roadblock over these less intrusive alternative means of deterrence. There is nothing in the record which shows that the only practical or effective means of catching drunk drivers is by arbitrarily subjecting all citizens to police scrutiny without suspicion of wrongdoing simply because they happen to be traveling on a particular road at a certain time. Further, we cannot describe as minimal the degree of intrusion caused by DUI roadblocks. In reality, DUI roadblocks are designed to be set up at night, without warning and at locations which are constantly changing. Motorists are often unaware of the reason for the stop prior to being asked to display their driver's license. Lights are shined into their eyes and officers peer into the passenger compartment of their automobile. Although field officers generally have no discretion over who to stop, we are unaware of any criteria used by supervisory officers in determining the need, location, time and duration of a roadblock. DUI roadblocks involve a significant degree of intrusion.

Based on the foregoing, we find that the government interest in detecting drunk drivers by employing roadblocks does not outweigh the resulting public inconvenience and interference with the individual's Fourth Amendment rights. DUI roadblocks involve a significant degree of intrusion and are of speculative deterrent value when compared to less intrusive means of enforcement. Therefore, we hold that roadblocks set up for the purpose of screening out drunk drivers violate Article I, section 6 of the Illinois Constitution and the Fourth and Fourteenth Amendments to the United States Constitution. This opinion does not purport to limit the authority of law enforcement officials to apprehend on the basis of probable cause those motorists guilty of driving while under the influence. The order of the circuit court of McDonough County granting the defendant's motion to suppress is affirmed.

REVIEW SECTION

READING COMPREHENSION

What did the court attempt to delineate in this case?

THINKING CRITICALLY

The subject of the validity of roadblocks, and roadblock arrests, is extremely difficult. The governing test which balances the public interest in apprehending DUI violators against motorists' rights to security and privacy may produce legitimate arguments either way. In light of the debate about balancing public interest in crime control and individual rights, articulate your position on this controversial issue.

CASE

In *People v Lidster,* the defendant was convicted of driving under the influence of alcohol after being stopped at an "informational roadblock" conducted by the police department. The defendant appealed, contending that the trial court erred in denying his motion to quash his arrest and suppress evidence because the roadblock was an unreasonable seizure. Can a warrantless temporary roadblock which stops automobiles without any articulable suspicion of illegal activity produce constitutionally permissible arrests?

PEOPLE V. LIDSTER
747 N.E.2d 419 (Ill.App. 2 Dist., 2001)

On August 30, 1997, Lombard police set up an "informative stop" at the location of a hit-and-run accident a week before. The officers intended to stop all eastbound traffic and pass out flyers about the accident, hoping that someone had witnessed the incident and could provide information about the offender or his vehicle. While conducting the roadblock, Detective Wayne Vasil was standing in the center lane and the defendant's Mazda almost struck Vasil as the defendant approached. At that point, Vasil was not aware that defendant had violated any state law or city ordinance, although he had "some sort of feeling that something might be wrong." Vasil stated that defendant's van had already been stopped pursuant to the roadblock before nearly striking him. Vasil approached the van to ask defendant why he had almost hit him. During the ensuing conversation, Vasil began to suspect that defendant might be under the influence of alcohol. As a result, he directed defendant to pull onto a side street for field sobriety tests. Another officer conducted the tests and defendant was arrested for driving under the influence of alcohol. Defendant moved to quash his arrest, arguing that the roadblock was unconstitutional. The trial court denied the motion. Subsequently, a jury found defendant guilty and the court sentenced him to court supervision. After the court denied his posttrial motion, defendant filed a timely notice of appeal.

On appeal, defendant renews his argument that the roadblock was unconstitutional. He contends that, under the balancing test developed by the state and federal courts, the public interest in conducting the roadblock--searching for evidence about a prior crime--did not outweigh the intrusion on the rights of innocent motorists. It is impossible to escape the conclusion that the roadblock's ostensible purpose was to seek evidence of "ordinary criminal wrongdoing." While the crime under investigation here, involving the death of an innocent person, is undoubtedly serious, equally serious crimes unfortunately happen every day in many jurisdictions. If investigating such a crime could be the basis for a roadblock, police could stop all cars entering or leaving town virtually every day on the chance that someone might have seen something that would aid the investigation. Such unbridled use of checkpoints also leaves open the possibility of police subterfuge, using the pretense of investigating some infamous crime to stop motorists based on the generalized possibility that interrogation and inspection may reveal that any given motorist has committed some crime. We note that in this case a second officer was stationed on a side street, apparently to prevent drivers from evading the roadblock. This tends to discredit the explanation that the police were merely seeking information. Presumably, if a motorist were willing to provide information to the police, he or she would not attempt to avoid the roadblock.

The State argues that the public interest in seeing the hit-and-run solved was not insubstantial and that the police took reasonable steps to minimize the intrusion on the motorists' rights. However, assuming for the sake of argument that the police did everything reasonably possible to minimize the intrusion, a criminal investigation can never be the basis for a roadblock, at least absent some emergency circumstance not present here. Such an interest is simply not sufficiently weighty to counterbalance even a minimal intrusion on the rights of drivers stopped at the checkpoint. Finally, although not itself dispositive, some mention should be made of the third element of the balancing equation, the degree to which the seizure advances the public interest. Here, the State presented no empirical evidence of the effectiveness of such a checkpoint program. In the absence of evidence to the contrary, it seems likely that more traditional law enforcement techniques would have been just as, if not more, effective than the roadblock without infringing on the constitutional rights of numerous motorists, none of whom was suspected of a crime.

Because the roadblock at which defendant was apprehended did not comply with constitutional standards, the trial court should have granted defendant's motion to quash his arrest and suppress evidence. Absent this evidence, there remains no evidence to support his conviction for driving under the influence of alcohol. The judgment of the circuit court is reversed.

REVIEW SECTION

READING COMPREHENSION

What did the court attempt to delineate in this case regarding the balance that must be used in establishing roadblocks?

SECTION 4: FRISKS AND THE FOURTH AMENDMENT

OVERVIEW

While a frisk and a stop are similar, it is important to distinguish between the two. A stop is a seizure of an individual, whereas a frisk is a search. Thus, a lawful stop must occur prior to the occurrence of a frisk. Furthermore, the facts that support a stop do not automatically support a frisk as well. Frisks are considered Fourth Amendment searches by the court and therefore to be lawful must be backed by a stop that involves a reasonable suspicion that a crime may have been underway and/or reasonable suspicion that the individual is armed and therefore an officer can do a once-over-lightly pat-down to detect only weapons to ensure their safety.

CASE

In *People v Sorenson,* the defendant was charged with one count of unlawful possession of a controlled substance after police discovered cocaine in one of his unlaced hiking boots during a pat-down search following a traffic stop. The circuit court denied the defendant's motion to suppress the evidence seized, finding that the search was valid because, under the totality of the circumstances, the officer had a reasonable belief that the search was necessary to protect himself from harm. Following a stipulated bench trial, the defendant was convicted of the charged offense and sentenced to two years of probation. The defendant appealed to the appellate court, and the appellate court affirmed the circuit court's denial of the motion to suppress, along with the defendant's conviction and sentence. The Supreme Court of Illinois affirms the judgment of the appellate court.

PEOPLE V. SORENSON
Supreme Court of Illinois
752 N.E.2d 1078 (Ill. 2001)

At the suppression hearing, Springfield police officer Jim Cordery testified that on the evening of September 16, 1997, around 9:10 p.m., he was conducting a surveillance from his police vehicle of a "known drug house" in Springfield, Illinois. Cordery explained that he lived in the area and that he had been told by numerous neighbors and other sources that the occupants of the house were dealing drugs at the location. He also had been informed that there was an extremely high amount of foot, bicycle and car traffic coming to the house, which involved the visitors staying for two or three minutes and then leaving. Cordery noted that the police had previously arrested the occupants of the house for dealing narcotics.

Officer Cordery stated that while he was parked outside the house, a vehicle pulled up with three persons inside. The defendant, a white male with red hair, was the sole backseat passenger. Cordery watched the defendant exit the vehicle and go inside the house. The defendant remained inside the house for about three or four minutes before returning to the same vehicle. Cordery suspected that a drug transaction had taken place in the house so he decided to follow the vehicle when it pulled away. After the driver failed to signal his intention to turn left at an intersection, the officer stopped the car. When asked if he felt particularly threatened at the time he made the traffic stop, Cordery responded affirmatively, stating, "I did feel uneasy, yes sir." He noted that his concern arose out of the location of the stop, that it was a dark road, that there were three persons in the vehicle, and that in his experience, persons involved in drugs are known to carry weapons. Cordery acknowledged that the occupants of the vehicle had not made any menacing or threatening gestures toward him.

Officer Cordery further testified that after he approached the vehicle, the driver produced his driver's license and proof of insurance. Cordery then asked him if he had "any weapons, drugs, needles." At that point, the driver consented to a pat-down search, which did not reveal any weapons or contraband. Cordery stated that following the pat-down of the driver, he turned his attention toward the defendant because the defendant was on his side of the vehicle and therefore would be the "quickest threat" to the officer. Cordery asked the defendant if he had any weapons, drugs, needles or anything on him that could hurt the officer. The defendant responded that he did not. According to Cordery, the defendant then gave his permission to be searched. The defendant stepped out of the vehicle and placed his hands on the trunk of the car. Cordery then conducted a frisk of the defendant. During the course of the frisk, Cordery asked the defendant to remove his boots and kick them to the side. Cordery noted that he asked the defendant to remove his boots because they were unlaced. The officer added that, in his experience, any time boot laces are untied there is a very strong possibility that a weapon may be located inside and that it allows quick access. After the defendant removed his boots, Cordery observed a white, rock-like substance in one of the boots. The officer recognized the substance as possibly being cocaine, and it subsequently tested positive for the presence of cocaine.

The defendant was the only other witness to testify at the suppression hearing. The defendant testified that on the evening in question, he went inside the house for about 5 or 10 minutes. When he left the house, he got into a vehicle with two of his friends. He stated that he thought the officer pulled the vehicle over because the driver had activated his signal late into the turn. The officer pulled the vehicle over about one block from the house the defendant had left. When the officer finished searching the driver, he told the driver to sit back down in the car. According to the defendant, the officer then told the defendant to "step out of the vehicle" and put his hands on the trunk. The defendant complied with the officer's instructions. The officer then conducted a pat-down search of the defendant. When the officer finished the pat-down, he noticed that the defendant's boots were unlaced. The officer then asked the defendant to remove his boots. The defendant described his boots as steel-toed hiking boots that came above his ankles.

At the conclusion of the hearing, the trial court denied the defendant's motion to suppress. It found that the State had failed to meet its burden of proof as to whether the defendant consented to the search, but it further found that the search of the defendant was valid under the standards enunciated Terry v. Ohio, 392 U.S. 1, 20 L. Ed. 2d 889, 88 S. Ct. 1868 (1968). In its written order denying the defendant's motion to reconsider, the trial court noted the following objective circumstances surrounding the stop, in concluding that Officer Cordery possessed a reasonable belief that the search was necessary to protect himself from harm: "The officer testified that he observed the defendant exit a known drug house, that he stopped the vehicle on a dark street, that the defendant was in closest proximity to the officer after the driver exited the vehicle, that he is trained to suspect that drug purchasers are armed with greater frequency than the norm, that his training instructs him that weapons are often carried in boots and that the fact that the boots were unlaced induced him to search those boots for weapons."

The cause subsequently proceeded to a stipulated bench trial. The defendant agreed to the stipulation presented by the prosecutor, with one notable exception. In that regard, defense counsel told the trial court that the defendant had "previously testified that consent was not volunteered, and that is the issue that will be appealed, along with some other issues along with the search." The trial court accepted the stipulation and found the defendant guilty of unlawful possession of a controlled substance. The appellate court affirmed the defendant's conviction and the trial court's denial of the defendant's motion to suppress. We granted the defendant leave to appeal.

The defendant challenges the propriety of the trial court's denial of his motion to suppress. Traditionally, this court has stated that when a trial court's ruling on a motion to suppress evidence involves factual determinations and credibility assessments, the ultimate ruling will not be disturbed on appeal unless it is manifestly erroneous. This deferential standard of review is grounded in the reality that the trial court is in a superior position to determine and weigh the credibility of witnesses, observe the witnesses' demeanor, and resolve conflicts in the witnesses' testimony. Accordingly, we will accord great deference to the trial court's factual findings, and we will reverse those findings only if they are against the manifest weight of the evidence; however, we will review *de novo* the ultimate question of the defendant's legal challenge to the denial of his motion to suppress.

The defendant argues that Officer Cordery lacked a reasonable belief that the defendant posed a danger necessary to justify a pat down search under Terry. The defendant further argues that the officer exceeded the bounds of a valid Terry frisk for weapons when he directed the defendant to remove his boots. The officer need not be absolutely certain that the individual is armed; the issue is whether a reasonably prudent man in the circumstances would be warranted in the belief that his safety or that of others was in danger. In determining whether the officer acted reasonably in such circumstances, due weight must be given to the specific reasonable inferences which he is entitled to draw from the facts in light of his experience.

The defendant does not challenge the stop in this case. The stop of the vehicle in which the defendant was a passenger was justified based on Officer Cordery's observation of a traffic violation. Furthermore, it is well established that following a lawful traffic stop, police may, as a matter of course, order the driver and any passengers out of the vehicle pending completion of the stop without violating the protections of the fourth amendment. The question of whether the investigatory stop was valid, however, is a separate question from whether the search for weapons was valid. Turning to the question of whether the frisk was valid, we initially note that the defendant claims that he is not contesting the facts relating to that issue, while at the same time arguing that the record does not support the trial court's finding that he left a known drug house prior to the stop or that he might have been involved in any illegal activity. The trial court determined that the defendant had left a known drug house and implicitly found that the officer had good reason to suspect that the defendant had been involved in purchasing illegal drugs. Given the appropriate deference to the facts found and the inferences drawn by the trial court, we find that its factual determinations were well supported by the record and were not against the manifest weight of the evidence.

The defendant also maintains that the record indicates that the officer was not so much concerned with his safety as he was in searching for illegal drugs. That notion, however, is belied by the record. Officer Cordery specifically testified that he turned his attention toward the defendant during the course of the stop because the defendant was on his side of the vehicle and was the "quickest threat" to the officer. The remainder of the officer's testimony indicates that he clearly was primarily concerned with the possibility that the defendant possessed a weapon. The fact that the officer may have also believed that the defendant possessed illegal drugs did not negate the officer's concern for his safety. Here, the trial court's findings indicated that Officer Cordery conducted the search for the discovery of weapons, and we note that that finding was not against the manifest weight of the evidence.

Relying on this courts decisions People v. Flowers, 179 Ill. 2d 257 (1997), and People v. Galvin, 127 Ill. 2d 153 (1989), the defendant argues that Officer Cordery improperly based his decision to search the defendant not on any specific concerns for his safety but rather on a series of general suppositions which were tantamount to a policy or procedure of searching every person during a routine traffic stop. The defendant further argues that there is not a sufficient nexus between illegal drug activity and a reasonable belief that a suspect is armed and dangerous. We believe that a comparison of the Flowers and Galvin cases with the present case supports the notion that the frisk was proper here.

The defendant relies on People v. Wright, 183 Ill. 2d 16 (1998), for his contention that we should reject any nexus between illegal drug activity and a reasonable belief that a suspect is armed and dangerous. The defendant's reliance on Wright, however, is misplaced. Wright involved the standard necessary to enter someone's home unannounced, and we do not find it applicable to the propriety of a Terry frisk in conjunction with a traffic stop. Instead, we note that it has been held that when a police officer possesses a reasonable articulable suspicion that automobile occupants were dealing drugs just prior to the stop, the officer's belief that the suspects were armed and dangerous was reasonable because weapons and violence frequently are associated with drug transactions.

We next must address the defendant's argument that Officer Cordery exceeded the bounds of a permissible Terry frisk for weapons when he directed the defendant to remove his hiking boots. The defendant maintains that the limited exception for a frisk for weapons permits a pat-down only of a person's outer clothing. The defendant is mistaken in his assertion that the scope of a Terry search is always limited to a pat-down of a person's outer clothing. The Terry Court noted that a weapons search must, like any other search, "be strictly circumscribed by the exigencies which justify its initiation." The Court in Terry, however, refrained from articulating the specific limitations that might be imposed in all cases, and instead stated that "limitations will have to be developed in the concrete factual circumstances of individual cases." The Terry Court further noted that the scope of the search must be confined to "an intrusion reasonably designed to discover guns, knives, clubs, or other hidden instruments for the assault of the police officer."

In evaluating the validity of an officer's protective conduct under Terry, the touchstone of the analysis is the reasonableness under the circumstances of the particular governmental invasion of a citizen's personal security. Under the circumstances of the present case, we find that Officer Cordery did not act unreasonably in directing the defendant to remove his unlaced boots to determine if they contained a weapon. Under the circumstances, we find that the scope of the search was sufficiently confined to "an intrusion reasonably designed to discover guns, knives, or other hidden instruments for the assault of the police officer" and therefore was proper. We note that most of the other state courts which have addressed the issue have found that a search involving the removal of a shoe or looking into a boot is within the permissible scope of Terry if the officer conducted the search with the intent of finding a weapon.

In the present case, Officer Cordery asked the defendant to remove his shoes out of a legitimate concern for his safety. Thus we find the removal of the defendant's shoes did not exceed the scope of a valid Terry search for weapons. For the foregoing reasons, we hold that the trial court properly denied the defendant's motion to suppress. Accordingly, we affirm the judgment of the appellate court.

REVIEW SECTION

READING COMPREHENSION

Detail the facts of this case and the relevance of consent by the suspect and perceived potential harm by the officer.

Detail the reasonableness of the officer's protective conduct under the Terry rule.

CONCLUSION

This chapter has reviewed stops, frisks, and the Fourth Amendment; stops and the Fourth Amendment; special situation stops; and frisks and the Fourth Amendment. You have become aware that government officials are free to approach individuals in public places to request response to inquiries or to request a search. As well, you know that according to the Fourth Amendment to the U.S. Constitution and Article One, Section Six of the Illinois Constitution, a seizure occurs when a government official removes an individual's right to leave or stay in a specific location. What should have become obvious in review of this chapter is that it is not always clear when an individual feels free to "go about their business" and when the police have created a situation of coercion. The courts attempt to define such scenarios in continually occurring interpretations of the Fourth Amendment.

Chapter Five

Seizures of Persons: Arrest

While we have previously discussed voluntary contact with government officials, stops by officers which must involve reasonable suspicion, we now turn to arrests. Because arrest is more intrusive than either a stop or voluntary contact, arrest involves more factual support by government officials in the form of probable cause. To make an arrest reasonable, the government must demonstrate that is was based on probable cause and the manner in which the arrest was made was reasonable. Arrest by a peace officer is detailed in 725 ILCS 5/107-2:

> A peace officer may arrest a person when: (a) He has a warrant commanding that such person be arrested; or (b) He has reasonable grounds to believe that a warrant for the person's arrest has been issued in this State or in another jurisdiction; or (c) He has reasonable grounds to believe that the person is committing or has committed an offense.

In Illinois, 725 ILCS 5/107-5 details the method of arrest:

> (a) An arrest is made by an actual restraint of the person or by his submission to custody. (b) An arrest may be made on any day and at any time of the day or night. (c) An arrest may be made anywhere within the jurisdiction of this State. (d) All necessary and reasonable force may be used to effect an entry into any building or property or part thereof to make an authorized arrest.

Keep in mind the guidelines as set forth in 725 ILCS 5/112A-26 elaborate arrest without a warrant:

> (a) Any law enforcement officer may make an arrest without warrant if the officer has probable cause to believe that the person has committed or is committing any crime, including but not limited to violation of an order of protection, under Section 12-30 of the Criminal Code of 1961, even if the crime was not committed in the presence of the officer.

This chapter will review:

(1)   The definition of arrest;

(2)   Probable cause; and

(3)   The manner of arrest.

SECTION 1: THE DEFININTION OF ARREST

OVERVIEW

By definition, an arrest involves the stop, seizure, or deprivation of one's liberty by virtue of legal authority. All individuals properly accused of a crime or misdemeanor, may be arrested, however by the laws of the United States, ambassadors and other public ministers are exempt from arrest. As defined by 725 ILCS 5/102-5, an 'arrest' means "the taking of a person into custody."

Whether a detention was an investigatory stop or a full-blown arrest is a question of law wherein the courts attempt to determine at what point, in view of the totality of the circumstances, a reasonable person would not feel free to leave a situation. This gets a little complicated however, because a person may feel detained by an investigative stop, yet this would not officially constitute an arrest. There is no bright-line test that separates an investigatory stop from an arrest, though the length of time of the detention certainly plays some role. Thus, whether a seizure constitutes an arrest is answered on a case-by-case basis in light of the totality of the circumstances.

The courts consider various factors in making this distinction, such as the number of officers present, the show of authority, and the use of physical restraint, though in the end the courts have indicated that 'common sense' and 'ordinary experience' must prevail in the analysis. Keep in mind that police must not necessarily recite the magic words, 'You are under arrest.' For example in Dunaway v. New York, 442 U.S. 200 (1979), whether the suspect was told that he was 'under arrest' was irrelevant to determining whether he was, in fact, under arrest. Thus, when officers use restrictive seizure to investigate suspicions of criminal activity, the detention of the suspect is sufficient to constitute an arrest even if the officer did not formally advise the suspect. Thus, you need to think of arrest as a zone, with the common element being the requirement of probable cause in order to be considered reasonable by the Fourth Amendment.

SECTION 2: PROBABLE CAUSE

OVERVIEW

Between reasonable suspicion and proof beyond a reasonable doubt, lies probable cause which is required by officers to make an arrest. This means that officers must have enough facts to reasonably believe that the arrested individual has committed, is committing, or is about to commit a crime. This reasonable belief can be based either on direct information or hearsay. While hearsay cannot be admitted in a court of law, it can be used to establish probable cause for arrest, though an anonymous tip in and of itself is insufficient in this regard. Courts employ the totality of circumstances of informant reliability test to determine whether or not hearsay evidence is reliable. You must keep in mind that when doubts arise as to reasonableness, courts tend to accept the facts as perceived by law enforcement officers.

CASE

Illinois v Gates involves a May 3, 1978, anonymous letter received by the Police Department of Bloomingdale, Illinois which included statements that respondents, husband and wife, were engaged in selling drugs to be transported by air. Acting on the tip, a police officer placed the flight under surveillance with the DEA. A search warrant for respondents' residence and automobile was obtained from an Illinois state-court judge. When respondents arrived at their home, the police were waiting and discovered marihuana and other contraband in respondents' car trunk and home. Prior to respondents' trial on charges of violating state drug laws, the trial court ordered suppression of all the items seized, and the Illinois Appellate Court affirmed. The Illinois Supreme Court also affirmed, holding that the letter and affidavit were inadequate to sustain a determination of probable cause for issuance of the search warrant since they failed to satisfy the two-pronged test of (1) revealing the informant's basis of knowledge and (2) providing sufficient facts to establish either the informant's veracity or the reliability of the informant's report.

ILLINOIS V. GATES
Supreme Court of the United States
462 U.S. 213, 103 S. Ct. 2317 (1983)

Respondents Lance and Susan Gates were indicated for violation of state drug laws after police officers, executing a search warrant, discovered marihuana and other contraband in their automobile and home. Prior to trial the Gateses moved to suppress evidence seized during this search. The Illinois Supreme Court affirmed the decisions of lower state courts granting the motion. It held that the affidavit submitted in support of the State's application for a warrant to search the Gateses' property was inadequate. We granted certiorari to consider the application of the Fourth Amendment to a magistrate's issuance of a search warrant on the basis of a partially corroborated anonymous informant's tip. After receiving briefs and hearing oral argument on this question, however, we requested the parties to address an additional question: " the rule requiring the exclusion at a criminal trial of evidence obtained in violation of the Fourth Amendment, should to any extent be modified, so as, for example, not to require the exclusion of evidence obtained in the reasonable belief that the search and seizure at issue was consistent with the Fourth Amendment." We decide today, with apologies to all, that the issue we framed for the parties was not presented to the Illinois courts and, accordingly, do not address it. Rather, we consider the question originally presented in the petition for certiorari, and conclude that the Illinois Supreme Court read the requirements of our Fourth Amendment decisions too restrictively. Initially, however, we set forth our reasons for not addressing the question regarding modification of the exclusionary rule.

Our certiorari jurisdiction over decisions from state courts derives from 28 U. S. C. § 1257, which provides that " judgments or decrees rendered by the highest court of a State in which a decision could be had, may be reviewed by the Supreme Court as follows: . . . (3) By writ of certiorari, . . . where any title, right, privilege or immunity is specially set up or claimed under the Constitution, treaties or statutes of . . . the United States." The application of these principles in the instant case is not entirely straightforward. It is clear in this case that respondents expressly raised, at every level of the Illinois judicial system, the claim that the Fourth Amendment had been violated by the actions of the Illinois police and that the evidence seized by the officers should be excluded from their trial. It also is clear that the State challenged, at every level of the Illinois court system, respondents' claim that the substantive requirements of the Fourth Amendment had been violated. The State never, however, raised or addressed the question whether the federal exclusionary rule should be modified in any respect, and none of the opinions of the Illinois courts give any indication that the question was considered.

The fact that the Illinois courts affirmatively applied the federal exclusionary rule -- suppressing evidence against respondents -- does not affect our conclusion. In the present case, although the Illinois courts applied the federal exclusionary rule, there was never "any real contest" upon the point. The application of the exclusionary rule was merely a routine act, once a violation of the Fourth Amendment had been found, and not the considered judgment of the Illinois courts on the question whether application of a modified rule would be warranted on the facts of this case. In such circumstances, absent the adversarial dispute necessary to apprise the state court of the arguments for not applying the exclusionary rule, we will not consider the question whether the exclusionary rule should be modified.

Likewise, we do not believe that the State's repeated opposition to respondents' substantive Fourth Amendment claims suffices to have raised the question whether the exclusionary rule should be modified. We now turn to the question presented in the State's original petition for certiorari, which requires us to decide whether respondents' rights under the Fourth and Fourteenth Amendments were violated by the search of their car and house. This totality-of-the-circumstances approach is far more consistent with our prior treatment of probable cause than is any rigid demand that specific "tests" be satisfied by every informant's tip. Perhaps the central teaching of our decisions bearing on the probable-cause standard is that it is a "practical, non-technical conception." Our decisions applying the totality-of-the-circumstances analysis have consistently recognized the value of corroboration of details of an informant's tip by independent police work. The anonymous letter contained a range of details relating not just to easily obtained facts and conditions existing at the time of the tip, but to future actions of third parties ordinarily not easily predicted. If the informant had access to accurate information of this type a magistrate could properly conclude that it was not unlikely that he also had access to reliable information of the Gateses' alleged illegal activities. It is apparent, therefore, that the judge issuing the warrant had a substantial basis for that probable cause to search the Gateses' home and car existed. The judgement of the Supreme Court of Illinois therefore must be reversed.

The Honorable Justice STEVENS, with whom JUSTICE BRENNAN joins, dissenting. The fact that Lance and Sue Gates made a 22-hour nonstop drive from West Palm Beach, Florida, to Bloomingdale, Illinois, only a few hours after Lance had flown to Florida provided persuasive evidence that they were engaged in illicit activity. That fact, however, was not known to the judge when he issued the warrant to search their home. What the judge did know at that time was that the anonymous informant had not been completely accurate in his or her predictions. The discrepancy between the informant's predictions and the facts known to Detective Mader is significant for three reasons. First, it cast doubt on the informant's hypothesis that the Gates already had "over $100,000 worth of drugs in their basement." Second, the discrepancy made the

Gates' conduct seem substantially less unusual than the informant had predicted it would be. Third, the fact that the anonymous letter contained a material mistake undermines the reasonableness of relying on it as a basis for making a forcible entry into a private home. No one knows who the informant in this case was, or what motivated him or her to write the note. Given that the note's predictions were faulty in one significant respect, and were corroborated by nothing except ordinary innocent activity, I must surmise that the Court's evaluation of the warrant's validity has been colored by subsequent events.

In apologizing for its belated realization that we should not have ordered reargument in this case, the Court today shows high regard for the appropriate relationship of this Court to state courts. When the Court discusses the merits, however, it attaches no weight to the conclusions of the Circuit Judge, of the three judges of the Second District of the Illinois Appellate Court, or of the five justices of the Illinois Supreme Court, all of whom concluded that the warrant was not based on probable cause. In a fact-bound inquiry of this sort, the judgment of three levels of state courts, all of which are better able to evaluate the probable reliability of anonymous informants in Bloomingdale, Illinois, than we are, should be entitled to at least a presumption of accuracy. I would simply vacate the judgment of the Illinois Supreme Court and remand the case for reconsideration.

REVIEW SECTION

READING COMPREHENSION

Detail the facts of this case and the arguments presented by the Supreme Court in contrast to those of all the lower Illinois courts.

THINKING CRITICALLY

Should an anonymous letter be sufficient grounds for determining probable cause?

In the dissenting opinion it is noted that the Supreme Court dismissed the conclusions of the Circuit Court, of the Second District of the Illinois Appellate Court, and of the Illinois Supreme Court, who all concluded that the warrant was not based on probable cause. In your opinion, should the Supreme Court have negated the "fact-bound inquiry of this sort . . . [by those] better able to evaluate the probable reliability of anonymous informants in Illinois?" Do you agree or disagree with the dissenting view to vacate the judgment of the Illinois Supreme Court and remand the case for reconsideration?

SECTION 3: THE MANNER OF ARREST

OVERVIEW

Aside from probable cause, the Fourth Amendment also includes a reasonable manner of arrest requirement. In Illinois, 725 ILCS 5/107-5 refers to the manner of arrest:

> (d) All necessary and reasonable force may be used to effect an entry into any building or property or part thereof to make an authorized arrest.

Thus, when you consider if the manner of an arrest was reasonable, you must also consider whether the level of force used by law enforcement personnel was reasonable. The courts employ an objective standard of reasonable force, wherein according to the Fourth Amendment, officers are entitled to employ the amount of force necessary to apprehend suspects.

CASE

In *Fantasia v Kinsella,* the plaintiff brings action against three police officers for the Village of Orland Park in connection with an altercation in his home and his subsequent arrest. Plaintiff alleges that defendants violated 42 U.S.C. § 1983 by using excessive force against him, failing to prevent the use of excessive force against him, falsely arresting him and conspiring to violate his constitutional rights. The plaintiff also brings a claim under Illinois state law for malicious prosecution.

FANTASIA V. KINSELLA
United States District Court, N.D. Illinois, Eastern Division
956 F.Supp. 1409

Early in the day on May 22, 1994, plaintiff went to his neighbor's house in Orland Park to watch a Chicago Bulls basketball game on television. Over the course of the day, plaintiff drank three "Rum and Cokes" and had a sip of a Bloody Mary drink. The Bulls lost the game and plaintiff returned home. Plaintiff's wife, Mary Fantasia, also had returned home from a trip to the grocery store a short time earlier. After returning home, plaintiff argued with his wife over the actions of one of his daughters. At some point, a container of dry dog food and a ceramic container fell to the floor and spilled all over the kitchen floor. Both plaintiff and Mrs. Fantasia agree that plaintiff accidentally knocked both to the floor. During the argument with plaintiff, Mrs. Fantasia stated that if plaintiff did not quiet down she would call the police because she did not want her neighbors to hear their argument. Plaintiff then picked up the telephone and dialed 911 himself and handed the telephone receiver to his wife. The 911 operator answered and asked Mrs. Fantasia if she wanted "police or fire." Mrs. Fantasia answered "police," but when the police answered she said "never mind" and hung up the receiver. Nevertheless, the 911 operator dispatched officers to plaintiff's home.

Responding to the call in separate squad cars, both officers Kinsella and Hartsock arrived at plaintiff's home between five and ten minutes after Mrs. Fantasia spoke to the 911 operator. Officer Hartsock went to the back door and attempted to follow plaintiff's daughter into the house through a screen door on the patio, but plaintiff slid the screen door closed before Officer Hartsock could enter. Plaintiff yelled to Officer Hartsock that he was not needed. Meanwhile, Officer Kinsella had entered the house through the front door. Upon his entry, Mrs. Fantasia told Officer Kinsella, "The Bulls lost. Maybe you can help him." When plaintiff saw Officer Kinsella, he demanded that Officer Kinsella leave the house. Using profanity, Officer Kinsella responded that he was going nowhere. Plaintiff, who was holding a broomstick, then told Officer Kinsella that "if you were not a police officer, I'd kick your f***ing ass." Officer Kinsella told plaintiff to release the broomstick or he would arrest plaintiff. After repeating the command twice — a time span of approximately five seconds — plaintiff released the broom. Officer Kinsella took the broomstick and threw it into the living room.

From this point on, the facts are disputed at nearly every turn. Because the facts must be viewed in a light favorable to the nonmovant, plaintiff's version of the facts will be used. After throwing the broomstick into the living room, Officer Kinsella threw his hat to the floor and told plaintiff, "come on ***hole, let's go outside right now." Plaintiff responded that he would not do that but "if you were not a police officer, I would beat the living sh** out of you." Officer Kinsella then hit plaintiff in the hip area with a baton. After several baton strikes to plaintiff's arm and elbow, plaintiff was pushed backwards into a set of closet doors, which then collapsed. Plaintiff got up and said, "Is that the best you can do?" Officer Kinsella punched plaintiff in the face. After recovering from the punch, plaintiff again asked Officer Kinsella, "Is that all you f***ing got?" Officer Kinsella responded with a second punch to plaintiff's face. After the second punch, Officer Hartsock pushed Officer Kinsella off of plaintiff and said "Do you know what you're doing?"

Plaintiff retreated into the kitchen and proceeded to pick up the telephone receiver. Officer Duggan, now in the kitchen, motioned to Officer Kinsella to relate to him what was happening. Officer Kinsella indicated that plaintiff was being arrested. Officer Duggan then asked plaintiff to hang up the telephone. Plaintiff hung up the telephone after Officer Duggan's second request to do so. Officer Duggan told plaintiff to step into the front room. With the assistance of Officer Kinsella, Officer Duggan placed handcuffs on plaintiff. Plaintiff was charged with aggravated assault. Later that day, plaintiff was treated at Palos Community Hospital for injuries he had sustained to his hip, upper left arm and left elbow. After a jury trial, plaintiff was acquitted of all charges against him.

On February 16, 1996, plaintiff filed this action in the Law Division of the Circuit Court of Cook County. Defendants removed the action to federal district court in a timely manner. In Count I, plaintiff alleges that Officer Kinsella violated § 1983 by using excessive force against him. In Count II, plaintiff alleges that all three defendants violated § 1983 by failing to prevent the use of excessive force against plaintiff. In Count III, plaintiff asserts a false arrest claim against all defendants under § 1983. In Count IV, plaintiff claims that Officer Kinsella is liable for malicious prosecution under Illinois law for filing a complaint of aggravated assault against plaintiff. In Count V, plaintiff alleges that defendants violated § 1983 by conspiring to deprive plaintiff of his constitutional rights. Defendants move for summary judgment on all counts.

Rule 56(c) of the Federal Rules of Civil Procedure provides that summary judgment "shall be rendered forthwith if the pleadings, depositions, answers to interrogatories and admissions on file, together with the affidavits, if any, show that there is no genuine issue as to any material fact and that the moving party is entitled to a judgment as a matter of law." The purpose of summary judgment is to assess the proof in order to see whether there is a need for trial. On a motion for summary judgment, the entire record is considered with all reasonable inferences drawn in favor of the nonmovant and all factual disputes resolved in favor of the nonmovant. The burden of establishing the lack of any genuine issue of material fact rests with the movant. The nonmovant, however must set forth specific facts showing there is a genuine issue for trial, and cannot rest merely on the allegations contained in the pleadings.

In Count I, plaintiff alleges that Officer Kinsella used excessive force against him in violation of his constitutional rights. Officer Kinsella claims that he is entitled to qualified immunity from liability in connection with the force he used against plaintiff. Although a police officer has the right to use some degree of physical coercion in making an arrest, the inquiry in an excessive force case is to determine how much force is "objectively reasonable." Officer Kinsella contends that numerous facts demonstrate that he did not use excessive force against plaintiff, but rather, that he engaged in "good, sound police work" during his stop at plaintiff's home. Officer Kinsella contends that he reasonably believed that he was entering into a violent domestic dispute. Plaintiff approached Officer Kinsella with a broom in his hands and began yelling obscenities at him. Officer Kinsella contends that after he took the broomstick, plaintiff leaned down to speak to his son and arose in a "bladed stance," prompting Officer Kinsella's first punch. Officer Kinsella asserts that plaintiff's continual forward motions towards him prompted his second punch and baton beatings. Officer Kinsella contends his response "was rather muted under the circumstances." The problem with this argument is that nearly all of the facts relied on by Officer Kinsella are contested by plaintiff. On a motion for summary judgment, all factual disputes must be resolved in favor of the nonmovant. Under the Seventh Circuit's guidelines, Officer Kinsella's actions must be judged in light of the severity of the crime at issue, whether plaintiff posed an immediate threat to the safety of the officers, and whether plaintiff was actively resisting arrest or attempting to evade arrest by flight. Plaintiff's alleged crime was aggravated assault on a police officer. From the facts as plaintiff alleges them, the officers may have been justified in believing plaintiff posed a threat to them as he appeared enraged and possibly intoxicated. Plaintiff, however, could not have been actively resisting or attempting to evade arrest, as he had no idea he was in danger of being arrested. At base, the question is what force is reasonable for three officers to take to bring an individual under control who is screaming obscenities at them at a close distance. Officer Kinsella's most compelling reason for a finding that the continued hits on plaintiff were objectively reasonable — that plaintiff went after Officer Kinsella after each hit — is disputed by plaintiff. Plaintiff claims he never approached Kinsella and that the officers never attempted to restrain him, rather than beat him.

Even under Officer Kinsella's version of the events, the question is raised as to why Officer Kinsella failed to tell plaintiff that he was under arrest before hitting him for the first time.

Officer Kinsella provides no explanation why he did not place plaintiff under arrest or attempt to restrain him without using force. More information is needed to determine which version is the more accurate description of events and whether Officer Kinsella's actions were objectively reasonable. A jury ultimately may find that Officer Kinsella's version of the events is the most accurate and it was reasonable to react to plaintiff by hitting him, but this determination cannot be made now on the disputed facts of the record. Defendants' motion for summary judgment on Count I will be denied.

In Count II, plaintiff alleges that defendants violated his constitutional rights by failing to prevent the use of excessive force against him. "An officer who is present at the scene and who fails to take reasonable steps to protect the victim of another officer's use of excessive force can be held liable under § 1983 for his nonfeasance." Thompson v. Boggs, 33 F.3d 847, 857 (7th Cir.1994). A police officer, however, "cannot be held liable for failing to intercede if he has no realistic opportunity to prevent an attack." The determination as to whether an officer had sufficient time to intervene or was capable of preventing the harm caused by the other officer is generally an issue for the trier of fact unless a reasonable jury could not possibly conclude otherwise in light of all of the evidence.

Officer Hartsock argues that he cannot be liable for failing to prevent excessive force because plaintiff's own allegations establish that Hartsock intervened in the dispute by attempting to keep plaintiff away from Kinsella. Officer Hartsock testified in his deposition that he was assisting Officer Kinsella in subduing plaintiff by shoving and pushing him. Officer Hartsock's deposition testimony regarding the events leading up to his involvement in the incident is undisputed. Under either parties' view of the facts, Officer Hartsock's intervention hastened the end of plaintiff's beating. The only question is whether his intervention was timely. The first realistic opportunity for Officer Hartsock to intervene was when he did — immediately after he made the call for backup units. Judgment as a matter of law will be granted in favor of Officer Hartsock on Count II.

Officer Duggan argues that he is not liable for failing to prevent the attack on plaintiff because he did not arrive at plaintiff's residence until after the incident had ended and plaintiff had gone into the kitchen to make a telephone call. Plaintiff argues that Officer Duggan arrived before Officer Kinsella's first hit; defendants concur that Officer Duggan arrived afterwards. Mrs. Fantasia's testimony corroborates the officers' testimony that Officer Duggan arrived subsequent to the attack on plaintiff. Nevertheless, plaintiff is entitled to have inconsistencies in testimony resolved in his favor. At the least, plaintiff's own testimony supports inference that Officer Duggan was present for the beating. Summary judgment will be denied as to Officer Duggan on Count II.

Defendants contend that they are entitled to summary judgment on plaintiff's conspiracy claim because plaintiff has brought forth no evidence of an express or implied agreement among the defendants. To establish a *prima facie* case of civil conspiracy, a plaintiff must demonstrate (1) an express or implied agreement among defendants to deprive plaintiff of secured constitutional rights and (2) an actual deprivation of those rights in the form of overt acts in furtherance of the agreement. A plaintiff need not establish these elements by direct evidence; circumstantial evidence of the conspiracy is sufficient. Plaintiff alleges that defendants conspired to use excessive force against him, falsify official reports relating to his case, falsely charge him with a crime, and falsely report and testify against him at his criminal trial. In support of his conspiracy theory, plaintiff states that all officers were present for the beating, arrested plaintiff and acquiesced when Officer Kinsella filed his complaint against plaintiff. Defendants contend that this evidence, even if true, does not support the inference of a meeting of the minds among defendants. As to the alleged conspiracy to use excessive force, plaintiff has brought forth no evidence that the officers agreed to use force against plaintiff. All three officers arrived separately and came in through different entrances. None of the officers was ever alone with any one of the other officers. Plaintiff has brought forth no evidence that Officer Kinsella's actions at the time of the beating were anything but independent. The only reasonable inference is that Officer Kinsella was the sole actor involved in the decision to use force against plaintiff.

As to the decision to arrest plaintiff, again there is no evidence to suggest that Officer Duggan or Officer Hartsock had any reason to doubt Officer Kinsella's statement that plaintiff had committed an assault on him. Officers Duggan and Hartsock were entitled to rely on Officer Kinsella's statement and participate in arresting plaintiff. It is not clear that either Officer Duggan or Hartsock was even in the house when the alleged assault occurred. Again, plaintiff has brought forth no evidence that the defendants ever had — or could have had — any sort of meeting of the minds with respect to arresting plaintiff. Finally, plaintiff has not brought forth any evidence that either Officer Hartsock or Officer Duggan had any involvement with the filing of Officer Kinsella's complaint, and only Officer Kinsella signed the complaint. Aside from the fact that plaintiff has not provided evidence of any alleged false testimony made by the defendants at his trial, defendants, as witnesses at plaintiff's trial, enjoy absolute immunity as to their testimony. In light of the overall failure to produce any evidence of an express or implied agreement, summary judgment will be granted as to Count V as to all defendants.

Although defendants' motion requests summary judgment on all counts of plaintiff's complaint, defendants failed to address plaintiff's false arrest and malicious prosecution claims in their motion for summary judgment and supporting memorandum. These claims may have been appropriate for resolution on a summary judgment motion, but defendants have provided no facts or argument from which to make this determination. Defendants' motion will be denied as to plaintiff's false arrest and malicious prosecution claims.

IT IS THEREFORE ORDERED that:

(1) Defendants' motion for summary judgment is granted in part and denied in part. Defendants' motion is granted as to Count II with respect to defendants William Kinsella and Donald Hartsock and Count V with respect to all defendants. Defendants' motion is denied as to Counts I, II, III and IV.

(2) The parties shall file a final pretrial order in open court.

REVIEW SECTION

READING COMPREHENSION

Delineate the facts and findings in this case.

THINKING CRITICALLY

Take a position on the following statement regarding the dual roles of officers in effectuating an arrest: "Law enforcement officers should not have to worry about being detectives concerning every potential cause of action flowing from discretionary police functions."

CONCLUSION

This chapter has established that arrest is more intrusive than either a stop or voluntary contact, and thus involves more factual support by government officials in the form of probable cause. To make an arrest reasonable, the government must demonstrate that is was based on probable cause and the manner in which the arrest was made was reasonable. Further elaborated were the factors considered in determining whether or not law enforcement personnel used excessive force in making an arrest.

Chapter Six

Searches for Evidence

The method of analysis used to examine government action, stop and frisk, and arrest, is also used for searches, whether conducted with or without a warrant. As a reminder, to determine whether or not the government has complied with the Fourth Amendment involves analysis of three questions:

(1)   Was the action by the government a search?

(2)   If considered a search, was it an unreasonable search?

(3)   If considered an unreasonable search, should the evidence obtained during the unreasonable search be excluded from consideration?

This chapter will review these questions in light of:

(1)   Searches with warrants; and

(2)   Searches without warrants.

SECTION 1: SEARCHES WITH WARRANTS

OVERVIEW

As a reminder, Article One, Section Six of the Illinois Constitution reads as follows regarding searches with warrants:

> The people shall have the right to be secure in their persons, houses, papers and other possessions against unreasonable searches, seizures, invasions of privacy or interceptions of communications by eavesdropping devices or other means. No warrant shall issue without probable cause, supported by affidavit particularly describing the place to be searched and the persons or things to be seized.

More specifically, three elements are required to meet the warrant requirement as outlined by the Fourth Amendment and elaborated in Article One, Section Six of the Illinois Constitution. These three requirements are:

(1)   The particularity requirement which means that the warrant must state the place(s) to be searched, the person(s) or thing(s) to be seized, the communication that will be intercepted, and the nature of the evidence;

(2)   The probable cause affidavit is the document which supports the notion that said information will be found in the location specified; and

(3)   The "knock and announce" rule which requires officers to announce their status and that they have a warrant in hand, prior to entering a location. This rule can be abandoned if officers need to prevent violence, prevent the destruction of evidence, or prevent the escape of a suspect.

As you read through several cases involving searches with warrants, keep in mind the requirements of a warrant and potential exceptions to the "knock and announce" rule.

CASE

In *People v Hardin,* the State appeals a suppression order of the circuit court. The issue on appeal is whether police officers' failure to knock and announce before entering the defendant's home to execute a valid search warrant was justified by exigent circumstances.

PEOPLE V. HARDIN
535 N.E.2d 1044, 179 Ill.App.3d 1072 (1989)

On March 31, 1987, the Kane County sheriff's department obtained a warrant to search the residence of defendant, Charles W. Hardin. The complaint requesting issuance of the search warrant states that a reliable, confidential source informed the police that defendant was selling cocaine from his residence. The complaint also states that in September 1986 another search warrant had been issued for the same residence and that 6.2 grams of cocaine had been seized in the search. During the execution of the September 1986 warrant, defendant stated to Detective Atchison of the sheriff's department that the officers executing the warrant were fortunate that defendant did not get to his gun. The police seized a .38 caliber handgun which had been in close proximity to defendant when the police entered the residence. The March 31, 1987, warrant was executed on April 1, 1987, and a quantity of cannabis was seized. Defendant was charged with possession of cannabis.

Defendant filed a motion to quash the search warrant and to suppress evidence. He alleged that the warrant was invalid for lack of probable cause and that the warrant was improperly executed in that the police failed to knock and announce before entering his residence. The trial court determined that there was probable cause and the warrant was valid. On the issue of execution, the State stipulated that the officers did not knock and announce their authority prior to executing the warrant. The State argued, however, that exigent circumstances existed which rendered the action excusable. Specifically, the State argued that defendant's prior threat created in the officers a reasonable fear for their safety if they proceeded with the usual announcement. The trial court found that there were no exigent circumstances to justify the officers' actions; therefore, the warrant was improperly executed. The court ordered the evidence seized pursuant to the search to be suppressed. The State appeals contending that the officers' reasonable apprehension of danger, based on defendant's prior threat, created exigent circumstances which justified entry without prior announcement.

Absent exigent circumstances, police officers executing a search warrant are expected to knock and announce their authority and purpose before entering the premises to be searched. The purpose of the "knock and announce" rule is to notify the person inside of the presence of police and of the impending intrusion, give that person time to respond, avoid violence, and protect privacy as much as possible. Although the failure of the police to announce their authority and purpose is not a per se violation of the fourth amendment, it may influence whether a subsequent entry of a premises to arrest or search is constitutionally reasonable. Where exigent circumstances exist, the failure of the police to knock and announce their authority and purpose in the execution of a search warrant for narcotics does not violate the fourth amendment right against unreasonable searches and seizures. Exigent circumstances that may justify the failure to announce authority and purpose include uselessness of the announcement, ease with which the evidence may be destroyed, and danger to the policeman executing the warrant.

The State contends that exigent circumstances did exist here. The facts establishing the exigency appear on the face of the complaint for the search warrant. The same officers involved with this search had executed a similar warrant on the same residence some eight months before. At that time a .38 caliber handgun was recovered. Defendant told the officers that they were fortunate that he did not get to his gun. The State urges that, based on the circumstances of the earlier encounter, the officers had a reasonable belief that a weapon would be used upon them if they proceeded with an ordinary announcement, and this reasonable apprehension of danger created an exigent circumstance sufficient to excuse their failure to knock and announce.

Defendant cites the holding People v. Marinez (1987), 160 Ill.App.3d 349, 112 Ill.Dec. 193, 513 N.E.2d 607, in support of the trial court's suppression order. In Marinez, the police officers knew the occupant of the house to possess firearms. The court stated, however, that information indicating the presence of weapons does not alone create exigent circumstances. The court found that the police had no further information which suggested that the occupant carried the weapon on his person, that he had ever used the gun, or that there was any danger to the police from the use of the weapon. On this basis the court found that there was no reason to excuse the police from failing to knock and announce their presence and intent.

We consider the reasoning in the recent case of People v. Trask (1988), 167 Ill.App.3d 694, 118 Ill.Dec. 529, 521 N.E.2d 1222, to be particularly applicable to this case. In Trask, the trial court, after finding that the police officers had knocked and had waited a reasonable time before entering the residence to execute a search warrant, also found that an exigent circumstance had existed. This finding was based on a police officer's testimony that he had arrested the defendant some 3 1/2 months earlier and the defendant had had a loaded semiautomatic pistol on his person. In affirming the trial court, we stated: "Although the officer did not know whether defendant had any other guns, any apprehension that defendant might be armed and dangerous would appear reasonable in light of the previous encounter. The police should not have to be certain that they will be shot at if they wait very long before entering; they just have to have a reasonable apprehension of danger. The trial court's finding of exigent circumstances was thus not erroneous." We believe that the reasoning in Trask applies here. In this case, as in Trask, the officers had no information that defendant currently possessed a weapon; however, in light of their previous encounter with defendant, the officers' apprehension that defendant might be armed and dangerous was reasonable.

Compliance with the "knock and announce" rule should be excused only where the officers reasonably believe that the weapon will be used against them if they proceed with the ordinary announcement. We consider that defendant's prior possession of a weapon and his threatening statement to the police officers was sufficient to create a reasonable apprehension of danger and to justify the officers' failure to knock and announce their presence and intent. The judgment of the circuit court is reversed, and the cause is remanded for further proceedings.

REVIEW SECTION

READING COMPREHENSION

Elaborate the fact of this case, including why officers deemed it necessary to enter the residence in violation of the knock and announce rule.

What is the rationale behind the knock and announce rule?

THINKING CRITICALLY

Should prior gun ownership provide exigent circumstances indefinitely for a violation of the knock and announce rule? Do you believe the case would have been decided the same absent any threatening comments in previous encounters between the defendant and law enforcement?

CASE

In *People v Tate,* the defendant was convicted after a bench trial for possession of heroin, cocaine, cannabis and unlawful use of a weapon. He was sentenced to concurrent terms of 10 years for possession of heroin, 6 years for each conviction of possession of cocaine and cannabis and 8 years for unlawful use of a weapon. The defendant appeals. We reverse.

PEOPLE V. TATE
753 N.E.2d 347 (Ill.App. 1 Dist. 2001)

Defendant was arrested in his apartment on October 2, 1996, after execution of a search warrant revealed that he was in possession of heroin, cocaine, cannabis and a .357-caliber revolver. These items were seized and inventoried by the police. Defendant filed two motions to suppress the evidence seized from his apartment. The first motion argued that the search warrant was invalid because it did not describe the place to be searched with particularity. The warrant listed the address to be searched as 6201 South Champlain, third floor. The warrant did not specify apartment 3N. This motion was denied. Defendant does not challenge the ruling on appeal.

Defendant's second motion to suppress argued that the seizure was invalid because of the police officers' failure to comply with the "knock and announce rule" before forcibly entering defendant's apartment. Carlos Hayes and defendant testified in support of this motion.

Hayes testified that, on October 2, he went to visit his girlfriend and arrived at 10:45 p.m., about 10 minutes before the police came. Hayes said his girlfriend was not home, but that her mother was home with four children. Hayes said he then heard two large booming noises from the front door. Hayes denied hearing a knock at the door, but admitted hearing someone yell "police" after the booming noises. Hayes then saw about 10 police officers come in with weapons drawn. Hayes and defendant were told to lie on the floor and not move. They were then led to the living room. Hayes denied that defendant was in the dining room when the police came into the apartment. Hayes also denied seeing a search warrant or that the police recovered anything from the dining room or anywhere else in the apartment.

Defendant said that, while he and Hayes were speaking in low voices in the kitchen, he heard two loud booms at the front door. Defendant denied hearing a noise before then. Defendant then saw police running down the hallway toward him in the kitchen with weapons drawn. He was told to lie down and was later led to the living room. Defendant denied that there was a gun on the dining room table. Defendant said that the door the police came through was split in half and off the hinges.

Officer John DuBoise testified that he executed a search warrant with 11 other officers. Two were uniformed, the rest were in plain clothes. DuBoise said he was in plain clothes. DuBoise testified that he arrived at the apartment at about 10:53 p.m. DuBoise said he heard a television on in the apartment as he stood outside the front door. He knocked on the door twice and announced his office twice but received no response. DuBoise then entered the apartment. He saw defendant sitting at a dining room table and Hayes in a front bedroom. DuBoise said that some officers entered from the rear of the apartment. DuBoise did not know whether those officers knocked first. DuBoise admitted, on cross-examination, that neither his arrest nor case reports mentioned that he knocked on the door before entering, announced his office or purpose, that a television was playing loudly or that he gave the occupants time to respond to his knocks. DuBoise admitted that a search warrant data sheet showed that 8, not 12, men entered the apartment that night. DuBoise denied forcing the door down with a battering iron, claiming the door came open after just a "gentle tap." DuBoise admitted he had no information that defendant was destroying contraband. On redirect examination, DuBoise said that his reports were intended as summaries, not detailed descriptions of everything that happened. DuBoise also said that he knocked on the door twice, "pretty hard."

The trial court then heard oral argument from defendant and the State. Defendant argued that the officers' failure to knock and announce violated the fourth amendment and that no recognized exception to the "knock and announce" rule applied. The State argued that the police did knock and announce. The State, relying on Wilson v. Arkansas, 514 U.S. 927, 934, 131 L. Ed. 2d 976, 982, 115 S. Ct. 1914, 1918 (1995), alternatively argued that the search and seizure here were nevertheless reasonable because the officers' awareness that drug transactions were taking place could have reasonably led them to believe that weapons would be present or evidence destroyed.

The trial court denied the motion to suppress in a written order read into the record. The court found that the officers failed to comply with the "knock and announce" rule: "Credible testimony at the pre-trial motion to suppress from Carlos Hayes and the defendant indicated that while the officers upon entry into the apartment did announce that they were the police, there was no knock prior to the use of force to open the front door to the apartment."

The trial court then considered whether the violation required suppression of the evidence seized: "This Court having found that the arresting officers failed to comply with the principle of 'knock and announce' by entering the apartment of Petitioner 'simultaneously' with their announcement (without having first knocked) there remains in this Court's mind the critical question of whether exclusion of evidence as a consequence is appropriate, i.e., whether exclusion of probative/reliable evidence is required." The court then reasoned that the independent source and/or inevitable discovery doctrines trumped the exclusionary rule: "It is this Court's view that contraband/evidence seized under the authority of a valid search warrant is admissible under the 'independent source' and 'inevitable-discovery' exceptions to the exclusionary rule, even where 'knock and announce' has not been complied with. The exclusionary rule should not be extended to bar admission of evidence that could have been seized-and, in fact, was seized under the authority of a valid search warrant."

A custodial search of defendant revealed he had $339 in cash and a state-issued identification. The parties then stipulated that forensic evidence from the Illinois State Police Crime Laboratory would show that the substance taken from the apartment tested positive for cocaine, heroin, and marijuana. The parties also stipulated that the chain of custody was maintained. The State then rested. Defendant rested after the parties stipulated to Hayes' testimony presented at the earlier motion to suppress hearing. The trial court found defendant guilty of possession of heroin, cocaine, cannabis and unlawful use of a weapon. He was sentenced to concurrent terms of 10 years for heroin possession, 6 years for each conviction of cannabis and cocaine possession and 8 years for the weapons violation.

Defendant raises five issues on appeal: whether (1) the trial court should have granted the motion to suppress based on the officers' failure to comply with the "knock and announce" rule; (2) the trial court can only impose one sentence for simultaneous possession of more than one controlled substance; (3) the mandatory Class X sentencing violates the rule set out <u>Apprendi v. New Jersey</u>, 530 U.S. 466, 147 L. Ed. 2d 435, 120 S. Ct. 2348 (2000); (4) the extended-term sentences are void as imposed; and (5) the mittimus should be corrected. We need not address the last four issues since we conclude that violation of the "knock and announce" rule requires suppression of the evidence seized.

We must determine whether the independent source and/or the inevitable discovery doctrines apply to save evidence seized under a valid search warrant when that warrant was executed in violation of the "knock and announce" rule. We conclude that neither exception to the exclusionary rule applies here. Implementation of the exclusionary rule assumes that the challenged evidence is the product of some illegal government activity. The record here shows that the trial court ruled and the State concedes the knock and announce violation. This violation makes the search presumptively unreasonable. The State does not contend that the unannounced entry was warranted by exigent circumstances. Our analysis considers only the application of the proffered exceptions to the exclusionary rule. Our supreme court has twice considered the constitutionality of search warrants executed under a so called "no knock" statute that authorized unannounced entries if certain circumstances were present.

People v. Krueger, 175 Ill. 2d 60, 675 N.E.2d 604 (1996), the court found unconstitutional a statute authorizing unannounced entry based solely on the occupant's possession of firearms. The court recognized that exigent circumstances could justify an unannounced entry but reasoned that the mere presence of firearms did not create an exigent circumstance. The Krueger court also declined to apply the "good-faith" exception articulated United States v. Leon, 468 U.S. 897, 82 L. Ed. 2d 677, 104 S. Ct. 3405 (1984), as extended Illinois v. Krull, 480 U.S. 340, 94 L. Ed. 2d 364, 107 S. Ct. 1160 (1987). Leon held that the exclusionary rule will not apply where an officer, in good faith, relies on a search warrant later found to be unsupported by probable cause. This rule was extended in Krull to apply to an officer's good-faith reliance on a search warrant issued under a statute later found unconstitutional.

People v. Wright, 183 Ill. 2d 16, 697 N.E.2d 693 (1998), our supreme court again found unconstitutional a statute authorizing an unannounced entry when firearms are accessible to an occupant. Relying on Krueger, the Wright court said that the presence of firearms will support an exigent circumstance if the officers have a reasonable belief that the firearms will be used against them. The Wright court then declined to apply the "good-faith" exception to the exclusionary rule.

We believe our supreme court would be equally reticent to apply the trial court's analysis here- that the independent source and inevitable discovery rules apply to trump the exclusionary rule. Last, we disagree with the State that application of the exclusionary rule here hampers the purpose of the rule. The exclusionary rule is invoked to deter future police misconduct. That purpose is served here, where the exclusionary rule in article I, section 6, of the Illinois Constitution affords greater protection than its federal counterpart. The motion to suppress evidence should have been granted once the trial court found that the officers failed to knock and announce their office before entering the apartment. Defendant's sentence and conviction are vacated. The judgment of the trial court is reversed.

REVIEW SECTION

READING COMPREHENSION

Elaborate the facts of this case, including a discussion of why the entry was not considered an exception to the knock and announce rule?

THINKING CRITICALLY

Is suppression of evidence if the knock and announce rule is violated an adequate deterrent to police misconduct?

SECTION 2: SEARCHES WITHOUT WARRANTS

OVERVIEW

Perhaps contrary to popular public perception, majority of searches are executed without warrants because the courts interpret broadly the exceptions provided to law enforcement. The U.S. Supreme Court has elaborated five major exceptions to the warrant requirement:

(1)   Searches incident to arrest are reasonable under the Fourth Amendment. In fact, 725 ILCS 5/108-1 elaborates the search of a person arrested without a warrant:

> (1) When a lawful arrest is effected a peace officer may reasonably search the person arrested and the area within such person's immediate presence for the purpose of: (a) protecting the officer from attack; or (b) preventing the person from escaping; or (c) discovering the fruits of the crime; or (d) discovering any instruments, articles, or things which may have been used in the commission of, or which may constitute evidence of, an offense.

(2)   Consent searches must be voluntary are needed when there is no probable cause to search and involve searches wherein an individual gave a law enforcement personnel permission to search belongings or conduct a pat-down;

(3)   Vehicle searches are permitted with probable cause due to a reduced expectation of privacy, though 725 ILCS 5/108-1 stipulates:

> (3) A law enforcement officer may not search or inspect a motor vehicle, its contents, the driver, or a passenger solely because of a violation of Section 12-603.1 of the Illinois Vehicle Code.

(4)   Container searches are permitted if the container is in a vehicle and an officer has probable cause to search; if there is only reasonable suspicion, an officer may briefly seize a container but must obtain a warrant backed by probable cause in order to search;

(5)   Exigent circumstances searches are based on an officer's reasonable suspicion and can involve a pat-down for weapons, a search if there is reasonable belief that evidence may be destroyed, entrance into a house without a warrant if the officer is in hot pursuit, or a search wherein an officer has probable cause that an individual is of danger to the community.

CASE

In *People v Tisler,* the court reviews an earlier finding. At a bench trial in the circuit court, the parties stipulated that the defendant had possessed less than 30 grams of LSD. This crime constituted a Class 4 felony. The defendant was convicted and sentenced to 24 months' probation and one weekend in a correctional center. In addition, defendant was fined $500 and ordered to pay costs of $120. Before trial, the defendant moved to suppress evidence that he claimed was obtained either through an illegal seizure or through a search incident to an illegal arrest. The trial court, after hearing testimony, denied the motions and allowed the evidence. The defendant appealed, and the appellate court reversed the judgment without remand. Finding that defendant's arrest was without probable cause, the appellate court held that all evidence obtained as a result of the arrest must be suppressed.

PEOPLE V. TISLER
469 N.E.2d 147, 103 Ill.2d 226 (1984)

Before this court, the State raises the issue whether the trial court properly denied defendant's motions to suppress evidence. We will address this question after a statement of the pertinent facts. Our disposition of this first issue renders it unnecessary to consider a second issue that the State raises in its brief.

James Hollenbeck, a police officer testified at the hearing on the motions to suppress. While off duty on Saturday, January 9, 1982, Hollenbeck received a telephone call at 2:30 p.m. from an informant. The caller identified himself, and the officer recognized him as an informant that he had dealt with before. The caller then related the following information: that at the time they were speaking, two residents were on their way to Streator to pick up "some hits" of LSD. After they obtained the LSD, the two individuals--defendant Tisler and a friend, Jerry Cox--would return to Marseilles at 3:40 p.m., a little over an hour hence. They would be riding in Tisler's car, a green, two-door Chevrolet Camaro with the letters "JAT" on its license plates. After they entered Marseilles via the river bridge, Tisler and Cox would proceed to the Number Nine Game Room. There, they would deliver the LSD. The informant also stated that the LSD would be in a very small container which easily could be disposed of if Hollenbeck were to detain Tisler and Cox with an ordinary traffic stop. Therefore, the informant advised, Hollenbeck should approach the subjects only after they had parked at the Game Room and were out of the car.

Hollenbeck had worked with this informant twice before, and the informant's tips had always been accurate. In one case, a single tip resulted in arrest and conviction. The other case involved the informant's supplying information at several times during a four- to six-week period. Again, the information led to an arrest and conviction. Tips supplied by this informant, however, had never been used by Hollenbeck or his police department to obtain a search or arrest warrant. Certain aspects of the tip were familiar to Hollenbeck. He knew Tisler and Cox, he knew Tisler's car, he also knew that its full license plate number was JAT 76. Hollenbeck recognized the Number Nine Game Room as a Marseilles business that served as a hangout for local teenagers.

After the telephone call, Hollenbeck sought help in obtaining a warrant. Since it was Saturday, he knew that judges' offices were closed. In such a case, the procedure was to contact an assistant State's Attorney and advise him of the facts on which the officer based his suspicions. If the assistant State's Attorney thought the facts would support a probable-cause finding, he would meet with the officer, draft a warrant, and contact a judge at home to request his signature. Although this procedure usually took from two to three hours, Hollenbeck attempted to contact the first assistant State's Attorney at home and at his office. Unsuccessful, he left a message for the attorney to call right away. After failing to reach another assistant State's Attorney at home, Hollenbeck proceeded without a warrant.

Hollenbeck and Officer Stevenson parked where they could watch the river bridge. They wore street clothes and traveled in Hollenbeck's private car with no police insignia or equipment. The winter weather that day was unusually severe: Hollenbeck testified that the temperature was 25 degrees below zero with a wind-chill factor of 60 degrees below zero. Snow fell, and area roads were becoming impassable. At 3:45 p.m., the officers saw a green Chevrolet Camaro approach. Defendant was driving, Jerry Cox sat in front on the passenger side, and a third male, unknown to the officers, rode in the back seat. Hollenbeck pulled in directly behind defendant's car and followed for about three blocks. When defendant parked across the street from the Number Nine Game Room, the officers left Hollenbeck's car and approached the Camaro. Defendant stepped out of his car and Hollenbeck saw that his left hand was closed. What looked like a plastic bag extended from defendant's fist, but the officer could not see what its contents might be. While defendant stood between his car and its still open door, Hollenbeck asked him what he was holding. Defendant replied, "Nothing," so Hollenbeck inquired again, explaining to defendant that he could see something in his hand. At this point, defendant started to move his left hand around behind his back.

Hollenbeck then took defendant's left hand and removed a small plastic bag. It contained several pills, which the officer recognized as "dots." As Hollenbeck retrieved the plastic bag, he placed defendant under arrest. The officers then searched the area immediately surrounding defendant. After being patted down and handcuffed, defendant was taken to the police station in a squad car that waited nearby. Sometime after the arrest, a forensic scientist's report disclosed that the pills taken from defendant contained LSD.

Before proceeding, we note that the trial court viewed the police conduct in this case as a warrantless arrest accompanied by a search incident to arrest. We will treat the facts in the same manner. It follows, then, that the central issue is the legality of the warrantless arrest. If probable-cause requirements were met before the arrest, then evidence seized during the search incident to arrest was properly admitted at trial. We now address whether the trial court correctly found that probable cause existed for defendant's arrest. While stressing the informant's past reliability, the State maintains that the tip in this case is sufficiently detailed to be self-verifying in nature. According to the State, the detailed tip, when considered in light of the officers' corroboration of the details, is sufficient to justify the trial court's finding of probable cause. Therefore, the State reasons, the LSD seized in the search incident to arrest was legally obtained and properly admitted into evidence. The State argues that the appellate court, which reversed and excluded the evidence, reached an incorrect result because it failed to consider either the self-verifying details or the subsequent corroboration.

Defendant, on the other hand, denies that the officers had probable cause for his arrest. Therefore, he argues, the police conduct violated his rights under the United States and Illinois constitutions. Defendant claims that, under these circumstances, the trial court should have excluded the LSD and other items seized at the time of the arrest. His theory is based on the informant's failure to explain how he learned the information that he related by telephone to Hollenbeck. Defendant explains that, for all Hollenbeck knew at the time of arrest, the tip was based on a casual rumor or even was wholly fabricated by someone who knew of defendant's routine visits to the Game Room. Given the absence of a statement from the informant assuring that he obtained his story reliably, defendant contends that the information known to the officers did not meet constitutional standards for probable cause. Defendant rejects the notion that the tip was sufficiently detailed or corroborated to cure this deficiency.

In reference to Federal and State warrant requirements, this court has explained that a detached judicial officer must resolve the question of whether probable cause exists to justify issuing a warrant. The decision is to be based on information contained in sworn statements or affidavits that are presented to the magistrate. Whether probable cause exists in a particular case turns on the totality of the circumstances and facts known to the officers and court when the warrant is applied for. The probability of criminal activity, rather than proof beyond a reasonable doubt, is the standard for determining whether probable cause is present. Whether the necessary probability exists is governed not by technical legal rules, but rather by common-sense considerations that are factual and practical. When a police officer has proceeded without a warrant to search, seize evidence, or arrest a person, the trial court making a probable-cause determination is to apply standards at least as stringent as those that guide a magistrate in deciding whether to issue a warrant. The Code of Criminal Procedure of 1963 allows a warrantless arrest only when a peace officer "has reasonable grounds to believe that the person is committing or has committed an offense." As used in the statute, "reasonable grounds" is considered to have the same substantive meaning as "probable cause."

To determine whether a warrantless arrest meets the reasonable-grounds/probable-cause requirement, the trial court must decide whether "a reasonable and prudent man, having the knowledge possessed by the officer at the time of the arrest, would believe the defendant committed the offense." (People v. Wright (1968), 41 Ill.2d 170, 174, 242 N.E.2d 180.) In determining whether the officer had probable cause, the officer's factual knowledge, based on his prior law-enforcement experience, is relevant. If the trial court finds that a warrantless arrest was based on probable cause, the arrest is deemed lawful, and evidence obtained during a warrantless search incident to that arrest is admissible to prove defendant's guilt. A police officer need not have observed personally the facts that he presents to a magistrate making a probable-cause determination. The officer's statements may be based on hearsay, and frequently such hearsay statements originate with an informant's tip. If facts supplied in a particular tip are essential to a finding of probable cause, the tip must meet standards of reliability before the magistrate may consider it in his determination.

Defendant asserts that article I, section 6, of the 1970 Illinois Constitution guarantees more individual rights than either the former State Constitution or the fourth amendment to the Federal Constitution. In the committee report to the constitutional convention that accompanied the present Illinois section, the drafters stated their intent that changes to the section would accomplish two specific goals: First, the new language would provide citizens with express protection against eavesdropping devices. Second, the section now would protect against invasions of privacy. Proposals to change other aspects of article I, section 6, were rejected in committee. As a result, the language pertinent to the case at bar--the warrant clause with its probable-cause requirement, and the guarantee against unreasonable search and seizure--remains nearly the same as that of the fourth amendment. Thus, the intent of the constitutional convention was to extend the protection afforded by the fourth amendment of the Federal Constitution and of our 1870 State Constitution to cover eavesdropping and to protect against invasions of privacy. The convention manifested no intent to expand the nature of the protection afforded by the fourth amendment of the Federal Constitution.

After having accepted the pronouncements of the Supreme Court in deciding fourth amendment cases as the appropriate construction of the search and seizure provisions of the Illinois Constitution for so many years, we should not suddenly change course and go our separate way simply to accommodate the desire of the defendant to circumvent what he perceives as a narrowing of his fourth amendment rights. Any variance between the Supreme Court's construction of the provisions of the fourth amendment in the Federal Constitution and similar provisions in the Illinois Constitution must be based on more substantial grounds. We must find in the language of our constitution, or in the debates and the committee reports of the constitutional convention, something which will indicate that the provisions of our constitution are intended to be construed differently than are similar provisions in the Federal Constitution, after which they are patterned.

Decisions involving the exclusionary rule and the Illinois Constitution's article I, section 6, require that we carefully balance the legitimate aims of law enforcement against the right of our citizens to be free from unreasonable governmental intrusion.

We now consider whether, in view of all the circumstances presented to the trial court, the arrest was unlawful under the holding in Gates. Initially, we note that a reviewing court will not disturb a trial court's finding on a motion to suppress, unless that finding is manifestly erroneous. In Gates, the Supreme Court stated that our task on review is simply to ensure that the trial court had a substantial basis for concluding that probable cause existed (Illinois v. Gates (1983), 462 U.S. 213, 238-39, 103 S.Ct. 2317, 2332, 76 L.Ed.2d 527, 548). There is no doubt that Hollenbeck could consider his informant to be a reliable source. This court has regarded as believable an informant whose past tips have led to "pending" arrests. We conclude that Hollenbeck had reasonable grounds to infer that defendant was committing a crime. His next act, that of arresting defendant, therefore comports with statutory and constitutional standards. Under these circumstances, the search incident to arrest and the seizure of the LSD tablets were also lawful. The informant's proven trustworthiness had been substantially reaffirmed during the moments preceding the arrest. Virtually every detail of the informant's tip was confirmed prior to the arrest.

Defendant claims that the corroboration in this case means little because the officers only confirmed innocent activity on defendant's part. He also contends that corroboration proves nothing about an informant's basis of knowledge, an aspect of the instant tip about which we concededly have no direct information. However, we are not persuaded that these considerations negate the existence of probable cause in this case. Turning next to defendant's claim that corroboration cannot prove a proper basis of knowledge, we again reject defendant's contention.

In our case, not only had the informant proved reliable in previous cases, but nearly every aspect of the information he supplied in the present case was corroborated. The balanced assessment of the informant's tip in this case causes us to conclude that the officer reasonably relied upon this information. The tip, in conjunction with the evasive conduct of the defendant when confronted by the officer, furnished probable cause to believe that he was engaged in unlawful conduct.

The trial court therefore did not err in failing to suppress the evidence. We find that the appellate court erroneously reversed the defendant's conviction. For the above reasons, the judgment of the appellate court is reversed and the judgment of the circuit court of La Salle County is affirmed.

GOLDENHERSH, Justice, dissenting: I dissent, and would affirm the judgment of the appellate court. Prior to discussing what I perceive to be the errors in the majority's holding the search valid, I state my concurrence with the views expressed by Justice Clark concerning this court's interpreting our constitution to afford greater protection than do purportedly similar provisions of the Federal Constitution. The record in this case contains no evidence of the informant's basis of knowledge and the allegedly corroborative evidence of defendant's activity, in lieu thereof, is utterly meaningless. The value of evidence as corroborative of a fact related by an informant must be determined by the surrounding circumstances, and as the Supreme Court and this court have said on numerous occasions, the presence of probable cause is to be determined on a common sense basis. In its opinion in Gates the Supreme Court did not obviate the requirement that there appear in "the totality of the circumstances" a basis for determining the basis of knowledge of the unnamed informant. The Supreme Court said: "We agree with the Illinois Supreme Court that an informant's 'veracity,' 'reliability,' and 'basis of knowledge' are all highly relevant in determining the value of his report" (Illinois v. Gates (1983), 462 U.S. 213, 230, 103 S.Ct. 2317, 2327, 76 L.Ed.2d 527, 543). The result of this decision is to apply an amorphous concept of "totality of the circumstances" without guidelines or minimum requirements. I am of the opinion that further application of this "test" will "foretell an evisceration of the probable cause standard." SIMON, J., joins in this dissent.

REVIEW SECTION

READING COMPREHENSION

Elaborate the facts of the case leading to the discovery of contraband and the relevance of probable cause.

Outline the findings of the lower courts in reference to this case.

THINKING CRITICALLY

According to the dissenting opinion: "the value of evidence as corroborative of a fact related by an informant must be determined by the surrounding circumstances." Discuss the presence, or lack thereof, of veracity, reliability, and basis of knowledge in the informant tip in this case.

CASE

In *People v James,* the appeal addresses the question of whether it is reasonable for a police officer to believe that he has been granted the right to search a closed purse that he finds on the passenger seat in an automobile, where the driver of the car, but not the passenger, has consented to a search of the vehicle.

PEOPLE V. JAMES
645 N.E.2d 195 (1994)

In April 1992, the defendant, Delores James, was a passenger in an automobile that was stopped by officers of the Urbana police department. The officers directed the driver and the passengers to step out of the car. When defendant exited the vehicle, she left her purse on the front, passenger-side seat of the car. One of the officers then escorted defendant away from the automobile. Although defendant was not aware of it, the driver of the car agreed to a police search of the vehicle. During this search, the officers opened and looked into defendant's purse, where they found cocaine. She was arrested and charged with unlawful possession of a controlled substance. Defendant filed a motion to suppress the evidence found by police officers during their search of her purse. She argued that she had not consented to the search and that the driver lacked the authority to consent to a search of her purse. Following an evidentiary hearing, the trial court allowed the defendant's motion to suppress. The appellate court reversed the trial court's ruling. We allowed the defendant's petition for leave to appeal.

At the trial court's hearing with respect to defendant's motion to suppress, the defendant testified that on April 1, 1992, at approximately 7 p.m., she was a passenger in a vehicle being driven by Ruth Boolman. Defendant was sitting in the front passenger seat of the car. A third passenger, Shirley James, was in the back seat of the car. They were stopped by an Urbana police department squad car. One officer approached the driver's side of the car, another officer came to the passenger side, and a third officer went to the rear of the vehicle. The officer near the driver spoke to her briefly. The officers then asked defendant and Shirley James to exit the car and they complied. One of the officers "walked defendant off a good piece by a tree" away from where the others were located. Defendant could not hear the conversations between the police officers and the other occupants of the vehicle. A short while later, one of the other officers approached defendant and asked her about her purse. Defendant had left the purse on the front passenger seat in the car. She stated that the officer told her he had looked in the purse and removed "a pipe and the bag and the tie." The officers never asked her permission to look inside her purse. Defendant admitted that the items found inside the purse belonged to her.

Officer Troy Phillips of the Urbana police department testified that on the night of the incident, he and his partner stopped a vehicle because it had no rear license plate and because a document, indicating that a license had been applied for, was torn and illegible. When the officers stopped the car, they examined the document and found it to be in order. Officer Phillips testified that there were three women passengers in the car and two small children. He spoke to the driver after she got out of the automobile. Officer Phillips explained to Boolman that they were working a special detail in the area because it was a "high traffic drug area." He asked Boolman if she had any contraband such as weapons or drugs on her person, and she said that she did not. She agreed to a search of her person, which produced no drugs or contraband. Officer Phillips then asked Boolman if he could search her car, advising her that he was looking for drugs or weapons. Boolman consented to a search of the automobile. Officer Phillips stated that all of the passengers had exited the car before he searched it. During the search, he noticed a purse on the front seat. He opened the purse and found drug paraphernalia inside it. Officer Phillips stated on cross-examination that when Boolman consented to the search of her vehicle, she was standing behind her car, in between her own vehicle and the squad car. The officer stated that he believed the other passengers were still in the vehicle at the time he sought Boolman's consent. After Boolman consented to the search, Officer Phillips asked the passengers to step out of the car. The officer admitted that he did not tell the passengers that he was going to search the vehicle.

Based on this testimony, the trial court allowed the defendant's motion to suppress the evidence taken from her purse. In its oral pronouncements, the trial court acknowledged that the officers had lawfully stopped the Boolman vehicle in order to check the validity of its license plates. The trial court also found no impropriety in Officer Phillips' request that Boolman permit him to search the vehicle. With respect to Officer Phillips' search of the defendant's purse, however, the trial court found it significant that the purse did not belong to Boolman, but belonged to the defendant. The trial court further found that defendant had not consented to the officer's search of the purse and that she "had no idea that car was going to be searched." The trial court observed that "where there is more than one person in the car, that would lead a person to presume that perhaps an article that was found on the passenger seat, which is somewhere other than where the owner/driver had been located, that it seems to me at the very least some reasonable inquiry as to whom that property belongs to would be necessary." The trial court noted that the officers were well aware that there were passengers in the vehicle, and observed that the officers found the purse "where one of those other persons who has not given consent to search the car or container was seated." The trial court held that the defendant "didn't abandon her purse under the circumstances." The trial court allowed the defendant's motion to suppress.

The State appealed from the trial court's ruling, arguing that the driver's consent to search the automobile reasonably included the contents of the purse found on the front passenger seat of the vehicle. The appellate court agreed and reversed the trial court's allowance of the defendant's motion to suppress. The appellate court reasoned that "driver consent to search for drugs extends to closed containers which may belong to others who have exited the vehicle." Indeed, the appellate court "pondered how the searching officers could distinguish between ownership of the various containers in the vehicle" and noted that "in the search process, such split-second decisions are likely given little thought." The appellate court also observed that a "third party may give legally sufficient consent for a search if he has actual authority over the property shared in common with the defendant." According to the appellate court, "by allowing the driver to exercise authority over a vehicle, a defendant assumes the risk that the driver will allow someone to look inside it." The court concluded that it could find "no justifiable reason to limit the effect of driver consent to search where a passenger aware or unaware of the consent to search leaves a container in the automobile." The appellate court held that, when the driver of a vehicle consents to a police officer's search of the car for narcotics, it is reasonable for the police officer to believe that the driver's consent to search the vehicle also extends to a search of a closed purse left in the vehicle by a passenger. One justice dissented from this disposition. This dissenting justice believed that defendant had a reasonable expectation of privacy in her purse, which was closed when she left it in the automobile. The dissent noted that a police officer is "not always entitled to accept a person's consent to search personal property." The dissenting justice concluded that the trial court's factual findings were not against the manifest weight of the evidence and that the cases cited by the majority were distinguishable and inapposite.

Defendant argues that the trial court's suppression of the evidence taken from her purse was correct and should be upheld by this court. Defendant contends that Boolman's consent to Officer Phillips' search of the automobile did not justify his search of defendant's purse. Defendant claims that Boolman did not have the authority to consent to a search of defendant's purse. Defendant notes that under United States Supreme Court precedent, a police officer must make an objectively reasonable determination of whether a person has the apparent authority to consent to a search (Illinois v. Rodriguez (1990), 497 U.S. 177, 110 S.Ct. 2793, 111 L.Ed.2d 148). The defendant asserts that other Supreme Court precedent is factually distinguishable from the instant cause and that decisions from other jurisdictions support her position. The defendant argues that the appellate court's decision did not take into account the factual findings made by the trial court, all of which were fully supported in the record.

The State responds that although the trial court's factual findings should be reversed only if manifestly erroneous, the trial court's legal determination regarding the reasonableness of the search is subject to *de novo* review. The State emphasizes that there is a lesser privacy interest in a vehicle than there is in a private dwelling and asserts that the Supreme Court "has accorded automobiles fewer constitutional protections than other non-mobile entities." The State suggests that the "fact that Officer Phillips may have incorrectly assumed that the purse belonged to the driver of the car is not a factor relevant to a Fourth Amendment analysis." The State relies upon the apparent authority rule enunciated by the Supreme Court. On this basis, the State contends that the driver of the vehicle, Boolman, had the apparent authority to consent to a search of defendant's purse. The State asserts that defendant assumed the risk that the driver of the automobile in which she was riding would agree to a police search of the vehicle and its contents, including defendant's purse. The State argues that it would be impractical to require police officers to "inquire of all of the occupants of an automobile whether they consent to the search of their belongings, and then sort out and classify all of those belongings."

The Illinois State Bar Association, as *amicus curiae*, agrees with the position advocated by the defendant. The Association contends that the appellate court's decision should be reversed as an improvident erosion of fourth amendment rights. Because the testimony provided by defendant and Officer Phillips was not wholly consistent or uncontradictory, we find the manifest error standard of review is applicable in the present cause. Under the fourth amendment to the United States Constitution, the fundamental purpose is to protect the legitimate expectations of privacy that citizens possess in their persons, their homes, and their belongings. The amendment seeks to balance and accommodate the often opposing interests of safeguarding citizens from unreasonable interferences with privacy and accord fair leeway for enforcing the law in the community's protection. The principles of the fourth amendment are applicable to the States through the due process clause of the fourteenth amendment, since the right to be free from

STUDENT SUPPORT SERVICES CENTER

arbitrary government intrusion is basic to a free society and implicit in the concept of ordered liberty.

Initially, we note that general principles of fourth amendment jurisprudence provide no validity for the law enforcement officers' actions in the case presently before us. The amendment explicitly requires that officers obtain a warrant, supported by probable cause, before they may search persons or property. The record does not show that Officer Phillips had a warrant for his search of the Boolman car or the defendant's purse. The United States Supreme Court has recognized an exception to the fourth amendment's warrant requirement, applicable where it is shown that there are exigent circumstances excusing the need to obtain the warrant. However, the police must still have probable cause to undertake the search. In the present case, there is no argument that exigent circumstances existed or justified the warrantless search undertaken by Officer Phillips. The State attempts to justify the search of the defendant's purse by relying upon another exception to the fourth amendment warrant requirement that has been recognized by United States Supreme Court precedent: the "automobile exception." However, that exception does not apply, and is inapposite, to the present cause.

Under the automobile exception, law enforcement officers may undertake a warrantless search of a vehicle if there is probable cause to believe that the automobile contains evidence of criminal activity that the officers are entitled to seize. In the case at bar, the State does not suggest that Officer Phillips had probable cause to believe that evidence of a crime would be found in either the Boolman vehicle or defendant's purse. In addition, there is nothing in the record to demonstrate that the police had such probable cause. Officer Phillips never testified that he believed that he had probable cause to search the car or the purse. The record offers only one reason for Officer Phillips' search of Boolman's vehicle: he undertook his search of the automobile because Boolman consented to this search. Therefore, if Officer Phillips' search of defendant's purse is to be justified under fourth amendment principles, the State must find refuge in Boolman's consent to the officer's search of the vehicle.

On the issue of consent, the State seeks to justify the officer's search of defendant's purse in light of the United States Supreme Court's decision Florida v. Jimeno (1991), 500 U.S. 248, 111 S.Ct. 1801, 114 L.Ed.2d 297. In Jimeno, a police officer stopped the vehicle which defendant was driving because of a traffic offense. The officer asked to search defendant's automobile for narcotics and the defendant consented. During the search, the officer saw a folded, brown bag on the floor of the vehicle. The officer opened the bag and found cocaine. The Supreme Court determined that the officer's search of the brown paper bag was authorized by the defendant's consent to a search of the vehicle. The Court reasoned that the "standard for measuring the scope of a suspect's consent under the Fourth Amendment is that of 'objective' reasonableness--what would the typical reasonable person have understood by the exchange between the officer and the suspect?" The Court noted that the parameters of a search are usually defined by the purpose of the search. The State argues that the Court's ruling in Jimeno shows that the officers in the instant case were justified in searching the purse found in Boolman's car. We disagree, because we find that Jimeno is significantly different from the present case.

The defendant in Jimeno was the driver of the vehicle. In his capacity as driver, the defendant had the authority to consent to a search of the car, because he had immediate possession and control of the entire vehicle. There was no question in Jimeno that the driver also had possession and control over the brown paper bag, and that he therefore had the authority to permit the police to search the bag. Although there was a passenger in Jimeno, there was no argument that the brown bag belonged to the passenger rather than the defendant driver. The question in Jimeno was whether the defendant, having the authority to consent to a search of both the vehicle and the paper bag, intended his consent to a search of the vehicle to also encompass a search of the paper bag. In the instant case, in contrast, Boolman did not own defendant's purse, nor is there any suggestion that she had common possession or control of the defendant's purse. Since Boolman did not own or share control of the purse, the precise question addressed in Jimeno is not presented in the case now before us.

Applying this jurisprudence to the present case, we conclude that Officer Phillips should have ascertained who owned the purse he found in the Boolman vehicle before he opened and searched the contents of the purse. In our view, it would have been objectively reasonable for the law enforcement officer to realize that the purse might belong to one of the passengers rather than to Boolman. The purse was found on a passenger seat in the car, not on the driver's seat, thereby tending to the conclusion that the purse belonged to the passenger, not the driver. It would have been unreasonable for the officer to believe that Boolman shared some common use in the purse with one of the passengers in the vehicle, since a purse is generally not an object for which two or more persons share common use and authority. Also, it is uncontradicted that defendant did not know that Boolman had given her consent to a search of the vehicle. It is also unrebutted that defendant did not know the police officers' purpose for the search, and that defendant was not aware that she was being asked to exit the vehicle so that the officers could search the automobile. Under these circumstances, the defendant did not abandon her purse in the vehicle, nor did she assume the risk that someone might look into her purse if she left it in the car.

Given all of these considerations, we conclude that Officer Phillips' actions were not objectively reasonable and that his search of defendant's purse was therefore invalid. By our holding we emphasize that the apparent authority rule does not allow law enforcement officers to "proceed without inquiry in ambiguous circumstances or always accept at face value the consenting party's apparent assumption that he has authority to allow the contemplated search." One commentator has succinctly remarked: "Under a sound application of the apparent authority rule the police must be required to make reasonable inquiries when they find themselves in ambiguous circumstances. This does not mean that the police must contest every claim of authority. But sometimes the facts known by the police cry out for further inquiry, and when this is the case it is not reasonable for the police to proceed on the theory that ignorance is bliss."

The appellate court found that further inquiry by Officer Phillips would not have been advisable because it would have been difficult for him to determine who owned the various pieces of property in the vehicle. The court also suggested that when a search is undertaken, "such split-second decisions are likely given little thought." Similar sentiments have been expressed in decisions from other courts regarding the apparent authority rule. We would agree that the apparent authority doctrine should not be applied so strictly that it becomes "unworkable and places too heavy a burden on the police." Also, the emergency nature of the circumstances confronting the police in various situations may not permit protracted investigation into the true ownership or authority over the property or premises which the police have been given the permission to search. Consent searches provide a valuable investigative tool for law enforcement authorities, by providing a lawful avenue for the officers to exonerate the innocent and focus their efforts on others who are more likely to be guilty of criminal activity.

However, neither police convenience nor the exigencies of the moment justified the officer's failure to ask Boolman in the present case if the purse belonged to her or to one of her passengers. This would not have been a cumbersome, time-consuming or complicated undertaking in the instant case. Also, there was no emergency nature to the officer's search, since the occupants of the vehicle were being detained by the officers, and there was no likelihood that the evidence of narcotics, if it were present, would be destroyed or hidden by Boolman or her passengers. There was no immediate threat that the evidence or the occupants would be affected by the short time it would have taken for the officer to simply inquire regarding ownership of the purse. As the Illinois State Bar Association aptly observes, the time that would be required to ask which passenger owned the purse "does not seem an onerous burden nor one which would place the officers in danger."

Based upon our review of the record and the pertinent precedent, we find no manifest error in the trial court's determination that Officer Phillips' search of the defendant's purse was not objectively reasonable. At no time did the defendant abandon her possessory interest in or control over her purse. The purse was closed when she left it on the passenger seat of the vehicle, where she had been riding, and she had a legitimate expectation of privacy in the contents of her purse. Accordingly, we affirm the trial court's allowance of the defendant's motion to suppress.

We reverse the appellate court's decision that the trial court's ruling was in error. We decline to consider the State's invitation that this court adopt the apparent authority rule as a matter of substantive Illinois constitutional law, pursuant to our State constitutional provision that bars unreasonable searches and seizures. This argument is waived, inasmuch as it was never presented to the trial court or the appellate court upon review. Also, we note that the cases upon which the State relies do not address the apparent authority rule in the context of our State constitutional provision, but rather analyzed and applied Federal fourth amendment jurisprudence regarding unreasonable searches and seizures. We need not and do not decide whether the apparent authority rule has not been, but should be, adopted as an element of our State constitutional jurisprudence prohibiting unreasonable searches and seizures. As stated more fully above, the apparent authority rule does not justify the officers' conduct in the present cause. As a result, our recognition of the rule as an element of Illinois constitutional law would not alter our conclusion that the trial court's decision was correct, and that the disposition of the appellate court should be reversed.

For the reasons stated, judgment of the appellate court is reversed and the judgment of the circuit court is affirmed. The cause is remanded to the circuit court for further proceedings consistent herewith. Appellate court reversed; circuit court affirmed; cause remanded.

REVIEW SECTION

READING COMPREHENSION

Detail the facts of this case, including a discussion of the findings of the lower courts.

Elaborate the issues to be decided in this case, including a discussion of precedent.

THINKING CRITICALLY

In your opinion, does an unreasonable search result, and thus a Fourth Amendment violation, when officers open a purse belonging to someone other than the driver of a vehicle stopped? Were the requirements met of a consensual search?

CONCLUSION

As the past several chapters have detailed, the method of analysis used to examine government action, stop and frisk, and arrest, is also used for searches. This involves analysis of whether the action constituted a search, its reasonableness, and the potential of exclusion of evidence if unreasonable. This chapter examined this analysis in greater detail with regard to searches with a warrant and searches without a warrant.

Chapter Seven

Special-Needs Searches

Our discussions up to this point have involved searches and seizures for the purpose of crime control. The U.S. Supreme Court however has applied the Fourth Amendment to a myriad of special needs that go beyond traditional enforcement of criminal laws. These are referred to as "special needs searches" and will be elaborated throughout this chapter including:

(1)   Special needs vs. the expectation of privacy;

(2)   Custody-related searches; and

(3)   Student searches.

SECTION 1: SPECIAL NEEDS VS. THE EXPECTATION OF PRIVACY

OVERVIEW

Although there are a variety of types of special needs searches, there are four main characteristics that link such searches:

(1)   The direction is at the populace generally, rather than suspects specifically;

(2)   The result can still be prosecution and conviction;

(3)   There is no requirement of a warrant or probable cause; and

(4)   The reasonableness of such a search depends on the balance of special needs of government and individual privacy.

Thus, while the goal is not crime control per se, special needs searches still have the underlying aim of protection of the citizenry. What you must keep in mind is that the special need of the government almost always outweighs an individual's right to privacy, and thus the search is considered reasonable.

SECTION 2: CUSTODY-RELATED SEARCHES

OVERVIEW

If you are a prisoner, a parolee or probationer, a defendant detained before trial, or even a prison visitor, you are subject to a significantly reduced expectation of privacy. While the courts have held that such individuals are not beyond the reach of the Constitution, the need to maintain safety and security outweighs individual privacy. Courts examine the particular circumstances of the case, however have repeatedly accepted that full-body, strip, and body-cavity searches are Fourth Amendment searches, yet are considered reasonable without a warrant or probable cause if overridden by safety concerns. Such searches do require reasonable suspicion as support and violate prisoner rights if conducted when not required to secure safety and discipline.

CASE

People v Lafayette details a case wherein the respondent was arrested for disturbing the peace and taken to the police station. There, without obtaining a warrant and in the process of booking him and inventorying his possessions, the police removed the contents of a shoulder bag and found amphetamine pills. The respondent was subsequently charged with violating the Illinois Controlled Substances Act, and at a pretrial hearing the trial court ordered suppression of the pills. The Illinois Appellate Court affirmed, holding that the shoulder bag search did not constitute a valid search incident to a lawful arrest or a valid inventory search of respondent's belongings. The Supreme Court reviews this case and holds that the search of the respondent's shoulder bag was a valid inventory search. Elaborated below is the relevant section from 725 ILCS 5/108-2 regarding custody and the disposition of things seized:

> An inventory of all instruments, articles or things seized on a
> search without a warrant shall be given to the person arrested and a
> copy thereof delivered to the judge before whom the person
> arrested is taken . . . If the person is released without a charge
> being preferred against him all instrument, articles or things seized,
> other than contraband, shall be returned to him upon release.

ILLINOIS V. LAFAYETTE
Supreme Court
462 U.S. 640, 103 S.Ct. 2605, 77 L.Ed.2d 65 (1983)

The question presented is whether, at the time an arrested person arrives at a police station, the police may, without obtaining a warrant, search a shoulder bag carried by that person. On September 1, 1980, at about 10 p.m., Officer Maurice Mietzner of the Kankakee City Police arrived at the Town Cinema in response to a call about a disturbance. There he found respondent involved in an altercation with the theatre manager. He arrested respondent for disturbing the peace, handcuffed him, and took him to the police station. Respondent carried a purse-type shoulder bag on the trip to the station. At the police station respondent was taken to the booking room; there, Officer Mietzner removed the handcuffs from respondent and ordered him to empty his pockets and place the contents on the counter. After doing so, respondent took a package of cigarettes from his shoulder bag and placed the bag on the counter. Mietzner then removed the contents of the bag, and found ten amphetamine pills inside a cigarette case package.

Respondent was subsequently charged with violating Section 402(b) of the Illinois Controlled Substances Act, on the basis of the controlled substances found in his shoulder bag. A pretrial suppression hearing was held at which the State argued that the search of the shoulder bag was a valid inventory search. Officer Mietzner testified that he examined the bag's contents because it was standard procedure to inventory "everything" in the possession of an arrested person. He testified that he was not seeking and did not expect to find drugs or weapons when he searched the bag and he conceded that the shoulder bag was small enough that it could have been placed and sealed in a bag, container or locker for protective purposes. After the hearing, but before any ruling, the State submitted a brief in which it argued for the first time that the search was valid as a delayed search incident to arrest. Thereafter, the trial court ordered the suppression of the amphetamine pills.

On appeal, the Illinois Appellate Court affirmed. It first held that the State had waived the argument that the search was incident to a valid arrest by failing to raise that argument at the suppression hearing. However, the court went on to discuss and reject the State's argument: "Even assuming, *arguendo,* that the State has not waived this argument, the stationhouse search of the shoulder bag did not constitute a valid search incident to a lawful arrest." The State court also held that the search was not a valid inventory of respondent's belongings.

The Illinois Supreme Court denied discretionary review. We granted certiorari because of the frequency with which this question confronts police and courts, and we reverse.

The question here is whether, consistent with the Fourth Amendment, it is reasonable for police to search the personal effects of a person under lawful arrest as part of the routine administrative procedure at a police stationhouse incident to booking and jailing the suspect. The justification for such searches does not rest on probable cause, and hence the absence of a warrant is immaterial to the reasonableness of the search. Indeed, we have previously established that the inventory search constitutes a well-defined exception to the warrant requirement. A so-called inventory search is not an independent legal concept but rather an incidental administrative step following arrest and preceding incarceration. To determine whether the search of respondent's shoulder bag was unreasonable we must "balance its intrusion on the individual's Fourth Amendment interests against its promotion of legitimate governmental interests."

In order to see an inventory search in proper perspective, it is necessary to study the evolution of interests along the continuum from arrest to incarceration. We have held that immediately upon arrest an officer may lawfully search the person of an arrestee; he may also search the area within the arrestee's immediate control. An arrested person is not invariably taken to a police station or confined; if an arrestee is taken to the police station, that is no more than a continuation of the custody inherent in the arrest status. Nonetheless, the factors justifying a search of the person and personal effects of an arrestee upon reaching a police station but prior to being placed in confinement are somewhat different from the factors justifying an immediate search at the time and place of arrest. The governmental interests underlying a stationhouse search of the arrestee's person and possessions may in some circumstances be even greater than those supporting a search immediately following arrest. Consequently, the scope of a stationhouse search will often vary from that made at the time of arrest. Police conduct that would be impractical or unreasonable—or embarrassingly intrusive—on the street can more readily—and privately—be performed at the station. At the stationhouse, it is entirely proper for police to remove and list or inventory property found on the person or in the possession of an arrested person who is to be jailed. Examining all the items removed from the arrestee's person or possession and listing or inventorying them is an entirely reasonable administrative procedure. It is immaterial whether the police actually fear any particular package or container; the need to protect against such risks arises independent of a particular officer's subjective concerns. Finally, inspection of an arrestee's personal property may assist the police in ascertaining or verifying his identity. In short, every consideration of orderly police administration benefiting both police and the public points toward the appropriateness of the examination of respondent's shoulder bag prior to his incarceration.

The Illinois court held that the search of respondent's shoulder bag was unreasonable because "preservation of the defendant's property and protection of police from claims of lost or stolen property, could have been achieved in a less intrusive manner." The real question is not what "could have been achieved," but whether the Fourth Amendment requires such steps; it is not our function to write a manual on administering routine, neutral procedures of the stationhouse. Our role is to assure against violations of the Constitution. The reasonableness of any particular governmental activity does not necessarily or invariably turn on the existence of alternative "less intrusive" means. We are hardly in a position to second-guess police departments as to what practical administrative method will best deter theft by and false claims against its employees and preserve the security of the stationhouse. It is evident that a stationhouse search of every item carried on or by a person who has lawfully been taken into custody by the police will amply serve the important and legitimate governmental interests involved.

Even if less intrusive means existed of protecting some particular types of property, it would be unreasonable to expect police officers in the everyday course of business to make fine and subtle distinctions in deciding which containers or items may be searched and which must be sealed as a unit. Applying these principles, we hold that it is not "unreasonable" for police, as part of the routine procedure incident to incarcerating an arrested person, to search any container or article in his possession, in accordance with established inventory procedures. The judgment of the Illinois Appellate Court is reversed and the case is remanded for proceedings not inconsistent with this opinion. It is so ordered.

REVIEW SECTION

READING COMPREHENSION

Detail the facts of this case and the grounds for searching the shoulder bag.

THINKING CRITICALLY

Elaborate the interplay between the state's interpretation of the Fourth Amendment and the interpretation provided by the Supreme Court. Do you agree with the decision in this case by the Illinois courts or the Supreme Court?

SECTION 3: STUDENT SEARCHES

OVERVIEW

The doctrine of *in loco parentis* means that while in school, administrators act as substitute parents. As such, the court has determined that the Fourth Amendment ban on unreasonable searches does apply to those conducted by school officials who need reasonable suspicion to perform such a search. In Illinois, the School Violence Tipline is one safety measure involving the Illinois State Police. The tipline encourages students to anonymously report weapons violations or threats of violence that occur on school grounds. The result is passage of the information to law enforcement authorities for further investigation.

CASE

Following a bench trial in circuit court, Kenneth Dilworth was convicted of unlawful possession of a cocaine with intent to deliver while on school property. The circuit court had earlier denied the defendant's motion to suppress evidence. The appellate court reversed the defendant's conviction, finding that his motion to suppress evidence should have been granted. In *People v Dilworth,* the Supreme Court of Illinois allows the State's petition for leave to appeal and reverses the appellate court.

PEOPLE V. DILWORTH
Supreme Court of Illinois
661 N.E.2d 310, 169 Ill.2d 195 (Ill., 1996)

Defendant was a 15-year-old student at the Joliet Township High Schools Alternate School. The Alternate School is unlike a regular public school in that only students with behavioral disorders attend it. A little more than 100 students attended the school at the relevant times. According to the Alternate School handbook, which was admitted into evidence, the goal of the school's program is to create an environment that will allow students to modify their behavior in a positive direction. Students who improve their behavior are allowed to return to regular school. The liaison officer at the school was Detective Francis Ruettiger. Ruettiger was a police officer employed by the Joliet police department and was assigned full-time to the Alternate School. His primary purpose at the school was to prevent criminal activity. If he discovered criminal activity, he had the authority to arrest the offender and transport the offender to the police station. Ruettiger also handled some disciplinary problems. Like the teachers, Ruettiger was authorized to give a detention, but not a suspension. Only the school principal and the director could suspend a student.

On November 18, 1992, two teachers asked Ruettiger to search a student, Deshawn Weeks, for possession of drugs. The teachers informed Ruettiger that they had overheard Weeks telling other students that he had sold some drugs and would bring more drugs with him to school the following day. The next day, Ruettiger searched Weeks' person in his office and found nothing. He then escorted Weeks back to his locker. Defendant and Weeks met at their neighboring lockers. According to Ruettiger, the two adolescents began talking and giggling "like they put one over on him." Ruettiger noticed a flashlight in defendant's hand and immediately thought that it might contain drugs. He grabbed the flashlight from defendant, unscrewed the top, and observed a bag containing a white chunky substance underneath the flashlight batteries. The substance later tested positive for the presence of cocaine. Defendant ran from the scene, but was captured by Ruettiger and transported to the police station. While there, defendant gave a statement admitting that he intended to sell the cocaine because he was tired of being poor.

Ruettiger explained that he had two reasons for seizing and searching the flashlight. He was suspicious that the flashlight contained drugs. Secondly, Ruettiger believed it was a violation of school rules to possess a flashlight on school grounds because a flashlight is a "blunt instrument." The school's disciplinary guidelines, of which all students must be informed when they enroll, prohibited the possession of "any object that can be construed to be a weapon." Ruettiger had never seen a student with a flashlight at the school before. He admitted, however, that students were never specifically informed that flashlights were prohibited. Also, he did not consider a flashlight to be "contraband per se." Ruettiger further related that he had daily contact with each student at the Alternate School. On one occasion, two weeks before the arrest, a teacher had suspected defendant of selling drugs in class and asked Ruettiger to search him. Ruettiger did so and found nothing. At that time, defendant told Ruettiger that he did not have any drugs, but named another student who did. A search of the other student revealed marijuana and resulted in the student's arrest.

Defendant's teacher, Danica Grabavoy, testified that sometime soon after defendant was enrolled in the Alternate School, she reviewed the entire school handbook with him and his guardian. Among other things, the handbook explains the school's policies and disciplinary guidelines. On a page entitled "Alternate School Search Procedures," the handbook states: "To protect the security, safety, and rights of other students and the staff at the Alternate School, we will search students. This search may include the student's person, his/her belongings, and school locker. Search procedures may result from suspicions generated from direct observation or from information received from a third party. Search is done to protect the safety of students. However, if in the process any illegal items or controlled substances are found in a search, these items and the student will be turned over to the police."

Prior to trial, defendant moved to suppress the evidence found in his flashlight. He argued that Ruettiger's seizure and search of the flashlight violated the fourth and fourteenth amendments to the United States Constitution. The circuit court conducted a hearing in which it denied the motion. The court found that Ruettiger was acting as an agent for the staff of the Alternate

School when he seized and searched the flashlight. Noting that the school staff must deal with difficult students, the court held that the proper fourth amendment standard to apply in this case was the reasonable suspicion standard for searches of students by school officials (New Jersey v. T.L.O. (1985), 469 U.S. 325, 105 S.Ct. 733, 83 L.Ed.2d 720), rather than the general standard of probable cause. Alternatively, the court found that even if Ruettiger was acting as a police officer, he had "reasonable cause" to believe that the flashlight contained contraband.

Defendant was tried as an adult in a stipulated bench trial. The circuit court found defendant guilty and sentenced him as an adult to the minimum four-year term of imprisonment. As previously noted, the appellate court reversed defendant's conviction outright based on its holding that his motion to suppress evidence should have been granted. The appellate court agreed with the lower court that the reasonable suspicion standard applied; however, it found that Ruettiger did not have reasonable suspicion to seize and search the flashlight. In the appellate court's opinion, Ruettiger had only a mere "hunch" that the flashlight contained drugs.

The State contends that the circuit court properly denied defendant's motion to suppress evidence for two reasons: (1) Ruettiger properly seized the flashlight as contraband because defendant's possession of the flashlight violated the school's disciplinary guidelines; and (2) Ruettiger had reasonable suspicion, as well as probable cause if required, to seize and search the flashlight. Defendant responds that Ruettiger's seizure and search of his flashlight contravened the fourth and fourteenth amendments to the United States Constitution. In New Jersey v. T.L.O. (1985), the United States Supreme Court addressed the constitutionality of searches of students by teachers and school officials. In T.L.O., a teacher discovered T.L.O., a 14-year-old high school student, smoking cigarettes in a lavatory in violation of a school rule. The teacher took T.L.O. to the principal's office, where she was questioned by an assistant vice principal. The school official demanded to see her purse, opened it, and found a pack of cigarettes. As the school official reached into the purse for the cigarettes, he noticed a package of cigarette rolling papers. In his experience, the possession of rolling papers by high school students was closely associated with the use of marijuana. A further, thorough search of the purse revealed a small amount of marijuana, a pipe, a number of empty plastic bags, a substantial quantity of one-dollar bills, a list of names of students who apparently owed T.L.O. money, and two letters implicating T.L.O. in marijuana dealing. The school official turned this evidence over to the police after notifying T.L.O.'s mother. T.L.O.'s mother accompanied T.L.O. to police headquarters, where T.L.O. confessed to selling marijuana at the high school. The State subsequently brought delinquency charges against her in juvenile court. T.L.O. sought to suppress the evidence of marijuana dealing, claiming the search was unconstitutional.

The Court initially determined that the fourth amendment to the United States Constitution applies to searches of students conducted by public school officials. In doing so, the Court rejected the argument that public school officials are exempt from the dictates of the fourth amendment because they act in *loco parentis* in their dealings with students. The Court emphasized that the State has a substantial interest in maintaining a proper educational environment for the schoolchildren entrusted to its custody and tutelage. The Court explicitly recognized that, under the fourth and fourteenth amendments, schoolchildren have legitimate expectations of privacy in possessions brought with them to school. "In short, schoolchildren may find it necessary to carry with them a variety of legitimate, noncontraband items, and there is no reason to conclude that they have necessarily waived all rights to privacy in such items merely by bringing them onto school grounds." In balancing the competing interests of a school's need to maintain a proper educational environment and the schoolchild's legitimate expectations of privacy, the Court held that teachers and school officials do not need a warrant before searching a student and need not adhere to the requirement that searches be based on probable cause. "Rather, the legality of a search of a student should depend simply on the reasonableness, under all the circumstances, of the search."

The Court set forth a twofold inquiry for determining the reasonableness of any search. First, the action must be " justified at its inception;" second, the search as actually conducted must be "reasonably related in scope to the circumstances which justified the interference in the first place" (T.L.O., 469 U.S. at 341, 105 S.Ct. at 743, 83 L.Ed.2d). Applying the test to the facts, the Court found that the school official's search of T.L.O.'s purse for cigarettes was reasonable. The Court proceeded to find the further search for marijuana reasonable as well, given the school official's observation of rolling papers. Consequently, the Court concluded that the evidence of marijuana dealing should have been admitted in T.L.O.'s juvenile delinquency proceedings.

The State first argues that Ruettiger properly seized defendant's flashlight based solely on the Alternate School's disciplinary guidelines. Although the circuit court made no ruling on this argument, a reviewing court may affirm the circuit court's decision based on any grounds in the record. Counsel for the State conceded at oral argument that, under the above logic, school officials could automatically seize and search any flashlight carried onto school grounds. Moreover, counsel admitted that, under his interpretation of the school's rule, any other blunt object, such as a book, could also be construed to be a weapon subject to automatic search and seizure. These are precisely the types of arbitrary invasions by government officials that the fourth amendment safeguards against. The State cannot compel attendance at public schools and then subject students to unreasonable searches of the legitimate, noncontraband items that they carry onto school grounds. Accordingly, we reject the State's initial argument.

The State next contends that, under the totality of the circumstances, Ruettiger had reasonable suspicion, as well as probable cause if required, to seize and search the flashlight. Defendant responds that Ruettiger had neither; rather, he seized and searched the flashlight on a mere hunch in violation of defendant's constitutional rights. Before addressing these contentions, we must determine whether the proper fourth amendment standard to apply in this case is the less stringent reasonable suspicion standard for searches of students by school officials or the general standard of probable cause. Defendant insists that because Ruettiger was a police officer, he was required to have probable cause to seize and search the flashlight.

The Court in T.L.O. stated that the standard of reasonableness applies to a search of a student "by a teacher or other school official." In so ruling, however, the Court noted: "We here consider only searches carried out by school authorities acting alone and on their own authority. This case does not present the question of the appropriate standard for assessing the legality of searches conducted by school officials in conjunction with or at the behest of law enforcement agencies, and we express no opinion on that question." Decisions filed after T.L.O. that involve police officers in school settings can generally be grouped into three categories: (1) those where school officials initiate a search or where police involvement is minimal, (2) those involving school police or liaison officers acting on their own authority, and (3) those where outside police officers initiate a search. Where school officials initiate the search or police involvement is minimal, most courts have held that the reasonable suspicion test obtains. However, where outside police officers initiate a search, or where school officials act at the behest of law enforcement agencies, the probable cause standard has been applied.

In the present case, the record shows that Detective Ruettiger was a liaison police officer on staff at the Alternate School. He worked there full-time, handling both criminal activity and disciplinary problems. Given the scenario, this case is best characterized as involving a liaison police officer conducting a search on his own initiative and authority, in furtherance of the school's attempt to maintain a proper educational environment. We hold that the reasonable suspicion standard applies under these facts.

Our holding in this case comports with Vernonia School District 47J v. Acton (1995), 515 U.S. There, the United States Supreme Court utilized a three-prong test for determining whether special needs beyond normal law enforcement require a departure from the usual fourth amendment standard of probable cause and a warrant. The competing interests of the individual and the State were balanced by an examination of the following: (1) the nature of the privacy interest upon which the search intrudes, (2) the character of the search, and (3) the nature and immediacy of the governmental concern at issue, and the efficacy of the means for meeting it. An analysis of each of these three factors supports our holding that reasonable suspicion, not probable cause, is the proper fourth amendment standard to be applied in this case.

As to the first factor, the nature of the privacy interest upon which the search intrudes, it must be remembered that we are dealing with schoolchildren here. In this respect, the Vernonia majority stated: "Fourth Amendment rights are different in public schools than elsewhere; the 'reasonableness' inquiry cannot disregard the schools' custodial and tutelary responsibility for children. For their own good and that of their classmates, public school children are routinely required to do a variety of things. Students within the school environment have a lesser expectation of privacy than members of the population generally." The second factor is the character of the search. The intrusion complained of in this case is the seizure and search of defendant's flashlight by a school liaison officer. Of utmost significance, the liaison officer had an individualized suspicion that defendant's flashlight contained drugs. We find this search as conducted to be minimally intrusive. The final factor--the nature and immediacy of the governmental concern at issue, and the efficacy of the means for meeting it--also weighs in favor of the reasonable suspicion standard here. There is no doubt that the State has a compelling interest in providing a proper educational environment for students, which includes maintaining its schools free from the ravages of drugs. As to the efficacy of the means for meeting this interest, it is relevant that the search at issue took place at an alternate school for students with behavioral disorders. In order to maintain a proper educational environment at this particular school, school officials found it necessary to have a full-time police liaison as a member of its staff. In sum, our consideration of the three Vernonia factors supports our application of the reasonable suspicion standard in the case at bar. For the reasons stated, we find that reasonable suspicion is the proper fourth amendment standard to be applied in the case *sub judice*.

As earlier noted, the Court in T.L.O. set forth a twofold inquiry for determining whether, under all the circumstances, a search of a student is reasonable: the action must be justified at its inception, and the search as actually conducted must be reasonably related in scope to the circumstances which justified the interference in the first place. For Ruettiger's search of defendant's flashlight to have been justified at its inception, Ruettiger must have had reasonable grounds for suspecting that the flashlight contained drugs in violation of the law and the school rules. The totality of the circumstances would lead a reasonable person to suspect that defendant was carrying drugs in his flashlight. Indeed, upon seeing the flashlight in defendant's hand, Ruettiger testified that he immediately thought that it might contain drugs. Although an objective standard must be used in determining whether reasonable suspicion was present, the testimony of an officer as to his subjective feelings is one of the factors that may be considered in the totality of the circumstances. Ruettiger's testimony as to his subjective belief can thus be considered as additional support for our conclusion. We also find that the search as conducted here was permissible in its scope. Ruettiger had individualized suspicion that defendant's flashlight contained drugs. He seized and searched only that flashlight. This measure was reasonably related to the objectives of the search and was not excessively intrusive.

For the foregoing reasons, we conclude that Ruettiger's seizure and search of defendant's flashlight was constitutional because it was reasonable under the totality of the circumstances. We therefore reverse the judgment of the appellate court and affirm the judgment of the circuit court. Appellate court judgment reversed; circuit court judgment affirmed.

Justice NICKELS, dissenting: I respectfully dissent. I cannot agree with the majority that a police officer whose self-stated primary duty is to investigate and prevent criminal activity may search a student on school grounds on a lesser fourth amendment standard than probable cause merely because the police officer is permanently assigned to the school and is listed in the student handbook as a member of the school staff. The majority's departure from a unanimous line of Federal and State decisions places form over substance and opens the door for widespread abuse and erosion of students' fourth amendment rights to be free from unreasonable searches and seizures by law enforcement officers.

The majority reaches its conclusion by: (1) relying on the faulty premise that Ruettiger is a school official for fourth amendment purposes; (2) misreading the line of school search decisions involving police; and (3) relying on conclusions from factually distinguishable United States Supreme Court decisions rather than utilizing the rationale the Court used to reach those conclusions. I address each issue in turn.

The majority takes the position that for the purposes of the fourth amendment, Ruettiger is a school official similar to a teacher or principal. However, Ruettiger is a police officer. He is employed by the City of Joliet police department and is assigned to patrol the Alternate School grounds as a police liaison officer. Ruettiger's self-stated primary duty at the school is to investigate and prevent criminal activity. When Ruettiger discovers such activity, he arrests the offender and takes him or her to the police station. Although Ruettiger is listed in the school handbook as a member of the school support staff, and had the authority to give a detention, and handles "some" disciplinary problems, these additional factors do not detract from the fact that Ruettiger was still a police officer whose primary duty was the same as any police officer assigned to patrol any area: to investigate and prevent criminal activity. In re E.M. (1994), 262 Ill.App.3d 302, 199 Ill.Dec. 556, 634 N.E.2d 395, where our appellate court noted that a school principal's interrogation of a student at school was for school disciplinary purposes while a police liaison officer's subsequent interrogation of that student at school regarding the same incident was for law enforcement purposes. People v. Bowers (1974), 77 Misc.2d 697, 356 N.Y.S.2d 432, where a school security officer, unlike a faculty member, was required to have probable cause rather than reasonable suspicion in searching a student because: (1) the security guard was under the control of the police commissioner and had to abide by the police department's guidelines; and (2) the security guard was placed on school grounds solely for security purposes and served no educational function at the school.

The majority, however, fails to acknowledge this clear point and argues that I place undue emphasis on Ruettiger's testimony that his primary purpose at the school was to investigate and prevent criminal activity. However, I only emphasize so strongly Ruettiger's testimony as to his primary duty at the school because the majority cannot see what is so obvious in this case: Ruettiger's self-stated primary duty at the school, as displayed by his actions in arresting defendant, is that of a police officer, not a school official. In addition to relying on the fiction that Ruettiger is a school official, the majority argues that support for its decision exists in previous case law, and specifically in two United States Supreme Court decisions, for its holding that Ruettiger was allowed to search defendant based only on reasonable suspicion. However, there is no support for the majority's conclusion in any previous decision.

The majority examines the line of Federal and State decisions involving police searches of students at school and concludes that the reasonable suspicion standard applies to Ruettiger's action here. This conclusion, however, is based on a misreading of two decisions. Every Federal and State decision on this matter has rejected the majority's view. All Federal and State decisions reviewed indicate that police officers, including police liaison officers, are required to have probable cause to search a student if they are significantly involved in the search. This was the law prior to T.L.O. (see Picha v. Wielgos (N.D.Ill.1976), 410 F.Supp. 1214, 1219) and has also been the law after T.L.O. Although several decisions have allowed student searches under the reasonable suspicion standard where police have participated in the search, these decisions have stressed that police involvement in the searches was minimal. The majority attempts to find support for its holding by stating that the reasonable suspicion standard applies in those cases "involving school police or liaison officers." The two decisions on which the majority relies for this assertion however, not only fail to address the issue of what fourth amendment standard applies, they do not involve police liaison officers. The two decisions involve "school police," which differ from police liaison officers in several significant respects. First, school police are employed by a school district while police liaison officers are employed by the local police department. Thus, while a school police officer is employed by and is ultimately responsible to the school district, a police liaison officer, such as Ruettiger, is employed by and ultimately responsible to local law enforcement authorities. Obviously, school districts and local law enforcement authorities have different missions.

The distinction between school police and police liaison officers is significant because every case involving police liaison officers has indicated that probable cause is required if the officer acts on his own initiative, as Ruettiger did here. Surely, if the reasonable suspicion standard is not applicable to a police liaison officer directing a school official to conduct a search, it is not applicable where that same police liaison officer conducts a search on his own initiative, without the involvement of any school official, as was done here. The majority also finds that Ruettiger initiated the search to further the school's attempt to maintain a proper educational environment. However, any police search at a school, or even of a schoolchild outside of school, can be said to have been performed to maintain a proper educational environment. This does not allow a police officer, whose primary duty is to investigate and prevent criminal activity, the right to search a student on mere whim and less than probable cause in direct contravention of a student's constitutional rights.

In sum, not one case involving a police search of a student at school, including cases involving police liaison officers, supports the majority's conclusion. In fact, every authority available has rejected the majority's view. The majority finds support only by misreading the facts of Wilcher and S.F., decisions that involve "school police" rather than police liaison officers. The result is that this court has for the first time in a long line of cases departed from the overwhelming view that police officers, even liaison police officers, are required to have probable cause to search a student on school grounds when instigating and carrying out a search.

The majority also attempts to find support for its position in two Supreme Court decisions, T.L.O. and Vernonia. However, the majority errs in relying simply on the results of those two factually distinguishable decisions rather than on the analysis which led the court to its conclusions. Both T.L.O. and Vernonia allowed school officials, not police authorities, to search students for noncriminal purposes based on only a reasonable suspicion. The results of T.L.O. and Vernonia thus do not apply to the instant case because the search here was conducted by a police officer investigating criminal activity for the purpose of facilitating a criminal case against defendant. A thorough examination of the three-part test enunciated by the Supreme Court in Vernonia reveals this distinction and the flaws in the majority's cursory analysis.

The first factor in balancing the competing interests of the individual and the State is the nature of the privacy interest upon which the search intrudes. The majority in the instant case concludes that because defendant was a child in school, he had a lowered expectation of privacy. This arbitrary and somewhat simplistic holding, however, fails to consider the factor the Vernonia Court found most relevant to this issue: defendant's privacy interest in relation to the State's role in conducting the search. The T.L.O. Court did not elaborate on the reasons for its finding that a schoolchild has a diminished expectation of privacy. The Court noted that the most important factor concerning the privacy interest of schoolchildren is the special relationship between the subject of the search, the schoolchildren, and the State in its role in conducting the search, as schoolmaster, guardian and tutor. In the instant case, the State did not act as guardian and tutor in conducting the search. Instead, the State acted as adversarial law enforcer. Thus, the special relationship did not exist between defendant and Ruettiger. Listing Ruettiger as a member of the school staff and allowing him to give a detention does not alter his primary role at the school, which Ruettiger readily admitted was to investigate and prevent criminal activity. To find that

Ruettiger acted as guardian and tutor for the purposes of the fourth amendment in his relationship with defendant denies the facts of the case. The relevant question to be asked here, then, is whether the search is one that a reasonable police officer might undertake, one based on probable cause. The answer is no.

Thus, while defendant was at school, his expectation of privacy was diminished in relation to school officials, such as teachers or principals, to whom he was entrusted and who served as guardian and tutor in a nonadversarial role. However, defendant's right to an expectation of privacy was not diminished in relation to the State in its adversarial role as law enforcer. A school child's expectation of privacy vis-a-vis the State as police officer, even a police liaison officer, is not diminished simply because the child is at school. It is also important to note that while the majority finds that defendant had a diminished right to privacy in school, defendant was charged and sentenced to four years in the penitentiary as an adult. I find it fundamentally unfair and inconsistent with compulsory school attendance laws to conclude that defendant had diminished privacy rights in relation to a police officer assigned to a school, whose primary duty was to investigate and prevent criminal activity, and then to charge and sentence defendant as an adult with evidence obtained by that officer.

The next factor considered in this balance is the character of the intrusion. The majority finds the intrusion minimal because Ruettiger limited his search to defendant's flashlight. However, the majority cannot reconcile this finding with the Supreme Court's holding in T.L.O. that a seizure and search of a child's possessions, such as the handbag or purse at issue in T.L.O., or the flashlight involved here, "no less than a similar search carried out on an adult, is undoubtedly a severe violation of privacy." The majority also cannot reconcile its finding with the readily apparent reason for the search, the investigation of criminal activity. It is significant that as a police officer, Ruettiger conducted the seizure and search of defendant's personal noncontraband item, the flashlight, in furtherance of his self-stated primary purpose at the school: "to take care of criminal activity." A search of a student by a school official, however, such as a teacher or principal, is conducted primarily to maintain discipline and decorum in the classroom. Thus, the second factor of the balancing equation, the character of the intrusion complained of, also favors the standard of probable cause. This is a classic fourth amendment search in which a police officer seizes and searches a defendant's noncontraband item in order to facilitate a criminal prosecution.

The final factor in the balance is the nature and immediacy of the governmental concern at issue, and the efficacy of the means used for meeting that concern. I agree with the majority that the State's interest in maintaining schools free from the ravages of drugs is compelling. Yet, I do not believe that this interest is sufficiently compelling, even at the Alternate School, in light of students' privacy interest vis-a-vis the State as law enforcer and the severe nature of the intrusion, to justify the lowering of the standard to search for a police officer in school from probable cause to reasonable suspicion. I believe this compelling interest has been met by allowing teachers and school administrators, who have almost constant contact with and supervision over students, the right to search students based on only reasonable suspicion. Moreover, in addressing this issue, the Vernonia Court concluded that accusatory searches by school officials are more negative than random searches. In the present case, the search was accusatory. The present search was also conducted by a police officer, and not a teacher untrained in the intricacies of fourth amendment jurisprudence and probable cause. T.L.O. stated that the lowered level of suspicion was proper for teachers untrained in fourth amendment jurisprudence. Police officers such as Ruettiger, however, are trained in fourth amendment jurisprudence. Thus, the lower standard is appropriate for teachers and school administrators, but not for police officers.

The majority tortures this logic by finding that because teachers and school administrators are not trained in the intricacies of the fourth amendment, police officers may patrol school hallways, searching and seizing based only on reasonable suspicion. However, the Supreme Court's point is that teachers and school administrators are allowed the lowered standard because they are untrained in fourth amendment jurisprudence. Conversely, since police officers are trained in fourth amendment jurisprudence, they are required to abide by its general requirement of probable cause to search.

Upon consideration of these three factors, I find only one, the compelling interest in protecting school children from the influx of drugs into the school that prompted the Supreme Court in T.L.O. and in Vernonia to lower the fourth amendment standard for school officials to search schoolchildren. This factor, however, is not sufficiently compelling to allow this court to lower the standard for a police officer to search a student, even a police liaison officer assigned to an alternate school, from probable cause to reasonable suspicion. More significant is the severe intrusion of a schoolchild's expectation of privacy vis-a-vis the State as law enforcer. My conclusion is supported by the Vernonia decision, which found the most important factor in balancing the interests between the individual and the State in a school search to be the relationship between the State as searcher and the subject of the search. The State conducted the seizure and search here as law enforcer and the standard required was probable cause. My conclusion is also consistent with the overwhelming weight of legal authority.

I note briefly that Ruettiger did not have probable cause to search defendant's flashlight. The majority's conclusion has been rejected by every decision addressing this issue. However, henceforth, a police officer assigned to a school whose primary duty at the school is that of a police officer, to investigate and prevent criminal activity, is now not a police officer, but a school official. The result is that local law enforcement agencies now have greater latitude to search students in school, based on the fact that they are children, and then have them charged and sentenced as adults with the evidence obtained. The majority's conclusion is a threat to the rights of all children in school to be free from unreasonable searches and seizures and from overzealous and aggressive police conduct. Children do not learn respect for their basic constitutional rights, or the rights of others, in such a setting. Instead, such a negative environment only fosters cynicism as well as suspicion of, and contempt for, all police activity. I cannot join the majority's departure from logic, good sense, and established case law. Accordingly, I dissent. Justices HARRISON and McMORROW join in this dissent.

REVIEW SECTION

READING COMPREHENSION

Elaborate the procedures used in school searches in this case.

Detail the facts of this case, including what standard for searches was used and the logic behind this decision.

Detail the requirements of a reasonable search at school.

THINKING CRITICALLY

Indicate your position on the following quote by the dissent: "The majority's departure from a unanimous line of Federal and State decisions places form over substance and opens the door for widespread abuse and erosion of students' fourth amendment rights to be free from unreasonable searches and seizures by law enforcement officers."

The majority in this case finds that "because teachers and school administrators are not trained in the intricacies of the fourth amendment, police officers may patrol school hallways, searching and seizing based only on reasonable suspicion." The problem according to the dissenting view however, is that "teachers and school administrators are allowed the lowered standard because they are untrained in fourth amendment jurisprudence. Conversely, since police officers are trained in fourth amendment jurisprudence, they are required to abide by its general requirement of probable cause to search." Which standard do you believe should have been applied to this case?

As a 15-year-old with a history of behavioral problems, do you believe the defendant should have been tried as an adult? Was the four year minimum term of imprisonment reasonable?

CASE

The three cases elaborated as one below, arise from searches of high school students in public schools by Chicago police officers. In each case the student was charged with possession of a firearm on school property. The charges were based on three separate incidents at three different schools. Two of the cases involved searches of students based on individualized suspicion. In the third case the weapon was discovered in the course of a random, mass search of the entire student body. In each case the trial judge held the seizure of a handgun violated the Fourth Amendment prohibition of unreasonable searches and seizures.

PEOPLE V. PRUITT, BROOKS AND CHEATHAM
278 Ill.App.3d 194, 662 N.E.2d 540 (1996)

The Fourth Amendment to the United States Constitution, as extended to the states by the Fourteenth Amendment, applies to searches of students conducted by public school officials. A student's subjective expectation of privacy, in his person and in the personal possessions he carries, is an expectation that society is prepared to recognize as legitimate. The State cannot compel attendance at public schools and then subject students to unreasonable searches of the legitimate, noncontraband items that they carry onto school grounds. School officials, when carrying out searches and other disciplinary functions in furtherance of school policies, cannot claim a parent's immunity from the restrictions of the Fourth Amendment. The main reason for lowering the Fourth Amendment standard applicable to searches of students in schools is to protect and maintain a proper educational environment for all students, not because of any real or imagined "special relationship" between students and teachers.

The legality of a search of a student should depend on the reasonableness, under all the circumstances, of the search. Determining reasonableness requires the answers to two questions: first, whether the action was justified at its inception; second, whether the search as actually conducted was reasonably related in scope to the circumstances which justified the interference in the first place. The reasonableness inquiry cannot disregard the schools' custodial and tutelary responsibility for children. The State's power over schoolchildren permits a degree of supervision and control that could not be exercised over free adults. The proper Fourth Amendment standard to apply in cases of school searches by a liaison police officer or any public school official is that of reasonable suspicion. A city police officer assigned to a school full-time as a "liaison officer" is in the same position as a school official for Fourth Amendment purposes, even though his primary purpose at the school was to prevent criminal activity. With these principles in mind, we turn to the individual cases before us. Each involved a hearing on the defendant's motion to suppress evidence. Since neither the facts nor the credibility of witnesses is seriously questioned in any of the cases, we will accept the trial judge's findings of fact and conduct a *de novo* review of each case.

Pruitt testified he was searched before he reached the two lines of metal detectors, one for boys and one for girls, that had been set up inside the Fenger High School on November 24, 1993. He admitted a loaded .38 caliber handgun was found in his pants pocket. The trial judge rejected Pruitt's testimony and accepted the police officer's testimony. The State called Officer Edward Sonne. He testified that on November 24, 1993, he was assigned to assist in a random metal detector search at Fenger. The school did not use metal detectors every day. When the school decided to conduct a metal detector search, the Chicago police department, by request of the school, would assist. On November 24, 1993, about 40 Chicago police officers were assigned to the Fenger School to assist in the metal detector operation. Officer Sonne, dressed in uniform, was stationed at the metal detector used to screen the boys. Pruitt passed through the metal detector at about 7:50 that morning. The machine registered a positive reading, indicating that he was carrying something metal on his person. Because of the positive reaction of the magnetometer, a protective pat-down search was made. In the pat-down, Officer Sonne felt a large metal object that felt like a gun. The object, located in Pruitt's pants pocket, was removed.

It proved to be a .38 caliber revolver with a 2 1/2-3 inch barrel. After the gun was discovered, Officer Sonne escorted Pruitt to a conference room where paper work regarding Pruitt's arrest was completed.

At the close of this evidence, the trial judge took the case under advisement. Due to comments made by the court, the State moved to reopen the case to offer further evidence to be considered on the motion. The trial court denied the request, but allowed the State to make an offer of proof for review purposes. As part of its offer of proof, the State presented the testimony of Linda C. Layne, principal at Fenger. She explained that the school's rules and regulations are set forth in a handbook, which all students are given and required to keep with them. In the "Safe School Zone" section, the handbook notified students that "possession of guns, knives, or other weapons is forbidden and will result in arrest and expulsion from Fenger ..." The school handbook and a written offer of proof were submitted to the court. While the trial judge did not change his mind about allowing the additional evidence, he did consider the contents of the offer of proof when announcing his decision. For that reason, and because we believe the trial judge should have allowed the additional evidence, we will consider the offer of proof as part of the record.

Magnetometers, or metal detectors, have become standard equipment in airports and public buildings. They are used to detect concealed weapons. When conducted by public officers, a metal detector walk-through is a search for Fourth Amendment purposes. In its amicus brief the Chicago Board of Education informs us that during the 1990-91 school year there were 183 weapons confiscated from students at the Board's 77 high schools, 11 of the weapons from Fenger. To meet the weapons problem, the Board began the random use of metal detectors in high schools. The Board's "Policy" statement contains little in the way of standards for when and how the metal detector searches are to be conducted. It is virtually no policy at all. The Chicago police department reports that 15 guns and 294 other weapons were confiscated from students during the 1991-92 school year as a result of 30 temporary metal detector screenings. In the 1992-93 school year, 21 screenings produced no guns and 42 other weapons. In each of the 1993-94 and 1994-95 schools years, four guns were seized from students in the screenings. The Board cites these statistics as proof of the success of the program.

The trial judge, in his carefully considered opinion, would require either an individualized reasonable suspicion of wrongdoing or some kind of specific school plan designed to address a compelling State interest before he would approve metal detector searches of students. We share the trial judge's high regard for the constitutional right to privacy, but we cannot find in the cases we are bound to follow the requirements he would exact. It is true that T.L.O. expressly reserved the question of whether individualized suspicion is an essential element of the reasonableness standard for school searches. At the same time, the Supreme Court observed that exceptions to the requirement of individualized suspicion can be appropriate "where the privacy interests implicated by a search are minimal and other safeguards are available to assure that the individual's reasonable expectation of privacy is not subject to the discretion of the official in the field" (T.L.O., 469 U.S. at 342, n. 8, 105 S.Ct. at 743, n. 8, 83 L.Ed.2d). Each of the suspicionless, administrative searches upheld by the Supreme Court was conducted as part of a general regulatory scheme to ensure public safety, not as a criminal investigation to secure evidence of crime. The analogy to the metal detector screening in this case is apt.

In Vernonia, the Supreme Court approved a school district drug policy that authorized random urinalysis drug testing of student athletes. The decision was based on the students' decreased expectation of privacy--they were public school students, the relative unobtrusiveness of the search--producing urine samples, and the severity of the need met by the search--deterring drug use by children. The policy satisfied the Fourth Amendment's reasonableness requirement, said the Court. No individualized suspicion was required.

There are two reported cases on the subject of metal detector screening in public schools: In re F.B. (1995), 442 Pa.Super. 216, 658 A.2d 1378, and People v. Dukes (City Crim.Ct.1992), 151 Misc.2d 295, 580 N.Y.S.2d 850. In In re F.B., the court found that individualized suspicion was not required for metal detector screening at a Philadelphia high school. First, the court held the search was justified at its inception because of the high rate of violence in the Philadelphia public schools. Second, the intrusion caused by the metal detector screening was no greater than necessary to satisfy the governmental interest justifying the search. The Philadelphia screening passed the balancing test established by T.L.O. Dukes was a trial court decision which ordinarily would be given little precedential weight. It is, however, the first reported case in the country on the subject of metal detector screening in public schools. The judge found that the extent of violence in the public schools justified the minimal intrusion caused by the metal detectors.

Although we are troubled by the failure of the Chicago Board of Education to establish strict standards for the use of metal detectors, we cannot say the screening in this case violated the Fourth Amendment. The searches of Pruitt and all the other Fenger students were directed and controlled by school officials, although actually carried out by Chicago police officers. The metal detectors belonged to the school board. The purpose of the screening was to protect and maintain a proper educational environment for all students, not to investigate and secure evidence of a crime. Because all students were required to walk through the detectors no official discretion or opportunity to harass was involved. The intrusion was minimal, not involving any physical touching until the metal detector reacted. Once the metal detector reacted, the facts were sufficient to justify a frisk.

We find, then, that the screening satisfied the Fourth Amendment reasonableness test established by T.L.O.: the action was justified at its inception by the reality of violence in the schools; the search as conducted was reasonably related in scope to the circumstances which justified the interference in the first place. The trial court's order suppressing Pruitt's gun as evidence is reversed and the cause is remanded for trial.

On April 13, 1993, Johnnie Cheatham was a 15-year-old student at Chicago Vocational High School. He was arrested that day after he was discovered carrying a loaded .22 caliber automatic pistol. The arresting officer, Kimberly Taylor, was a Chicago police officer assigned as a school patrol officer to Chicago Vocational. She and her partner, Officer Grissett, were permanently assigned to the school as liaison officers. Under an agreement between the Board of Education and the Chicago police department two officers are assigned to each Chicago public school to work with the school administration. Their purpose is to maintain security in the school.

Officer Taylor was the only witness to testify at the hearing on defendant's motion to suppress the gun. On April 13, 1993, she received a message from a school security agent, Jesse Richardson, regarding a student having a weapon. Immediately, Officer Taylor contacted Richardson. He told her that a student informed him that Cheatham had a gun in school that day. Officer Taylor, accompanied by her partner, Officer Grissett, obtained Cheatham's class schedule and then went to his classroom. Officer Grissett approached Cheatham and asked if they "could have a word with him." Cheatham nodded and then left the classroom with the officers. They went to a disciplinary office shared by the school patrol officers and the dean of boys. The room was located four doors down from the classroom Cheatham had been in. Inside the office, Cheatham was asked "if he had anything in his possession that could get him in trouble." Cheatham pointed to his left coat pocket. He then was asked what it was. He told them it was a gun. Officer Grissett then removed the gun from Cheatham's pocket.

The trial judge held Cheatham was illegally seized when the police officers approached him in a classroom and asked if they "could have a word with him." The judge recognized that the applicable standard was reasonable suspicion, but concluded that an "uncorroborated tip from an unidentified informant is insufficient to form a basis of a reasonable suspicion." T.L.O. reminds us that reasonableness under the Fourth Amendment "depends on the context within which the search takes place." We must balance "the need to search against the invasion which the search entails." We will assume, without deciding, that Cheatham was seized within the meaning of the Fourth Amendment when Officer Grissett, in uniform and armed, asked if he could have a word with him outside the classroom, then brought him to an 8' X 10' room 100 feet away. We believe the information from a fellow student that Cheatham was carrying a gun on that day created a reasonable suspicion that justified the initial intrusion. The officers could not ignore the information. The intrusion, asking him to leave the classroom, was slight, certainly more reasonable, less intrusive, and less embarrassing than questioning him in the presence of classmates. After that, there was no search until Cheatham told the officers he had a gun in his left coat pocket. Based on the totality of the circumstances in this case, we find the trial judge erred when he suppressed Cheatham's gun. That order is reversed and the cause is remanded for trial.

Two witnesses testified at the hearing--Isaiah Kurry, Dean of Students at Simeon Vocational High School, and Chicago police officer David Rozell. Kurry testified that on December 3, 1993, he received a communication from another teacher, Mrs. Vaughn, regarding a stranger in the school. She told him the stranger (later identified as Brooks) was seen coming up the rear staircase. Students are restricted from using that staircase. In addition, he was wearing a jacket. Students are not allowed to wear jackets in the school. She told Kurry the boy's behavior had been suspicious, "unnatural, he seemed to be nervous about something." Mrs. Vaughn told Kurry she saw the boy do something with his hand: "it was a movement and a reaching inside of the jacket that he had on, something of that nature." Kurry then confronted Brooks, whom he did not recognize as a student at Simeon. Brooks told Kurry his name and said that he was a student. Kurry asked Brooks to come to the office with him so he could verify his identity. Kurry described Brooks as "cooperative and relaxed" as they walked to the office. When Kurry asked why he was not in class and had no hall pass, Brooks said he had just been reinstated at the school. Kurry took Brooks to an administrative room that is also used by two Chicago police officers assigned to the school on a full-time basis. They went to this room because the other disciplinary room was in use. While in the office, a school administrator, Mr. Evans, came in and identified Brooks as a Simeon student.

Kurry had notified Officer Rozell, one of the two officers assigned to the school. Kurry told Officer Rozell about Mrs. Vaughn's report and her concerns about the suspicious stranger. Kurry asked Rozell "to be present in the room with me" during the interview with Brooks. Officer Rozell, in uniform, came into the office to observe the interview with Brooks. After 45 minutes to an hour in the room, Kurry told Brooks to empty his pockets: "I asked him to empty out his pockets to, you know, further see just who he was and what, because the actual suspicion was that he had something on him that was suspicious--by his movements." Before that moment, Brooks had been "totally cooperative," and had caused no difficulties. He had been identified as a Simeon student and he provided proof that he had been reinstated. When told to empty his pockets, Brooks began to comply. At that point, Officer Rozell conducted a pat-down of Brooks. He did that, he testified, because of what Kurry had told him about Brooks and because he noticed "a bulge" in Brooks' inside jacket pocket. During the pat-down Rozell felt a metal object in Brooks' inside jacket pocket. He immediately arrested Brooks, handcuffed him, and advised him of his rights. Then he reached into Brooks' pocket and retrieved the handgun.

The trial judge held, and we agree, that the defining moment in the seizure of the gun took place when Dean Kurry ordered Brooks to empty his pockets. Although Kurry testified he "asked" Brooks to empty his pockets, a request to a student from the dean of students in the presence of a uniformed police officer in a room used by the police assumes the dimension of an order. Forty-five to 60 minutes had gone by between the time Brooks was brought to the administrative office and the request to empty his pockets. Officer Rozell did nothing until the "empty your pockets" order by Kurry. We find no reason to believe he would have conducted the pat-down had Kurry not issued that order. Everyone in the trial court, including the prosecutor, ignored Officer Rozell's claim he saw a "bulge" in Brooks' inside jacket pocket, but did nothing about it until Dean Kurry ordered Brooks to empty his pockets. So shall we. The question, then, is whether Dean Kurry had a reasonable suspicion that justified the order to Brooks to empty his pockets. Dean Kurry was acting on "an inchoate and unparticularized suspicion or hunch" when he ordered Brooks to empty his pockets. Public school student or not, Brooks possessed a Fourth Amendment expectation of privacy as he sat in that administrative office. The expectation was not realized.

We conclude the seizure of the gun from Brooks' jacket was not based on the reasonable suspicion. We affirm the trial judge's decision to suppress the evidence.

We have concluded, as we must, that a public school student does not lose his or her constitutional expectation of privacy simply by entering the schoolhouse, but that expectation is reduced because of the need to create a safe educational environment. Lines must be drawn. That some Fourth Amendment protection remains is a point we make in the case of Anthony Brooks. We affirm the trial judge's order suppressing the gun found in his jacket. At the same time, we find that the seizures of guns from Serrick Pruitt and Johnnie Cheatham were justified by the standards of Fourth Amendment reasonableness established in Vernonia, T.L.O., and Dilworth.

The trial judge's orders suppressing those guns are reversed and those cases are remanded for trial. We have drawn lines.

REVIEW SECTION

READING COMPREHENSION

Elaborate the procedures used in school searches in this case.

THINKING CRITICALLY

Take a position on whether you believe random searches in schools for guns and drugs are acceptable? Because school violence certainly occurred prior to recent occurrences that have become widely publicized such as Columbine, what do you feel the role of the media is in creating a perception of danger at schools?

Agree or disagree with the findings of the court in this case as articulated in their conclusion: "We have concluded, as we must, that a public school student does not lose his or her constitutional expectation of privacy simply by entering the schoolhouse, but that expectation is reduced because of the need to create a safe educational environment. Lines must be drawn. That some Fourth Amendment protection remains is a point we make in the case of Anthony Brooks. We affirm the trial judge's order suppressing the gun found in his jacket. At the same time, we find that the seizures of guns from Serrick Pruitt and Johnnie Cheatham were justified by the standards of Fourth Amendment reasonableness established in Vernonia, T.L.O., and Dilworth. The trial judge's orders suppressing those guns are reversed and those cases are remanded for trial. We have drawn lines."

CONCLUSION

While most searches and seizures are conducted for the purpose of crime control, the U.S. Supreme Court has applied the Fourth Amendment to a myriad of special needs that are beyond traditional enforcement of criminal laws. Such "special needs searches" include inventory searches, international border searches, airport searches, custody-related searches, student searches, and employee drug searches. What you should have noticed is that "special needs searches" require far less evidence to conduct, and therefore involve a lower expectation of privacy by the citizenry than found in many traditional searches.

Chapter Eight

Police Interrogation and Confessions

Three provisions in the U.S. Constitution, which are mirrored in the Illinois Constitution, develop guidelines to oversee police interrogation and confession. The first is the Fifth Amendment, as well as Article One, Section Ten of the Illinois Constitution in the self-incrimination clause:

> No person shall be compelled in a criminal case to give evidence
> against himself.

The self-incrimination clause is used by the courts to determine if coercion was used before formal charges have been filed. The landmark case was *Miranda v. Arizona* in 1966 where the court implemented this clause to determine the constitutionality of interrogation.

The second is the Fourteenth Amendment, as well as Article One, Section Two of the Illinois Constitution, the due process clause:

> No person shall be deprived of life, liberty or property without due
> process of law.

The due process clause is designed to ensure the voluntary nature of a confession. A coerced confession violates due process not only because it was compelled, but also because the reliability rationale dictates that the admission of unreliable evidence to demonstrate guilt denies individuals the right to their life. Further, the accusatory system rationale suggests that coerced confessions, even if true, undermine the criminal justice system wherein the burden of proving guilt beyond a reasonable doubt is placed on the state. Finally, there is a fundamental fairness rationale behind due process which requires that fundamental fairness in our society be upheld.

The third is the Sixth Amendment right-to-counsel clause, as well as Article One, Section Eight of the Illinois Constitution:

> In criminal prosecutions, the accused shall have the right to appear
> and defend in person and by counsel.

The right-to-counsel clause has been the subject of debate because what does "in all criminal prosecutions" mean? The courts use this clause to determine if coercion was used after formal charges have been filed.

To examine police interrogation and confession, this chapter will elaborate:

(1)   The interrogation and confession setting;

(2)   The Constitution and self-incrimination;

(3)   The application of *Miranda v. Arizona* in Illinois case law; and

(4)   The waiver of rights to counsel and to remain silent.

SECTION 1: THE INTERROGATION AND CONFESSION SETTING

OVERVIEW

What has become known as the *Miranda* warning is the subject of much debate and controversy in American culture. While some view it as an integral tool in maintaining the integrity of the judicial system, many see it as a technicality that clever criminals exploit only to cause harm once again to an innocent society. Once we reach the accusatory stage of the criminal justice system the stakes become higher both for those involved as suspects and those who work in law enforcement. The balancing act between crime control and individual liberty and privacy becomes even more precarious. Because interrogation is an act that occurs privately between an officer of the law and an individual suspect, the balance in question is between obtaining a correct result in the specific case in question and also guaranteeing fairness in cases generally. With specific regard to homicide in Illinois, HB 223/SB 15 mandates that any statement made as a result of a custodial interrogation is inadmissible in court unless it is electronically recorded. While there are exceptions written into the law, the bill allows interrogations to be recorded without the suspect's knowledge or permission, if the subject is aware the interviewer is an officer. The presumption against admissibility of an unrecorded statement can be overcome "by a preponderance of the evidence that the statement was voluntary based on the totality of the circumstances."

CASE

In *People v Hawthorn,* the Illinois Appellate Court reviews an appeal from the state in which the circuit court suppressed certain inculpatory statements made by the defendant, Carolyn Hawthorn. After an evidentiary hearing, the circuit court found that Hawthorn had been subject to a custodial interrogation without the requisite Miranda warnings. The circuit court held that the statements made during this interrogation were inadmissible because they were obtained in violation of the defendant's Fifth and Sixth Amendment rights. In addition, the circuit court held that the defendant's subsequent statements must be suppressed pursuant to the fruit of the poisonous tree doctrine. This court reversed the decision.

PEOPLE V. HAWTHORN
613 N.E.2d 1274, 244 Ill.App.3d 687 (1993)

On July 16, 1986, the body of Glen Johnson was found in a dumpster in Skokie, Illinois. Johnson had been beaten and shot with a .32 caliber gun. The Skokie police detectives ascertained that Johnson had been the defendant's boyfriend and had lived with the defendant and her two sons until the date of his death. From July until September 4, 1986, the detectives spoke with Hawthorn approximately a dozen times. They discussed the murder with her and questioned her about Johnson's habits, friends, and hang outs. Sometimes they went to Hawthorn's home or office, other times she came to the police station. The police subpoenaed her telephone records for the entire month of July to find out what phone calls were made by Hawthorn and Johnson. In addition to Hawthorn, the police interviewed about 100-200 other individuals in connection with the investigation. During their investigation the police learned that there had been fights between Hawthorn and Johnson, and that Johnson had caught Harry Ollie, another boyfriend of Hawthorn, in her bedroom. Ollie told the police that he had given Hawthorn a .32 caliber gun to use as protection against Johnson. The police learned that Ollie had taken an unauthorized leave from his job on July 15, 1986, the day before the body was discovered.

The officers testified that, as of September 4, 1986, they did not believe Hawthorn was a suspect, but they did believe she knew more abut the murder than she had told them. The information that Hawthorn gave the police contained a number of inconsistencies. For example, Hawthorn told Officer Jones that the last time she saw Johnson, he left in his car. However, Johnson's car was at Hawthorn's residence the first time the police came by after the discovery of Johnson's death. In addition, evidence indicated that Hawthorn was driving Johnson's car, rather than her own, during the time that Johnson was missing. Officer Silverberg testified that he became concerned when other persons gave him information which Hawthorn withheld. Finally, all of Johnson's associates suggested that Hawthorn must have played a part in Johnson's death. Despite this information, the officers testified that on September 4, 1986, they felt that the investigation had come to a dead end. Therefore, as a last shot, they decided to ask Hawthorn to submit to a polygraph examination. Officer Jones testified that on September 4, he called Hawthorn and invited her to come to the Skokie police station for another interview about the Johnson homicide. Hawthorn agreed to come to the station and arrived around noon. At this time, Jones told Hawthorn that he believed that she was being untruthful, and asked her to take a polygraph examination. Jones had received authorization from the department to incur the expense of the polygraph test prior to her arrival. When Hawthorn agreed to take the polygraph examination, Jones called Reid and Associates in Chicago and made an appointment for 1:30 p.m. Jones and Silverberg drove Hawthorn to the polygraph appointment in an unmarked police car.

Upon arriving at Reid and Associates, Hawthorn and the officers waited in the lobby prior to the examination. The officers remained with Hawthorn during this time, and Hawthorn slept while she waited. Jones testified that he had a conversation with the polygraph examiner or his assistant prior to the polygraph test, but did not tell him what he wanted discovered or discussed. Silverberg testified that he gave the examiner a list of questions he wanted the examiner to ask Hawthorn. The questions included: whether Hawthorn killed Johnson, whether she shot him with a handgun, whether she knew who killed him, and whether she was involved in his killing. Michael Masokas, who was employed by Reid and Associates as a polygraph examiner, testified that he met with Jones and Silverberg at 1:15 p.m. for approximately 20 to 25 minutes. At this time he obtained background information from which to develop polygraph questions, and received a list of questions from the officers.

Masokas then went into the room where Hawthorn had been placed by one of the receptionists. Jones and Silverberg waited in the lobby. Upon entering the room, Masokas observed that Hawthorn had a release form in front of her. Masokas asked Hawthorn if she had time to read it and, upon receiving an affirmative response, asked her to sign it. He signed the form as a witness to her signing. Masokas then proceeded to examine Hawthorn in three distinct stages: the pre-test interview, the polygraph test itself, and the post-test interrogation. During the initial interview, Masokas obtained general background information including her medical and work history. He asked Hawthorn if she knew why she was in the office. She responded that her boyfriend had been killed and she was a suspect in the murder so they wanted her to take the polygraph test. Masokas also asked her if she was involved in causing Johnson's death, and Hawthorn said no. Masokas observed her behavior as he asked these questions. After 45 minutes to an hour, Masokas took Hawthorn into another room with a polygraph instrument. Prior to the actual examination, they reviewed the questions which would be asked during the test. Masokas then attached her to the instrument and proceeded with the examination. Masokas asked ten questions, four of which were relevant to the investigation. This procedure took 30-35 minutes. Masokas then returned Hawthorn to the initial interview room, and left to review the polygraph results for ten or fifteen minutes. Masokas concluded that Hawthorn was not telling the truth.

Upon returning to the interview room, Masokas confronted Hawthorn with the fact that she was not telling the truth, and began the post-test interrogation. At the beginning of the interrogation Masokas told Hawthorn that the door was unlocked and she was free to leave. Masokas used an interrogation procedure known as the Reid Nine Steps of Interrogation. One of the primary goals of this procedure is to minimize the moral guilt and responsibility associated with a crime, thereby inducing a suspect to confess. This goal is accomplished, in part, through the development of themes which explain why the suspect may have committed the offense, and, at the same time, provide justification for committing the offense. Approximately an hour into the interrogation, Louis Senese, then the chief examiner of Reid and Associates, entered the room. Prior to his entry, he had been monitoring the interrogation via an intercom system. Since Masokas appeared to be at an impasse, Senese offered his assistance. Senese continued to interrogate Hawthorn until he induced an admission. At that point he left the room.

When Senese stepped out of the room, Hawthorn provided Masokas with a ten to fifteen minute detailed account of the occurrence. Among other things Hawthorn told Masokas that her two sons had beaten Johnson in her apartment, knocked him unconscious, tied him up and taken him out through a window. At this point, Officer Jones, who had been summoned by Senese from the lobby, entered the room. Masokas summarized for Jones what Hawthorn told him. When Masokas finished, either Masokas or Officer Jones asked Hawthorn if the story was true and she agreed. It was approximately 5:30 p.m. at the time Hawthorn made this admission, and she had been in the continuous company of either police officers or polygraph examiners for approximately 5 1/2 hours. No Miranda warnings were given prior to this admission.

Following her admission to Jones, Silverberg administered Miranda warnings to Hawthorn in the lobby, while Jones made some phone calls. Then they drove to Hawthorn's apartment where Jones advised both Hawthorn and her 16-year-old son, Frank Robinson, of their Miranda rights. Hawthorn told Frank to go ahead and tell them what happened. Frank made a statement and was arrested. The officers took Frank to the police station. Hawthorn was not arrested, but she also went to the station via her own transportation. Frank was placed alone in a room, until Hawthorn arrived and joined him. Shortly before 9 p.m., Assistant State's Attorney Mermel arrived at the police station and was briefed by the detectives. After Frank and Hawthorn executed Miranda waiver forms, Mermel had a 20-25 minute conversation with them, and then took a court-reported statement. After the statement was transcribed, Frank and Hawthorn signed it in the presence of Detective Brezezicki. Hawthorn was arrested three months later and indicted for murder, armed violence, concealment of a homicidal death, aggravated kidnapping, aggravated unlawful restraint, solicitation, conspiracy and obstruction of justice. Hawthorn moved to suppress the statements she made on the ground that they were obtained in violation of Miranda, and her Fifth Amendment rights. On March 28, 1990, the circuit court ordered that all statements given by Hawthorn would be suppressed. The circuit court found that Hawthorn had been subject to a custodial interrogation without the requisite Miranda warnings. Therefore, the circuit court held that the statements made during this interrogation were inadmissible because they were obtained in violation of the defendant's Fifth and Sixth Amendment rights. In addition, the circuit court held that the defendant's subsequent statements must be suppressed pursuant to the fruit of the poisonous tree doctrine. The State appeals from the order of suppression.

Initially we note that both the State and the defendant have agreed that no Sixth Amendment violation occurred. The Sixth Amendment guarantee of counsel attaches only at the initiation of adversarial judicial proceedings. On September 4, 1986, the day of the interrogation, no adversarial proceedings had commenced. Therefore, no Sixth Amendment violation occurred when Hawthorn was questioned in the absence of counsel. The circuit court erred in holding that a Sixth Amendment violation had occurred.

Two issues remain before this court. First, we must determine whether the trial court's holding that the defendant was "in custody" and, therefore, entitled to Miranda warnings is against the manifest weight of the evidence. Second, assuming that a Miranda violation took place, we must determine whether the trial court erred in concluding that the defendant's subsequent statement made to the assistant States Attorney should be suppressed pursuant to the fruit of the poisonous tree doctrine. Miranda v. Arizona (1966), 384 U.S. 436, 86 S.Ct. 1602, 16 L.Ed.2d 694, the United States Supreme Court held that in order to safeguard the Fifth Amendment right to be free from self-incrimination, Miranda warnings must be given to any defendant subject to custodial interrogation. The Miranda court defined a "custodial interrogation" as questioning initiated by law enforcement officers after a person has been taken into custody or has otherwise been deprived of his freedom of action in any significant way.

The determination of whether an interrogation is custodial should focus on all of the circumstances surrounding the questioning, including: the location, length, mood and mode of the interrogation; the number of police officers present; any indicia of formal arrest or evidence of restraint; the intentions of the officers; the extent of the officers' knowledge; and the focus of the investigation. The trial court must examine and weigh these factors, along with the credibility of the witnesses. It must then make an objective determination as to what a reasonable person, innocent of any crime, would perceive if he or she were in the defendant's position. The burden of proving that a defendant was not in a custodial situation and had not been deprived of his freedom of action in any significant way is on the State. When reviewing the trial court's ruling on a motion to suppress, a court of review will not disturb the trial court's finding unless it is manifestly erroneous.

The circuit court below did in fact consider each factor and made the following findings of fact. At the time of the interrogation, Hawthorn was a primary suspect. The police officers knew that Hawthorn had lived with Johnson, and that she had a reason to fear Johnson because he had abused her in the past. The officers had reasonable grounds to believe that Hawthorn had been provided with a pistol which was the same caliber as the gun used to kill Johnson. They knew that this gun had been provided so that she could protect herself against Johnson. Finally, the police knew that Hawthorn showed very little emotion when informed of Johnson's death. The court also found that the police officers employed subterfuge in requesting that Hawthorn come to the station for an interview when their actual, but unexpressed, motive was to induce her to submit to a polygraph test. Furthermore, instead of allowing Hawthorn to drive herself to the exam in her own car, the police drove her to the offices of Reid and Associates in an unmarked police car. With respect to the place of interrogation, the circuit court found that in Hawthorn's case, the place of interrogation was a room or office which was specifically designed and intended for interrogation. At no time was Hawthorn ever outside of the presence of police; she was taken directly from the police station to another place which was specifically designed for interrogation purposes. The court found that the polygraph examiners were acting as agents of the police. The police gave Masokas, one of the examiners, a list of questions to ask during the examination, and he did in fact ask those questions. Upon completion of the polygraph test, Masokas confronted Hawthorn with the fact that she had failed the test and, therefore, was not telling the truth. Masokas and later Senese commenced an interrogation using the most scientifically efficient method of interrogation permissible under our judicial system. Finally, the court found that the interrogation took place at a time which had long surpassed the investigation stage and, in fact was at the accusatorial stage. Considering all of the above factors together, the circuit court found that Hawthorn's freedom had been significantly impaired throughout the entire day of September 4, 1986.

Initially the State contends that the circuit court's finding that Hawthorn was a primary suspect is against the manifest weight of the evidence. The State correctly points out that both Officer Jones and Officer Silverberg testified that they did not believe that Hawthorn was a suspect prior to September 4, 1986, the day of the interrogation. We note, however, that the record also contains evidence that the police possessed information which could lead a reasonable police officer to view Hawthorn as a suspect. Contrary to the State's argument, the trial court did not ignore the testimony of the officers. Instead, the trial court stated that in light of the evidence of the officers' knowledge about Hawthorn as of September 4th, it found the testimony of the officers to be incredulous. It is the function of the trial court to determine the credibility of the witnesses and to resolve any conflict in their testimony. In light of all the evidence before the trial court, we cannot say that its conclusion that Hawthorn was a suspect on September 4th was against the manifest weight of the evidence.

Next, the State argues that the trial court erred in finding that the polygraph examiners were acting as agents of the police. We disagree. Our supreme court has previously recognized that polygraph examiners may become agents of the police during an interrogation. Whether or not the polygraph examiners have become agents of the police in a particular case depends upon the unique facts of that case. The facts in this case indicate that the polygraph examiners went far beyond merely administering a polygraph test. Masokas confronted Hawthorn with the fact that she failed the examination and, therefore, was not telling the truth. He then commenced a highly structured and stressful interrogation aimed at inducing a confession. When it became apparent that Masokas would not obtain a confession, Senese intervened and completed the interrogation. Only after the examiners had induced a confession did the examiners return Hawthorn to the police officers. Based upon the facts of this case, we hold that the trial court's conclusion that the examiners were acting as agents of the police is not against the manifest weight of the evidence.

The State next contends that the trial court's conclusion that Hawthorn was in custody on September 4th is erroneous because the trial court applied the wrong standard. The State maintains that the trial court determined that Hawthorn was in custody because the officers considered her a primary suspect and focused their investigation on her. Therefore, the State asserts that the trial court improperly focused on the subjective intent of the police officers instead of the objective perceptions of a reasonable, innocent person in Hawthorn's position. It is well established that Miranda warnings are not triggered solely by the government's focusing on a particular suspect. However, the knowledge possessed by the police, as well as the focus of their investigation are two of many factors that may be considered in determining whether a particular interrogation was custodial. The subjective intent of the police officers is relevant to the extent that it might color their outward behavior toward an individual who is the subject of an interrogation.

The State is correct in asserting that these factors should not control a trial court's determination of whether an interrogation is custodial. However, the State is mistaken in asserting that the subjective intentions of the police officers did control the outcome of the trial court's decision in this instance. After discussing the officers conduct toward Hawthorn, the court stated "the actions of the Skokie Police would indicate that a reasonable person would be at least apprehensive as to whether or not they were free to go." Moreover, after carefully considering all the circumstances surrounding the questioning, the trial court stated, "taking all those factors together, the Court is satisfied that throughout the entire day of September 4 that Carolyn Hawthorn's freedom had been significantly impaired and that she was a suspect and that she would be interrogated at an accusatorial stage and not an investigation stage." Although we do not agree with the trial court's finding that Hawthorn's freedom was significantly impaired throughout the entire day of September 4th, we are satisfied that the circuit court considered all of the factors surrounding the questioning of Hawthorn. The trial court did not focus exclusively on the subjective intent of the officers, but instead, applied the proper standard in determining whether the interrogation of Hawthorn was custodial. We hold that the trial court's conclusion that the interrogation of Hawthorn by the police was custodial is not against the weight of the evidence in so far as it applies to the questioning by the police after they were informed of her admission.

The State next contends that the Illinois Supreme Court (Melock, 149 Ill.2d 423, 174 Ill.Dec. 857, 599 N.E.2d 941) dictates that we reverse the trial court's suppression order. We disagree. In Melock, the defendant was suspected of murdering his grandmother. The police went to Melock's home and requested that he accompany them to the police station. Melock was taken to an interview room and questioned for two hours. While Melock was at the station, he offered to take a polygraph examination to prove that he was telling the truth. Melock was transported from the police department to the offices of John Reid and Associates by the interrogating officers. Upon arriving, Melock sat alone in an unsecured waiting room for about 30 minutes while the police officers spoke with the polygraph examiners. Like the case at bar, Masokas, the polygraph examiner, questioned Melock in three distinct stages. As in Hawthorn's case, the polygraph examiner induced an admission during the post-test interrogation, and then summoned the police officers. However, before eliciting any statement from Melock, the police read Melock his Miranda rights. The trial court held that Melock was not in custody prior to the point in time that Melock made the admission to Masokas and the Supreme Court affirmed.

We disagree with the State's contention that Melock controls the outcome of this case. The facts of the instant case differ from those of Melock in one critical respect. In Melock, the defendant was given Miranda warnings as soon as he made an admission to the polygraph examiners and before he made any statement to the police officers. In contrast, Hawthorn was not given Miranda warnings as soon as the polygraph examiners induced an admission from her. Instead, the police elicited a second admission from Hawthorn before they gave her Miranda warnings. In light of the facts of this case, it is our view that Miranda warnings should have been given after the polygraph examiners induced an admission, and before the police elicited any further statements. The facts before the court present an extremely close case. We are mindful of the limited scope of our review; the trial court's determination will not be reversed unless it is manifestly erroneous. In light of all the circumstances surrounding the questioning of Hawthorn, we cannot say that the circuit court's conclusion that Hawthorn was in custody and, therefore, entitled to Miranda warnings at the point she made her initial admission to the police officers following the polygraph examination is against the manifest weight of the evidence. Therefore, the trial court did not err in suppressing Hawthorn's initial statement.

We now turn to Hawthorn's subsequent statement which was made to Assistant States Attorney Mermel at the police station later that evening. The trial court found this statement to be the "fruit" of the initial custodial interrogation conducted in violation of Miranda. The trial court further found that no attenuation occurred between the initial violation and the subsequent statement. Therefore, the trial court held that these statements were inadmissible pursuant to the fruit of the poisonous tree doctrine. We disagree. Oregon v. Elstad (1985), 470 U.S. 298, 105 S.Ct. 1285, 84 L.Ed.2d 222, the United States Supreme Court held that the fruit of the poisonous tree doctrine is not applicable to Miranda violations. As the Miranda Court observed, however, Miranda violations differ significantly from Fourth Amendment violations which have traditionally warranted a broad application of the "fruits" doctrine. The Fourth Amendment exclusionary rule is designed to deter unreasonable searches, no matter how probative their fruits. In contrast, the Miranda exclusionary rule was created to safeguard Fifth Amendment rights and sweeps more broadly than the Fifth Amendment itself. Miranda warnings are not themselves rights protected by the Constitution. Instead, the requirement that Miranda warnings be given is a prophylactic measure designed to insure that the right against compulsory self incrimination is protected. As such, the Miranda exclusionary rule may be triggered even in the absence of a Fifth Amendment violation. The Supreme Court in Elstad concluded: "It is an unwarranted extension of Miranda to hold that a simple failure to administer the warnings, unaccompanied by any actual coercion or other circumstances calculated to undermine the suspect's ability to exercise his free will, so taints the investigatory process that a subsequent voluntary and informed waiver is ineffective for some indeterminate period. Though Miranda requires that the unwarned admission must be suppressed, the admissibility of any subsequent statement should turn in these circumstances solely on whether it is knowingly and voluntarily made."

The principle set forth in Elstad is clear. The failure to administer Miranda in the absence of coercion does not implicate the fruit of the poisonous tree doctrine. In the case at bar the trial court did not make a finding of coercion. The defendant urges this court to impute a finding of coercion to the trial court. Defendant asserts that since the trial court failed to apply Elstad, it "apparently recognized" that more than a mere failure to administer Miranda warnings occurred. We disagree. The trial court suppressed the initial statements solely because the Hawthorn was not given Miranda rights. Furthermore, there is no basis in the record to support a finding of coercion. The facts of this case indicate that the only violation of Hawthorn's rights that occurred was the failure to administer Miranda warnings. Therefore, the trial court erred in applying the fruit of the poisonous tree doctrine.

As discussed in Elstad, the only relevant issue concerning Hawthorn's subsequent statement is whether it was made voluntarily. A statement is voluntary where under the totality of the circumstances, it is given freely, voluntarily and without compulsion or inducement. On the other hand a statement is involuntary if the defendant's will was overcome at the time he confessed. Factors the court should consider when making a determination of voluntariness include the age, education and intelligence of the accused, the duration of the questioning, whether the accused was apprised of his constitutional rights, and whether the accused was subjected to any physical punishment, such as the deprivation of food or water. No single fact is dispositive; the question must be answered on the facts of each case. The facts of this case indicate that after Hawthorn made an initial admission at the polygraph office she was given Miranda warnings. The police then drove her home. Upon arriving at Hawthorn's home, the officers gave Miranda warnings to both Hawthorn and her son, Frank. At this time Frank admitted his involvement in the murder and gave a statement to the police. The officers then placed Frank under arrest and took him to the police station. Hawthorn was not arrested, but instead was left at home, alone. Hawthorn then went to the station of her own volition in order to be with her son. At the station, Assistant State's Attorney Mermel gave Miranda warnings to both Hawthorn and her son before taking a joint statement. Both Hawthorn and Frank waived their Miranda rights and gave a statement. Considering the totality of the circumstances surrounding Hawthorn's subsequent statement, we hold that the statement was voluntary and, therefore, admissible. The trial court erred in suppressing the statement.

For the foregoing reasons, the decision of the trial court is affirmed in part and reversed in part and remanded.

REVIEW SECTION

READING COMPREHENSION

Detail the facts of this case and the main distinctions between the findings of the trial court and the appellate court.

SECTION 2: THE CONSTITUTION AND SELF-INCRIMINATION

OVERVIEW

What does it mean to be considered a witness against yourself? It means that government officials cannot compel you to give testimony against yourself in a court of law. In essence, what this means is that confessions and other incriminating statements must meet the voluntariness test of self-incrimination. The totality circumstances surrounding one's statement must demonstrate that the confession was given voluntarily.

CASE

In *People v Dmitriyev,* the defendant pled guilty to two counts of burglary and implicated Igor Naydenov, his codefendant. The trial court sentenced the defendant the same day. Fifteen days later, the State called the defendant to testify against Naydenov. Finding that defendant did not have a Fifth Amendment right to remain silent, the trial court ordered defendant to testify. When he contradicted the factual basis for his guilty plea, the trial court found the defendant in direct contempt for lying. Because the Supreme Court allows a defendant to file a motion to withdraw a guilty plea within 30 days from the date of sentencing, the appellate court believes the defendant continued to have a Fifth Amendment right to remain silent at the time he was ordered to testify.

PEOPLE V. DMITRIYEV
707 N.E.2d 121, 302 Ill.App.3d 814 (1998)

On May 20, 1997, defendant pled guilty to two counts of burglary. The assistant State's Attorney read a stipulated factual basis for the plea, providing that defendant and Naydenov were found by police while in the process of removing airbags from a vehicle. It also provided that, if a trial was held, defendant would testify that he was indeed working with Naydenov to remove airbags from two vehicles without the owners' permission. While under oath, the defendant agreed with the factual basis, stating "yes, that's what happened." The trial court sentenced defendant to 48 months of probation and ordered him to pay $300 in restitution. On June 4, 1997, the State called defendant to testify against Naydenov. Because defendant's attorney failed to appear, the trial court directed Assistant Public Defender Mr. Slonim to give advice. Before defendant was sworn, Slonim stated to the court that he advised defendant to decline to answer any questions concerning the case based on the fifth amendment right against self-incrimination and that defendant intended to follow his advice. He explained that the basis for invoking the fifth amendment was that defendant's testimony might be deemed contrary to anything he had testified to before and that such could be used against him. After a short colloquy between the court and Slonim, the court informed defendant that it did not believe the fifth amendment applied since he pled guilty to the charges against him and no other charges were pending. The trial court then ordered him to testify.

Defendant denied involvement in the crime and also denied that Naydenov was involved. Moreover, defendant testified that the stipulated facts he agreed to when he pled guilty were not true. Subsequently, the trial court questioned defendant. The trial court asked defendant whether he lied to the court when he agreed to the stipulated factual basis for his guilty plea. Upon the trial court's repeated demands for a yes or no answer, defendant said yes. Consequently, the trial court found defendant in direct contempt for lying to the court when he pled guilty and sentenced him to six months of imprisonment. The trial court also denied defendant's motion for reconsideration. This appeal followed.

Although defendant raises four points of error on appeal, we find his contention that the trial court improperly denied him the fifth amendment right against self-incrimination to be dispositive. Under the fifth amendment to the United States Constitution, a witness is guaranteed the right to remain silent if his testimony might incriminate him. In People v. Edgeston, 157 Ill.2d 201, 220, 191 Ill.Dec. 84, 623 N.E.2d 329 (1993), the court noted: "The fifth amendment not only protects the individual against being involuntarily called as a witness against himself in a criminal prosecution but also privileges him not to answer official questions put to him in any other proceeding, civil or criminal, formal or informal, where the answers might incriminate him in future criminal proceedings." A witness may only exercise the right against self-incrimination where he reasonably suspects the possibility of subsequent prosecution if he answers. However, it is the trial court and not the witness that determines whether there is a real danger of incrimination under the particular facts of the case. "A witness may be denied the privilege only when it is perfectly clear, considering all the circumstances, that the answer sought cannot possibly have a tendency to incriminate."

Generally, once a defendant has entered a plea of guilty, he waives his right against compulsory self-incrimination. A defendant who has entered into a plea agreement continues to be shielded by the right against self-incrimination until the 30-day period for withdrawing his plea has expired. In the instant case, defendant was called to testify 15 days after he pled guilty. The State argues that the premise for defendant's desire to invoke his fifth amendment right related only to his fear of perjury and not to any fear related to jeopardizing a motion to withdraw his plea or an appeal of his conviction. In particular, the State contends that defendant's premise for invoking the fifth amendment renders the rule inapplicable. It also contends that any fifth amendment right is not triggered since defendant had not filed a motion to withdraw his plea. We disagree with both contentions.

That defendant sought to avoid testifying in fear of committing perjury does not exempt application of the rule. The fifth amendment right to silence is properly raised where the question calls for an answer that might incriminate the witness; all that must be apparent is a "real danger" that the witness will incriminate himself. As such, the focus is on the ability to raise the shield when presented with questions that call for a potentially incriminating answer and not on whether the witness's actual answer will implicate him further. In this case, it is clear that the questions the State posed to defendant went to the core of the charges lodged against him. Thus, the fifth amendment right to silence was applicable. We also reject the State's argument that the trial court properly compelled defendant to testify since he had yet to file a motion to withdraw his guilty plea. Whether a defendant has filed a motion to withdraw is not determinative. Moreover, the State's argument begs the question of whether a defendant actually has a 30-day window in which to file his motion to withdraw. Under the State's approach, the rule allowing 30 days for filing a motion to withdraw would be rendered nearly meaningless if the witness further incriminates himself.

Contrary to the State's arguments, we believe that bright line application of the above rule is necessary to ensure predictability and the rights of defendants. The court in Morales explained that the policy supporting maintaining one's right to invoke the fifth amendment in this situation is to ensure that the ability to withdraw a plea remains unfettered by additional incriminating admissions. The court explained that if the witness was compelled to testify, his answers, if incriminating, would be persuasive grounds for a court to exercise its discretion and deny any subsequent motion to withdraw the plea. "Forcing the witness to testify would tend, as a practical matter, to make the guilty plea irrevocable" (Morales, 102 Ill.App.3d at 904, 58 Ill.Dec. 408, 430 N.E.2d 350). In a broader context, the rule is only a small segment supporting the prophylactic policy behind the fifth amendment of protecting defendants against self-incrimination until their cases have reached final adjudications. The policy is best illustrated People v. Den Uyl, 318 Mich. 645, 29 N.W.2d 284 (1947). There, although defendant's conviction and sentence had been affirmed on appeal, his petition for certiorari was still pending before the United States Supreme Court when he was called to testify. The Michigan Supreme Court approved of the trial court's reason for upholding the defendant's fifth amendment rights. The trial court stated: "I do not believe that the verdict of guilty concludes that case in the Federal Court, nor does it render the danger of self-incrimination remote or fanciful or speculative, as alleged in this motion; and that does not become true, in my judgment, until such time as the time for appeal passes and the person convicted commences to serve the sentence imposed upon him without further right of appeal except by a special leave of the court, because, in my judgment, if the case should for any reason be reversed and sent back for a new trial, the danger of self-incrimination again arises."

Lastly, we summarily address the State's contention that defendant waived his fifth amendment right when he began answering questions. The State contends that the right is personal and that, to properly invoke it, the witness must raise it himself while on the stand. Under the facts of this case, the State's argument is without merit. Here, the trial court specifically ordered defendant to testify regarding the matters to which he pled guilty. Thus, it cannot be said that he voluntarily waived his right to remain silent. For the foregoing reasons, we reverse the circuit court of Cook County. Reversed.

REVIEW SECTION

READING COMPREHENSION

Detail the facts of this case and the applicability of the Fifth Amendment.

THINKING CRITICALLY

Should the courts err on the side of the defendant and adopt the policy that a party can invoke the Fifth Amendment as long as their case is still under review?

SECTION 3: *MIRANDA V. ARIZONA* IN ILLINOIS

OVERVIEW

Because suspects are confined to a strange location where psychological pressure and tricks are used in an attempt to secure a confession, the court created a measure to prevent involuntary confessions. In *Miranda v. Arizona* in 1966 the courts, by a bare majority, deemed interrogation inherently coercive and created the *Miranda* warning in an attempt to create a balance and overcome the pressures of interrogation. Keep in mind that this warning must be given only if officers intend to take the suspect into custody and interrogate the suspect. Thus, questioning of people at crime scenes, questioning of individuals prior to them being considered an official suspect, and questioning of people during Fourth Amendment stops do not require the *Miranda* warning. The *Miranda* warning includes four warnings that are now famous due to the proliferation of police shows on television:

(1)   Right to remain silent;

(2)   Anything you do say can and will be used against you in a court of law;

(3)   Right to an attorney; and

(4)   If you cannot afford an attorney, one will be appointed for you.

In addition to the standard *Miranda* warning, there are five more rules that the court has created to balance the coercion involved in interrogation, however the suspect does not have to be informed of these rules:

(1)   An individual can claim their right to silence at any time and the interrogation must stop immediately upon this request;

(2)   If an individual indicates they want an attorney present prior to the start of an interrogation, government officials may not begin interrogation. Further, if already begun, interrogation must cease once an individual requests and attorney;

(3)   If an individual gives a statement without an attorney present, the burden is on the state to prove that the right against self-incrimination and the right to an attorney were waived;

(4)   Any statement that is obtained in violation of these rules is inadmissible in a court of law; and

(5)   Should an individual employ the right against self-incrimination, s/he cannot be penalized through an inference of guilt.

As you read cases that address the *Miranda* warning, keep in mind the rights of the individual and at what point the burden shifts to the state if these rights are violated.

CASE

Patterson v Illinois is a case before the U.S. Supreme Court that addresses both the *Miranda* warning and an individual's right to counsel. After being informed by police that he had been indicted for murder, the petitioner, who was in police custody, twice indicated his willingness to discuss the crime during interviews initiated by the authorities. On both occasions, he was read a form waiving his rights under Miranda v. Arizona (384 U.S. 436), initialed each of the five specific warnings on the form, and signed the form. He then gave inculpatory statements to the authorities. The Illinois trial court denied his motions to suppress his statements on constitutional grounds, and the statements were used against him at trial. The State Supreme Court affirmed his conviction, rejecting his contention that the warnings he received, while adequate to protect his Fifth Amendment rights as guaranteed by Miranda, did not adequately inform him of his Sixth Amendment right to counsel. The U.S. Supreme Court determines that the postindictment questioning that produced incriminating statements did not violate the individual's Sixth Amendment right to counsel.

PATTERSON V. ILLINOIS
U.S. Supreme Court
487 U.S. 285 (1988)

In this case, we are called on to determine whether the interrogation of petitioner after his indictment violated his Sixth Amendment right to counsel. Before dawn on August 21, 1983, petitioner and other members of the "Vice Lords" street gang became involved in a fight with members of a rival gang, the "Black Mobsters." Some time after the fight, a former member of the Black Mobsters, James Jackson, went to the home where the Vice Lords had fled. A second fight broke out there, with petitioner and three other Vice Lords beating Jackson severely. The Vice Lords then put Jackson into a car, drove to the end of a nearby street, and left him face down in a puddle of water. Later that morning, police discovered Jackson, dead, where he had been left.

That afternoon, local police officers obtained warrants for the arrest of the Vice Lords, on charges of battery and mob action, in connection with the first fight. One of the gang members who was arrested gave the police a statement concerning the first fight; the statement also implicated several of the Vice Lords (including petitioner) in Jackson's murder. A few hours later, petitioner was apprehended. Petitioner was informed of his rights and volunteered to answer questions put to him by the police. Petitioner gave a statement concerning the initial fight between the rival gangs, but denied knowing anything about Jackson's death. Petitioner was held in custody the following day, August 22, as law enforcement authorities completed their investigation of the Jackson murder.

On August 23, a Cook County grand jury indicted petitioner and two other gang members for the murder of James Jackson. Police Officer Michael Gresham, who had questioned petitioner earlier, removed him from the lockup where he was being held, and told petitioner that because he had been indicted he was being transferred to the Cook County jail. Petitioner asked Gresham which of the gang members had been charged with Jackson's murder, and upon learning that one particular Vice Lord had been omitted from the indictments, asked: "Why wasn't he indicted, he did everything." Petitioner also began to explain that there was a witness who would support his account of the crime. At this point, Gresham interrupted petitioner, and handed him a Miranda waiver form. The form contained five specific warnings, as suggested by this Court's Miranda decision, to make petitioner aware of his right to counsel and of the consequences of any statement he might make to police. Gresham read the warnings aloud, as petitioner read along with him. Petitioner initialed each of the five warnings, and signed the waiver form. Petitioner then gave a lengthy statement to police officers concerning the Jackson murder; petitioner's statement described in detail the role of each of the Vice Lords - including himself - in the murder of James Jackson.

Later that day, petitioner confessed involvement in the murder for a second time. This confession came in an interview with Assistant State's Attorney (ASA) George Smith. At the outset of the interview, Smith reviewed with petitioner the Miranda waiver he had previously signed, and petitioner confirmed that he had signed the waiver and understood his rights. Smith went through the waiver procedure once again: reading petitioner his rights, having petitioner initial each one, and sign a waiver form. In addition, Smith informed petitioner that he was a lawyer working with the police investigating the Jackson case. Petitioner then gave another inculpatory statement concerning the crime. Before trial, petitioner moved to suppress his statements, arguing that they were obtained in a manner at odds with various constitutional guarantees. The trial court denied these motions, and the statements were used against petitioner at his trial. The jury found petitioner guilty of murder, and petitioner was sentenced to a 24-year prison term.

On appeal, petitioner argued that he had not "knowingly and intelligently" waived his Sixth Amendment right to counsel before he gave his uncounseled postindictment confessions. Petitioner contended that the warnings he received, while adequate for the purposes of protecting his Fifth Amendment rights as guaranteed by Miranda, did not adequately inform him of his Sixth Amendment right to counsel. The Illinois Supreme Court, however, rejected this theory. In reaching this conclusion, the Illinois Supreme Court noted that this Court had reserved decision on this question on several previous occasions and that the lower courts are divided on the issue. We granted this petition for certiorari to resolve this split of authority and to address the issues we had previously left open.

There can be no doubt that petitioner had the right to have the assistance of counsel at his postindictment interviews with law enforcement authorities. Our cases make it plain that the Sixth Amendment guarantees this right to criminal defendants. Petitioner asserts that the questioning that produced his incriminating statements violated his Sixth Amendment right to counsel in two ways. Petitioner's first claim is that because his Sixth Amendment right to counsel arose with his indictment, the police were thereafter barred from initiating a meeting with him. He equates himself with a preindictment suspect who, while being interrogated, asserts his Fifth Amendment right to counsel; under Edwards v. Arizona, 451 U.S. 477 (1981), such a suspect may not be questioned again unless he initiates the meeting.

Petitioner, however, at no time sought to exercise his right to have counsel present. The fact that petitioner's Sixth Amendment right came into existence with his indictment does not distinguish him from the preindictment interrogatee whose right to counsel is in existence and available for his exercise while he is questioned. Had petitioner indicated he wanted the assistance of counsel,

157

the authorities' interview with him would have stopped, and further questioning would have been forbidden (unless petitioner called for such a meeting). Petitioner's principal and more substantial claim is that questioning him without counsel present violated the Sixth Amendment because he did not validly waive his right to have counsel present during the interviews. Since it is clear that after the Miranda warnings were given to petitioner, he not only voluntarily answered questions without claiming his right to silence or his right to have a lawyer present to advise him but also executed a written waiver of his right to counsel during questioning, the specific issue posed here is whether this waiver was a "knowing and intelligent" waiver of his Sixth Amendment right.

In the past, this Court has held that a waiver of the Sixth Amendment right to counsel is valid only when it reflects "an intentional relinquishment or abandonment of a known right or privilege." In other words, the accused must "know what he is doing" so that "his choice is made with eyes open." Was the accused, who waived his Sixth Amendment rights during postindictment questioning, made sufficiently aware of his right to have counsel present during the questioning, and of the possible consequences of a decision to forgo the aid of counsel? In this case, we are convinced that by admonishing petitioner with the Miranda warnings, respondent has met this burden and that petitioner's waiver of his right to counsel at the questioning was valid. First, the Miranda warnings given petitioner made him aware of his right to have counsel present during the questioning. There is little more petitioner could have possibly been told in an effort to satisfy this portion of the waiver inquiry. Second, the Miranda warnings also served to make petitioner aware of the consequences of a decision by him to waive his Sixth Amendment rights during postindictment questioning. Petitioner knew that any statement that he made could be used against him in subsequent criminal proceedings. This warning also sufficed - contrary to petitioner's claim here. By knowing what could be done with any statements he might make, and therefore, what benefit could be obtained by having the aid of counsel while making such statements, petitioner was essentially informed of the possible consequences of going without counsel during questioning. If petitioner nonetheless lacked "a full and complete appreciation of all of the consequences flowing" from his waiver, it does not defeat the State's showing that the information it provided to him satisfied the constitutional minimum.

Our conclusion is supported by petitioner's inability, in the proceedings before this Court, to articulate with precision what additional information should have been provided to him before he would have been competent to waive his right to counsel. All that petitioner's brief and reply brief suggest is petitioner should have been made aware of his "right under the Sixth Amendment to the broad protection of counsel" - a rather nebulous suggestion - and the "gravity of his situation." But surely this latter "requirement" (if it is one) was met when Officer Gresham informed petitioner that he had been formally charged with the murder of James Jackson. Under close questioning on this same point at argument, petitioner likewise failed to suggest any meaningful additional information that he should have been, but was not, provided in advance of his decision to waive his right to counsel. The discussions found in favorable court decisions, on which petitioner relies, are similarly lacking.

As a general matter, then, an accused who is admonished with the warnings prescribed by this Court in Miranda has been sufficiently apprised of the nature of his Sixth Amendment rights, and of the consequences of abandoning those rights, so that his waiver on this basis will be considered a knowing and intelligent one. We consequently reject petitioner's argument, which has some acceptance from courts and commentators, that since "the sixth amendment right to counsel is far superior to that of the fifth amendment right" and since "the greater the right the greater the loss from a waiver of that right," waiver of an accused's Sixth Amendment right to counsel should be "more difficult" to effectuate than waiver of a suspect's Fifth Amendment rights. While our cases have recognized a "difference" between the Fifth Amendment and Sixth Amendment rights to counsel, and the "policies" behind these constitutional guarantees, we have never suggested that one right is "superior" or "greater" than the other, nor is there any support in our cases for the notion that because a Sixth Amendment right may be involved, it is more difficult to waive than the Fifth Amendment counterpart.

Instead, we have taken a more pragmatic approach to the waiver question - asking what purposes a lawyer can serve at the particular stage of the proceedings in question, and what assistance he could provide to an accused at that stage - to determine the scope of the Sixth Amendment right to counsel, and the type of warnings and procedures that should be required before a waiver of that right will be recognized.

Before confessing to the murder of James Jackson, petitioner was meticulously informed by authorities of his right to counsel, and of the consequences of any choice not to exercise that right. On two separate occasions, petitioner elected to forgo the assistance of counsel, and speak directly to officials concerning his role in the murder. Because we believe that petitioner's waiver of his Sixth Amendment rights was "knowing and intelligent," we find no error in the decision of the trial court to permit petitioner's confessions to be used against him. Consequently, the judgment of the Illinois Supreme Court is Affirmed.

JUSTICE BLACKMUN, dissenting. I agree with most of what JUSTICE STEVENS says in his dissenting opinion, I however, merely would hold that after formal adversary proceedings against a defendant have been commenced, the Sixth Amendment mandates that the defendant not be "subject to further interrogation by the authorities until counsel has been made available to him, unless the accused himself initiates further communication, exchanges, or conversations with the police." The Court's majority concludes: "The fact that petitioner's Sixth Amendment right came into existence with his indictment . . . does not distinguish him from the preindictment interrogatee whose right to counsel is in existence and available for his exercise while he is questioned." I must disagree. "When the Constitution grants protection against criminal proceedings without the assistance of counsel, counsel must be furnished whether or not the accused requested the appointment of counsel." (Carnley v. Cochran, 369 U.S. 506, 513 1962). In my view, the Sixth Amendment does not allow the prosecution to take undue advantage of any gap between the commencement of the adversary process and the time at which counsel is appointed for a defendant.

JUSTICE STEVENS, with whom JUSTICE BRENNAN and JUSTICE MARSHALL join, dissenting. The Court should not condone unethical forms of trial preparation by prosecutors or their investigators. In civil litigation it is improper for a lawyer to communicate with his or her adversary's client without either notice to opposing counsel or the permission of the court. An attempt to obtain evidence for use at trial by going behind the back of one's adversary would be not only a serious breach of professional ethics but also a manifestly unfair form of trial practice.

In the criminal context, the same ethical rules apply and, in my opinion, notions of fairness that are at least as demanding should also be enforced.

After a jury has been empaneled and a criminal trial is in progress, it would obviously be improper for the prosecutor to conduct a private interview with the defendant for the purpose of obtaining evidence to be used against him at trial. Even if such an interview were to be commenced by giving the defendant the five items of legal advice that are mandated by Miranda, I have no doubt that this Court would promptly and unanimously condemn such a shabby practice. As our holding in Michigan v. Jackson, 475 U.S. 625 (1986), suggests, such a practice would not simply constitute a serious ethical violation, but would rise to the level of an impairment of the Sixth Amendment right to counsel.

The question that this case raises, therefore, is at what point in the adversary process does it become impermissible for the prosecutor, or his or her agents, to conduct such private interviews with the opposing party? Several alternatives are conceivable: when the trial commences, when the defendant has actually met and accepted representation by his or her appointed counsel, when counsel is appointed, or when the adversary process commences. In my opinion, the Sixth Amendment right to counsel demands that a firm and unequivocal line be drawn at the point at which adversary proceedings commence.

In prior cases this Court has used strong language to emphasize the significance of the formal commencement of adversary proceedings. Such language has been employed to explain decisions denying the defendant the benefit of the protection of the Sixth Amendment in preindictment settings, but an evenhanded interpretation of the Amendment would support the view that additional protection should automatically attach the moment the formal proceedings begin. Today, in reaching a decision similarly favorable to the interest in law enforcement unfettered by process concerns, the Court backs away from the significance previously attributed to the initiation of formal proceedings. In the majority's view, the purported waiver of counsel in this case is properly equated with that of an unindicted suspect. The return of an indictment, or like instrument, substantially alters the relationship between the state and the accused. Moreover, the return of an indictment also presumably signals the government's conclusion that it has sufficient evidence to establish a prima facie case. As a result, any further interrogation can only be designed to buttress the government's case; authorities are no longer simply attempting to solve a crime. Given the significance of the initiation of formal proceedings and the concomitant shift in the relationship between the state and the accused, I think it quite wrong to suggest that Miranda warnings - or for that matter, any warnings offered by an adverse party - provide a sufficient basis for permitting the undoubtedly prejudicial - and, in my view, unfair - practice of permitting trained law enforcement personnel and prosecuting attorneys to communicate with as-of-yet unrepresented criminal defendants.

It is well settled that there is a strong presumption against waiver of Sixth Amendment protections. Warnings offered by an opposing party, whether detailed or cursory, simply cannot satisfy this high standard. The majority premises its conclusion that Miranda warnings lay a sufficient basis for accepting a waiver of the right to counsel on the assumption that those warnings make clear to an accused "what a lawyer could `do for him' during the postindictment questioning: namely, advise him to refrain from making any incriminating statements." Yet, this is surely a gross understatement of the disadvantage of proceeding without a lawyer and an understatement of what a defendant must understand to make a knowing waiver. The Miranda warnings do not, for example, inform the accused that a lawyer might examine the indictment for legal sufficiency before submitting his or her client to interrogation or that a lawyer is likely to be considerably more skillful at negotiating a plea bargain and that such negotiations may be most fruitful if initiated prior to any interrogation. Rather, the warnings do not even go so far as to explain to the accused the nature of the charges pending against him - advice that a court would insist upon before allowing a defendant to enter a guilty plea with or without the presence of an attorney. Without defining precisely the nature of the inquiry required to establish a valid waiver of the Sixth Amendment right to counsel, it must be conceded that at least minimal advice is necessary - the accused must be told of the "dangers and disadvantages of self-representation."

Yet, once it is conceded that certain advice is required and that after indictment the adversary relationship between the state and the accused has solidified, it inescapably follows that a prosecutor may not conduct private interviews with a charged defendant. As at least one Court of Appeals has recognized, there are ethical constraints that prevent a prosecutor from giving legal advice to an uncounseled adversary. Thus, neither the prosecutor nor his or her agents can ethically provide the unrepresented defendant with the kind of advice that should precede an evidence-gathering interview after formal proceedings have been commenced. Indeed, in my opinion even the Miranda warnings themselves are a species of legal advice that is improper when given by the prosecutor after indictment.

Moreover, there are good reasons why such advice is deemed unethical, reasons that extend to the custodial, postindictment setting with unequaled strength. First, the offering of legal advice may lead an accused to underestimate the prosecuting authorities' true adversary posture. For an incarcerated defendant - in this case, a 17-year-old who had been in custody for 44 hours at the time he was told of the indictment - the assistance of someone to explain why he is being held, the nature of the charges against him, and the extent of his legal rights, may be of such importance as to overcome what is perhaps obvious to most, that the prosecutor is a foe and not a friend. Second, the adversary posture of the parties, which is not fully solidified until formal charges are brought, will inevitably tend to color the advice offered. As hard as a prosecutor might try, I doubt that it is possible for one to wear the hat of an effective adviser to a criminal defendant while at the same time wearing the hat of a law enforcement authority. Finally, regardless of whether or not the accused actually understands the legal and factual issues involved and the state's role as an adversary party, advice offered by a lawyer (or his or her agents) with such an evident conflict of interest cannot help but create a public perception of unfairness and unethical conduct. This interest is a factor that may be considered in deciding whether to override a defendant's waiver of his or her Sixth Amendment right to conflict-free representation, and likewise, should be considered in determining whether a waiver based on advice offered by the criminal defendant's adversary is ever appropriate.

In sum, without a careful discussion of the pitfalls of proceeding without counsel, the Sixth Amendment right cannot properly be waived. An adversary party, moreover, cannot adequately provide such advice. As a result, once the right to counsel attaches and the adversary relationship between the state and the accused solidifies, a prosecutor cannot conduct a private interview with an accused party without "diluting the protection afforded by the right to counsel." Although this ground alone is reason enough to never permit such private interviews, the rule also presents the added virtue of drawing a clear and easily identifiable line at the point between the investigatory and adversary stages of a criminal proceeding. Such clarity in definition of constitutional rules that govern criminal proceedings is important to the law enforcement profession as well as to the private citizen. It is true, of course, that the interest in effective law enforcement would benefit from an opportunity to engage in incommunicado questioning of defendants who, for reasons beyond their control, have not been able to receive the legal advice from counsel to which they are constitutionally entitled. But the Court's singleminded concentration on that interest might also lead to the toleration of similar practices at any stage of the trial. I think it clear that such private communications are intolerable not simply during trial, but at any point after adversary proceedings have commenced. I therefore respectfully dissent.

REVIEW SECTION

READING COMPREHENSION

What is the purpose of a *Miranda* warning?

Detail the logic of the court in *Miranda v. Arizona* (1966).

Detail the facts of this case, including a discussion of the Sixth Amendment.

THINKING CRITICALLY

Do you believe *Miranda* has had a positive, negative, or neutral effect on law enforcement? Elaborate your rationale.

Use majority and dissenting opinions to articulate how you would decide this case.

SECTION 4: THE WAIVER OF RIGHTS TO COUNSEL AND TO REMAIN SILENT

OVERVIEW

So, how do we decide if an individual has waived their right to remain silent and to have an attorney present? The court has adopted an implied waiver test which essentially means that the totality of the circumstances in each individual case must prove that the suspect was aware of their rights and gave those rights up voluntarily. A confession is thus considered involuntary if government officials engaged in coercion during interrogation and that this coercion caused the suspect to make incriminating statements. Interrogating officers are still permitted to make promises, false and misleading statements, or appeal to the defendant's emotions, without risking the voluntary nature of the confession. The essential element to remember is that *Miranda* was intended to remove coercion from the interrogation process, not to remove the element of pressure.

CASE

At issue in *People v Villalobos* is whether the defendant invoked his fifth amendment right to counsel by filing a form at a bond hearing that stated defendant would not participate in "any questioning, identification process or other procedures on any case or matter" without his counsel present. The appellate court concluded that he did not. This case allows the defendant's petition for leave to appeal and affirms the judgment of the appellate court.

PEOPLE V. VILLALOBOS
737 N.E.2d 639 (2000)

On November 13, 1994, Ronnie Johnson was shot and killed. The evidence at defendant's trial for Johnson's murder established that at 3:30 a.m. on November 13, defendant and four friends drove south on the Dan Ryan Expressway, with defendant in the front passenger seat of the car. The car encountered a white Cadillac, driven by Johnson. Although the testimony is conflicting, it appears that Johnson increased his speed, and defendant told the driver of his car to accelerate and follow Johnson. Defendant then leaned out of the car and fired nine shots at Johnson's car. One bullet entered the left side of Johnson's head and killed him. Roughly 45 minutes after this shooting, defendant and his friends were arrested for possession of cannabis and drinking on a public way-an offense unrelated to Johnson's killing.

On November 14, 1994, defendant appeared at a bond hearing on the possession of cannabis charge. At the bond hearing, defendant signed a form entitled "Appearance, Notice of Representation and Demand for Preliminary Hearing/Trial" (hereinafter, appearance form). In addition to documenting both the assistant public defender's and defendant's demand for a preliminary hearing and trial, the appearance form contained a section stating: "BE ADVISED, the under-signed defendant serves this NOTICE OF REPRESENTATION on the State, its agents and on all law enforcement officers barring the defendant's participation, without the presence of his/her counsel, in any questioning, identification process or other procedures on any case or matter whatsoever." Defendant did not post bond and proceeded to Cook County jail.

On November 16, 1994, pursuant to a writ, two Chicago police officers removed defendant from jail and brought him to police headquarters in order to question him relative to Johnson's death. After being advised of his Miranda rights and waiving them in writing, defendant provided a written statement in the presence of an assistant State's Attorney and a police officer, in which he confessed to the shooting. Defendant was subsequently arrested and charged with Johnson's murder. Defendant moved to suppress his statement prior to the murder trial. In his motion to suppress, defendant argued that by signing and filing the appearance form, which attempted to bar his participation in any questioning on any case or matter, he provided notice to the prosecution that he did not wish to speak to any law enforcement personnel without the assistance of counsel. The assistant public defender who represented defendant at his bond hearing on the cannabis charge testified at defendant's motion to suppress that the appearance form was a "standard form" that she prepared for every defendant whom she represented. The circuit court denied defendant's motion to suppress, finding that the additional language on the appearance form regarding defendant's unwillingness to speak with law enforcement personnel in "any case" was "surplusage" and bound law enforcement personnel only on the cannabis offense. The inculpatory statement was subsequently introduced at defendant's bench trial for the murder of Ronnie Johnson. The circuit court found defendant guilty.

Defendant appealed his conviction on the ground that the denial of his motion to suppress constituted error. He argued that, by signing and filing the appearance form during his bond hearing on the cannabis charge, he invoked his fifth amendment right to counsel pursuant to Miranda. Police officers violated that right when they subsequently questioned him on an unrelated offense without his counsel being present. The appellate court affirmed defendant's conviction. Defendant appeals the appellate court's determination that the motion to suppress was properly denied because defendant failed to invoke his fifth amendment right to counsel pursuant to Miranda.

Miranda v. Arizona, 384 U.S. 436, 16 L. Ed. 2d 694, 86 S. Ct. 1602 (1966), the United States Supreme Court required that certain procedural safeguards be provided to a suspect before custodial interrogation. Although not enumerated in the Constitution, the Supreme Court found these safeguards necessary in order to protect the privilege against compulsory self-incrimination under the fifth amendment. Specifically, the Court required that a person in custody be advised of certain rights, including the right to remain silent and the right to an attorney, prior to any interrogation by law enforcement. Edwards v. Arizona further expanded Miranda and held that once a person invokes his right to counsel during custodial interrogation, he "is not subject to further interrogation by the authorities until counsel has been made available to him, unless the accused himself initiates further communication, exchanges, or conversations with the police."

The single issue presented in this appeal is whether defendant invoked his Miranda right to counsel when, at a bond hearing, the defendant signed a notice of appearance form which included a statement that the defendant would not participate in any future questioning on any matter without his attorney present. There is no dispute that defendant was in custody while at his bond hearing. There is also no dispute that defendant was not subject to interrogation at that time. Nevertheless, defendant argues that he effectively invoked his Miranda right to counsel by filing the appearance form at his bond hearing. Therefore, defendant argues his Miranda right to counsel may be invoked prior to custodial interrogation.

The United States Supreme Court has not directly answered the issue before this court. However, the Court has strongly suggested that a defendant cannot anticipatorily invoke his Miranda right to counsel at a preliminary hearing. An overwhelming number of federal courts have also held that a defendant cannot invoke his Miranda rights outside the context of custodial interrogation. It is not surprising that virtually every Supreme Court opinion involving Miranda has used the phrase "custodial interrogation." It is custodial interrogation with which Miranda was concerned. It is the right to an attorney during custodial interrogation that Miranda and its progeny protects. That right does not exist outside the context of custodial interrogation. One cannot invoke a right that does not yet exist. While in court on a bond hearing, a defendant is not subject to interrogation, and the need for Miranda is not yet present.

In support of the argument that his Miranda rights had attached at his bond hearing, defendant cites to <u>United States v. Kelsey, 951 F.2d 1196 (10th Cir. 1991)</u>, and <u>North Carolina v. Torres, 330 N.C. 517, 412 S.E.2d 20 (1992)</u>. Defendant's reliance on these decisions is misplaced, as both cases are factually inapposite. Unlike the matter at bar, both Kelsey and Torres involved situations where the defendant's interrogation was imminent when he or she requested counsel. Interrogation was not imminent in the case at bar. Defendant was in court on an unrelated crime when he attempted to invoke his Miranda right to counsel. There was no suggestion that defendant would be questioned on the crime with which he was charged or any other crime subsequent to his bond hearing. In fact, defendant's interrogation regarding the Johnson murder occurred two days after his bond hearing.

The defendant points out that under <u>Edwards and Arizona v. Roberson, 486 U.S. 675, 100 L. Ed. 2d 704, 108 S. Ct. 2093 (1988)</u>, once a suspect invokes his right to counsel pursuant to Miranda, he may not be interrogated again regarding any offense unless he initiates the conversation. Therefore, the defendant further notes, if an accused invokes his Miranda right to counsel when in custody for one offense, law enforcement personnel cannot question him on that offense or any unrelated offense without counsel present. However, the suspect must invoke the right to counsel during custodial interrogation or when custodial interrogation was imminent. Defendant also argues that he should be allowed to assert his Miranda rights at a bond hearing because "if a defendant remains in continuous custody the only verifiable assertion of his Fifth Amendment right to counsel is one made before a judge." According to defendant, unless the Miranda right to counsel is asserted in open court in the presence of a judge, "the only witnesses to a request for counsel would be the very officers whose objective it is to obtain a statement." We disagree. If we were to accept defendant's argument, we would have to require a judge to be present every time a suspect receives Miranda warnings. Although Miranda and its progeny demand certain procedural safeguards to uphold a person's fifth amendment right against compulsory incrimination, no case has required that an independent third party be present to attest that a suspect was advised of or waived his Miranda rights.

Stretching Miranda to allow anticipatory invocations of the right to counsel would extend Miranda far beyond its boundaries and upset the very balance that Miranda sought to protect-the balance between effective law enforcement and protection of individual rights. In order to invoke the Miranda right to counsel, an individual must be both in custody and subject to interrogation or under imminent threat of interrogation. In the case at bar, defendant was not subject to interrogation at the bond hearing. We therefore hold that defendant could not effectively invoke his Miranda right to counsel at the bond hearing. Defendant's motion to suppress was correctly denied. We note that the State moved to strike portions of defendant's reply brief. We ordered that motion taken with the case and now deny it. For the foregoing reasons, we affirm the judgment of the appellate court. Affirmed.

JUSTICE HEIPLE, dissenting: Today's majority opinion erroneously holds that police may interrogate a criminal suspect in their custody without an attorney present, even after that suspect has clearly and unambiguously requested the assistance of an attorney in dealing with custodial interrogation. I therefore dissent. From a purely policy perspective, the rule announced by the majority is a bad one. After today, police arresting a suspect will no longer have any reason to inform a suspect of his Miranda rights until immediately before they initiate questioning. Indeed, under the rationale of the majority, police may now freely interrogate a suspect who states "I refuse to answer questions without a lawyer" as the police are applying the handcuffs, as long as the police wait until later to ask any questions. In such a scenario, the suspect's request for counsel would have been made at a time when interrogation was not imminent. Accordingly, the majority would hold that such a suspect had no fifth amendment right to invoke. Such a result is clearly inconsistent with the values which the Miranda decision was meant to protect.

The majority's concern that a person could invoke the fifth amendment right to counsel even before arrest, is directed at a straw man. The defendant in this case did not attempt to invoke his right to counsel by letter prior to arrest. On the contrary, defendant was in continuous police custody from the time he requested an attorney to assist him during interrogation until the time when the interrogation took place. In any event, giving effect to the defendant's clear and unambiguous request for counsel under the facts of this case would not require this court to expand the right to the extremes supposed by the majority. Rather, this court should rule that the fifth amendment right to counsel attaches and may be invoked by a defendant at any time after he is taken into custody. This rule would strike a proper balance between the recognition of a suspect's right to be free from compelled self-incrimination and the interests of law enforcement in obtaining evidence. This court should further hold that the State was bound in this case to honor defendant's request not to be questioned without his attorney present, and that police questioning in spite of this request violated defendant's constitutional rights under the fifth amendment. Accordingly, the trial court erred when it denied defendant's motion to suppress his confession. Defendant is entitled to a new trial. Accordingly, I respectfully dissent. CHIEF JUSTICE HARRISON joins in this dissent.

REVIEW SECTION

READING COMPREHENSION

Detail the facts of this case and the relevance, or lack thereof, of the appearance form.

THINKING CRITICALLY

Agree or disagree with the following statement made by the majority: "Stretching Miranda to allow anticipatory invocations of the right to counsel would extend Miranda far beyond its boundaries and upset the very balance that Miranda sought to protect-the balance between effective law enforcement and protection of individual rights. In order to invoke the Miranda right to counsel, an individual must be both in custody and subject to interrogation or under imminent threat of interrogation."

CONCLUSION

Three provisions in the U.S. Constitution, which are mirrored in the Illinois Constitution, develop guidelines to oversee police interrogation and confession: the self-incrimination clause, the due process clause, and the right-to-counsel clause. This chapter examined police interrogation and confession through an elaboration of the interrogation and confession setting, the Constitution and self-incrimination, the application of *Miranda v. Arizona* in Illinois case law, and the waiver of rights to counsel and to remain silent. This chapter made evident several of the court's 'bright-line' rules with respect to garnering of evidence by government officials.

Chapter Nine

Identification Procedures

For government officials to determine that a crime was committed is significantly less intensive than proving who committed such a crime. While recent technological advances such as DNA have improved the ability of the government to identify a suspect, eyewitness identification in the form of lineups, show-ups, and photo identification is debatable in its reliability, especially when the suspect is of another race than the person involved in identification.

This chapter will review:

(1)   The risks of mistaken eyewitness identification;

(2)   The Constitution and identification procedures; and

(3)   DNA profile identification.

SECTION 1: THE RISKS OF MISTAKEN EYEWITNESS IDENTIFICATION

OVERVIEW

If the goal of the American criminal justice system is punishment of those who are guilty and freedom for the innocent, then eyewitness identification throws a wrench into this goal. As mentioned in your text, almost half of all wrongful convictions occur due to mistaken identifications. These mistakes are a result of a myriad of elements such as perception, memory, suggestion, and recall. Both perception and attention influence how we see events and psychologists have determined that our brain does not record images exactly as we see them. When examining a crime committed by a stranger, our perception is influenced by how long we observed the stranger, any distractions that may have been occurring simultaneously, our focus of observation, any stress we may have been under at the time, and the race of both you and the stranger in question. As well, our memory fades during the first few hours after an event, however our confidence in our recollection increases. Finally, when presented with a lineup, shop-up or photo identification by police, most individuals feel they need to choose the best likeness of the perpetrator given the choices provided. 725 ILCS 5/Art. 107A elaborates the procedure in Illinois regarding lineups and photo spreads:

> (a) All lineups shall be photographed or otherwise recorded. These
> photographs shall be disclosed to the accused and his or her
> defense counsel during discovery proceedings as provided in
> Illinois Supreme Court Rules. All photographs of suspects shown
> to an eyewitness during the photo spread shall be disclosed to the
> accused and his or her defense counsel during discovery

proceedings as provided in Illinois Supreme Court Rules. (b) Each eyewitness who views a lineup or photo spread shall sign a form containing the following information: (1) The suspect might not be in the lineup or photo spread and the eyewitness is not obligated to make an identification. (2) The eyewitness should not assume that the person administering the lineup or photo spread knows which person is the suspect in the case. (c) Suspects in a lineup or photo spread should not appear to be substantially different from "fillers" or "distracters" in the lineup or photo spread, based on the eyewitness' previous description of the perpetrator, or based on other factors that would draw attention to the suspect.

All of these factors combine to form very shaky ground on which the criminal justice system relies in proving guilt beyond a reasonable doubt. The problem: given all these obstacles to observing and recalling an event involving a stranger, are eyewitness testimonies enough to prove guilt beyond a reasonable doubt?

CASE

A jury convicted defendant of first degree murder. The State's evidence consisted of four eyewitnesses who identified the defendant as the shooter in a drive-by shooting. The trial court sentenced him to 35 years in prison. In *Tisdel v People,* the defendant appeals, arguing that the trial court erred in (1) refusing to allow expert testimony regarding eyewitness identification; (2) admitting nonidentification lineup testimony; (3) admitting testimony regarding the identification of his codefendant; and (4) allowing lineup photographs to go back to the jury. Defendant also argues that he received ineffective assistance of counsel based on his trial counsel's failure to object to the nonidentification testimony and testimony regarding his codefendant. As you read this case, ponder the question: When the sole issue in a criminal prosecution is one of identity and the sole incriminating evidence is eyewitness testimony, should the court admit expert testimony upon the factors that affect the reliability of eyewitness identification?

TISDEL V. PEOPLE
739 N.E.2d 31 (2000)

On August 19, 1996, three eyewitnesses identified defendant from a lineup as the passenger who shot Julio Lagunas in a September 3, 1995, drive-by shooting. He was arrested and charged with first degree murder. The driver of the car, Mark Robinson, had already been arrested and charged in connection with the crime. On September 12, 1997, a fourth eyewitness picked defendant out of a lineup as the shooter. Defendant filed motions in *limine* to quash his arrest and suppress the lineup identifications. The trial court denied the motions. Defendant also filed a motion in *limine* to allow expert testimony on eyewitness identification. Defense counsel asserted that Dr. Elizabeth Loftus would testify regarding the scientific bases for eyewitness identification and identify certain areas where jurors hold misconceptions about the identification process. Defendant's written offer of proof alleged that Dr. Loftus would discuss several factors beyond the knowledge of the average lay person that affect a witness' ability to recall. Specifically, she would have testified about the latest scientific research concerning the passage of time between the incident and the identification; the lack of correlation between the certainty with which a witness makes an identification and the validity of that identification; the effect of stress on a witness; weapon focus; and cross-racial identification. Although the trial court found Dr. Loftus' curriculum vitae to be "extremely impressive," it determined that her testimony would not ordinarily be beyond the normal knowledge of the average person and in this case would be more confusing than it would be helpful; however, it did not deny the motion because such testimony might not, in the appropriate case, be proper. Consequently, the trial court denied the motion.

At trial, the State called Gerardo Quiroz. Gerardo testified that on September 3, 1995, he was standing on the sidewalk outside Clark Mall. His friend Jose Ramos was making a call on a pay phone at the mall entrance. The parking lot was next to the entrance of the mall. Gerardo's brother, Osvaldo, was standing near Jose. Gerardo observed a car black Camaro with tinted windows, chrome wheels, and two tailpipes. The side windows of the car were down. The car pulled into the mall entrance and stopped near the phones. The two men inside the car attempted to talk to some girls who were heading toward the mall entrance. After the girls entered the mall, the car drove toward the back of the parking lot, turned right, and came through the middle of the lot. The car stopped on the sidewalk before turning into the street. At this point, Gerardo was closer to Jose, and the car was approximately 30 to 40 feet from them when Gerardo saw the passenger pull out a gun and point it at them. Gerardo testified that he tried to hide behind a nearby brick pillar but was able to focus on the face of the passenger. Gerardo identified defendant as the passenger.

Gerardo saw Francisco Curonel standing across the street in front of Touhy Park as Gerardo and Jose followed the car on the Touhy Park side of the street. Osvaldo remained on the mall side of the street. Francisco attempted to "hit" the car with something but missed. The passenger took out the gun and pointed it at Francisco, who ducked. Osvaldo crossed the street from the mall side. Gerardo saw Julio Lagunas and Ulysses Renteria, who died before the trial started. The car stopped, and Gerardo "saw a hand sticking out" from the passenger side of the car. At this point, Gerardo was at the Jarvis intersection north of the mall. There was a gun in the passenger's hand, and it was pointed toward Julio and Ulysses when Gerardo heard a gunshot. The car then sped up and took off. Gerardo ran up to Julio and Ulysses. Jose was already there, and Osvaldo arrived immediately thereafter. Osvaldo went home before the police arrived. Gerardo, Jose, Francisco, and Ulysses described the car to the police and were taken to the 24th District police station where they viewed the car.

Gerardo testified that he was then taken to Belmont and Western station to talk to detectives. Gerardo described the passenger as a 23-year-old skinny black male with braided hair and a light complexion. He viewed a lineup but was unable to identify anyone. On August 16, 1996, Gerardo viewed another lineup and recognized the second person from the left as the passenger, whom he identified as the defendant, and he also identified People's exhibit 14 as a picture of the lineup placing an "X" over the passenger's head. During cross-examination, when defense counsel asked Gerardo if he was initially 30 to 40 feet away from Jose and Osvaldo, he answered "no." Defense counsel attempted to impeach him with testimony he apparently gave during

Robinson's trial. Gerardo did not remember testifying that Jose and Osvaldo were 30 to 40 feet away from him. The parties stipulated that on July 10, 1997, Gerardo testified that he was on the sidewalk on the side of the mall and that Osvaldo and Jose were 30 or 40 feet away from him. Gerardo explained that when the car first pulled into the lot, he saw two black males but couldn't tell what they looked like at that point. Gerardo admitted that he talked with the others about what they saw when they went to view the first lineup. He did not remember talking to Osvaldo and Francisco when he viewed the lineup a year later nor did he remember what the passenger was wearing, but he did remember that the passenger had braids close to his head with beads on the end. He told the police at the scene about the braids.

The State called Osvaldo Quiroz next. Osvaldo identified defendant as the passenger. On September 12, 1995, Osvaldo spoke with the police at Belmont and Western and looked at some pictures. He identified the driver from a photograph the police showed him. Osvaldo told them he was "pretty sure that was the guy but he needed to see him in person." Osvaldo went back to the station on September 21, 1995, to view a lineup. Gerardo was there too, but Osvaldo did not talk to Gerardo before viewing the lineup. He identified Robinson as the driver. There was a person in the lineup who had corn rows or braids in his hair, but it was not defendant. On August 16, 1996, Osvaldo saw another lineup. Ulysses, Gerardo, Jose, and Francisco were also there but Osvaldo did not talk with them before viewing the lineup. Osvaldo identified People's exhibit 17 as a picture of the lineup and identified defendant as the person he identified. Osvaldo put an "X" over defendant's head.

The State called Francisco Curonel next, who testified that he was by himself near Touhy Park. The driver was black and had short hair, a bald head, a goatee, and was wearing a black T-shirt. The car turned into the mall, which was approximately 15 feet away from where he was standing. The police took him, Ulysses, Jose, and Gerardo to the 24th District, where he saw the car. The police then took them to view a lineup. Francisco was "90 percent sure" he saw the driver. He described the passenger as a black male, about 25 to 28, with a skinny face and braided hair close to his head. Francisco went back to Belmont and Western on August 16, 1996, to view another lineup. He identified People's exhibit 26 as a picture of the lineup. He identified the shooter and put an "X" over the head of that person. Francisco testified that he saw the lineup by himself and did not have a chance to talk with Gerardo or Osvaldo after viewing it.

The State then called Jose Ramos, who testified that he was on the pay phone. A black IROC Camaro stopped right in front of him on the sidewalk. The windows were down, and he could see two males. The passenger was smoking marijuana, and there was a gun between the seats. The passenger grabbed the gun and put it between his legs. The passenger had braids. He identified defendant as the passenger. The car went around the lot and came out the middle. Before turning left onto Clark, defendant pointed the gun at him. Jose saw Francisco across the street. Francisco tried to throw something at the car and then hit the ground when defendant pointed the gun at him. Jose ran across the street to Francisco. The car went through a red light. Jose saw Julio trying to cross the street. The car pulled up to the sidewalk right next to Julio. A shot came from the passenger side of the car, after which the car kept going. Jose and Francisco ran up to where Julio was lying. Osvaldo and Gerardo were there too. After giving a description of the car to the police, they were taken to the 24th District. Jose saw the car in the parking lot in back of the station. Jose described the passenger as 21 to 25 years old, dark skinned, with braids. He looked at a lineup that night but was unable to identify anyone. On September 12, 1997, Jose saw another lineup and identified defendant as the passenger. Jose identified People's exhibit 30 as a picture of the lineup and put an "X" over the person he identified.

Officer Gaskew testified that he obtained a description of the car from the witnesses at the scene. The witnesses told him the passenger was wearing dark clothing and had braids or corn rows in his hair. Their description did not include beads in the passenger's hair. Officer Floyd Eppling testified that he was driving a squad car when he received a message about a vehicle wanted in connection with a shooting. Officer Eppling saw a car that matched the description. The driver's window was down part way, and he saw two black people in front. The passenger had either braids or waves with multicolored beads. He could not tell if the person was male or female. There was too much traffic to make an immediate U-turn, but he eventually caught up to the car and pulled it over; however, the passenger was no longer in the car. He brought the driver to the 24th District and his partner drove the car to the station. The crime scene was about 2-1/2 miles from where he pulled the car over. During cross-examination, Officer Eppling stated that he saw the car about five minutes after receiving the message. The passenger's braids were about shoulder length, hanging, with multicolored beads. He could not see the passenger's face.

Detective Greg Pattitsis interviewed Francisco at the 24th District. Francisco tentatively identified Robinson as the driver. Francisco said "it looked like the individual that was driving the car, but he wasn't sure." Gerardo and Jose did not identify anyone. He also interviewed Osvaldo a few days later. Osvaldo described the passenger as 23 to 28 years old, dark complected, with braided hair and curls or strands in the back with black, white, and blue beads. Osvaldo picked Robinson out of a photo array as the driver but asked to see him in person. Osvaldo picked Robinson out of a lineup as the driver.

On August 16, 1996, defendant was brought to Area 3. Gerardo, Osvaldo, and Francisco came to the station and viewed a lineup. They identified defendant as the passenger. Detective Pattitsis identified People's Exhibit 41 as an individual picture of defendant taken from the lineup. Defendant was 21 years old at the time, 5 feet 9 inches, 155 pounds, and had a braided hairstyle. On September 12, 1997, Jose viewed a lineup at the county jail. Jose identified defendant as the passenger. Detective Pattitsis identified People's exhibit 42 as an individual picture of defendant taken from the lineup. Defendant had a different hairstyle than the one he had in August.

During cross-examination, Detective Schorsch admitted that he had complained about the lighting conditions during the second lineup but was told they could not be improved. On redirect, he testified that he could see the participants before they stepped up to the viewing window. Defendant's motion for a directed finding was denied.

The defense first called Patrick Moran, the forensic investigator who lifted fingerprints from the car. The defense next called Richard McGrath, an expert in latent fingerprint identification. He examined the latent fingerprints recovered from the car. Only two were suitable for comparison with fingerprints in the automated fingerprint identification system. There were no positive comparisons. He was asked to compare the latent prints to fingerprints of Robinson and defendant. Robinson's matched, but defendant's did not. On cross-examination, he testified that fingerprints are not necessarily left behind every time a person touches a surface and that it cannot be determined how long a fingerprint has been in a particular place. The trial court's instruction to the jury included the following: "When you weigh the identification testimony of a witness, you should consider all the facts and circumstances in evidence including but not limited to the following: The opportunity the witness had to view the offender at the time of the offense or the witness's degree of attention at the time of the offense; or the witness' earlier description of the offender; or the level of certainty shown by the witness when confronting the defendant; or the length of time between the offense and the identification confrontation."

The trial court allowed the lineup photographs to go back with the jury over defense counsel's objection. The jury found defendant guilty of first degree murder.

On November 21, 1997, defendant filed a motion for a new trial or judgment notwithstanding the verdict. At the hearing, defense counsel argued that the defense should have been allowed to present expert testimony concerning eyewitness identification. Before ruling, the trial judge stated that he "would have weighed the evidence differently and that he was not personally convinced based on the evidence that defendant was proven guilty beyond a reasonable doubt." However, the trial court denied the motion, finding that there was a rational basis to find defendant guilty. The trial court sentenced defendant to 35 years' imprisonment.

Defendant argues that he is entitled to a new trial because the State impermissibly attempted to bolster its case by having Gerardo, Osvaldo, and Jose testify that, prior to viewing the lineup from which they identified defendant, they viewed another lineup from which they did not identify anyone as being the passenger. Defendant was not in this initial lineup. Defendant concedes that he has waived this issue for review since he did not object to the testimony at trial or in his posttrial motion. However, defendant urges us to apply the plain error rule. The plain error doctrine may be applied where the evidence is closely balanced or where the error is of such magnitude that it denied the accused a fair trial. The State maintains that the evidence is overwhelming since four eyewitnesses identified defendant as the shooter.

Unless vague or doubtful, eyewitness identification of an accused will sustain a conviction if the witness viewed the accused under circumstances permitting a positive identification. Factors to consider in determining whether an identification is reliable are: (1) the opportunity the witness had to view the offender at the time of the offense; (2) the witness' degree of attention; (3) the accuracy of the witness' prior description of the offender; (4) the level of certainty demonstrated by the witness at the identification confrontation; and (5) the length of time between the incident and the identification confrontation. A reviewing court cannot substitute its own judgment for that of the trier of fact on questions involving the credibility of witnesses or the weight of the evidence.

In this case, none of the eyewitnesses knew defendant or viewed him for a considerable length of time. There was no physical evidence linking defendant to the crime, and defendant was not arrested near the scene. Defendant did not confess, and Robinson did not testify. Although all four eyewitnesses independently identified defendant in lineups and in court, we cannot ignore the substantial amount of time that elapsed between the offense and the lineup identifications. Osvaldo, Gerardo, and Francisco picked defendant out of a lineup almost a year after the shooting. Jose picked defendant out of a lineup two years later. Although Osvaldo and Jose had the best opportunity to view the passenger, the driver was in their line of sight when the car was closest to them. Therefore, we agree with defendant that the evidence was closely balanced.

The State may not bolster a witness' identification of a defendant by introducing evidence that the witness failed to identify anyone else during pretrial identification procedures. Witnesses cannot testify as to statements made out of court in an effort to corroborate their trial testimony on the same subject. Here, defendant complains that the prosecutor relied on the nonidentifications to show how careful the witnesses were in their identifications of defendant. Gerardo and Jose testified that they viewed a lineup on September 3, 1995, but were unable to identify anyone. Osvaldo testified that he viewed a lineup on September 21, 1995, from which he identified the driver but not the passenger. The record establishes that the prosecutor relied on this testimony during closing argument. It is clear that the nonidentification testimony should not have been allowed because it was presented simply to corroborate the witnesses' subsequent identification of defendant. However, the error cannot be considered harmless. The cases the State relies on are inapplicable. Therefore, the trial court's error in admitting the testimony warrants reversal. As an intermediate reviewing court, we are bound to follow mandates; however, it is difficult to imagine that this is the issue upon which the jury determined the credibility of the witnesses. We agree with defendant that his trial attorney should have objected to the nonidentification testimony and raised the issue in the posttrial motion. However, defendant's ineffective assistance argument is immaterial, given our consideration of the issue under the plain error doctrine.

We now consider an issue likely to arise on remand. Defendant argues that the trial court erred by denying his motion in *limine* to admit the expert testimony of Dr. Loftus on the subject of eyewitness identification. The State argues that the trial court correctly denied defendant's request because the reliability of eyewitness identifications is not beyond the common knowledge of the average juror. In Illinois, expert testimony is generally allowed if (1) the testimony reflects generally accepted scientific or technical principles; (2) the expert's experience and qualifications afford him knowledge that is not common to lay persons; and (3) the testimony will aid the trier of fact in reaching its conclusion. The admission of eyewitness identification expert testimony is within the sound discretion of the trial court and its ruling should not be reversed absent a clear showing of abuse of that discretion. Illinois courts have uniformly upheld a trial court's refusal to allow such testimony. Again, we note that the court here has properly weighed the benefits of such testimony and has exercised its discretion in not allowing the expert to testify, rather than ruling outright that such testimony can never be probative. Other jurisdictions have found that the exclusion of expert testimony regarding eyewitness identification is an abuse of discretion.

Numerous studies in the area of eyewitness psychology indicate that there is significant potential for eyewitness error and that jurors have misconceptions about the abilities of eyewitnesses. There are two types of eyewitness identification expert testimony. The first dispels myths or attacks commonsense misconceptions about eyewitness identifications, such as the effects of stress and weapon focus on the accuracy of identifications. The second provides the jury with useful information about the kinds of mental factors involved in the identification process, such as the effect of time on the reliability of identifications, the forgetting curve, and problems with cross-racial identifications. Trial courts should carefully scrutinize the proffered testimony to determine its relevance--that is, whether there is a logical connection between the testimony and the facts of the case. Normally, expert testimony that is probative and relevant should be allowed. The trial court must also determine whether the proffered testimony would confuse or mislead the jury. We realize that other jurisdictions have formulated guidelines for trial courts to follow when considering whether to allow such testimony. However, a trial court's decision to allow or exclude eyewitness identification expert testimony must be made on a case-by-case basis. Even where cross-examination of an eyewitness and an instruction are sufficient, allowing expert testimony may still be helpful to the trier of fact.

Defendant contends that Dr. Loftus' testimony should have been admitted because it would have aided the jury in reaching a more informed decision as to the credibility of the eyewitness testimony. We find that the trial court properly exercised its discretion. The record shows that the judge considered the reliability and potential helpfulness of the testimony, balanced the proffered testimony against cases in which this court has upheld the exclusion of such evidence, and found that the testimony would not assist the jury. Additionally, the record establishes that defense counsel thoroughly cross-examined all of the eyewitnesses and that the trial court instructed the jury on the reliability of eyewitness identification. However, the trial court would not have abused its discretion had it allowed the testimony given the facts of this case.

Under certain circumstances, eyewitness identification expert testimony can assist the jury in reaching a correct decision. This is such a case. The central issue at trial involved the accuracy of the eyewitness identifications. The circumstances surrounding those identifications are questionable. Most troubling is the significant amount of time that elapsed between the crime and the identifications. There was no corroborating evidence linking defendant to the crime. Dr. Loftus' testimony would have been relevant because she would have discussed the factors that affected the reliability of the identifications in the instant case without directly commenting on the eyewitnesses' credibility. We acknowledge that the use of expert testimony could lead to battles between experts over the value of eyewitness identifications. However, "given the high stakes in criminal cases and the proven ability of judges to tailor issues and limit witnesses, a little extra time does not seem wasteful even if expert witnesses are competing for the jury's attention." As the Illinois Supreme Court noted People v. Gardner, 35 Ill. 2d 564, 572 (1966), "of all the factors that account for the conviction of the innocent, the fallibility of eye-witness identification ranks at the top."

We decline to address defendant's remaining arguments. Reversed and remanded for a new trial.

REVIEW SECTION

READING COMPREHENSION

Detail the facts of this case and the relevance of the plain error rule.

When is expert testimony permitted in Illinois?

THINKING CRITICALLY

When the sole issue in a criminal prosecution is one of identity and the sole incriminating evidence is eyewitness testimony, should the court admit expert testimony upon the factors that affect the reliability of eyewitness identification?

Should eyewitness identification alone be enough to establish proof beyond a reasonable doubt? What if the sentence is death?

SECTION 2: THE CONSTITUTION AND IDENTIFICATION PROCEDURES

OVERVIEW

As you can probably imagine, the unreliable identification that often results from eyewitness testimony can violate the Fifth and Fourteenth Amendment rights to due process. The violation of course would be that misidentification could lead to deprivation of life, liberty, or property without due process of law. While the might-or-might-not-be-present instruction and blind administrators decrease somewhat the likelihood of a misidentification, courts rarely throw out such testimony regardless of how high the misidentification risk. The problem however, is jurors usually believe this testimony.

CASE

A jury convicted the defendant of residential burglary and after denying his posttrial motion, the trial court sentenced Gonzalez to nine years' imprisonment. On appeal in *People v Gonzalez,* the defendant wants reversal of his conviction because (1) the trial court erred in admitting testimony concerning the sole eyewitness' prior identification of defendant, and (2) the State did not prove defendant's guilt beyond a reasonable doubt.

PEOPLE V. GONZALEZ
685 N.E.2d 661, 292 Ill.App.3d 280 (1997)

We first address the admissibility of the prior identification. The State called Michelle Marquez as its sole identification witness. Ms. Marquez testified that, on the afternoon of February 6, 1995, she was home watching television. After hearing a loud banging noise outside, she looked out the window but could not identify the source of the noise. A few moments later, after hearing the back gate of her neighbors' fence open and close, she again looked out the window. This time, she saw two men leaving her neighbors' backyard through the gate. Ms. Marquez went to the front window of her house and watched as the two men, who were carrying loaded grocery bags, walked away down the street. When asked to describe the two men, Ms. Marquez stated that they were both Hispanic with light brown skin, dark brown hair, and dark eyes. One of the men, who was wearing dark pants and a blue windbreaker, carried a pair of gold work gloves in the rear right pocket of his pants. The other man wore blue jeans, a waist-length tweed jacket, and a black and white "beanie." The State's Attorney then asked Ms. Marquez whether she saw either of the two men in the courtroom. Although defendant was seated at the defense table, Ms. Marquez responded, "No." Ms. Marquez explained that, although she is able to identify and describe accurately a person's clothing, she is "not good with faces at all."

Over defense counsel's objection, and notwithstanding Ms. Marquez' inability to identify defendant in open court, the trial court permitted the State then to question Ms. Marquez regarding her prior out-of-court identification of defendant. The trial court ruled that Ms. Marquez' prior identification was an exception to the hearsay rule and therefore admissible as substantive evidence under 725 ILCS 5/115-12. Ms. Marquez testified that, as the men continued to walk away, she got into her car and began to follow them. At no time while she was following the men did they dispose of the bags, split up, or join with others. After several blocks, the men entered an apartment house. Ms. Marquez returned home and called the police. The police met Ms. Marquez at her home and drove her to the apartment house. Leaving Ms. Marquez in the backseat of a squad car parked two houses down, the police entered the apartment house and arrested defendant and his brother, Ismael. After bringing defendant and his brother out of the house, the police asked Ms. Marquez whether she saw the two men who had robbed her neighbors. Pointing to the two men who the police had brought out of the house, Ms. Marquez responded, "Yes." Ms. Marquez explained that, although she never got a good look at the men's faces, she was able to identify their clothing.

The State then called Officer Zegar of the Aurora police department to identify defendant as one of the two men whom Ms. Marquez identified from the backseat of the squad car. Defendant argues that, because Ms. Marquez was unable to identify defendant in open court, the trial court should not have admitted as substantive evidence Ms. Marquez' prior identification of defendant. Instead, the trial court should have ruled the testimony inadmissible under 725 ILCS 5/115-10.1 as a prior inconsistent statement. The State responds that, under section 115-12, an in-court identification is not a prerequisite to the substantive admission of a prior out-of-court identification. This issue requires us to consider the application of potentially competing evidentiary rules. On the one hand, section 115-10.1 precludes the trial court from admitting as substantive evidence a witness' prior inconsistent statement unless (1) the witness is subject to

177

cross-examination concerning the statement; and (2) the statement was made under oath. In light of Ms. Marquez' inability to identify defendant in open court, Ms. Marquez' prior identification of defendant could be construed as a prior inconsistent statement. Because Ms. Marquez' prior identification statement was not made under oath, defendant argues that, under section 115-10.1, Ms. Marquez' prior identification was inadmissible as substantive evidence. On the other hand, section 115-12 allows the trial court to admit as substantive evidence a prior statement of identification if (1) the declarant testifies at trial; and (2) the declarant is subject to cross-examination. In this case, Ms. Marquez testified at trial and was vigorously cross-examined by defense counsel. Thus, under section 115-12, Ms. Marquez' prior identification appears to be admissible as substantive evidence.

We perceive two possible resolutions to the apparent conflict between sections 115-10.1 and 115-12. The first, which defendant advocates, is that section 115-12 authorizes the substantive admission of all prior statements of identification that corroborate a witness' in-court identification. Thus, defendant argues, had Ms. Marquez identified defendant in open court as one of the two men she saw robbing her neighbors' house, the trial court's substantive admission of Ms. Marquez' prior identification of defendant would have been proper. In this case, however, where Ms. Marquez was unable to identify defendant in open court, defendant argues that the trial court should have treated Ms. Marquez' prior identification of defendant as a prior inconsistent statement under section 115-10.1. Thus, defendant reads section 115-10.1 as an exception to section 115-12. That is, a prior identification is admissible under section 115-12 unless it is a prior inconsistent statement as defined in section 115-10.1.

Defendant's position is not without support in the law. People v. Davis, 137 Ill.App.3d 769, 92 Ill.Dec. 243, 484 N.E.2d 1098 (1985), the Appellate Court, First District, faced a set of facts virtually identical to that presented in this appeal. In Davis, on the day after he was shot, the complaining witness identified the defendant as his assailant. At the preliminary hearing, the witness again identified the defendant as his assailant. At trial, however, the witness testified that, although defendant may have been the man who shot him, he was uncertain. The trial court then permitted the prosecution to question the witness regarding his prior identifications of the defendant. On appeal, the Davis court held that the trial court should not have admitted the witness' prior statements of identification as substantive evidence. In so ruling, the court noted that, three years prior to the enactment of section 115-12, the Illinois Supreme Court, in People v. Rogers, 81 Ill.2d 571, 44 Ill.Dec. 254, 411 N.E.2d 223 (1980), held that evidence of a witness' prior identification was admissible solely for purposes of corroborating an in-court identification and not as substantive evidence. Given the temporal proximity between the Rogers decision and the legislature's enactment of section 115-12, the Davis court concluded that section 115-12 represented a direct response to Rogers. The Davis court therefore read section 115-12 narrowly and concluded that it merely expanded the holding in Rogers to permit the admission of prior consistent identification statements as both corroborative and substantive evidence. Because the complaining witness was unable to identify Davis in open court, the Davis court held that the witness' prior identifications were not admissible as substantive evidence under section 115-12.

Defendant's reading of sections 115-10.1 and 115-12 is not, however, the only reading. As noted above, section 115-12 on its face permits the substantive admission of all prior identification statements without regard to whether the witness makes an in-court identification. Thus, it is also possible to read section 115-12 as an exception to section 115-10.1. That is, a prior inconsistent statement is inadmissible under section 115-10.1 unless it is a prior statement of identification as defined in section 115-12. This position, which the State advocates, also finds ample support in the law. First, the plain language of section 115-12 neither requires an in-court identification nor prohibits the introduction of a prior identification statement where the witness is unable to identify the defendant in open court.

Section 115-12, in its entirety, provides: "Substantive Admissibility of Prior Identification. A statement is not rendered inadmissible by the hearsay rule if (a) the declarant testifies at the trial or hearing, and (b) the declarant is subject to cross-examination concerning the statement, and (c) the statement is one of prior identification of a person made after perceiving him."

We read nothing in this statute that prohibits the introduction of a prior identification where the witness is unable to identify the defendant in open court. Had the legislature intended such a prohibition, it easily could have drafted a section 115-12(d) reading "and the statement corroborates the declarant's identification of the person in open court." The legislature did not, however, attach this final condition.

Second, the Illinois Supreme Court has issued two opinions that can be read to support the State's reading of section 115-12. People v. Holveck, 141 Ill.2d 84, 152 Ill.Dec. 237, 565 N.E.2d 919 (1990), the Illinois Supreme Court held that, under section 115-12, an in-court identification is not a prerequisite to the substantive admission of a prior identification. In Holveck, without ever attempting an in-court identification, the State questioned its identification witness about her out-of-court identification of the defendant. In affirming the trial court's substantive admission of the testimony, the Holveck court held that, because the witness testified at trial and was subject to cross-examination, the elements of section 115-12 were satisfied and the trial court's admission of the prior identification was proper. Read narrowly, Holveck permits the substantive admission of a prior identification statement where the State does not attempt an in-court identification. Read broadly, Holveck rejects the Davis court's holding that a prior identification is inadmissible where the witness is unable to identify the defendant in open court.

More problematic is the Illinois Supreme Court's decision People v. Lewis, 165 Ill.2d 305, 209 Ill.Dec. 144, 651 N.E.2d 72 (1995), a case upon which both defendant and the State rely. In Lewis, the defendant sought to introduce his arrest report as a prior identification statement under section 115-12. Defendant argued that, because the physical description contained in the arrest report differed from that contained in the incident report, the arrest report was admissible to rebut the complaining witness' identification of defendant. In rejecting this argument, the court stated: "Born out of this court's decision People v. Rogers (1980), 81 Ill.2d 571, section 115-12 is designed to permit the use of prior consistent out-of-court statements as corroborative or substantive evidence of a witness' prior identity of a defendant. Defendant's proffer of the arrest report description was neither corroborative of the complaining witness' prior identification of defendant nor was it substantive evidence of such. The rule has no application here."

Defendant argues that, because the court in this passage both emphasized the word "consistent" and cited Davis, the court effectively endorsed the holding of Davis. The State, by contrast, argues that Lewis represents an endorsement of Holveck and thus, by implication, a rejection of Davis. We agree with the State. Defendant's reading of Lewis is flawed for two reasons. First, although we concede that the first sentence read alone may support defendant's interpretation, the first sentence must be read in the context of both the entire passage and the facts of the case. Again, the defendant in Lewis argued that section 115-12 permits the substantive admission of a prior statement that misidentified him as the offender. The passage set forth above is a direct response to this argument. Indeed, in the second and third sentences of the passage, the court makes clear that its purpose is to confine the scope of section 115-12 to prior statements that identify the defendant as the offender. Stated differently, the court rejects the defendant's argument that section 115-12 permits the substantive admission of prior statements that misidentify the defendant as the offender. Contrary to defendant's assertion, we do not believe that Lewis necessarily represents an embrace of Davis. Second, defendant's reading of this passage is precluded by an examination and understanding of the authority cited by the court. At first blush, the court appears to be citing patently contradictory authority. On the one hand, the court cites Davis which holds that a prior identification is inadmissible where the witness is unable to identify the defendant in open court. On the other hand, the court cites Holveck which holds that an in-court identification is not a prerequisite to the introduction of a prior identification which both endorses the view that section 115-12 permits the introduction of a prior identification even where the witness is unable to identify the defendant in open court and expressly rejects the holding of Davis.

We fail to see how the court, as defendant contends, could embrace Davis while simultaneously citing authority that expressly rejects Davis. Defendant offers no explanation for the apparent conflict, and we therefore decline to read Lewis as an endorsement of Davis. We believe that there is only one way to reconcile the Lewis court's reliance on apparently contradictory authority. The manner in which the court cited Davis demonstrates that the court did not attribute as much weight to Davis as it did to Holveck. Thus the Lewis court's reading of section 115-12 ultimately is consistent with that set forth in Holveck and not with that set forth in Davis. Finally, sound public policy supports the proposition that section 115-12 permits the introduction of a prior identification even where the witness is unable to identify the defendant in open court. Whereas a witness' initial identification of the defendant often occurs within days, hours, or even minutes of the crime, the defendant's trial typically occurs several months after the initial identification. A reliable identification occurring only minutes after the crime should not be kept from the jury solely because the witness is unable, several months later and under the pressure of testifying in court, to identify the defendant who, in many cases, will have modified his appearance since the time of the initial identification. Indeed, we believe that the legislature sought to avoid precisely that result when it enacted section 115-12.

Accordingly, we respectfully decline to follow the decision in Davis and instead adopt the position set forth by the Illinois Supreme Court in Holveck and Lewis. We therefore hold that, notwithstanding Ms. Marquez' inability to identify defendant in open court, the trial court properly admitted as substantive evidence Ms. Marquez' prior identification of defendant.

Defendant's second argument is that the State failed to prove defendant's guilt beyond a reasonable doubt. When determining whether the State proved the defendant's guilt beyond a reasonable doubt, this court's duty is not to ask itself whether it believes that the evidence establishes the defendant's guilt. Rather, our duty is to ask whether the evidence viewed in a light most favorable to the prosecution would allow any rational trier of fact to find the essential elements of the crime proved beyond a reasonable doubt. The reversal of a conviction is required only where the defendant can show that the evidence is so unsatisfactory or improbable as to create a reasonable doubt of the defendant's guilt. The trial court convicted defendant of residential burglary. Under section 19-3 of the Criminal Code of 1961, a person commits residential burglary when he or she "knowingly and without authority enters the dwelling place of another with the intent to commit therein a felony or theft." In Illinois, the defendant's possession of recently stolen property is sufficient to support a burglary conviction if (1) there is a rational connection between his recent possession of property stolen in the burglary and his participation in the burglary; (2) his guilt of burglary more likely than not flows from his recent, unexplained possession of the burglary proceeds; and (3) there is evidence corroborating the defendant's guilt. In addition, the identification testimony of a single eyewitness is sufficient to sustain the defendant's conviction.

A rational connection exists between recent possession of stolen property and participation in the burglary if the inference that defendant obtained the items by burglary is not unreasonable. Of paramount concern in determining whether the inference is reasonable is whether defendant's possession of the stolen property is proximate to both the time and place of the burglary. In this case, the State demonstrated proximity of both time and distance. Ms. Marquez testified that approximately 20 minutes passed between the time she watched defendant leave her neighbors' house and the time she identified defendant for the police at the apartment house. In addition, Officer Zegar described the distance between the victims' house and the apartment house as a two- to three-minute drive. Finally, Officers Woods and Zegar testified that, when they arrived at the apartment house approximately 20 minutes after the burglary, they found defendant in possession of the property stolen from the victims' house.

Accordingly, because the State presented evidence of an eyewitness' positive identification of defendant, we hold that the State proved defendant's guilt beyond a reasonable doubt. For the foregoing reasons, the judgment of the circuit court of Kane County is affirmed.

REVIEW SECTION

READING COMPREHENSION

Detail the facts of this case.

Distinguish 725 ILCS 5/115-12 and 725 ILCS 5/115-10.1 and the relevance of each for this case.

SECTION 3: DNA PROFILE IDENTIFICATION

OVERVIEW

DNA (deoxyribonucleic acid) testing has the power to potentially identify suspects or absolutely exclude an individual from consideration as a suspect. Courts have adopted a variety of standards for admission of DNA evidence at the trial stage and 725 ILCS 5/116-3 delineates the guidelines for a motion for fingerprint or forensic testing not available at trial regarding actual innocence:

> (a) A defendant may make a motion before the trial court that entered the judgment of conviction in his or her case for the performance of fingerprint or forensic DNA testing, including comparison analysis of genetic marker groupings of the evidence collected by criminal justice agencies pursuant to the alleged offense, to those of the defendant, to those of other forensic evidence, and to those maintained under subsection (f) of Section 5-4-3 of the Unified Code of Corrections, on evidence that was secured in relation to the trial which resulted in his or her conviction, but which was not subject to the testing which is now requested because the technology for the testing was not available at the time of trial. Reasonable notice of the motion shall be served upon the State. (b) The defendant must present a *prima facie* case that: (1) identity was the issue in the trial which resulted in his or her conviction; and (2) the evidence to be tested has been subject to a chain of custody sufficient to establish that it has not been substituted, tampered with, replaced, or altered in any material aspect. (c) The trial court shall allow the testing under reasonable conditions designed to protect the State's interests in the integrity of the evidence and the testing process upon a determination that: (1) the result of the testing has scientific potential to produce new, noncumulative evidence materially relevant to the defendant's assertion of actual innocence even though the results may not completely exonerate the defendant; (2) the testing requested employs a scientific method generally accepted within the relevant scientific community.

The goal of DNA testing should be to balance both the finality of litigation and protection of the rights of prisoners whose cases may need future review due to advances in the development of DNA technology.

CASE

People v Battles is a case wherein the State wanted to obtain refuge from an approaching speedy trial deadline and waited until just before the expiration of a statutory term to inform the court of a DNA testing request.

PEOPLE V. BATTLES
724 N.E.2d 997 (2000)

The advent of DNA forensic technology in the late 1980s presented a dilemma for our legislators. On the one hand, the speedy trial statute forbad trial detention beyond 120 days without a trial. On the other hand, DNA evidence could take more than 120 days to generate. The DNA analysis method exclusively in use at that time involved a test series that spanned several months. By the very nature of the method employed, any DNA testing was going to take a long time to complete. Moreover, several factors converged to assure significant delay before DNA testing could begin. Normally, testing could not begin until after a suspect was in custody and time toward a speedy trial deadline was already running. The samples necessary for testing could not be harvested without a court order. Once the court-ordered samples were gathered, they had to be packaged and sent to one of a select few forensic labs that specialized in the new technology. These labs serviced DNA testing requests from all over the country. Their services were in high demand. Thus, a confluence of circumstances present at the inception of DNA testing pressed the State's ability to develop DNA evidence in time for use at the trial of anyone being held in custody. It was clear that DNA testing might not be completed in time for use at a speedy trial setting, no matter how diligent an effort the State made to procure the tests results within the required 120-day time span.

Therefore, our legislature amended the speedy trial statute to accommodate use of DNA evidence that might otherwise be lost to a speedy trial deadline. In 1990, lawmakers added a sentence to the statute. It empowers the State to hold a defendant in custody beyond 120 days without a trial where a diligent effort to obtain DNA evidence within 120 days fails. The amendment reads: "If the court determines that the State has exercised without success due diligence to obtain results of DNA testing that is material to the case and that there are reasonable grounds to believe that such results may be obtained at a later day, the court may continue the cause on application of the State for not more than an additional 120 days" (725 ILCS 5/103-5). The original passage of this provision came at a time when testing labs were in short number and the methods those labs employed were slow. Yet, legislators did not provide a sanctuary from the normal speedy trial term for every case that involved, or potentially could involve, DNA testing. The amendment was designed for use only in those cases where a diligent effort to obtain DNA evidence within the 120-day term had proven unsuccessful. The State was not empowered to expand the normal speedy trial term without showing a diligent but failed attempt to secure DNA testing within the 120-day term. There was no refuge provided for cases where the need for additional time to conduct testing stemmed from the State's neglect or lack of effort.

We are presented a case where the State invoked 725 ILCS 5/103-5(c) to obtain refuge from an approaching speedy trial deadline. The State appeared 13 days prior to expiration of the 120-day statutory term and informed the court that it had requested DNA testing. The State asked for another 120 days within which to commence trial. On the 113th day of pretrial confinement, the trial court granted the State's request to hold defendant in custody without a trial for an additional 120 days. Consequently, the State maintained its hold on defendant's freedom while it awaited the outcome of DNA testing. Defendant remained in a Jackson County jail cell for 314 days without a trial. When the State filed its motion to continue, defendant contested its use and insisted that trial commence as scheduled. Defendant claimed that the State failed to demonstrate a diligent effort to obtain DNA evidence in time for use at the impending trial. His argument proved to be of no avail.

Defendant renewed his complaint in a motion for discharge filed prior to the belated trial. In that motion, he claimed that the State's use of section 103-5(c) to delay proceedings deprived him of his right to a speedy trial. The motion reiterated defendant's earlier argument. Defendant challenged the trial court's finding that the State had made a diligent effort to obtain DNA testing before it employed section 103-5(c) to postpone trial. The argument failed again.

Defendant elected to proceed by way of a stipulated bench trial. He stipulated to the State's case, which included the DNA evidence developed during trial's delay. The trial court found defendant guilty of home invasion. Defendant currently serves a 20-year prison term imposed upon that finding. There is only one issue preserved for review. We are asked to decide whether defendant received his statutory right to a speedy trial. Since defendant did nothing to delay trial during the first 197 days of pretrial confinement, the answer to this question resides in the State's use of section 103-5(c). If the State cannot rely upon its use as a sanctuary from the law's normal 120-day speedy trial term, trial's delay beyond 120 days at the State's behest would constitute a breach of the law's guarantee to a speedy trial.

At issue is whether the State made a sufficient showing that it exercised due diligence in its attempt to accomplish DNA testing within the 120-day speedy trial term. We examine what the State presented in support of the due diligence determination in order to unearth whether a basis exists for such a finding. We will not overturn a due diligence determination unless it amounts to a clear abuse of discretion. The ultimate question for decision is whether the trial judge abused her discretion when she found that the State had established a diligent effort to procure DNA testing within the 120-day time frame that would have normally defined this defendant's statutory right to a speedy trial. We turn to a closer examination of the events that led the State to delay trial beyond the 120-day speedy trial term in order to obtain DNA test results.

On the evening of December 18, 1996, Jack Trammel hosted a small party at his Carbondale home. He and his seven guests were rudely interrupted when three men sporting ski masks and bearing arms crashed the party. The intruders assaulted two of the guests during the armed robbery that ensued. The assaults drew blood and some of that blood splattered onto the assailants. Jack Trammel escaped to a neighbor's home. He was able to summon the police while the crime was still in progress. The intruders made off with the partygoers' marijuana, an assault rifle, and $700 in cash. The intruders did not get far. As they departed the scene of the crime, the police arrived and gave chase. The ensuing escape attempt failed when the getaway car spun out of control and crashed. One of the suspects was able to run and did elude capture that evening. The other two, defendant Brent Battles and Stanley Algee, were arrested as they exited the car.

There were blood stains on the car's front seat and floor, on a ski mask removed from the car, and on the suspects' clothing. Two other ski masks were found on the side of the road along the attempted escape route. These items were turned over to the State crime lab, together with samples from the victims and the suspects. The following list chronicles the process by which these evidentiary materials found their way to the Carbondale State crime lab for testing.

December 20, 1996: The blood from the front seat of the getaway car and the blood-stained ski masks were delivered to the crime lab.

December 30, 1996: The defendant's blood-stained coveralls were delivered to the crime lab.

January 3, 1997: The blood samples were drawn from the two assault victims.

January 14, 1997: The State filed its motion for an order requiring the defendant to give blood, hair, and saliva samples.

February 4, 1997: After a hearing on the State's motion, defendant was ordered to provide the State with the requested samples.

February 6, 1997: The defendant's blood, hair, and saliva samples were gathered.

February 24, 1997: Defendant's samples were delivered to the crime lab.

All materials necessary to begin DNA testing were in the lab technicians' hands by February 24, 1997. However, Carbondale lab technicians could only perform standard blood analysis. They were not equipped to test for DNA matches. Any DNA work required transfer of the evidence to the State crime lab in Joliet, where there were two DNA lab technicians trained to conduct DNA testing. On February 4, 1997, the trial court set this case for a trial on April 14, 1997. This setting allowed for almost all of the 120 days within which trial had to begin. The State had 117 days of the speedy trial term within which to complete blood, hair, and fiber analysis. The State knew that it had 72 of those days remaining in its effort to procure DNA test results in time for use at trial. The samples drawn from defendant remained at the Jackson County Sheriff's Department for 18 of those days.

On March 31, 1997, the State filed its motion to continue trial for 120 days. It relied upon section 103-5(c) and claimed that added time was needed in order to procure DNA test results. The State presented its motion on April 4, 1997, and six days later, the trial court composed a docket entry that allowed the request. The ruling was entered without findings. Since the continuance was allowed pursuant to section 103-5(c), the trial court must have found the exercise of due diligence to accomplish DNA testing during the 104 days of custody that preceded the request. It also must have found that a diligent effort to procure the tests within the time that remained on the speedy trial term would not meet with success. These implicit findings are what defendant challenges on appeal.

The speedy trial statute enforces a constitutional right. Therefore, the statute, including the provision at issue here, must be liberally construed in defendant's favor. The parties have not provided, nor have we found, a case that discusses what it means to exercise due diligence in the DNA-testing context. The word "diligence" is generally defined to mean prudence, vigilant activity, or attentiveness. The term "due diligence" means: "Such a measure of prudence, activity, or assiduity, as is properly to be expected from, and ordinarily exercised by, a reasonable and prudent man under the particular circumstances; not measured by any absolute standard but depending on the relative facts of the special case" (Black's Law Dictionary 544,

589, 4th ed. 1968). Whether due diligence has been exercised is a question determined on a case-by-case basis after careful review of the particular circumstances presented.

When confronted with a section 103-5(c) request, the trial court should anticipate a showing from the State that law enforcement authorities have made a prudent and assiduous effort to complete DNA testing before expiration of the 120-day speedy trial term. The State needs to show that it did what our legislature wanted done--that it made a serious attempt to accomplish testing in time to meet its primary speedy trial obligation. The State bears the burden of proof on the question of due diligence. In order to meet this burden, the State should tender a full explanation of each and every step taken to complete DNA testing within the 120-day speedy trial term. The steps articulated should comprise a course of action that a reasonable and prudent person intent upon completing tests within 120 days would follow. Further, the showing should explain why the efforts engaged in fell short of their objective and resulted in an unavoidable need for delay.

The exercise of due diligence is measured by assessing the effort made to accomplish testing within the 120-day speedy trial term, not the effort made to complete testing in time for use at an earlier trial setting. Thus, where section 103-5(c) is invoked to delay a trial scheduled to begin far in advance of the 120-day expiration date, the State should make a further showing that explains why continued efforts to procure DNA test results within the 120-day term would prove unsuccessful. With these principles in mind, we examine what the State provided the trial court when it successfully pursued a 120-day trial delay.

The State's motion to continue pled the following: "(1) This matter is currently set for trial on April 14, 1997 at 8:00 a.m. (2) The court has previously granted the People's Motion for Taking of Samples of Defendant Battles, Algee, and Gates. (3) Those samples were taken in a timely fashion and submitted to the crime lab for analysis. The most recent communication from the crime lab was received from Stacey Speith, Forensic Scientist on March 19, 1997. (4) Samples regarding hair and fibers have not yet been received from the crime lab. Blood comparisons will be done after the hair and fiber analysis. (5) Blood stains were recovered from the coveralls of Stanley Algee as well as the seat of the automobile in which the defendants were traveling the night in question. The People have requested DNA analysis to compare the blood stains found on the coveralls and the car seat to the samples submitted by the defendants and the victims in this matter. The crime lab has not yet conducted their basic blood work analysis comparison; no DNA testing has commenced by the crime lab. (6) Since no blood work comparisons or DNA blood work has begun, and the People have not yet received results of hair and fiber comparisons, the People are not prepared to go forward with this case on its current setting. (7) Chapter 725, Section 5/103-5 provides for an extension of the speedy trial time upon request of the State for an additional 120 days to obtain the results of DNA testing. WHEREFORE, the People respectfully pray this Court enter an Order pursuant to Chapter 725 Section 5/103-5 extending the speedy trial time for a period of 120 days and authorize continuing the trial setting of April 14, 1997."

Nothing in this pleading speaks to the effort made to obtain DNA testing before the delay was requested. It does not say what the State tried to do in order to complete testing either in time for use at trial or within the 120-day speedy trial term. There is no mention of what was done between February 24, 1997, and March 31, 1997, in order to procure, or attempt to expedite, DNA testing. The pleading lacks any factual assertion from which to infer a prudent and assiduous effort to complete DNA testing before section 103-5(c) was invoked to postpone trial. The pleading does not provide a basis for the due diligence finding.

However, on April 4, 1997, an assistant State's Attorney presented the motion and stated the following: "Your Honor, each of the defendants is being held in the Jackson County Jail for speedy trial. The 120-day period would run either on April 16 or 17. The Speedy Trial Statute, section 103-5, does allow the People to ask for an additional time to try the defendants, that additional time being up to 120 days in a case where DNA evidence is to be sought. The People have requested that DNA analysis be performed on the blood stains, as well as for comparison purposes the samples which this Court has previously authorized. I would note for the Court that with regard to Defendant Battles, there was a Motion for Samples granted on February 4, file-stamped February 5. Your Honor, the samples were taken February 6, within one day, and they were transported to the Crime Lab within 13 days. In that 13-day period there were four days which were weekends. There was one day which was a holiday. And on February 11 there was a homicide which occurred that mandated the presence of detectives from the Jackson County Sheriff's Department to investigate. Your Honor, the samples are at the Crime Lab as we speak. They are currently conducting their analysis. After they are completed, those samples will then be transferred to the Serology Section of the Crime Lab in Carbondale for their preliminary analysis, and then the blood and the blood stains will be transferred to the State Crime Lab in Springfield for DNA analysis and comparison. It is anticipated that the DNA will take anywhere from eight to twelve weeks once it's received in Springfield. I cannot give the Court a more accurate figure than that. The Springfield Crime Lab is the only agency doing DNA analysis in criminal cases in the state of Illinois, and they are quite backlogged at this point in time. I cannot tell the Court that the DNA will be done within twelve weeks; however, it may take longer than that. And that's why, in this circumstance, I'm asking the Court to continue the matter for 120 days from the current trial setting, and I ask for the extension of the speedy trial time pursuant to statute."

These comments lack any mention of the effort made to obtain DNA test results either in time for use at the impending trial or within the 120-day speedy trial term. They do not articulate a course of action that a reasonable and prudent person intent on obtaining DNA test results within 120 days would follow. The comments made in support of the motion to continue fail to augment the pleadings with any information from which to infer that authorities made a serious effort to complete DNA testing within the 120-day speedy trial term. Initially, we are not particularly impressed with the effort authorities made to deliver the samples to the lab. By our count, they wasted 18 days that might otherwise have been used to complete testing. However, the State's reliance upon the effort made to deliver the samples to the crime lab is misplaced. Standing alone, rapid retrieval of testing materials and delivery of those materials to a crime lab for testing is not enough to show a prudent and assiduous effort to complete DNA testing within the 120-day speedy trial term. If the State gathered and delivered everything needed for DNA testing on the day of arrest, but thereafter crime lab technicians stood idly by and ignored those materials for 120 days, if the State did not even try to test the materials within the 120-day speedy trial term, a court would be hard-pressed to find that authorities pursued a course that a reasonable and prudent person intent on procuring DNA tests within 120 days would follow.

We believe that the State should have provided the trial court with an account of what transpired after the samples were delivered to the crime lab. It should have addressed those things that were done in an attempt to promote, or expedite, the testing of the materials after their delivery to the lab. We cannot eliminate the exercise of due diligence as a prerequisite to an extension of speedy trial constraints. If the mere assertion of a backlog's existence could constitute reason enough for use of section 103-5(c), its 120-day extension would become automatic. A showing of due diligence would become a thing of the past.

We find that the information conveyed to and possessed by the trial court at the time of its ruling did not support a due diligence determination. However, we would add that even if the statements made could support such a finding, those statements proved to be inaccurate. In its brief, the State points out in a footnote that the assistant State's Attorney mistakenly informed the court that the crime laboratory conducting DNA analysis was located in Springfield, when in fact it is located in Joliet. This mistake is not as insignificant as its treatment might suggest. The assistant's remarks to the trial court leave the distinct impression that the information conveyed came from sources at the State crime lab.

When the State submitted its motion to continue for decision, it failed to present anything from which to infer that a diligent effort had been made to complete DNA testing within the 120-day speedy trial term. It was impossible for the trial court to determine what kind of effort was made. The trial court was simply not told of that effort. Accordingly, we conclude that the trial court abused its discretion when it found that the State had exercised due diligence to obtain DNA testing before it invoked section 103-5(c) to delay trial. The State cannot rely on the statute's refuge from the normal speedy trial term. Hence, we conclude that defendant did not receive his statutory right to a speedy trial.

There was good reason why the State's motion to continue and the prosecutor's comments in support of it failed to explain the effort made to complete DNA testing within the 120-day speedy trial term. The State did not explain its effort because there was none. The State did nothing to process the blood delivered to the crime lab prior to invoking section 103-5(c). It took the State 103 days of defendant's pretrial confinement to decide whether to test for DNA matches. Once the decision to test was reached, the State did not attempt to test in the remaining time available. There was no effort to expedite DNA testing. Instead, the State chose to forestall all testing and invoke section 103-5(c). The State did not use section 103-5(c) as a refuge from an approaching deadline after a diligent but failed effort to obtain tests in time for use at trial. Rather, it used section 103-5(c) as a vehicle to cure the time problem created by its lack of effort. The State could not complete DNA testing within the 120-day speedy trial term because the State never attempted to test.

There have been dramatic advances in the methods employed to analyze DNA since the passage of section 103-5(c). As this case demonstrates, the State is no longer shackled to a test series that spans several months. The circumstances that gave rise to section 103-5(c) are not what they once were. We believe that if authorities pursue a prudent and reasonable course and are assiduous in their efforts, the 120-day extension provision found in section 103-5(c) should find rare use. Here, the State waited 104 days before deciding to test. But had the State made an effort to test as soon as it decided to do so, and acted with the April 14, 1997, trial deadline in mind, it is conceivable that DNA testing could have been completed in time for use at trial; it is conceivable that the State could have met its primary speedy trial obligation. For the reasons stated, we reverse defendant's conviction.

REVIEW SECTION

READING COMPREHENSION

Detail the facts of this case.

THINKING CRITICALLY

In your opinion, did this case violate the speedy trial rule when keeping the defendant in jail for 314 days without a trial?

CONCLUSION

Proving who committed a crime is far more difficult than mere proof that a crime occurred. Recent developments in DNA technology have improved the ability of the government to identify a suspect. While this is a vast improvement on eyewitness identification in the form of lineups, show-ups, and photo identification all of which are debatable regarding reliability, DNA technology has difficulties of its own. This chapter examined the risks of mistaken eyewitness identification, the Constitution and identification procedures, and DNA profile identification. What you may want to give some thought to is the complicated nature of the presentation of DNA evidence in a court of law. Have we progressed to the point where scientists can adequately explain to everyday citizens the intricacies of this technology? Or are jurors merely left to sift through evidence that they do not fully comprehend in assessing an individual's guilt or innocence?

Chapter Ten

Constitutional Violations: Exclusionary Rule and Entrapment

During the trial stage there are two remedies that can affect the outcome of the state's criminal case and which are the subject of this chapter:

(1)   The exclusionary rule; and

(2)   The defense of entrapment.

These remedies are not mutually exclusive, but it is important to remember that while each is created by the U.S. Supreme Court with the intent to enforce constitutional rights, neither is backed by any constitutional right.

SECTION 1: THE EXCLUSIONARY RULE

OVERVIEW

The exclusionary rule is a frequently used remedy against state power which involves throwing out illegally obtained evidence against a defendant. The landmark case was the U.S. Supreme Court ruling in Mapp v. Ohio, 367 U.S. 643, 81 S.Ct. 1684, 6 L.Ed.2d 1081 (1961) which required state courts to follow the prohibition imposed on the federal courts through the Weeks v. United States, 323 U.S. 383, 34 S.Ct. 341, 58 L.Ed. 652 (1914) decision. Courts in Illinois have placed high value on constitutional rights and have established that the right to be free from unreasonable invasions of privacy is expressed and more broadly stated under the Illinois Constitution than under United States Constitution. Further, while the primary purpose of the exclusionary rule has been to deter police misconduct, its use in preserving judicial integrity should not be overlooked.

When the government obtains evidence that assists in determining the guilt of a defendant, the exclusionary rule allows this evidence to be excluded from trial if it was obtained in violation of any of the below amendments:

(1)   Fourth Amendment ban on unreasonable search and seizure;

(2)   Fifth Amendment ban on coerced statements that are incriminating;

(3)   Sixth Amendment right to counsel; or

(4)   Fifth and Fourteenth Amendment right of due process.

The exclusionary rule is used only in the United States and is an attempt to maintain police and judicial integrity, as well as to deter government officials from violating the law. In the dissenting words of Justice Brandeis in *Olmstead v. United States* (227 U.S. 438 1928), the effect of the exclusionary rule is that:

> The criminal goes free, if he must, but it is the law that sets him free. Nothing can destroy a government more quickly than its failure to observe its own laws, or worse, its disregard of the charter of its own existence.

Unlike the portrayal by mainstream media, the exclusionary rule affects a miniscule portion of cases, and has virtually no effect on violent crimes and serious property offenses. What the exclusionary does accomplish is a fundamental fairness of constitutional government for all citizens.

CASE

In *Kirby v Illinois,* the petitioner and a companion were stopped for interrogation. When they produced identification in the name of a robbery victim, the petitioner and companion were arrested and later identified as the robbers. The petitioner and his companion were not advised of the right to counsel, nor did either ask for or receive legal assistance. Six weeks later, both were indicted for robbery. At the trial, after a pretrial motion to suppress testimony had been overruled, the victim testified as to his previous identification of petitioner and his companion, and again identified them as the robbers. The defendants were found guilty and petitioner's conviction was upheld on appeal, the appellate court holding that the per se exclusionary rule of United States v. Wade, 388 U.S. 218 , and Gilbert v. California, 388 U.S. 263 , did not apply to pre-indictment confrontations. This case is now heard by the U.S. Supreme Court.

KIRBY V. ILLINOIS
U.S. Supreme Court
406 U.S. 682 (1972)

In United States v. Wade, 388 U.S. 218 , and Gilbert v. California, 388 U.S. 263 , this Court held "that a post-indictment pretrial lineup at which the accused is exhibited to identifying witnesses is a critical stage of the criminal prosecution; that police conduct of such a lineup without notice to and in the absence of his counsel denies the accused his Sixth [and Fourteenth] Amendment right to counsel and calls in question the admissibility at trial of the in-court identifications of the accused by witnesses who attended the lineup." Those cases further held that no "in-court identifications" are admissible in evidence if their "source" is a lineup conducted in violation of this constitutional standard. "Only a per se exclusionary rule as to such testimony can be an effective sanction," the Court said, "to assure that law enforcement authorities will respect the accused's constitutional right to the presence of his counsel at the critical lineup." In the present case we are asked to extend the Wade-Gilbert per se exclusionary rule to identification testimony based upon a police station showup that took place before the defendant had been indicted or otherwise formally charged with any criminal offense.

On February 21, 1968, a man named Willie Shard reported to the Chicago police that the previous day two men had robbed him on a Chicago street of a wallet. On February 22, two police officers stopped the petitioner and a companion, Ralph Bean. When asked for identification, the petitioner produced a wallet that contained three traveler's checks and a Social Security card, all bearing the name of Willie Shard. Papers with Shard's name on them were also found in Bean's possession. When asked to explain his possession of Shard's property, the petitioner first said that the traveler's checks were "play money," and then told the officers that he had won them in a crap game. The officers then arrested the petitioner and Bean and took them to a police station. Only after arriving at the police station, and checking the records there, did the arresting officers learn of the Shard robbery. A police car was then dispatched to Shard's place of employment, where it picked up Shard and brought him to the police station. Immediately upon entering the room in the police station where the petitioner and Bean were seated at a table, Shard positively identified them as the men who had robbed him two days earlier. No lawyer was present in the room, and neither the petitioner nor Bean had asked for legal assistance, or been advised of any right to the presence of counsel.

More than six weeks later, the petitioner and Bean were indicted for the robbery of Willie Shard. Upon arraignment, counsel was appointed to represent them, and they pleaded not guilty. A pretrial motion to suppress Shard's identification testimony was denied, and at the trial Shard testified as a witness for the prosecution. In his testimony he described his identification of the two men at the police station on February 22, and identified them again in the courtroom as the men who had robbed him on February 20. He was cross-examined at length regarding the circumstances of his identification of the two defendants. The jury found both defendants guilty, and the petitioner's conviction was affirmed on appeal. The Illinois appellate court held that the admission of Shard's testimony was not error, relying upon an earlier decision of the Illinois Supreme Court, People v. Palmer, 41 Ill. 2d 571, 244 N. E. 2d 173, holding that the Wade-Gilbert per se exclusionary rule is not applicable to pre-indictment confrontations. We granted certiorari, limited to this question.

We note at the outset that the constitutional privilege against compulsory self-incrimination is in no way implicated here. It follows that the doctrine of Miranda v. Arizona, 384 U.S. 436, has no applicability whatever to the issue before us; for the Miranda decision was based exclusively upon the Fifth and Fourteenth Amendment privilege against compulsory self-incrimination, upon the theory that custodial interrogation is inherently coercive. The Wade-Gilbert exclusionary rule, by contrast, stems from a quite different constitutional guarantee - the guarantee of the right to counsel contained in the Sixth and Fourteenth Amendments. Unless all semblance of principled constitutional adjudication is to be abandoned, therefore, it is to the decisions construing that guarantee that we must look in determining the present controversy.

In a line of constitutional cases in this Court stemming back to the Court's landmark opinion in Powell v. Alabama, 287 U.S. 45, it has been firmly established that a person's Sixth and Fourteenth Amendment right to counsel attaches only at or after the time that adversary judicial proceedings have been initiated against him. This is not to say that a defendant in a criminal case has a constitutional right to counsel only at the trial itself. The Powell case makes clear that the right attaches at the time of arraignment, and the Court has recently held that it exists also at the time of a preliminary hearing. But the point is that, while members of the Court have differed as to existence of the right to counsel in the contexts of some of the above cases, all of those cases have involved points of time at or after the initiation of adversary judicial criminal proceedings - whether by way of formal charge, preliminary hearing, indictment, information, or arraignment.

The only seeming deviation from this long line of constitutional decisions was Escobedo v. Illinois, 378 U.S. 478 . But Escobedo is not apposite here for two distinct reasons. First, the Court in retrospect perceived that the "prime purpose" of Escobedo was not to vindicate the constitutional right to counsel as such, but, like Miranda, "to guarantee full effectuation of the privilege against self-incrimination . . . ." Secondly, and perhaps even more important for purely practical purposes, the Court has limited the holding of Escobedo to its own facts, and those facts are not remotely akin to the facts of the case before us.

The initiation of judicial criminal proceedings is far from a mere formalism. It is the starting point of our whole system of adversary criminal justice. For it is only then that the government has committed itself to prosecute, and only then that the adverse positions of government and defendant have solidified. It is then that a defendant finds himself faced with the prosecutorial forces of organized society, and immersed in the intricacies of substantive and procedural criminal law. It is this point, therefore, that marks the commencement of the "criminal prosecutions" to which alone the explicit guarantees of the Sixth Amendment are applicable. In this case we are asked to import into a routine police investigation an absolute constitutional guarantee historically and rationally applicable only after the onset of formal prosecutorial proceedings. We decline to do so. Less than a year after Wade and Gilbert were decided, the Court explained the rule of those decisions as follows: "The rationale of those cases was that an accused is entitled to counsel at any critical stage of the prosecution, and that a post-indictment lineup is such a critical stage." We decline to depart from that rationale today by imposing a per se exclusionary rule upon testimony concerning an identification that took place long before the commencement of any prosecution whatever.

What has been said is not to suggest that there may not be occasions during the course of a criminal investigation when the police do abuse identification procedures. Such abuses are not beyond the reach of the Constitution. As the Court pointed out in Wade itself, it is always necessary to "scrutinize any pretrial confrontation." The Due Process Clause of the Fifth and Fourteenth Amendments forbids a lineup that is unnecessarily suggestive and conducive to irreparable mistaken identification. When a person has not been formally charged with a criminal offense, there is a constitutional balance between the right of a suspect to be protected from prejudicial procedures and the interest of society in the prompt and purposeful investigation of an unsolved crime. The judgment is affirmed.

MR. JUSTICE BRENNAN, with whom MR. JUSTICE DOUGLAS and MR. JUSTICE MARSHALL join, dissenting. After petitioner and Ralph Bean were arrested, police officers brought Willie Shard, the robbery victim, to a room in a police station where petitioner and Bean were seated at a table with two other police officers. Shard testified at trial that the officers who brought him to the room asked him if petitioner and Bean were the robbers and that he indicated they were. The prosecutor asked him, "And you positively identified them at the police station, is that correct?" Shard answered, "Yes." Consequently, the question in this case is whether, under Gilbert v. California, 388 U.S. 263 (1967), it was constitutional error to admit Shard's testimony that he identified petitioner at the pretrial station-house showup when that showup was conducted by the police without advising petitioner that he might have counsel present. Gilbert held, in the context of a post-indictment lineup, that "only a per se exclusionary rule as to such testimony can be an effective sanction to assure that law enforcement authorities will respect the accused's constitutional right to the presence of his counsel at the critical lineup." I would apply Gilbert and the principles of its companion case, United States v. Wade, 388 U.S. 218 (1967), and reverse.

In Wade, after concluding that the lineup conducted in that case did not violate the accused's right against self-incrimination, the Court addressed the argument "that the assistance of counsel at the lineup was indispensable to protect Wade's most basic right as a criminal defendant - his right to a fair trial at which the witnesses against him might be meaningfully cross-examined." The Court began by emphasizing that the Sixth Amendment guarantee "encompasses counsel's assistance whenever necessary to assure a meaningful defence." After reviewing Powell v. Alabama, 287 U.S. 45 (1932); Hamilton v. Alabama, 368 U.S. 52 (1961); and Massiah v. United States, 377 U.S. 201 (1964), the Court, 388 U.S., at 225, focused upon two cases that involved the right against self-incrimination. The Court then pointed out that "nothing decided or said in the opinions in Escobedo and Miranda links the right to counsel only to protection of Fifth Amendment rights." To the contrary, the Court said, those decisions simply reflected the constitutional "principle that in addition to counsel's presence at trial, the accused is guaranteed that he need not stand alone against the State at any stage of the prosecution, formal or informal, in court or out, where counsel's absence might derogate from the accused's right to a fair trial. The security of that right is as much the aim of the right to counsel as it is of the other guarantees of the Sixth Amendment . . . ."

This analysis led to the Court's formulation of the controlling principle for pretrial confrontations: "In sum, the principle of Powell v. Alabama and succeeding cases requires that we scrutinize any pretrial confrontation of the accused to determine whether the presence of his counsel is necessary to preserve the defendant's basic right to a fair trial as affected by his right meaningfully to cross-examine the witnesses against him and to have effective assistance of counsel at the trial itself. It calls upon us to analyze whether potential substantial prejudice to defendant's rights inheres in the particular confrontation and the ability of counsel to help avoid that prejudice." It was that constitutional principle that the Court applied in Wade to pretrial confrontations for identification purposes. The Court first met the Government's contention that a confrontation for identification is "a mere preparatory step in the gathering of the prosecution's evidence," much like the scientific examination of fingerprints and blood samples. The Court responded that in the latter instances "the accused has the opportunity for a meaningful confrontation of the Government's case at trial through the ordinary processes of cross-examination of the Government's expert witnesses and the presentation of the evidence of his own experts." The accused thus has no right to have counsel present at such examinations: "they are not critical stages since there is minimal risk that his counsel's absence at such stages might derogate from his right to a fair trial."

In contrast, the Court said, "the confrontation compelled by the State between the accused and the victim or witnesses to a crime to elicit identification evidence is peculiarly riddled with innumerable dangers and variable factors which might seriously, even crucially, derogate from a fair trial." Most importantly, "the accused's inability effectively to reconstruct at trial any unfairness that occurred at the lineup may deprive him of his only opportunity meaningfully to attack the credibility of the witness' courtroom identification." The Court's analysis of pretrial confrontations for identification purposes produced the following conclusion: "Insofar as the accused's conviction may rest on a courtroom identification in fact the fruit of a suspect pretrial identification which the accused is helpless to subject to effective scrutiny at trial, the accused is deprived of that right of cross-examination which is an essential safeguard to his right to confront the witnesses against him. And even though cross-examination is a precious safeguard to a fair trial, it cannot be viewed as an absolute assurance of accuracy and reliability. Thus in the present context, where so many variables and pitfalls exist, the first line of defense must be the prevention of unfairness and the lessening of the hazards of eye-witness identification at the lineup itself. The trial which might determine the accused's fate may well not be that in the courtroom but that at the pretrial confrontation, with the State aligned against the accused, the witness the sole jury, and the accused unprotected against the overreaching, intentional or unintentional, and with little or no effective appeal from the judgment there rendered by the witness - that's the man."

The Court then applied that conclusion to the specific facts of the case. "Since it appears that there is grave potential for prejudice, intentional or not, in the pretrial lineup, which may not be capable of reconstruction at trial, and since presence of counsel itself can often avert prejudice and assure a meaningful confrontation at trial, there can be little doubt that for Wade the post-indictment lineup was a critical stage of the prosecution at which he was as much entitled to such aid of counsel . . . as at the trial itself." While it should go without saying, it appears necessary, in view of the plurality opinion today, to re-emphasize that Wade did not require the presence of counsel at pretrial confrontations for identification purposes simply on the basis of an abstract consideration of the words "criminal prosecutions" in the Sixth Amendment. Counsel is required at those confrontations because "the dangers inherent in eyewitness identification and the suggestibility inherent in the context of the pretrial identification," mean that protection must be afforded to the "most basic right of a criminal defendant - his right to a fair trial at which the witnesses against him might be meaningfully cross-examined." Indeed, the Court expressly stated that "legislative or other regulations, such as those of local police departments, which eliminate the risks of abuse and unintentional suggestion at lineup proceedings and the impediments to meaningful confrontation at trial may also remove the basis for regarding the stage as critical." Hence, "the initiation of adversary judicial criminal proceedings," is completely irrelevant to whether counsel is necessary at a pretrial confrontation for identification in order to safeguard the accused's constitutional rights to confrontation and the effective assistance of counsel at his trial.

In view of Wade, it is plain, and the plurality today does not attempt to dispute it, that there inhere in a confrontation for identification conducted after arrest the identical hazards to a fair trial that inhere in such a confrontation conducted "after the onset of formal prosecutorial proceedings." The plurality apparently considers an arrest, which for present purposes we must assume to be based upon probable cause, to be nothing more than part of "a routine police investigation," and thus not "the starting point of our whole system of adversary criminal justice." An arrest, according to the plurality, does not face the accused "with the prosecutorial forces of organized society," nor immerse him "in the intricacies of substantive and procedural criminal law." Those consequences ensue, says the plurality, only with "the initiation of judicial criminal proceedings," "for it is only then that the government has committed itself to prosecute, and only then that the adverse positions of government and defendant have solidified." If these propositions do not amount to "mere formalism," it is difficult to know how to characterize them. An arrest evidences the belief of the police that the perpetrator of a crime has been caught. A post-arrest confrontation for identification is not "a mere preparatory step in the gathering of the prosecution's evidence." A primary, and frequently sole, purpose of the confrontation for identification at that stage is to accumulate proof to buttress the conclusion of the police that they have the offender in hand. The plurality offers no reason, and I can think of none, for concluding that a post-arrest confrontation for identification, unlike a post-charge confrontation, is not among those "critical confrontations of the accused by the prosecution at pretrial proceedings where the results might well settle the accused's fate and reduce the trial itself to a mere formality."

The plurality today "declines to depart from the rationale" of Wade and Gilbert. The plurality discovers that "rationale" not by consulting those decisions themselves, which would seem to be the appropriate course, but by reading one sentence in Simmons v. United States, 390 U.S. 377, 382 -383 (1968), where no right-to-counsel claim was either asserted or considered. The "rationale" the plurality discovers is, apparently, that a post-indictment confrontation for identification is part of the prosecution. The plurality might have discovered a different "rationale" by reading one sentence in Foster v. California, 394 U.S. 440, 442 (1969), a case decided after Simmons, where the Court explained that in Wade and Gilbert "this Court held that because of the possibility of unfairness to the accused in the way a lineup is conducted, a lineup is a critical stage in the prosecution, at which the accused must be given the opportunity to be represented by counsel." In Foster, moreover, although the Court mentioned that the lineups took place after the accused's arrest, it did not say whether they were also after the information was filed against him. Instead, the Court simply pointed out that under Stovall v. Denno, 388 U.S. 293 (1967), Wade and Gilbert were "applicable only to lineups conducted after those cases were decided." Similarly, in Coleman v. Alabama, 399 U.S. 1 (1970), another case involving a pre-Wade lineup, no member of the Court saw any significance in whether the accused had been formally charged with a crime before the lineup was held.

In short, it is fair to conclude that rather than "declining to depart from the rationale" of Wade and Gilbert, the plurality today, albeit purporting to be engaged in "principled constitutional adjudication," refuses even to recognize that "rationale." For my part, I do not agree that we "extend" Wade and Gilbert by holding that the principles of those cases apply to confrontations for identification conducted after arrest. Because Shard testified at trial about his identification of petitioner at the police station showup, the exclusionary rule of Gilbert, 388 U.S., at 272 -274, requires reversal.

REVIEW SECTION

READING COMPREHENSION

Delineate the status of the exclusionary rule in Illinois as opposed to its federal application.

Detail the facts of this case and the relevance of prior decisions.

CASE

In <u>People v. Ross, 168 Ill.2d 347, 213 Ill.Dec. 672, 659 N.E.2d 1319 (1995)</u>, the court held that 725 ILCS 5/108-3(a)(1) does not authorize issuance of anticipatory search warrants. The issue in *People v Carlson* is whether evidence seized pursuant to an anticipatory search warrant issued and executed prior to our decision in Ross may be admitted into evidence pursuant to the good-faith exception to the exclusionary rule.

PEOPLE V. CARLSON
708 N.E.2d 372, 185 Ill.2d 546 (1999)

The Illinois State Police obtained a warrant to search defendant Jodi Kae Carlson's residence for, *inter alia*, psilocybin mushrooms, a controlled substance. The warrant was issued based on the affidavit of Special Agent Joseph Bolino. According to Agent Bolino's affidavit, a United States postal inspector searched an express mail package. The postal inspector had applied for and received a federal search warrant to search the package after a narcotics-trained police dog had alerted to it. The package contained approximately 400 grams of psilocybin. The postal inspector resealed the package and contacted Agent Bolino. The next day, Agent Bolino requested issuance of an anticipatory search warrant to be executed only upon the conditions that a postal inspector, posing as a postal carrier, deliver the package to 804 Midway Drive in Batavia, and that an occupant of the residence accept the package. The affidavit also described defendant's residence. The warrant was issued at 9:25 a.m. on July 13, 1994, and executed at 10:35 a.m. that same day.

After the police executed the warrant, defendant was arrested and charged in the circuit court with unlawful possession of a controlled substance and unlawful possession of a controlled substance with intent to deliver. Defendant filed a motion to quash the search warrant and suppress the evidence seized pursuant to the warrant. The circuit court initially denied defendant's motion. Shortly thereafter, however, this court delivered the opinion in Ross, holding that anticipatory search warrants were not authorized by statute and are therefore invalid. Based on Ross, defendant moved for reconsideration of the denial of her motion to suppress. The circuit court granted the motion for reconsideration and suppressed the evidence in question. The State filed a motion to reconsider, arguing that the evidence should be admissible under the good-faith exception to the exclusionary rule. The circuit court denied the motion. The State filed a certificate of impairment and appealed. The appellate court reversed the circuit court's suppression order. We allowed defendant's petition for leave to appeal. For the reasons set forth below, we affirm the judgment of the appellate court.

An anticipatory search warrant is a warrant based upon an affidavit showing probable cause that at a future time certain evidence of a crime will be located at a specific place. A common situation in which police officers seek anticipatory search warrants is where postal authorities notify the police that they have intercepted from the mail a package containing drugs. The police then seek issuance of a search warrant to be executed when the intercepted package is delivered. Section 108-3(a)(1) of the Code of Criminal Procedure of 1963 governs the issuance of search warrants in Illinois. At the time the anticipatory search warrant in this case was issued, section 108-3(a)(1) authorized search warrants for the seizure of "any instruments, articles or things which have been used in the commission of, or which may constitute evidence of, the offense in connection with which the warrant is issued." In Ross, we held that this language did not authorize the issuance of anticipatory search warrants.

It is undisputed that, pursuant to Ross, the anticipatory search warrant in this case was not authorized by statute. Therefore, defendant argues, the evidence seized pursuant to the invalid anticipatory search warrant should be inadmissible under the exclusionary rule. The State, however, argues that this evidence is admissible under the good-faith exception to the exclusionary rule as set forth United States v. Leon, 468 U.S. 897, 104 S.Ct. 3405, 82 L.Ed.2d 677 (1984). In Leon, the United States Supreme Court held that the fourth amendment exclusionary rule does not bar evidence obtained by a police officer who reasonably relied, in objective good faith, on a search warrant issued by a neutral and detached magistrate, but later found to be unsupported by probable cause. Defendant, relying on People v. Krueger, 175 Ill.2d 60, 221 Ill.Dec. 409, 675 N.E.2d 604 (1996), responds that the good-faith exception is not applicable here because of the nature of the holding in Ross.

A circuit court's ruling on a motion to quash arrest and suppress evidence is generally subject to reversal on appeal only if manifestly erroneous. Where only a question of law is involved, however, the circuit court's ruling is subject to *de novo* review. In this case, the issue raised is a question of law, and our review is therefore *de novo*.

Defendant contends that evidence seized pursuant to an anticipatory search warrant issued and executed prior to our decision in Ross is not admissible under the Leon good-faith exception to the exclusionary rule. In support, defendant argues that the anticipatory search warrant in this case was void *ab initio* because a crime had not been committed when the judge issued it. This, of course, is true of all anticipatory search warrants. In essence, defendant contends that anticipatory search warrants are unconstitutional. We note that, in Ross, we held that anticipatory search warrants were statutorily invalid, not that they were constitutionally invalid. Defendant asserts, however, that the analysis in Ross depended in part on Illinois constitutional principles. Specifically, defendant points out that Ross relied upon legislative history indicating that the drafters of the statute governing search warrants intended to follow the applicable existing case law (Lippman v. People, 175 Ill. 101, 113, 51 N.E. 872 1898). That decision, in interpreting the search and seizure provision of the Illinois Constitution of 1870, stated that a search warrant may be issued only after a showing that a crime has been committed. Thus, defendant argues, Ross found anticipatory search warrants to be not only statutorily invalid, but also violative of constitutional principles. We disagree. We hold that anticipatory search warrants are valid under both the fourth amendment to the United States Constitution and article I, section 6, of the Illinois Constitution of 1970.

Initially, we note that this court has not previously addressed the constitutionality of anticipatory search warrants. Our appellate court has explicitly held that anticipatory search warrants are valid under the Illinois Constitution. Several federal courts and other state courts have likewise upheld the constitutionality of anticipatory search warrants. The search and seizure clause of the Illinois Constitution provides: "The people shall have the right to be secure in their persons, houses, papers and other possessions against unreasonable searches, seizures, invasions of privacy or interceptions of communications by eavesdropping devices or other means. No warrant shall issue without probable cause, supported by affidavit particularly describing the place to be searched and the persons or things to be seized." Accordingly, both the fourth amendment and the Illinois search and seizure clause set forth two underlying requirements: searches and seizures must be reasonable, and probable cause must support search warrants. Anticipatory search warrants do not violate either requirement.

First, a search and seizure conducted pursuant to an anticipatory search warrant is reasonable. Where police officers know that a package containing contraband is going to be delivered to a certain residence at a certain time, there is nothing inherently unreasonable about allowing the issuance of a search warrant which will be executed only upon the occurrence of these conditions. The other options available in this scenario have significant drawbacks. For instance, the police could apply for a search warrant after the package is delivered, or simply conduct no search at all. Both of these options present the possibility that law enforcement authorities will lose track of both the criminal and the contraband. In addition, in some cases, the exigent circumstances exception to the warrant requirement may allow the police to conduct a lawful search without a warrant. A search pursuant to an anticipatory search warrant, however, is more reasonable than proceeding under the exigent circumstances exception because a neutral judge, rather than a police officer acting in the heat of the moment, makes the critical determination of whether probable cause for a search exists. Moreover, we find nothing inherently unreasonable about the option of obtaining an anticipatory search warrant, where, as discussed below, the police have probable cause to believe that a package containing contraband will be delivered to a certain place at a certain time.

Second, a properly issued anticipatory search warrant is based on probable cause. When a law enforcement official presents reliable evidence that a contraband delivery will occur at a certain place and at a certain time, and execution of the warrant is conditioned upon that delivery, there is sufficient probable cause to uphold the warrant. The fact that the contraband is not presently at the residence described in the warrant at the time the warrant is issued is inconsequential. The requirement that certain events must take place before the execution of an anticipatory search warrant assures that a search will take place only when justified by probable cause. Indeed, the information necessary to support issuance of an anticipatory search warrant is more likely to establish that probable cause will exist at the time of the search than the information necessary to support issuance of a typical search warrant. We therefore hold that anticipatory search warrants do not violate either the fourth amendment to the United States Constitution or the search and seizure clause of the Illinois Constitution.

Although we hold that anticipatory search warrants are constitutionally valid, it is undisputed that the anticipatory search warrant in this case was statutorily invalid under our decision in Ross. Consequently, we must determine whether the evidence seized from defendant's residence pursuant to a statutorily invalid anticipatory search warrant is admissible under the good-faith exception to the exclusionary rule. The United States Supreme Court first articulated the good-faith exception to the exclusionary rule United States v. Leon, 468 U.S. 897, 104 S.Ct. 3405, 82 L.Ed.2d 677 (1984). In Leon, the Supreme Court held that the fourth amendment exclusionary rule does not bar evidence obtained by a police officer who reasonably relied, in objective good faith, on a search warrant issued by a neutral and detached magistrate, but later found to be unsupported by probable cause. The Court in Leon noted that the purpose of the exclusionary rule is to deter police misconduct, not to punish the errors of magistrates and judges. The exclusionary rule cannot deter a police officer who reasonably believes in good faith that he possesses a valid search warrant from conducting a search pursuant to this warrant. This court adopted the Leon good-faith exception for Illinois in People v. Stewart (104 Ill.2d 463, 477, 85 Ill.Dec. 422, 473 N.E.2d 1227 1984). Later in Illinois v. Krull, 480 U.S. 340, 107 S.Ct. 1160, 94 L.Ed.2d 364 (1987), the United States Supreme Court extended the Leon good-faith exception. The Court held that the fourth amendment exclusionary rule does not bar evidence seized by a police officer who reasonably relied, in objective good faith, on a statute that authorized a warrantless administrative search, where the statute is later held unconstitutional. The Krull majority concluded that application of the exclusionary rule in situations where police officers conducted a search in objective good faith reliance on a statute, which is only later declared unconstitutional, would not deter future police misconduct.

This court People v. Krueger, 175 Ill.2d 60, 73-74, 221 Ill.Dec. 409, 675 N.E.2d 604 (1996), however, determined that the Krull good-faith exception is not compatible with the exclusionary rule arising out of the Illinois Constitution. After declaring unconstitutional 725 ILCS 5/108-8(b)(2) (allowing police to make "no-knock" entries under certain circumstances when executing a search warrant)), we held that evidence seized by virtue of an unconstitutional statute is not admissible under the good-faith exception to the exclusionary rule. Our opinion in Krueger discussed at length Justice O'Connor's dissent in Krull. Justice O'Connor explained that the extended good-faith exception to the fourth amendment exclusionary rule, as recognized by the Krull majority, provides a "grace period" for unconstitutional search and seizure legislation, during which time the State can "violate constitutional requirements with impunity." "Not only were such statutes the core concern of the Framers of the Fourth Amendment, the exclusionary rule had regularly been applied to suppress evidence gathered under unconstitutional statutes."

Based on reasoning similar to the reasoning in Justice O'Connor's dissent, this court in Krueger declined to interpret our state constitution in lockstep with the Krull majority. We explained that our state exclusionary rule has always been understood to bar evidence seized under the authority of an unconstitutional statute, and that to adopt Krull 's extended good-faith exception would drastically change this state's constitutional law. We then set forth the central basis for our rejection of Krull 's extended good-faith exception: "We are not willing to recognize an exception to our state exclusionary rule that will provide a grace period for unconstitutional search and seizure legislation, during which time our citizens' prized constitutional rights can be violated with impunity. We are particularly disturbed by the fact that such a grace period could last for several years and affect large numbers of people. This is simply too high a price for our citizens to pay." Significantly, however, we explicitly noted in Krueger that our decision to reject the Krull extended good-faith exception "does not impact the Leon good-faith exception."

Defendant argues that the Krueger rationale should be extended to apply to the instant case. Alluding to language in Krueger and in Justice O'Connor's dissent in Krull, defendant reasons that an invalid warrant resulting from a judicial error affects only one individual, whereas Ross 's declaration that anticipatory search warrants are statutorily invalid affects numerous individuals, including defendant. Defendant asserts that, since the reason for the invalidity of the warrant in her case resulted from legislative action, the evidence seized pursuant to this warrant should not be admissible under the Leon good-faith exception to the exclusionary rule. Defendant's argument is without merit. Most importantly, application of the Leon good-faith exception in the instant case does not present the threat to our citizens' constitutional rights that was present in Krueger. Both Krueger and Krull involved searches that were based on statutes later declared unconstitutional. Conversely, the instant case involves a search that was based on a constitutional anticipatory search warrant. This court in Ross found anticipatory search warrants to be statutorily invalid, not constitutionally invalid. Illinois citizens were never subjected to a grace period during which their constitutional rights could be violated with impunity-the fundamental concern set forth by this court in Krueger.

Furthermore, defendant's argument rests upon two inaccurate premises. First, defendant asserts that the warrant in her case was invalid as a result of legislative action. This is not correct. Anticipatory search warrants were declared invalid in Ross because the legislature had never approved of their use. This is best described as legislative inaction. Certainly the legislature did nothing to threaten the constitutional rights of Illinois citizens in this regard. Second, defendant contends that Krueger's rationale should apply here because large numbers of people may be affected by the holding in Ross. We disagree. The mere fact that large numbers of people may be affected was not dispositive in Krueger. Our concern in Krueger was that large numbers of people would be subjected to unconstitutional searches and seizures without any recourse. Defendant's argument must therefore be rejected.

We note that, if we were to accept defendant's position, we would implicitly be using Krueger's rationale to swallow the Leon good-faith exception. In fact, defendant contended at oral argument that we should reject Leon entirely. We decline to do so. Defendant offers no persuasive reason why we should depart from our previous adherence to the Leon good-faith exception. Consequently, the Leon good-faith exception remains valid. We therefore apply the Leon good-faith exception to the facts here. The Illinois legislature codified the Leon good-faith exception in 725 ILCS 5/114-12(b)(1), (b)(2). Section 114-12(b)(1) provides that a court should not suppress otherwise admissible evidence if a police officer seized the evidence in good faith. Section 114-12(b)(2)(i) sets forth the definition of "good faith" applicable to the case at bar: " 'Good faith' means whenever a peace officer obtains evidence: (i) pursuant to a search or an arrest warrant obtained from a neutral and detached judge, which warrant is free from obvious defects other than non-deliberate errors in preparation and contains no material misrepresentation by any agent of the State, and the officer reasonably believed the warrant to be valid." The actions of the police in this case meet this definition of good faith. The record reveals that the police obtained the anticipatory search warrant from a neutral and detached judge; the warrant was free from obvious defects; the warrant contained no material misrepresentations; and the police could have reasonably believed the warrant to be valid.

That the anticipatory search warrant was issued pursuant to the former section 108-3(a)(1) does not change our conclusion that the police acted in objective good-faith reliance on that warrant. At the time the police obtained the warrant, no Illinois case law held that anticipatory search warrants were statutorily or constitutionally invalid. Although this court in Ross ultimately concluded that the language of the former section 108-3(a)(1) did not authorize anticipatory search warrants, we specifically stated that this statutory provision was subject to "evenly plausible but divergent interpretations" as to whether it allowed anticipatory search warrants. Therefore, the police could have reasonably believed that section 108-3(a)(1) specifically authorized the anticipatory search warrant that they executed.

In sum, we hold that anticipatory search warrants are valid under both the fourth amendment to the United States Constitution and article I, section 6, of the Illinois Constitution. We further hold that the evidence seized in this case pursuant to the anticipatory search warrant issued and executed prior to our decision in Ross is admissible pursuant to the good-faith exception to the exclusionary rule. Accordingly, the circuit court erred in suppressing the evidence obtained pursuant to the anticipatory search warrant. For the reasons stated, we affirm the judgment of the appellate court, which reversed the judgment of the circuit court and remanded the cause to the circuit court for further proceedings. Affirmed.

Justice HEIPLE, dissenting: The warrant at issue was issued and executed before this court's decision People v. Ross, 168 Ill.2d 347, 213 Ill.Dec. 672, 659 N.E.2d 1319 (1995). In that case, we held that anticipatory search warrants were not authorized by section 108-3 of the Code of Criminal Procedure, as then in effect. This case presents the related question of whether evidence obtained pursuant to an anticipatory search warrant, issued and executed prior to our decision in Ross, is admissible against a defendant under the good-faith exception to the exclusionary rule. Article I, section 6, of the Illinois Constitution of 1970 provides, "No warrant shall issue without probable cause." Today the majority construes this clear constitutional command to permit a judge to issue a search warrant without probable cause to believe that a crime has been committed. In so doing, the majority abandons more than 100 years of precedent interpreting the right of the people of this state.

This court has had frequent occasion to consider the type of probable cause necessary to support the issuance of a search warrant. In the past, we have identified two core requirements: First, facts must be related which would cause a reasonable man to believe a crime had been committed. Secondly, facts must be set forth which would cause a reasonable man to believe the evidence was in the place to be searched. The warrant at issue satisfies neither of these requirements. At the time the warrant issued, defendant had not yet committed any crime, and the evidence was not located in her home. Thus, it cannot be disputed that there was neither probable cause to believe that a crime had been committed, nor probable cause to believe that the evidence was located at the premises to be searched. The majority dismisses these important constitutional infirmities. The majority posits that this court's prior holding invalidating anticipatory search warrants was decided merely as a matter of statutory construction; therefore, it treats the constitutionality of such warrants as a question of first impression. However, although we found it unnecessary to decide the constitutional question in Ross, our analysis in that case depended in large part upon Illinois constitutional jurisprudence in the area of searches and seizures. In concluding that section 108-3 of the Code of Criminal Procedure, as then in effect, prohibited anticipatory search warrants, we relied upon legislative history indicating that the drafters of that provision intended to follow existing case law.

In addition to rewriting well-settled constitutional law, today's decision represents astonishingly bad public policy. The majority's holding allows a court to authorize the invasion of a citizen's constitutionally protected privacy based upon information that, at some point in the future, the citizen may commit a crime and may have evidence of that crime in his home or on his person. Just as it is impermissible for police to detain a citizen based upon suspicion that the citizen may commit a crime, so too, it is inappropriate for a court to issue a search warrant in anticipation of criminality which has not yet occurred. Such action constitutes an overreaching and gross expansion of the police powers of this state, a terrible invasion of a citizen's privacy, and an incompatibility with the concepts of ordered liberty embodied in our Illinois Constitution. Finally, because the good-faith exception to the exclusionary rule is not applicable to evidence seized in violation of the Illinois Constitution, evidence seized pursuant to the anticipatory search warrant is inadmissible. For these reasons, I would affirm the judgment of the circuit court and reverse the judgment of the appellate court. Accordingly, I dissent.

REVIEW SECTION

READING COMPREHENSION

Why was the anticipatory search warrant in this case valid?

Detail the facts of this case, including the applicability of the constitution.

THINKING CRITICALLY

Which opinion of the court do you agree with and why?

Articulate the advantages and disadvantages of the exigent circumstances exception to the warrant requirement as compared to an anticipatory search warrant.

SECTION 2: THE DEFENSE OF ENTRAPMENT

OVERVIEW

What if you are going about your routine business and an undercover officer convinces you to commit a crime you would not have committed without his/her encouragement? Though attitudes have shifted remarkably, this is the purpose of the defense of entrapment. The logic behind this defense is to balance the need to cast a net for habitual criminals, while attempting not to capture otherwise law-abiding citizens. Historically, this practice arose to capture those involved in consensual crimes such as gambling and prostitution. This is known as an affirmative defense, not a constitutional right, and requires defendants have the burden of proving some evidence of entrapment. There is both a subjective and an objective test for entrapment.

The subjective test has been adopted by most states and the federal government, and requires the defendant to show that encouragement on the part of law enforcement crossed the line from acceptable to unacceptable. Defendants must demonstrate both that there existed no desire to commit the crime prior to the act of encouragement, and that the government's encouragement caused them to commit the crime in question. The question rests solely on intent. If intent was with the defendant, no entrapment occurred. If intent was with the government, entrapment did occur. Once a defendant has produced some evidence of persuasion, the government then must prove that indeed the defendant was predisposed to commit such a crime, thus shifting back the balance of intent.

The objective test of entrapment is also known as the hypothetical person test, and is adopted by a minority, but increasing number, of the courts. In this test, regardless of the defendant's past record or criminal inclination, the question is whether or not a reasonable, law-abiding citizen would have been induced to commit the crime with encouragement from law enforcement.

CASE

The following is from the case below, *People v Garcia:* "MILLS, Justice: Was Garcia entrapped by the police into committing this burglary? We think not. He was already predisposed to perpetrate the offense." Found guilty by a jury of committing burglary, Garcia was sentenced to imprisonment for 5 years. On appeal, the defendant contends that the State failed to prove beyond a reasonable doubt that he was not entrapped into committing this offense, that his representation by appointed counsel was ineffective, and that the victim was erroneously permitted to testify that her home had been burglarized on a prior occasion.

PEOPLE V. GARCIA
420 N.E.2d 221, 95 Ill.App.3d 377 (1981)

The evidence presented at trial focused on the defense of entrapment. On the evening of May 12, 1980, Detectives Randy Duvendack and Dale McKenna were positioned in the bushes behind the Corey residence and observed defendant and another man enter the backyard of the residence.

Officer John Lael and Detective Gerry Lieb, who had been cruising the area in a pickup truck, went to the Corey residence when they heard Officer McKenna yell. Lael testified that Randy Walden who was with defendant was working with the police in exchange for an agreement that he would not be prosecuted for certain alleged offenses. Detective Lieb and Officer Lael had discussed Walden's willingness to work with the police. Walden had informed Detective Lieb of earlier occasions when he and defendant had committed burglaries. (The defendant had already been investigated for an earlier burglary.) During the afternoon of May 12, Walden informed Detective Lieb that defendant would do a burglary with him that evening. It was Detective Lieb's idea to use the Corey residence as the site of this burglary.

Randy Walden the informer testified that the police officers wanted to catch defendant. Walden suggested committing this specific burglary to defendant after Garcia expressed a willingness to commit a burglary and led the defendant to the Corey residence. Officer Lieb had earlier told Walden to be there between 9 and 11 p.m. Walden denied, however, that he and defendant had ever committed any other burglary. Assistant State's Attorney Tim Olsen was called as a witness by defense counsel. He had discussed entrapment with Detective Lieb in March 1980. Lieb had asked whether it would be entrapment for an informant, who had committed burglaries with a certain person, to set up a burglary and tell the police when the burglary would occur. Olsen told Lieb that such a situation is not entrapment.

Defendant contends he was entrapped into committing this offense and requests this court to reverse his conviction. The defense of entrapment is found in section 7-12 of the Criminal Code of 1961: "A person is not guilty of an offense if his conduct is incited or induced by a public officer or employee, or agent of either, for the purpose of obtaining evidence for the prosecution of such person. However, this Section is inapplicable if a public officer or employer, or agent of either, merely affords to such person the opportunity or facility for committing an offense in furtherance of a criminal purpose which such person has originated." Once the entrapment defense is raised, it becomes incumbent upon the State to prove beyond a reasonable doubt that entrapment did not occur.

The question of whether entrapment exists is ordinarily reserved for the jury and should not be disturbed on appeal unless the reviewing court concludes that entrapment exists as a matter of law. Based on the evidence presented, the jury could have found that defendant was predisposed to commit this burglary. The fact that the police officers planned this particular offense does not require the reversal of defendant's conviction because entrapment does not exist where the law enforcement officers merely provide an opportunity for the commission of a crime by one who is already so predisposed. The evidence of defendant's predisposition is sufficient to defeat his claim of entrapment. From the testimony of both Detective Lieb and Randy Walden, it is clear that defendant Garcia wanted and agreed to commit a burglary before it was suggested that the Corey residence be the property hit. We find no basis in this record for setting aside the jury's verdict.

Defendant next asserts he was deprived of his due process right to a fair trial because of trial counsel's incompetence. In particular, defendant attacks the evidence elicited by his defense counsel that indicates he had been involved in other burglaries. Defendant contends his counsel should have moved to strike this extremely prejudicial evidence. In order to prevail in a claim of his counsel's incompetence, a defendant represented by court-appointed counsel must establish (1) actual incompetence and (2) substantial prejudice resulting therefrom. We agree with the State that defense counsel's decision not to react to this evidence of predisposition is properly characterized as trial tactics. Errors in judgment or trial strategy do not establish incompetence. The record does not support defendant's contention that he did not receive effective assistance of counsel. A defendant is entitled to a fair trial, but not a perfect trial. In retrospect, we can see that defense counsel's tactic of eliciting this testimony was perhaps unwise. But there undoubtedly are many trials in which lawyers realize after the fact that they should not have pursued a particular line of questioning. The distinction between improvident trial tactics and actual incompetence is a hazy one. In placing a case within one category or the other, a reviewing court is not in the business of second-guessing counsel. In this case, we do not see the defense attorney's error as rising to the level of actual incompetence.

Finally, defendant claims the trial court erred in allowing the victim to testify that her home had been burglarized on a prior occasion. We agree that this evidence is irrelevant and should not have been admitted. We find, however, the error in admitting this evidence is harmless and does not justify reversing defendant's conviction. Consequently, defendant's conviction is hereby affirmed.

CRAVEN, Justice, dissenting: I disagree with the majority opinion in two respects. First, this record establishes the existence of entrapment as a matter of law, and, second, if one is not persuaded to that conclusion then the defendant is entitled to a new trial by reason of incompetence of trial counsel. It is simply incomprehensible to me that the majority opinion categorizes the actions of the trial counsel here as mere "trial tactics." The precise question presented here is whether the evidence presented is sufficient to negate the defense of entrapment, beyond a reasonable doubt. The prohibition against police action designed to create and induce criminal acts in order to prosecute those persons who commit them underlies the entrapment defense. Two questions must be answered when determining if entrapment occurred: (1) whether the defendant was induced to commit a criminal offense by a government official or agent; and (2) whether the defendant was predisposed to commit the type of offense with which he is charged. The State argues that the police officers did not induce this burglary, but merely suggested the site. The record, however, refutes this contention. Randy Walden, who was working with the police, suggested committing this burglary to the defendant. Detective Lieb chose the Corey residence as the site of the burglary, and told Walden to be there. A closer question concerns the predisposition of the defendant. Predisposition means an already formed intent to commit the offense charged. The State argues that defendant's history of burglary involvement shows he was predisposed to commit this crime and supports the jury's determination of no entrapment. The record does show that the officers involved suspected that defendant had committed prior burglaries; and, according to the officers' testimony, Randy Walden had committed burglaries with the defendant in the past. At trial, Walden denied that he and defendant had ever committed a burglary. The question is not whether the defendant intended to commit the crime, but whether the intent originated in his mind. The evidence is simply insufficient to support a finding of predisposition on the part of the defendant.

We turn now to the issue of whether the defendant was denied the effective assistance of counsel. Interestingly enough the State does not assert waiver of any issue although no post-trial motion was filed by counsel. On appeal, the defendant attacks the evidence insinuating that he had been involved in other burglaries. That evidence was elicited by defense counsel even after the prosecutor informed counsel and the court that the State was not going to attempt to have such suspicions introduced in evidence. Counsel for the defendant responded that he was pursuing that line of examination of a witness and that he did not know what the witness was going to say. This was a clear indication that counsel did not interview the witness he was examining prior to the examination. That testimony was inadmissible if offered by the State and it was clearly severely prejudicial to the defendant. An attorney representing a defendant charged with a burglary who elicits evidence of his client's propensity to commit burglaries and the fact that his client was involved in other burglaries is hardly using trial tactics. It was a grievous error.

I am aware that in order to prevail in a claim of incompetence of counsel a defendant must establish that there was actual incompetence and that such resulted in substantial prejudice to his case. In this case, defense counsel raised the valid defense of entrapment, and then through his examination of witnesses introduced evidence, the substantive effect of which would be to tend to defeat that defense. Defense counsel elicited evidence tending to show that the defendant charged with burglary was a burglar. Effective representation of a defendant in a criminal case requires some familiarity with what testimony witnesses are going to give and pretrial preparation sufficient to enable counsel to anticipate witnesses' answers and to avoid questions that would tend to inculpate his client. Finally, the total failure of defense counsel to file a post-trial motion in view of the errors found in this record is but further evidence of the fact that the defendant here did not have that quality of representation necessary in order to obtain a fair trial. Thus, although I would reverse finding entrapment as a matter of law, if one is not persuaded to that view, then at a minimum this defendant is entitled to a new trial. For those reasons, I dissent.

REVIEW SECTION

READING COMPREHENSION

What are the facts of this case, including a detailed examination of what actions constitute entrapment?

THINKING CRITICALLY

In your opinion, should the state or the defendant bear the burden of persuading a jury of entrapment? Should a 'propensity to commit a crime' be a part of the consideration?

CASE

In *People v Wielgos,* the defendant was charged with delivery of more than 30 grams of cocaine. He was convicted by a jury, sentenced to six years imprisonment, and now appeals.

Eric Bjankini, a Northeast Metropolitan Enforcement Group undercover narcotics agent, in the summer of 1985, testified for the State. Working undercover as "Steve Hilton," Bjankini met with Edward Ruschinski on June 12, 1985 to discuss the purchase of cocaine. Ruschinski told Bjankini that he had access to cocaine. Three days later, Bjankini and Ruschinski again discussed the purchase of narcotics. Bjankini told Ruschinski that if he wanted to negotiate any transactions he could contact Bjankini via his pager. A week later, Ruschinski contacted Bjankini and asked if he was still interested in purchasing narcotics. Bjankini responded that he was, that he was always looking for a new supplier and that he would be willing to purchase whatever Ruschinski could get for him. Ruschinski told Bjankini that "he had a possibility of getting multiple ounces of cocaine" but did not name his source. Bjankini told Ruschinski to call him and let him know how much he could get and the price. Ruschinski contacted Bjankini a week later and told him that it looked like "we" would be able to get four ounces of cocaine around the 4th of July for $8,600.

Ruschinski contacted Bjankini on July 3 and informed him that he could get him four ounces of cocaine that day for $8,600. Bjankini picked Ruschinski up later that day and drove to the area of 70th and Harlem. During the drive, Bjankini and Ruschinski spoke about the impending transaction, about the fact that they would both benefit financially therefrom, about the fact that future transactions would be mutually beneficial, that "this could be a lucrative business" and that they "could have a long, permanent partnership." Ruschinski directed Bjankini to Burbank, Illinois, and they were admitted by defendant into his home. Bjankini introduced himself to defendant as "Steve Hilton" and informed him that he was interested in purchasing four ounces of cocaine. Defendant told Bjankini that he did not have the cocaine at that time, that Bjankini should return in half an hour and that there was a possibility that he would have it at that time. While in his home, neither Bjankini nor Ruschinski threatened defendant. After leaving defendant's home, Bjankini had Ruschinski count the $8,600. Upon returning, defendant informed Bjankini that his supplier had nine ounces of cocaine but could not drop off the amount defendant had ordered because the supplier was at the Taste of Chicago festival. Bjankini told defendant that he was always interested in a new supplier, that he would still like to purchase more cocaine, that, if the cocaine came later that evening, Ruschinski could take possession and that he would get it from him. After defendant told Bjankini that he would try to get the cocaine on Friday, Bjankini left and Ruschinski stayed with defendant.

Ruschinski informed Bjankini on July 5 that defendant was having trouble getting the cocaine. Bjankini told Ruschinski to give defendant his pager number so that Bjankini could talk to him directly. Thereafter, Bjankini was paged with the code he had given Ruschinski for defendant. Bjankini called defendant and defendant told him that he would be going over to his "connect's" house about 3:30 p.m. to get the okay to pick up the cocaine. Bjankini called defendant later and told him that he would be at his house at 3:45 to pick up the cocaine. Bjankini then called Ruschinski and told him he would meet him at 79th and Mobile at 3:30. Defendant paged Bjankini at 3:45 to tell him that he was on his way to pick up the cocaine. After meeting Ruschinski, Bjankini had him count the $8,600 to be paid defendant for the cocaine. Upon arriving at defendant's home, defendant led them into the kitchen and Bjankini observed a scale, some plastic "baggies" and a mound of white powder on a plate on the kitchen table. Defendant told Bjankini that "it was quality coke," and that "the weight was exact." He also asked Bjankini if he wanted to "zero out the scale," which meant to set the weight on the scale before weighing at no weight. Bjankini weighed the cocaine and informed defendant that it was correct. Ruschinski then advised defendant that he had counted the money and that it was in Bjankini's car. Bjankini took the cocaine, walked out to his car and gave a pre-arranged arrest signal. He and the team of agents surveilling the scene placed defendant and Ruschinski under arrest.

Defendant testified in his own behalf. In the summer of 1985, defendant was unemployed and was living with his mother. At that time, he had known Ruschinski for almost three years as a friend. Defendant had known Tony Creagh all of his life. Defendant denied ever having used, delivered or sold cocaine before June 1985. At that time, Ruschinski began telephoning defendant and asking for Creagh's phone number because he wanted to buy some cocaine from him. Defendant told Ruschinski that he did not "want to have any part of it." Between June and July 3, Ruschinski called defendant about 25 times and visited him about seven times. In one day during that period, Ruschinski called defendant five times. Ruschinski wanted defendant "to get a hold of Creagh for the purchase of cocaine." Defendant did not put Ruschinski in touch with Creagh nor did he agree to do anything with Ruschinski.

When Bjankini and Ruschinski came to his home on July 3, Bjankini asked defendant if the four ounces of cocaine were there. He also told defendant that he could make large amounts of money. Defendant responded that he did not have the cocaine and did not want any part in dealing with Bjankini and Ruschinski. Ruschinski, who was very upset, told defendant he thought the "arrangements were going to be worked out that day with Steve." Ruschinski also shook defendant by the shoulders and told him "that Steve had warned him and told him that it better be there that day." Ruschinski also told defendant "that Steve carried a gun at times." In response to defendant's statements, Bjankini asked defendant what was going on and said he "thought it was going to be here today." Bjankini also asked defendant whether he had gotten hold of Creagh. Defendant responded that he had not. Ruschinski again told defendant "that he meant business" and "that he wanted these four ounces of cocaine." Defendant then told Bjankini and Ruschinski that he would contact Tony and for them to come back in half an hour. However, defendant did not call Creagh. When Bjankini and Ruschinski returned, they again told defendant that he could make thousands of dollars and asked if he "was going to set them up with Tony." Defendant again refused. Defendant had made no arrangements prior to this meeting to supply or deliver any cocaine to Bjankini or Ruschinski and never had any intention to do so. After Bjankini left defendant's home, Ruschinski asked defendant to take him to Creagh's house and defendant agreed. However, Creagh was not home. Defendant had not decided to deliver any cocaine to Bjankini when he returned from Creagh's house. He decided to do so later that evening when Ruschinski called him and told him that Steve was threatening Ruschinski and telling him that "his people were waiting for this product" and that "he was very fed up with it." Ruschinski also told defendant that he was in a bad situation and needed defendant's help. Thereafter, defendant called Creagh.

Upon calling Creagh, defendant told him that he knew that he dealt cocaine, that he knew someone interested in buying four ounces and that he wanted to send Bjankini and Ruschinski to his house. After telling defendant that "he didn't want any part of anyone he didn't know," Creagh agreed to "do the four ounces of cocaine" directly with defendant. Creagh and defendant then agreed on a price of $7,500 for the cocaine. Defendant spoke with Ruschinski on the morning of July 5. Ruschinski told defendant he would bring a scale to defendant's home because it would be needed that afternoon. Defendant spoke with Ruschinski again in the afternoon and told him that he was scared, wanted to change his mind about doing the transaction and did not want any part in it. Ruschinski told defendant "that Steve would definitely do something" to both of them. He also told defendant to contact Bjankini via his beeper. Upon doing so, defendant told Bjankini that the transaction would take place around 4 p.m. On cross-examination, defendant testified that he decided to take part in the transaction because he felt threatened. He was pressured very heavily by both Bjankini and Ruschinski. When he spoke with him on July 5, Ruschinski told him that Bjankini was waiting for the cocaine and that, if he did not "come through with it, certain things would be happening."

On appeal, defendant chiefly asserts that a new trial is required due to: (1) the State's failure to tender, during discovery, statements which its witnesses testified defendant made during his arrest; and (2) prosecutorial misconduct during the course of his trial. However, we find no need to address those contentions of error inasmuch as we find dispositive the third error alleged, viz., the trial court's failure to instruct the jury properly on the defense of entrapment. Defendant tendered two instructions on the defense of entrapment. The first stated, *inter alia*, that it was a defense to the offense charged that defendant was entrapped, i.e., "that for the purpose of obtaining evidence against him, he was incited or induced by a public officer and/or agent of a public officer to commit an offense." The second instruction substituted the names of Bjankini and Ruschinski in the appropriate places in the first instruction. The trial court rejected defendant's entrapment instructions and charged the jury with the State's instruction on the defense, which omitted the "and/or agent of a public officer" language of defendant's first instruction.

Defendant asserts that, in rejecting the tendered instructions, the trial court rejected the defense theory of vicarious entrapment and committed reversible error. A defendant is entitled to a jury instruction on any defense which is supported by even very slight evidence. This rule applies to the entrapment defense. Applying this very liberal standard, we conclude that the evidence in this case was sufficient to warrant inclusion of the language omitted by the trial court from the entrapment instruction. Specifically, we find that Bjankini's own testimony amply revealed that Bjankini, a public officer, employed Ruschinski, albeit unwittingly, as his agent for the purchase of cocaine from third parties in general and from defendant specifically. Moreover, defendant's testimony was sufficient to have supported a jury finding that Ruschinski incited or induced defendant to deliver cocaine to Bjankini, had the jury been properly instructed. Beyond the fact that the evidence was sufficient to reveal that Ruschinski acted as Bjankini's agent and that Ruschinski induced or incited defendant to deliver cocaine to Bjankini, the instruction tendered by defendant was proper as a matter of law.

As noted above, section 7-12 of the Criminal Code of 1961 establishes that a defendant may be entrapped by an agent of a public officer or employee as well as such officer or employee. Moreover, while no Illinois case has reviewed the propriety of a jury instruction on entrapment where, as here, the alleged agent of a public officer or employee acted unwittingly, i.e., without the knowledge that his principal was a public officer, some Federal courts have approved an entrapment defense in such cases. In United States v. Anderton (5th Cir.1980), 629 F.2d 1044, the defendant tendered a jury instruction defining the term "law enforcement officer," used in a standard entrapment instruction, as including any person acting solely for or on behalf of a person actually in the employment of a federal or state agency in the pursuit of such occupation. The trial court instructed the jury, instead, that entrapment occurred when law enforcement officers or their agents induced the commission of a crime but that a private citizen who was not a government officer nor agent thereof could not commit entrapment. In reversing the defendant's conviction based on error in the jury instruction, the Anderton court held that a person who was "an ignorant pawn of the government" could commit entrapment.

Admittedly, the majority of Federal Courts of Appeal do not recognize the defense of vicarious entrapment. However, we believe that the plain and unambiguous language of section 7-12 of the Criminal Code must be read as allowing that defense in Illinois. Section 7-12 provides, *inter alia* that "a person is not guilty of an offense if his conduct is incited or induced by a public officer or employee, or agent of either." The statute does not require that the agent of the public officer or employee know the true identity of the public officer or employee. Moreover, it does not require that the agent communicate only inducements flowing directly from or originating with the officer or employee. Thus, the latter requirement, which the Federal courts impose in determining whether an entrapment defense is valid is inapplicable in Illinois. Giving effect to the plain and unambiguous language of the statute has the salutary result of recognizing that entrapment does not turn on the government's control of every detail of the discussions between its unwitting middlemen and defendants but, rather, that, once the government employs unsavory characters as such to ferret out crime, it should be fairly charged with responsibility for their actions.

Moreover, the State offers no cogent reason for holding otherwise in this case. The State argues that the jury was properly instructed on the defense of entrapment based upon the evidence presented at trial. Specifically, it asserts that, based upon the evidence, Ruschinski was not an agent of the police but rather a friend of defendant who merely solicited him to help Ruschinski commit the crime. It concludes that, as Ruschinski was neither a public officer nor agent thereof, but, rather, defendant's accomplice and codefendant, defendant was not entitled to the rejected instructions. Beyond the fact that our review of the evidence persuades us otherwise, we must note that neither of the cases the State cites for its latter conclusion, People v. Jarvis (1987), 158 Ill.App.3d 415, 110 Ill.Dec. 636, 511 N.E.2d 813 and People v. Miller (1980), 90 Ill.App.3d 422, 45 Ill.Dec. 810, 413 N.E.2d 143, in any way support it. The State also asserts that defendant's alleged use of the phrase "zero out the scale" and the fact he was able to procure a large amount of extremely pure cocaine (92%) in a short period of time reveal that he was entrapped by no one and was, instead, predisposed to commit the crime charged. We cannot agree that this evidence justified rejecting defendant's entrapment instructions.

Defendant denied that he used the phrase "zero out the scale." That the jury found him guilty does not require the conclusion that it also resolved this dispute against him. More importantly, we cannot agree that obtaining four ounces of cocaine in a short amount of time necessarily reveals a predisposition to commit the crime charged because, as the State implies, defendant had committed it in the past. This fact would reveal criminal predisposition only if Bjankini had explicitly sought extremely pure cocaine. In that case, obtaining 92% pure cocaine would reveal a familiarity with the criminal underworld of narcotics and narcotics peddlers and a predisposition to participate therein. But where, as here, the buyer does not stipulate the purity of the narcotics sought and it does not appear that the defendant was aware of the purity of the narcotics supplied, delivering such pure cocaine reveals nothing with respect to familiarity with that underworld and predisposition.

The State also contends that, in enacting section 7-12, the legislature did not intend to recognize the defense of vicarious entrapment. While this argument presents a difficult question theoretically, it does not do so practically as the State fails to cite any authority in support and to address the recognition of the defense in Federal jurisprudence. The recognition of vicarious entrapment as a valid defense in Federal caselaw, the plain and unambiguous language of section 7-12 and the State's aforementioned failures, we are compelled to conclude that the defense is valid in Illinois. For all the foregoing reasons, defendant's conviction is reversed and the cause is remanded for a new trial. Reversed and remanded.

REVIEW SECTION

READING COMPREHENSION

Detail the facts of this case and the relevance of the entrapment defense.

Discuss vicarious entrapment and the view of this defense by both the Illinois and federal courts.

THINKING CRITICALLY

Elaborate the elements of the objective and subjective tests. Defend which test you believe should be used in the entrapment defense.

CONCLUSION

This chapter addressed in detail the exclusionary rule and the defense of entrapment. Though neither are backed directly by constitutional rights, each has been established by the U.S. Supreme Court with the intent to enforce constitutional rights. Both the exclusionary rule and the entrapment defense have been the subject of much debate in this country, both expressed in case law and in the legislature.

Chapter Eleven

Constitutional Violations: Other Remedies Against Government Misconduct

We have elaborated the exclusionary rule and the defense of entrapment which are remedies available to defendants in criminal trial cases, however there are also remedies an individual may pursue against an officer that are not available at the trial stage. Such remedies include prosecuting the officer through criminal law which rarely occurs as police misconduct is infrequently viewed by the courts as a criminal action, suing a government official or entity through civil law in a state or federal court, or administrative discipline of an officer outside of the judicial system.

This chapter will review:

(1)   Remedies for official misconduct; and

(2)   Failure to protect by law enforcement.

SECTION 1: REMEDIES FOR OFFICIAL MISCONDUCT

OVERVIEW

Because criminal prosecution of an officer is rare, we will turn our attention to suing a government official or entity through the use of civil law at the state or federal level. An individual can sue a federal law enforcement officer for a constitutional tort action or *Bivens* action named for the case decided in 1971 (*Bivens . Six Unnamed FBI Agents*). This case created a private right to sue federal officers who have violated a constitutional right of an individual. Plaintiffs are required to prove that officers were acting under color of authority and that the action of the officer did indeed deprive the individual of a constitutional right. Proof of these two elements however, does not automatically translate into a successful outcome of the case. Law enforcement personnel may employ the qualified immunity or 'good faith' defense wherein they demonstrate the action in question met the test of objective legal reasonableness which is measured by the legal rules established at the time of the officer's action. This defense was created as a balance to prevent frivolous lawsuits arising from actions that officers must use broad discretion in making in performance of job duties and protection of the public.

A lawsuit filed against the federal government for the constitutional torts of their officers is a Federal Tort Claims Act (FTCA) action. Under the held-over doctrine of sovereign immunity, a government cannot be sued without their consent, though laws that at least to some degree waive this immunity are employed by most states and U.S. governments.

If an individual wants to sue a state officer, they can use either a state tort lawsuits or a federal U.S. Civil Rights Act lawsuit. Keep in mind that when pursuing a state tort action, officers are afforded the defense of official immunity. A Civil Right Act action allows plaintiffs to use the federal court to sue state, county, and municipal officers for violations of federal constitutional rights. The standard of proof required is very similar to that in a *Bivens* action. Finally, to sue a state or local government, a suit can be brought as a state tort action or as a U.S. Civil Rights Action.

CASE

On August 18, 1984, Steven Poole was shot by Michael Conroy, an on-duty police officer with the Rolling Meadows police department. In *Poole v The City of Rolling Meadows,* the plaintiff brings an action to recover damages for injuries he sustained as a result of the shooting. As amended, plaintiff's two-count complaint alleged that the defendants were guilty of willful and wanton misconduct which resulted in Poole's injuries. The complaint further alleged that the officer violated section 1983 of the Federal civil rights statute.

POOLE V. THE CITY OF ROLLING MEADOWS
656 N.E.2d 768, 167 Ill.2d 41 (1995)

With respect to the section 1983 claim, the jury returned a verdict in favor of Conroy. On the State-law claim that defendants acted willfully and wantonly, the jury found in favor of plaintiff and assessed compensatory damages in the amount of $199,164.81. Because the jury further determined that plaintiff was 75% contributorily negligent, the trial judge reduced the award by that percentage and entered judgment on the verdict for $49,791.20. Plaintiff challenged the reduction of damages, arguing that damages based on willful and wanton misconduct could not be reduced by a plaintiff's contributory negligence. The trial judge granted plaintiff's motion to reinstate the full jury award and entered judgment notwithstanding the verdict in the amount of $199,164.81. Defendants' post-trial motion challenging the modified judgment was denied. On appeal, the appellate court affirmed the trial judge's reinstatement of the full award of damages. We thereafter granted defendants' petition for leave to appeal.

The incident giving rise to the complaint filed against defendants occurred during the early evening hours of August 18, 1984. On that date, Conroy and three other police officers responded to a call from a neighbor that an individual had been seen entering the home of plaintiff's mother through a second-floor window. While investigating the incident, Conroy mistakenly shot plaintiff, who was coming out of the home's basement into a first-floor hallway. As a result of the shooting and plaintiff's injury, plaintiff filed suit against defendants. As amended, plaintiff's two-count complaint alleged that defendants were guilty of willful and wanton misconduct in causing plaintiff's injuries and that Conroy violated section 1983 of the Federal civil rights statute (42 U.S.C. § 1983). In their answer to the count of the complaint alleging willful and wanton misconduct, defendants pled as an affirmative defense that plaintiff's injuries resulted, in whole or in part, from plaintiff's willful and wanton misconduct or omissions. On the last day that evidence was heard at trial, defendants filed an amended answer. The amended answer was identical in all respects to the original answer except that defendants alleged plaintiff's contributory negligence, rather than plaintiff's willful and wanton misconduct, as an affirmative defense. Plaintiff's motion to strike the amended answer was denied.

During the conference on jury instructions, plaintiff argued that any contributory negligence on his part should not reduce a damage award based on defendants' willful and wanton misconduct. At the time of trial, however, two decisions from the Fourth District of the Appellate Court sanctioned a comparison of plaintiff's contributory negligence with defendant's willful and wanton misconduct under the doctrine of comparative fault. (Yates v. Brock (1989), 191 Ill.App.3d 358, 361, 138 Ill.Dec. 605, 547 N.E.2d 1031; State Farm Mutual Automobile Insurance Co. v. Mendenhall (1987), 164 Ill.App.3d 58, 61, 115 Ill.Dec. 139, 517 N.E.2d 341). The trial judge ruled that the jury could consider plaintiff's contributory negligence in reducing the damages awarded for defendants' willful and wanton misconduct, and over plaintiff's objection, instructed the jury accordingly. The jury subsequently returned a verdict in favor of Conroy on the section 1983 claim. On the State-law claim based on allegations of willful and wanton misconduct, the jury found for plaintiff and assessed damages in the amount of $199,164.81. The amount of damages was reduced by 75%, the percentage of contributory negligence the jury attributed to plaintiff. Judgment for plaintiff was, therefore, entered on the jury's verdict in the amount of $49,791.20.

In his post-trial motion, plaintiff challenged the reduction of damages, arguing that the amount of defendants' liability award could not be reduced by the percentage of plaintiff's contributory negligence. Between the time judgment was entered on the verdict and the filing of the post-trial motion, the First District of the Appellate Court issued its opinion in Burke v. 12 Rothschild's Liquor Mart, Inc. (209 Ill.App.3d 192, 154 Ill.Dec. 80, 568 N.E.2d 80 1991). The Burke court disagreed with the Fourth District cases and held that a defendant who was found guilty of willful and wanton misconduct was not entitled to a reduction in damages based on a plaintiff's contributory negligence. In light of the appellate court's decision in Burke, the trial judge granted plaintiff's request for post-trial relief and entered judgment notwithstanding the verdict in the amount of $199,164.81. Defendants' post-trial motion challenging the modified judgment was denied.

On appeal, defendants argued, among other things, that the trial judge erred in reinstating the full award of damages. Defendants contended that because of the change in law engendered by Burke, the appropriate remedy was a remand for a new trial to allow the jury to determine whether plaintiff acted willfully and wantonly and, if so, to compare plaintiff's willful and wanton misconduct with defendants' willful and wanton misconduct. Because Burke held that a plaintiff's contributory negligence could not reduce a defendant's liability based on willful and wanton misconduct, defendants contended that a new trial was warranted to allow them to proceed on a correct theory of the law. After the appeal was filed in the appellate court, but before the case was decided, this court affirmed the appellate court's decision in Burke. In Burke, this court held that a plaintiff's negligence could not reduce a damage award based on the willful and wanton misconduct of a defendant. This determination was based on the "qualitative distinction" between acts of simple negligence and willful and wanton misconduct. Based on this court's decision in Burke, the appellate court in the present case found that the trial judge's decision to reinstate the full damage award was proper. The appellate court also rejected defendants' argument that the appropriate remedy was a new trial to allow defendants to assert the affirmative defense of plaintiff's willful and wanton misconduct. Following the appellate court's decision in the present case, defendants petitioned this court for leave to appeal. We subsequently granted defendants' petition and, for the following reasons, reverse the judgment of the appellate court and remand for a new trial.

On appeal to this court, defendants argue that it was error for the trial judge to reinstate the full jury award. Defendants contend that they asserted plaintiff's contributory negligence as an affirmative defense based on the state of the law at the time the case was tried. Because Burke was read to mean that it was error to instruct the jury to compare plaintiff's contributory negligence with any form of defendants' willful and wanton misconduct, defendants argue that the trial judge should have granted them a new trial to assert an affirmative defense based on plaintiff's willful and wanton misconduct, rather than reinstating the jury verdict. By the trial judge's reinstatement of the full verdict, defendants maintain that they have been deprived of the opportunity to present a viable defense based on plaintiff's willful and wanton misconduct. We agree that the reinstatement of the verdict was error and that a new trial is warranted in this case, but for a different reason than that advanced by defendants.

As previously noted, this court in Burke held that because of the "qualitative difference" between simple negligence and willful and wanton misconduct a plaintiff's negligence could not be compared with a defendant's willful and wanton misconduct. Although the Burke court ruled that a plaintiff's negligence could not be compared with a defendant's willful and wanton misconduct, Burke does not completely dictate the outcome of this case. Before oral arguments were heard here, we filed our opinion in Ziarko v. Soo Line R.R. Co. (161 Ill.2d 267, 204 Ill.Dec. 178, 641 N.E.2d 402 1994), in which a plurality of this court reviewed the decision in Burke and limited its application and analysis to those cases in which the willful and wanton misconduct was intentional. In Ziarko, we recognized that the label "willful and wanton misconduct" has developed in this State as a hybrid between acts considered negligent and those found to be intentionally tortious. "Under the facts of one case, willful and wanton misconduct may be only degrees more than ordinary negligence, while under the facts of another case, willful and wanton acts may be only degrees less than intentional wrongdoing." In acknowledging that willful and wanton acts share similar characteristics with acts of ordinary negligence in some cases, a plurality of this court believed that Burke's holding that there was a "qualitative distinction" between willful and wanton acts and negligent acts did not consider the dual characteristics of willful and wanton misconduct. The plurality in Ziarko therefore distinguished Burke, stating that the Burke court limited its analysis to willful and wanton acts that were committed intentionally, and did not consider willful and wanton acts committed recklessly. In Ziarko, the plurality found no injustice to the rule adopted in Burke to the extent that it applied to willful and wanton misconduct amounting to intentional behavior. However, the plurality found that the rule in Burke was not valid when applied to willful and wanton acts that were simply reckless, rather than intentional.

Although Ziarko involved principles of contribution, rather than contributory fault principles, the plurality specifically discussed the ruling in Burke and to what extent a plaintiff's contributory negligence could be compared with a defendant's willful and wanton misconduct in apportioning damages. Under the plurality's analysis of Burke in Ziarko, a jury would therefore be precluded from reducing a defendant's damages by a plaintiff's contributory negligence if the defendant's willful and wanton misconduct was intentional. On the other hand, if a defendant's conduct amounted to reckless willful and wanton behavior, plaintiff's damages could be reduced by the percentage of his contributory negligence. Although only a plurality in Ziarko subscribed to the preceding analysis of Burke, we adhere to those views here.

In rendering their decisions, both the trial court and the appellate court in the present case relied on authority which held that a plaintiff's contributory negligence could not be compared with a defendant's willful and wanton misconduct. However, under the Ziarko plurality's interpretation of this court's opinion in Burke, a plaintiff's contributory negligence may be compared to a defendant's willful and wanton misconduct, if that willful and wanton misconduct was committed recklessly, rather than intentionally. Consequently, whether reinstatement of the full award of damages was appropriate here depends, in part, on whether defendants' willful and wanton misconduct was committed intentionally or recklessly.

Here, the jury was given the following instruction on the definition of willful and wanton misconduct: "When I use the expression 'willful and wanton misconduct,' I mean a course of action which shows actual or deliberate intention to harm or which, if not intentional, shows an utter indifference to or conscious disregard for the safety of others." As we noted in Ziarko, this particular instruction recognizes that a distinction should be drawn between willful and wanton acts that are intentional and misconduct that is reckless. The jury in the present case found that defendants were guilty of willful and wanton misconduct. However, the instruction was not limited to a particular kind of willful and wanton misconduct, and no special interrogatory was submitted to the jury to determine whether the type of willful and wanton misconduct defendants were guilty of was reckless or intentional. Moreover, the complaint alleged that the willful and wanton misconduct of defendants was committed both intentionally and with "conscious, reckless disregard or indifference." It is therefore unclear from the jury's verdict which type of willful and wanton misconduct defendants were found guilty of because the distinction between intentional and reckless willful and wanton misconduct neither was plead nor was the jury specifically asked to characterize defendants' misconduct.

Because we cannot determine whether defendants were guilty of intentional or reckless willful and wanton misconduct, we are also unable to determine whether plaintiff's contributory negligence could be compared to defendants' misconduct in apportioning damages. Further, in viewing the evidence in the light most favorable to defendants, we cannot say that the evidence so overwhelmingly indicated that defendants' conduct was intentionally willful and wanton that plaintiff's contributory negligence could not be taken into consideration in reducing the jury award. Because it is unclear whether defendant's willful and wanton misconduct was committed intentionally or recklessly, the trial court erred in reinstating the verdict. We therefore remand to the trial court for a new trial consistent with our opinion here. For the foregoing reasons, the decisions of the trial and appellate courts are reversed and the cause is remanded to the trial court for a new trial. Appellate court reversed; trial court reversed; cause remanded.

Justice NICKELS, dissenting: I respectfully dissent from the majority's holding that liability for willful and wanton conduct may be reduced based on the injured party's ordinary negligence, so long as the tortfeasor's willful and wanton conduct is merely "reckless" rather than "intentional." In Burke v. 12 Rothschild's Liquor Mart, Inc. (1992), this court held that willful and wanton conduct is qualitatively different from ordinary negligence and carries a degree of opprobrium not found in ordinary negligence. In so holding, the court suggested no distinction, such as the majority draws today, between "intentionally" and "recklessly" willful and wanton conduct. Nor was Burke 's vitality affected by Ziarko v. Soo Line R.R. Co. (1994). The six members of the court who participated in the decision of Ziarko were evenly divided on the question of whether Burke should be limited to cases involving "intentionally" willful and wanton misconduct. Lacking the support of a majority of the members of the court, this suggested limitation did not achieve the status of a precedential holding. Burke supplies the rule of decision for the case at bar, and in my view the majority's departure from Burke is ill-advised.

Citing the plurality opinion in Ziarko, the majority contends that willful and wanton misconduct has developed in Illinois as a hybrid between acts considered negligent and those considered intentionally tortious, and that in some cases willful and wanton acts share similar characteristics with acts of ordinary negligence. The majority maintains that the Burke court failed to consider the "dual characteristics" of willful and wanton conduct, and that Burke 's holding should be limited to cases involving willful and wanton conduct amounting to intentional behavior. The resultant rule: liability for "recklessly" willful and wanton conduct may be reduced on account of the plaintiff's ordinary negligence while liability for "intentionally" willful and wanton conduct may not. I disagree with the majority's reasoning. As indicated in my dissent in Ziarko, although willful and wanton conduct shares characteristics of both intentional and negligent conduct, it is analytically distinct from either concept. Willful and wanton conduct involves acts performed in conscious disregard of a known risk or with utter indifference to the consequences. While such conduct may be less opprobrious than the deliberate infliction of injury, it is still significantly more blameworthy and qualitatively different from ordinary negligence. According to the leading text on the subject of tort law, the terms "willful," "wanton" and "reckless," individually or in combination, mean essentially the same thing, and refer to conduct involving a state of mind that has been described as "quasi-intent." Thus, willful and wanton conduct is properly viewed as an aggravated form of negligence, differing in quality rather than in degree from ordinary lack of care. Accordingly, while the majority's characterization of willful and wanton conduct as a hybrid between intentional and negligent conduct is correct, it does not undermine the reasoning in Burke that all willful and wanton conduct is qualitatively different from ordinary negligence. I see no persuasive reason to depart from or revise Burke, and thus I respectfully dissent. HEIPLE and HARRISON, JJ., join in this dissent.

REVIEW SECTION

READING COMPREHENSION

Detail the logic of the court in making its finding.

Discuss the relevance of *Ziarko v. Soo Line R.R. Co* (1994) to this case.

THINKING CRITICALLY

The resulting rule of this case, according to the dissent entails "liability for recklessly willful and wanton conduct may be reduced on account of the plaintiff's ordinary negligence while liability for intentionally willful and wanton conduct may not." Agree or disagree with the premise of this rule.

Is there a qualitative difference between simple negligence and willful and wanton misconduct? How clear are these distinctions?

CASE

Jenkins v Meyers is a civil rights action brought by a prisoner at the Illinois State Penitentiary against various prison officials arising out of the defendants' failure to mail a trial transcript to the plaintiff's attorney.

JENKINS V. MEYERS
338 F.Supp. 383 (1972)

Plaintiff alleges that on August 31, 1970 he delivered the trial transcript in his case to Defendant Meyers, a clerk in the Record Office at Stateville to be mailed to his attorneys. Plaintiff was subsequently informed by his counsel that the transcript never arrived. Plaintiff's repeated inquiries to prison officials as to the whereabouts of the transcript were allegedly met with indifference. On February 9, 1971, Defendant Meyers returned the transcript to Plaintiff but refused to inform him as to where the transcript had been in the interim and Plaintiff's request for an investigation was turned down. As a result of these alleged acts Plaintiff contends that his rights under the First, Fourth, Sixth and Fourteenth Amendments have been violated; that his civil rights under 42 U.S.C. § 1983, have been violated; that he has lost a post conviction hearing and that his direct appeal was delayed and denied. He seeks injunctive relief and $10,000 in the actual and punitive damages. In Count II of Plaintiff's Second Amended Complaint he alleges that his transcript was seized from his person while he was on his way to his work assignment pursuant to a prison regulation forbidding possession of legal papers at job assignments and that as a result of his resistance he was punished with one day in isolation and the loss of the privilege of attending two movies. Plaintiff alleging violations of his First, Fourth, Sixth and Fourteenth Amendment rights seeks an additional $5,000 in actual and punitive damages on this Count and injunctive relief. Pursuant to an agreement made at the time of the submission of the pre-trial order, the issue of liability under Count I of the Second Amended Complaint has been separated from the issue of relief under Count I and from all of the issues under Count II, for disposition on the basis of the facts stipulated to in the pre-trial order.

In disposing of the issue of liability under Count I we must first determine the factual setting and then decide whether the acts involved are violations of the Civil Rights Act. Defendants do not controvert the fact that the transcript was indeed delivered to them for forwarding to Plaintiff's counsel; that it was not forwarded as directed and that it did not again turn up until February of 1971. The dispute centers around the whereabouts of the transcript during that five-month period and how it came to be lost. This Court is convinced that Defendants' version of the facts as substantiated by exhibits and other evidence is the true course of events that led to the disappearance of the record. Due to the large volume of mail handled by the prison record office, the transcript was inadvertently placed in an envelope along with some other papers addressed to Mrs. Rose Edmonds, the mother of another prisoner. Mrs. Edmonds, unaware that the misplaced documents were among the other papers correctly sent to her did not send them back until she returned her son's entire file. It was at this time that the error in regard to Plaintiff's transcript was discovered. Our factual finding, therefore, is that Defendants did not intend to deny or violate Plaintiff's constitutional right of access to the courts. This factual conclusion, however, in view of various interpretations given the Civil Rights Act is not sufficient in itself to dispose of the issue in this case.

Assuming as we have that the documents were negligently handled, we must now decide whether mere negligence, such as the mailing of Plaintiff's transcript, is not actionable under the Civil Rights Act as Defendants argue or whether Plaintiff is correct in his position that under the Civil Rights Act the fact that the prison officials did not intend to deprive him of his unimpeded access to the courts is irrelevant since "improper motive" is not an element of a § 1983 suit. Monroe v. Pape, 365 U.S. 167, 81 S.Ct. 473, 5 L.Ed.2d 492 (1961) determined that 42 U.S.C. § 1983 "should be read against the background of tort liability that makes a man responsible for the natural consequences of his actions" and that specific intent to violate the rights protected by the Act is not necessary for a cause of action. Early cases took this to mean that a § 1983 cause of action was possible for all torts so long as the tortious act was done by individuals acting under color of state law. The later trend was to move away from this absolute position. A great deal of debate centers on the question of whether "improper motive" must accompany an invasion of constitutional rights to make the violation actionable under § 1983.

In Joseph v. Rowlen, 402 F.2d 367 (1968), relied on by Plaintiff, the court rejected the notion that ulterior motive is a requisite of a § 1983 cause: "Federal courts, including this one have expressed the policy view that sec. 1983 should not be construed to make cognizable in a federal court any and all false imprisonment causes of action against police officers where the unlawfulness of the arrest is a violation of federal constitutional requirements. The formulae suggested at times for distinguishing causes of action which are cognizable in federal court from those which are not have usually required for a federal cause of action facts indicating flagrancy or an improper motive. One serious difficulty with such formulae is that there is nothing in the language of sec. 1983, or the fourth and fourteenth amendments as presently construed, on which to base such tests. Although the Supreme Court has found that certain defenses to a sec. 1983 cause of action exist, apparently by implication, they are defenses typical of tort causes of action. Thus common law defenses of legislative immunity and judicial immunity exist under sec. 1983. A police officer is not liable if he acted in good faith and with probable cause in making an arrest under a statute he believed to be valid even though the statute be later held invalid."

Whirl v. Kern, 407 F.2d 781 (5th Cir. 1969) also heavily relied on by Plaintiff, the court cites the Seventh Circuit trend as reflected in Rowlen, to disregard motive as an element of a § 1983 offense. Kern, was a false imprisonment rather than a false arrest case, where the Plaintiff was detained in prison for nine months after charges against him had been dismissed because the sheriff in whose custody he was, was unaware of the dismissal. The sheriff's defense to plaintiff's § 1983 suit was that the Civil Rights Act applied only to reprehensible or improperly motivated conduct. The court held good faith not to be an adequate defense.

The rule that we derive from these cases — a rule certainly adhered to by this Circuit — is that improper motive is not an element of a § 1983 action and that the Civil Rights Act must be read in a manner consistent with the background of common law tort liability which allows only for recognized tort defenses. Plaintiff would therefore have us find Defendants liable for its inadvertent act of incorrectly mailing the transcript although Defendants were merely negligent, on the theory that negligence is not a proper defense to a tort and thus cannot be a defense to a § 1983 action. The short answer to Plaintiff's contentions in this case would be that the fundamental tort element of injury is here absent. Thus, even if all the other ingredients of a tort case are present and cognizable under the Statute including negligence (a point which we do not concede) Plaintiff could not succeed given the fact that he has not been injured by Defendants' acts. Under the Illinois Post Conviction Hearing Act (Ill.Rev.Stat. Ch. 38 § 122-1) a proceeding may be commenced at any time within twenty years of the final judgment and Plaintiff can therefore still proceed with his attempt to secure post-conviction relief. Furthermore, the filing of the transcript is not necessary to set the appeal procedure in motion within the requisite time limit and Plaintiff's attorney could have taken proper action to inform the Supreme Court of the difficulty in locating the transcript. This lack of injury to Plaintiff would be entirely sufficient grounds for this Court to find for Defendants on the issue of liability under Count I.

However, since Plaintiff does present the important issue as to whether mere negligence of the sort involved in this case is cognizable under § 1983, we will rule on that portion of the Complaint. We hold that mere negligence involving an act void of not only specific intent but intent as such, is not grounds for a § 1983 suit. To better understand where on the Civil Rights spectrum in terms of intent our case lies, we must first chart out the various factual permutations possible under the Act:

(1) The most readily recognizable violation of a constitutionally secured right occurs where the act is wilfully done under color of law with the specific intent to deprive a person of a Federal right. The act is consciously motivated with the intended result of violating a constitutional right. This violation is cognizable not only under 42 U.S.C. § 1983 but also under the more limited 18 U.S.C. § 242 which requires that the act be "wilfully" done.

(2) A less easily recognizable though no less clear-cut violation of 42 U.S.C. § 1983 occurs where there is no "specific intent" to violate a constitutional right but where the act itself and its result were intended under color of law sans improper motive. Though ulterior motive is absent, the acts will "be read against the background of tort liability that makes a man responsible for the natural consequences of his actions" (Monroe v. Pape, 365 U.S. 167 at 187, 81 S.Ct. 473 at 484, 5 L.Ed.2d 492 1961). In such a case the elements of the offense are a violated constitutional right, a conscious act, an intended result and a result that should have been contemplated under the common law tort doctrine of foreseeability. Good faith or proper motive is no defense.

221

(3) The third category constitutes cases where the act is conscious, the result is intended, improper motive is absent and constitutional right is violated but the lack of an improper motive is a defense. The defense of good faith would be adequate when in applying common law tort background the defendant could not be held responsible for the natural consequences of his actions.

(4) The fourth category consists of cases where there is a deprivation of a constitutional right but the act bringing about that violation was an unconscious one, a pure mistake, and the factual as well as the legal result were unintended. Thus, not only was there an absence of both improper motive and specific intent —there was no motive and no intent whatsoever since the defendant was not cognizant that the act was taking place no less the legal implications of that act.

(5) The fifth category includes cases where there is no violation of a constitutional right as such, there was no improper motive and the act and the result were not intended. The injury in such a case is the result of a "pure tort" rather than a constitutional tort, such as personal injury and such an action cannot be maintained under 42 U.S.C. § 1983.

We maintain that 42 U.S.C. § 1983 was not meant to apply to unintentional torts where both the act is unconscious and the result unintended not only where the tort is a "pure" common law tort, but also where the result is a constitutional tort. The question of whether improper motive need be present applies only to those cases where some form of conscious intent was present. Our case, falling in the fourth category, would therefore not be actionable under 42 U.S.C. § 1983.

The cases interpreting lack of specific intent cover the full spectrum of degrees of intent of the first three categories mentioned yet no cited case has found a party liable where the very act itself was unintended. The common thread running through all of the "improper motive", "good faith" situations is the fact that the result of the act was intended and that a certain threshold cognizance of the act being performed, albeit an innocent one, was present. That a certain result be intended and that the act mounted to accomplish that result must be a conscious one is therefore a basic requisite for a § 1983 suit. Simply stated, this means that although specific intent need not be present some intent must be involved.

Our case falls within the fourth aforementioned category since the Defendants did not intend to mail the transcript to the mother of another prisoner, were not conscious of doing the act and did not intend the result. Plaintiff's attempt to apply the tort law en masse to § 1983 therefore cannot meet with success. To do so would convert every minor mistake, especially in the milieu of the prison, into a violation of § 1983. To hold prison officials to such a high standard of strict liability would impose such an impossible burden as to render prisons totally inoperable. As to the issue of liability under Count I we therefore find that Defendants' error in the mailing of the transcript is not an action cognizable under 42 U.S.C. § 1983.

REVIEW SECTION

READING COMPREHENSION

Detail the facts of this case.

Delineate the possible permutations of a suit filed under 42 U.S.C. § 1983 as addressed in this case.

THINKING CRITICALLY

Articulate how you would decide this case, including a discussion of the relevance of intent and subsequent injury.

CASE

Following a jury trial, defendant Gregory Becker, a Chicago police officer, was convicted of one count of armed violence, one count of involuntary manslaughter and three counts of official misconduct involving the shooting death of Joseph Gould. On appeal in *People v Becker,* the defendant asserts that: (1) his armed violence conviction was improperly based upon the same conduct found to be unintended by the jury's simultaneous verdict of guilty on involuntary manslaughter; (2) the verdicts for involuntary manslaughter and armed violence were legally inconsistent because their respective mental states of recklessness and knowledge were mutually inconsistent; (3) his armed violence charge constituted an impermissible double enhancement; (4) the indictment did not sufficiently allege a charge of armed violence; (5) the section 33-3(a) official misconduct conviction violated his fifth amendment privilege against compulsory self-incrimination; and (6) the State failed to prove him guilty beyond a reasonable doubt of official misconduct and armed violence where the acts performed were in his individual, not official, capacity.

PEOPLE V. BECKER
734 N.E.2d 987 (2000)

After dismissing 7 counts of the original 13-count indictment, the State proceeded to trial on the following counts against defendant: armed violence; involuntary manslaughter; and official misconduct. Count I alleged defendant committed armed violence in that he, while armed with a handgun, committed official misconduct. Count II alleged that defendant committed involuntary manslaughter in that he without lawful justification, acting in a reckless manner, unintentionally killed Joseph Gould when he discharged a handgun in the presence of Joseph Gould, causing a fatal gunshot wound to Gould's head. Count V alleged section 33-3(a) official misconduct in that defendant intentionally or recklessly violated Rule 6 of Article V of the Rules and Regulations of the Chicago Police Department by failing to follow procedures after discharging his firearm. Count IX alleged that defendant knowingly violated Rule 38 of Article V when he unnecessarily displayed his weapon and struck Joseph Gould with the weapon. Count XII alleged defendant knowingly violated Rule 9 of Article V when he engaged in an unjustified physical altercation using excessive force with Joseph Gould. Count XIII alleged that defendant knowingly violated Rule 9 when he engaged in an unjustified physical altercation with Joseph Gould.

At trial, the testimony indicated that on July 30, 1995, at 12:30 a.m., the defendant was off duty from his job as a Chicago police officer. Defendant and his girlfriend, Joey Preston, left America's Bar in Chicago and began to walk toward the defendant's car, parked on the corner of Huron and Franklin Streets. Defendant and Preston walked down Franklin Street, Joseph Gould approached them, and Gould engaged Preston in a conversation while defendant walked ahead of them. Preston yelled at Gould and told him to leave her alone, but Gould refused. Preston and Gould caught up to the defendant and the defendant told Gould to get away. Defendant and Preston then crossed Franklin with Gould just behind them. When they reached defendant's car, defendant walked to the trunk of the car and then walked back toward Gould. The defendant and Gould were facing each other. According to the State's witness, defendant, with a black object in his hand swung his arm towards Gould's face. A gun went off, and Gould fell to the ground. Defendant entered his car and left. Gould died from a single gunshot wound to the head. The police arrested him at his home and recovered the 9 millimeter weapon used in the shooting.

Charles Roberts testified that he was the assistant deputy superintendent for training for the Chicago police department. Roberts stated that defendant was trained at the Chicago Police Department Training Academy, where defendant received a copy of the rules and regulations of general and special orders of the Chicago police department. The rules and regulations govern the conduct of a police officer both on and off duty. Defendant was trained in the use of force, use of a weapon, and the requirement to notify his supervisor immediately upon discharge of his weapon. He was taught that his gun was never to be used as an impact weapon.

Lieutenant James K. Hickey testified that he was the commander in charge of the policy and procedure section of the research and development division for the Chicago police department. Lieutenant Hickey testified that General Order 85-1, in effect on July 30, 1995, required a police officer whether on or off duty at the time when he discharged a firearm to: (1) notify immediately the communications section and desk sergeant of the district where the firearm is discharged; (2) attend to required emergency assistance; (3) assist and provide information to department members investigating the discharge; (4) perform required duties including filing reports; and (5) submit a firearms use report to the watch commander without unnecessary delay. Lieutenant Hickey testified to general orders in effect on July 30, 1995, which governed the conduct, demeanor, and use of nondeadly and deadly force by a police officer. According to the general orders, a police officer should only use deadly force when he reasonably believes such force is necessary to prevent death or great bodily harm to himself or others. Lieutenant Hickey stated that the general orders restrict a police officer's use of a firearm until all other means to apprehend and control an individual have been employed without success. The use of a firearm in any case is a last resort measure. The rules prohibit police officers from using excessive force while on or off duty and prohibit unjustified altercations of any kind with any person while on or off duty. Hickey testified that an officer is expected "to render the highest order of police service to all citizens, whether or not during specifically assigned hours."

Defendant testified that while walking from America's Bar to his car with Preston, Gould asked him for money. Defendant refused the request. Gould followed them for about a half block and was agitated, mumbling continuously. Preston yelled at Gould to get away from her. Defendant told Gould to stay away from them or he would lock Gould up because he was a Chicago police officer. Gould then told defendant that he would "kick his ass." When Preston and defendant reached defendant's car, defendant went to the trunk and got Preston's purse and his gun. Defendant stated that he was putting the gun in his waistband when Gould pulled on his jacket. Both Gould and defendant pulled at the gun, defendant lost balance, and a struggle ensued over the weapon. Regarding the struggle defendant testified that Gould "pulled me off balance. I think I grabbed onto the shirt. He was pulling on it. I was pulling back. Excuse me. And I was just trying to get, gain control of it, and then I think it hit him in the head once, and then he pulled it back again, and I, when I pulled it, I extended my whole arm and I pulled back, and the gun fired." Defendant stated that he unintentionally pulled the trigger when he was trying to gain control of the gun. He testified that the gun was fully loaded, a bullet was in the chamber and the external safety was not engaged. After the gun went off, Gould fell to the ground but defendant testified that he did not believe Gould was shot. He and Preston drove to Preston's apartment, and he did not notify the police regarding the discharge of his weapon or the incident.

The State proceeded to trial on six counts of the indictment; however, when instructing the jury, count XII and count XIII were combined and the jury received the following five verdict forms: (1) armed violence predicated on section 33-3(b) official misconduct charge alleging defendant's unjustified altercation with Gould; (2) involuntary manslaughter; (3) section 33-3(a) official misconduct; (4) section 33-3(b) official misconduct based on defendant's unnecessary use or display of his weapon; and (5) section 33-3(b) official misconduct based on defendant's unjustified altercation. The jury found defendant guilty on all counts, including armed violence, involuntary manslaughter, and the three counts of official misconduct. The trial court merged the two section 33-3(b) official misconduct convictions into the armed violence conviction and sentenced defendant to concurrent sentences of 15 years on his conviction for armed violence, 5 years for involuntary manslaughter, and 5 years for the section 33-3(a) official misconduct.

The armed violence statute under which defendant was originally sentenced was part of Public Act 88-680 commonly known as the Safe Neighborhoods Law. People v. Cervantes, 189 Ill. 2d 80, 91 (1999), the supreme court declared Public Act 88-680 unconstitutional in that its provisions lacked a natural and logical connection and therefore violated the single subject clause of the Illinois Constitution. Public Act 88-680 included a provision increasing the minimum sentence for armed violence committed with a handgun from a minimum of 6 years to a minimum of 15 years. When an act is declared unconstitutional, the state of the law is as if the act had never been passed. As the result of Public Act 88-680 being declared unconstitutional, the original armed violence statute providing a 6 year minimum sentence applied to defendant's armed violence conviction. Since the Cervantes ruling, the trial court resentenced defendant to 10 years for armed violence based on the sentencing provisions in effect before the enactment of Public Act 88-680.

Defendant contends that his conviction for armed violence must be vacated because the armed violence conviction was based on unintentional and undeterrable conduct. Defendant argues that the State used the section 33-3(b) official misconduct charge as a predicate felony only because the State was precluded by law from using involuntary manslaughter as a predicate felony. Defendant further contends that the conduct underlying the official misconduct charge was the same conduct underlying the involuntary manslaughter charge and, therefore, was not a proper predicate for the armed violence charge. The Criminal Code of 1961 provides that "a person commits armed violence when, while armed with a dangerous weapon, he commits any felony defined by Illinois Law." An issue of statutory interpretation is a question of law and our review is *de novo*. The plain language of a statute is the best indicator of legislative intent. Our supreme court, under certain circumstances, has limited the type of felonies contemplated by the "any felony" language of the armed violence statute. Finding the words, "any felony" within the armed violence statute ambiguous, the supreme court has held that the offenses of voluntary and involuntary manslaughter cannot serve as predicate felonies for an armed violence charge and conviction because the legislature never intended for the armed violence statute to apply to conduct that is not deliberate.

Defendant's official misconduct charge, which served as the predicate felony for the armed violence conviction, was for a knowing violation of police rules and regulations. The purpose of the official misconduct statute is to compel public officials to act in a lawful manner and to maintain the public trust. The statute provides that: "A public officer or employee commits misconduct when, in his official capacity, he (b) knowingly performs an act which he knows he is forbidden by law to perform." Here, there was evidence which demonstrated that defendant knowingly performed an act which he knew was forbidden by law when he engaged in an unjustified altercation with Gould. Defendant knowingly engaged in a physical altercation with Gould while armed with his gun which escalated the possibility of violence and injury and ultimately ended in the death of the victim. It is the use or presence of a weapon that increases the chances of violence, great bodily harm or death and justifies an enhanced penalty under the armed violence statute. If the decision to use a weapon is not forced upon the defendant or a result of a spontaneous decision, then the defendant's conduct can be deterred and the purpose of the armed violence statute is satisfied. Here, there was evidence that defendant knowingly engaged in both a verbal and a physical altercation with the victim and knowingly violated Chicago police department rules by deliberately choosing not only to arm himself but to display and use his weapon during the altercation. The jury's guilty verdict on the section 33-3(b) official misconduct offense based on defendant's unjustified altercation with the victim indicates that the jurors found defendant's conduct to be a knowing violation of the law, and thereby deterrable conduct which provided a legally proper predicate felony for armed violence.

The purpose of the armed violence statute is to discourage those who contemplate a felonious act beforehand from carrying a weapon when they set forth to perform the act. Under the facts of this case we decline to find a legislative intent to exclude the section 33-3(b) official misconduct offense based on defendant's knowing violation of the law from being a predicate felony for an armed violence charge, since knowing conduct can be deterred and the purpose of the armed violence statute is thereby satisfied. Defendant's conviction for armed violence was based on evidence of knowing and deterrable official misconduct. The section 33-3(b) official misconduct allegation of defendant's unjustified altercation with Gould was a proper predicate felony for defendant's armed violence conviction.

We address defendant's alternative argument that the jury returned legally inconsistent verdicts by finding defendant guilty of armed violence and involuntary manslaughter because the mental states of recklessness and knowledge are mutually inconsistent. Defendant argues that if the jury found him guilty for armed violence based on his act of knowingly engaging in an unjustified altercation with the victim, the jury could not also consistently find that he acted recklessly for the same criminal conduct and return a verdict of guilty for involuntary manslaughter. Defendant contends that his armed violence verdict of guilty based on a section 33-3(b) official misconduct predicate felony, alleging the knowing rule violation of engaging in an unjustified altercation is legally inconsistent with the guilty verdict for involuntary manslaughter, based on recklessly causing Gould's death. The State counters that the section 33-3(b) official misconduct offense is not a lesser included offense of involuntary manslaughter but an offense based on a knowing rule violation. The State contends that because armed violence and involuntary manslaughter require proof of different elements, the jury could find that while defendant was engaging in conduct he knew he was forbidden to perform, he was also recklessly causing Gould's death.

In this case, the involuntary manslaughter count and the section 33-3(b) official misconduct count upon which the armed violence was based charged defendant with essentially one criminal act or course of conduct. In addition, the issues instructions given to the jury support a finding that the jury convicted defendant for knowing and reckless offenses for the same criminal conduct. The involuntary manslaughter instruction required the jury to find that "defendant performed the acts which caused the death of Joseph Gould" and that the "defendant performed those acts recklessly." The armed violence instruction and the section 33-3(b) official misconduct instruction that provided the predicate felony for the armed violence instruction required the jury to find that "defendant knowingly performed an act which he knew was forbidden by law, to wit: he engaged in an unjustified verbal or physical altercation with Joseph Gould in that he shot Joseph Gould in the head." The other section 33-3(b) official misconduct instruction required the jury to find that defendant knowingly performed an act which he knew was forbidden by law when "he unlawfully or unnecessarily used or displayed his weapon." The instructions and verdict forms provided to the jury rely on essentially the same conduct for the involuntary manslaughter, armed violence, and section 33-3(b) official misconduct offenses. The State's theory as articulated in rebuttal argument was that defendant committed one criminal act that caused the death of Gould, specifically, the act of pistol whipping Gould. Therefore, the record does not support a finding that defendant committed separate knowing and reckless acts, or that the defendant's mental state changed during his altercation with the victim.

In this case, the jury received conflicting testimony regarding the shooting of Gould and defendant's mental state at the time he armed himself, engaged in the verbal and physical altercation with the victim, and shot the victim. The State argued that defendant knowingly armed himself with his weapon, knowingly displayed his weapon, and knowingly engaged in an unjustified verbal and physical altercation during which the victim was shot; the defense argued that Gould was the aggressor and Gould was shot accidentally. The jury was instructed on knowing and reckless offenses arising from essentially the same conduct and returned guilty verdicts for each offense it was instructed on, thereby convicting defendant of offenses that contained mutually inconsistent mental states. We conclude that based on the evidence, the jury could have found that defendant acted either knowingly or recklessly, but it could not render inconsistent multiple guilty verdicts with both mental states for essentially the same conduct. The trial court's failure to send the jury back for further deliberations to resolve the inconsistent verdicts mandates a reversal and a new trial on all the inconsistent verdicts including involuntary manslaughter, armed violence, which was based on the section 33-3(b) knowing official misconduct charge alleging an unjustified altercation, and the section 33-3(b) knowing official misconduct charges. We further indicate that, on retrial, the trial court should take the preventative step of instructing the jury before it deliberates that it cannot consistently return simultaneous guilty verdicts for both reckless and knowing offenses. If after deliberation the jury again returns guilty verdicts for a reckless offense and a knowing offense, the trial court must send the jury back for further deliberation with additional instructions to resolve the inconsistency.

Defendant next contends that his armed violence conviction constitutes a double enhancement. Defendant argues that proof of a weapon was an essential element of his section 33-3(b) official misconduct charge, that served as the predicate felony for the armed violence charge, and the legislature did not intend armed violence to apply to a felony that required proof of a weapon as an element. The State claims that because the section 33-3(b) official misconduct charge that served as the predicate felony for armed violence did not allege defendant's use of a weapon but alleged a rule violation, there is no double enhancement. Double enhancement exists "when a factor previously used to enhance an offense or penalty is again used to subject a defendant to a further enhanced offense or penalty." In the context of armed violence, the State cannot seek to enhance an offense through the presence of a weapon and then use the weapon as a basis for an armed violence charge. However, where a defendant possesses a weapon during the commission of a felony, an armed violence charge does not constitute improper enhancement if the elements of the predicate felony require no presence or use of a weapon. However, defendant's armed violence charge does not constitute a double enhancement if the section 33-3(b) official misconduct charge that provides the predicate felony for the armed violence does not require a weapon as an element of the offense or is not enhanced by the presence of a weapon. Here, the armed violence predicate was an official misconduct charge alleging that defendant had engaged in an unjustified verbal or physical altercation with Gould. The predicate felony of official misconduct did not require proof of the use or presence of a weapon as an element of the offense; rather, the State was required to prove that defendant knowingly engaged in an unjustified altercation with Gould. The elements of the official misconduct that provided the predicate offense for the charge of armed violence are: (1) that the defendant was a public officer or employee; (2) that in his official capacity the defendant knowingly performed an act he knew was forbidden by law to perform, to wit: violated the rules and regulations of the Chicago police department; (3) that defendant engaged in an altercation with Joseph Gould; and (4) that the altercation was unjustified.

Therefore, this official misconduct charge could properly serve as a predicate felony for armed violence because the possession, use, or presence of a weapon was not an essential element of the predicate felony nor did the weapon enhance the predicate felony of official misconduct. Defendant was not subjected to double enhancement because the State did not need to prove that defendant used or possessed a weapon to sustain its burden of proving the elements of the official misconduct charge which served as the predicate felony for the armed violence. The issues instruction provided for the jury contained the essential elements of the offense and did not allow for conviction on legally impermissible grounds.

Defendant next contends that the trial court erred in denying his motion to dismiss the armed violence charge where the indictment failed to specify the law and the conduct that formed the basis for the official misconduct predicate felony for the armed violence charge. Defendant argues that because the armed violence charge only alleged that defendant committed official misconduct while armed with a dangerous weapon but described no rule violation or conduct underlying the charge, he was not sufficiently informed of the nature and elements of the armed violence charge and could not prepare an adequate defense. The standard of review of a defendant's motion to dismiss an indictment is whether the indictment strictly complies with the pleading requirements of section 111-3 of the Code of Criminal Procedure of 1963. Section 111-3(a)(3) of the Code of Criminal Procedure of 1963 requires that an indictment adequately inform an accused of a charged offense by "setting forth the nature and elements of the offense charged." The question is not whether the alleged offense could have been described with greater certainty, but whether there is sufficient particularity to enable the accused to prepare a proper defense. The official misconduct statute, standing alone, does not particularize the offense. Where a statute does not specifically define the crime, or does so only in general terms, the charge must go beyond the words of the statute; it must allege some act showing the statute was violated. "It is a well-established rule in Illinois that all counts of a multiple-count indictment should be read as a whole and that elements missing from one count of an indictment may be supplied by another count" (People v. Morris, 135 Ill. 2d 540, 544 1990). As a result, although an indictment must identify the elements of a predicate felony in an armed violence charge, those elements can be supplied by other counts of a multiple-count indictment.

Defendant suggests that he was required to defend against uncharged conduct, but his argument is not persuasive. Official misconduct counts XII and XIII properly served as a predicate felony for the armed violence charge by alleging that defendant engaged in an unjustified altercation with Gould. We further note that these two section 33-3(b) official misconduct counts informed the defendant of the nature of the official misconduct and relied on the same specific police department rule that defendant allegedly violated as contained in Article V. Moreover, those same two counts were the subject of defendant's bill of particulars regarding the physical altercation that provided the basis for the section 33-3(b) official misconduct predicate for the armed violence charge. Defendant also had available the preliminary hearing transcript. While the State's response to the bill of particulars and the preliminary hearing transcript cannot substitute for a valid indictment, they can supplement, as here, a sufficient indictment with more specificity to enable a defendant to better understand the nature of the charges against him, or to better prepare a defense. Therefore, the multiple-count indictment sufficiently notified defendant of the nature of the armed violence charge. We find the indictment does comply with Section 111-3(a)(3) of the Code of Criminal Procedure and affirm the ruling of the trial judge in denying defendant's motion to dismiss the armed violence charge.

Defendant contends that the judge erred in denying his motion to dismiss the section 33-3(a) official misconduct charge based on his failure to comply with General Order 85-1 of the Chicago police department. General Order 85-1 of the Chicago police department required that defendant provide the police department with information regarding the circumstances of the discharge of his weapon. Defendant claims that General Order 85-1 violates defendant's protection from compulsory self incrimination under the fifth amendment of the U.S. Constitution. Defendant was charged with section 33-3(a) official misconduct in that he intentionally or recklessly failed to perform a mandatory duty as required by law by violating the rules and regulations of the Chicago police department in not following required procedures after discharging his firearm. The purpose of the official misconduct statute is to compel public officials and employees, while acting in their official capacity, to do so in a lawful manner. An official misconduct charge can be based on a violation of an administrative rule or regulation, although that rule or regulation does not itself carry any penalty. A court inquires into the constitutionality of a statute only to the extent necessary to the particular case before it. Where no facts demonstrate an unconstitutional application of the statute or law to defendant, defendant cannot challenge the statute on grounds that it might conceivably be applied unconstitutionally in some hypothetical case. A reviewing court will not consider objections to an allegedly unconstitutional feature if the complaining party is not in any way aggrieved by the complained-of feature. Here, defendant has failed to demonstrate sufficient facts to establish that General Order 85-1 violated his protection from compulsory self-incrimination.

The standard for application of the fifth amendment privilege has been whether the person claiming it is confronted by substantial and real, not merely trifling or imaginary, hazards of incrimination. Application of the fifth amendment privilege to defendant is established by showing that defendant's compliance with General Order 85-1 would have resulted in evidence being used against defendant in a criminal proceeding. However, in this case, the defendant's statements were not used against him. Moreover, we would have to speculate as to whether defendant's compliance with General Order 85-1 would have generated statements by defendant that would have been used against him in a criminal proceeding. Such speculation cannot support a claim of standing or establish violation of the privilege against compulsory self-incrimination. Defendant asks this court to find the official misconduct statute unconstitutional as applied to the rules and regulations of the Chicago police department even though no direct constitutional right relating to the defendant has been violated. In the absence of facts demonstrating an unconstitutional application of the statute in this case, the defendant may not challenge the statute on the ground that it might have been applied to deprive him of his constitutional rights in some hypothetical sense.

In this case, the connection between the information required by General Order 85-1 and any actual incrimination of the defendant is too speculative to form a basis for a claim of privilege or to establish a violation of defendant's fifth amendment privilege. Defendant has not shown that, if he had complied with General Order 85-1, the information he would have provided would have been used against him in the prosecution of his criminal case. The privilege against compulsory self-incrimination does not apply unless the complainant faces a real and substantial risk of incrimination, rather than a remote risk. Based on the foregoing analysis we conclude the trial court properly denied defendant's motion to dismiss the section 33-3(a) official misconduct charge alleging defendant's failure to comply with General Order 85-1 of the Chicago police department.

Defendant lastly claims that the State failed to prove him guilty beyond a reasonable doubt of official misconduct and armed violence where the evidence demonstrated the acts of the defendant were committed in his individual, not official, capacity. If the evidence at trial was insufficient to support defendant's official misconduct and armed violence convictions, then double jeopardy bars the retrial of these counts. When the sufficiency of the evidence is challenged on appeal, the relevant inquiry is whether, when viewed in the light most favorable to the State, any rational trier of fact could have found that all of the elements of the crime were proven beyond a reasonable doubt. A police officer need not be on duty and in uniform to commit an act of official misconduct. A police officer commits an act of official misconduct when the officer exploits his official position and acts in detriment to the public good.

In this case, defendant interjected his public office and authority as a police officer to the detriment of the victim and the public. Defendant's actions cannot be severed from his sworn duties as a Chicago police officer.

After thoroughly reviewing the evidence, we find it to have been sufficient to support each of the guilty verdicts. If upon retrial and after deliberation the jury returns guilty verdicts for a reckless offense and a knowing offense, the trial court must send the jury back for further deliberations with additional instructions to resolve the inconsistent verdicts. We find no double jeopardy impediment to a new trial. We note that we have made no findings as to defendant's guilt that would be binding on retrial. For the reasons previously stated, we reverse defendant's armed violence, involuntary manslaughter and official misconduct section 33-3(b) convictions, vacate the sentences on those convictions and remand for a new trial consistent with this opinion. We affirm defendant's section 33-3(a) official misconduct conviction and sentence. Affirmed in part and reversed in part; cause remanded.

REVIEW SECTION

READING COMPREHENSION

Detail the charges and facts of this case, including relevant jury instructions.

THINKING CRITICALLY

According to the court: "the jury returned legally inconsistent verdicts by finding defendant guilty of armed violence and involuntary manslaughter because the mental states of recklessness and knowledge are mutually inconsistent." Do you agree that this case hinged on charges involving mutually exclusive mental states? Elaborate your position.

SECTION 2: FAILURE TO PROTECT BY LAW ENFORCEMENT

OVERVIEW

According to the U.S. Supreme Court's interpretation of the Fifth and Fourteenth Amendments, there is a no-affirmative-duty-to-protect rule. What this means in practice is that law enforcement has no affirmative duty to protect individuals from other individuals attempting to inflict injury. When however, the government imprisons individuals against their will, the special relationship exception prevails, indicating this is a violation of the Eighth Amendment as these individuals cannot protect themselves. As such, there exists a duty to protect in such situations.

So, what if your rights are violated and you decide to sue the government or its officers? Realistically, you should know you will be faced with many legal hurdles, and the citizen rarely prevails in such a suit. Such a lawsuit is both difficult and expensive to pursue, the U.S. Supreme Court has limited the ability of citizens to garner relief from police techniques even if they result in excessive force, and jurors are more likely to believe the testimony of an officer. In addition, qualified and absolute immunity protect most officials from successful lawsuits.

Where then does the average citizen seek accountability? The most common method by which officials are held accountable is through administrative review, including internal affairs units and external civilian reviews. While external civilian reviews would certainly appear to give the appearance of a fairer assessment, they were vehemently opposed during the 1960s when first suggested by liberal reformers. By the 1990s, most large cities had external civilian review procedures in place, though they are still opposed by government officials who believe the public cannot fully understand the complexities of the job and do not want the 'blue curtain' scrutinized.

CASE

The principal issue in *Zimmerman for Zimmerman v Village of Skokie* is whether the "special duty" doctrine violates the Illinois Constitution of 1970 when it is applied by the courts to override the immunities and defenses afforded to governmental entities by the Illinois General Assembly. The defendants contend that when the special duty doctrine operates to nullify the immunities and defenses available under the Tort Immunity Act, two provisions of the Illinois Constitution of 1970 are violated: article XIII, section 4, which provides that the doctrine of sovereign immunity is abolished "except as the General Assembly may provide by law;" and the separation of powers clause under article II, section 1 which provides that no branch of government "shall exercise powers properly belonging to another." The Supreme Court of Illinois holds that the operation of the special duty doctrine to negate the immunities and defenses provided to governmental entities violates both constitutional provisions.

ZIMMERMAN FOR ZIMMERMAN V. VILLAGE OF SKOKIE
Supreme Court of Illinois
697 N.E.2d 699, 183 Ill.2d 30 (1998)

The "special duty" doctrine was first recognized by this court <u>Huey v. Town of Cicero, 41 Ill.2d 361, 243 N.E.2d 214 (1968)</u>, as an exception to the common law "public duty" rule. The public duty rule is a long-standing precept which establishes that a governmental entity and its employees owe no duty of care to individual members of the general public to provide governmental services. This rule of nonliability is grounded in the principle that the duty of the governmental entity to preserve the well-being of the community is owed to the public at large rather than to specific members of the community. The special duty doctrine arose as a judicially

232

created exception to the nonliability principles of the public duty rule, and is applicable in certain limited instances where a governmental entity has assumed a special relationship to an individual.

This appeal arises from a series of occurrences initiated on July 25, 1982, when Scott Zimmerman was arrested at 11:20 p.m. by Skokie police after he broke a glass mug as he was leaving Houlihan's Restaurant & Bar. At the outset, we note that for purposes of the narrow legal issue presented in this appeal, the parties do not dispute the underlying facts in this litigation. Therefore, we include only a general discussion of these background facts. Upon Zimmerman's arrest, he was taken to the Skokie police station/jail, where he refused to be fingerprinted and became extremely upset. As a result of his refusal to cooperate with the fingerprinting procedure, the police placed Zimmerman alone in a cell in the men's cellblock at approximately 1 a.m. After he was placed in the cell, Zimmerman punched and kicked at the walls, screamed, and rattled his cell bars. At about the same time Zimmerman was placed into the cell, his family members arrived at the Skokie jail. Zimmerman's parents informed the officers that their son had been medically diagnosed as a claustrophobe, that he was under the care of a psychiatrist, and that he should be removed from the cell because he could not tolerate such confinement. At her request, Zimmerman's mother was allowed into the cellblock to calm Zimmerman. However, her efforts were unsuccessful, and she returned to the public area of the jail. Although the statements made by Zimmerman's parents to the Skokie police concerning Zimmerman's claustrophobia were true, the police refused to believe these declarations and informed Zimmerman's family members that he would not be removed from the cell until he calmed down and could be fingerprinted. The relationship between Zimmerman's parents and the police thereafter became confrontational, and the family members were ordered to leave the police station. Zimmerman's family members complied after being assured by the officers that the officers would keep a watch over Zimmerman.

During that evening, Zimmerman was removed from his cell for a second attempt at fingerprinting, and, upon his removal, he calmed down. However, Zimmerman once again refused to comply with the fingerprinting procedure and was replaced in the cell, where his violent behavior resumed. Thereafter, one of the officers checked on Zimmerman every 15 minutes and marked Zimmerman's physical condition as "okay" on the jail log. When an officer looked in on Zimmerman at approximately 2:45 a.m., Zimmerman was found lying in the cell with his hands around his neck, complaining that he could not breathe and gasping for air. At that time, Zimmerman was also screaming that he was going to kill himself because police had beaten him up for no reason. Fifteen minutes later, at approximately 3 a.m., when Zimmerman was again looked in on by an officer, Zimmerman was found hanging from the bars of his cell with his jeans around his neck, his body facing away from the bars and his legs looped through the bars. Zimmerman was resuscitated at the Skokie jail by the officers, who administered CPR. Zimmerman was thereafter transported to a hospital where it was determined that blood loss to his brain as a result of the hanging caused him to suffer permanent brain damage that impaired his ability to work and care for himself. Medical workers also found that Zimmerman had a cut under his right eye, contusions and bruises on his chest and arms, and a deep gash on his shin, which resembled the shape of a shoe or boot tip.

Subsequently, Zimmerman was declared a disabled person by the probate court of Cook County and his father, Irving, was appointed his guardian. Irving (plaintiff) thereafter filed suit on behalf of his son to recover damages for personal injuries Zimmerman suffered during the period he was in the custody of the Skokie police. Plaintiff's cause of action, originally filed on February 23, 1983, named as defendants the Village of Skokie and the police officers involved in these incidents.

Plaintiff's case was dismissed with prejudice as a sanction by the trial court on March 27, 1986, after plaintiff failed to comply with trial court orders directing Zimmerman to appear for a deposition and requiring plaintiff to respond to defendants' written discovery. Upon the trial court's denial of plaintiff's petition under section 2-1401 of the Code of Civil Procedure to vacate its dismissal order, plaintiff appealed. The appellate court vacated the circuit court's denial of plaintiff's section 2-1401 petition and remanded the cause to the trial court for further proceedings. Defendants' petition for rehearing was denied by the appellate court, and this court denied defendants' petition for leave to appeal.

Following remand to the trial court, plaintiff's case proceeded against defendants. On January 18, 1994, shortly before trial in this matter, the circuit court ruled on defendants' motion to strike and dismiss all counts of plaintiff's complaint. Defendants moved to dismiss plaintiff's claims on the pleadings on the basis that they were barred by various provisions of the Tort Immunity Act. Pursuant to section 4-105 of the Tort Immunity Act and section III(D) of the Municipal Jail and Lockup Standards as they read in 1982, the trial court granted defendants' motion only as to count V of the complaint, which asserted a cause of action in negligence. Section 4-105 of the Act read as follows: "Neither a local public entity nor a public employee is liable for injury proximately caused by the failure of the employee to furnish or obtain medical care for a prisoner in his custody; but a public employee, and the local public entity where the employee is acting within the scope of his employment, is liable if the employee knows or has reason to know from his observation that the prisoner is in need of immediate medical care and fails to take reasonable action to summon medical care. Nothing in this Section requires the periodic inspection of prisoners." In count V, plaintiff alleged that defendants breached their duty to take reasonable action to summon medical care for Zimmerman. The trial judge determined that section 4-105 did not establish a cause of action in negligence when read in conjunction with section 2-202 of the Tort Immunity Act, which provides: "A public employee is not liable for his act or omission in the execution or enforcement of any law unless such act or omission constitutes willful and wanton negligence."

Although the allegations sounding in negligence in count V were dismissed, the trial judge commented that plaintiff could offer evidence that the defendants' alleged failure to provide medical care amounted to willful and wanton misconduct. The trial judge denied the defendants' motion to strike and dismiss the remaining five counts of the complaint. Counts I and II asserted causes of action based upon alleged acts of willful and wanton misconduct, including defendants' placement of Zimmerman in a cell despite their awareness that he was claustrophobic and unstable. Counts III and IV of plaintiff's complaint, according to the trial judge, were "virtual mirror images of Counts 1 and 2, but they sound in negligence." Although the trial court agreed with defendants' assertion that section 2-202 of the Tort Immunity Act applied to these counts, he determined that at the pleading stage such a finding was not dispositive, because whether a police officer was engaged in the "execution and enforcement of any law" as contemplated under section 2-202 is a factual determination which could not be made at the pleading stage. Defendants also unsuccessfully argued four other defenses under the Tort Immunity Act to counts III and IV. Defendants first asserted protections pursuant to section 4-102 of the Act, which provides: "neither a local public entity nor a public employee is liable for failure to establish a police department or otherwise provide police protection service or, if police protection service is provided, for failure to provide adequate police protection or service." The trial court determined that "section 4-102 is not applicable to this case because it is not intended to apply to a jail lockup situation such as this. That section applies to the general public's right to police protection."

Defendants next argued the defenses contained in section 4-103 of the Act, which provides: "Neither a local public entity nor a public employee is liable for failure to provide a jail, detention or correctional facility, or if such facility is provided, for failure to provide sufficient equipment, personnel or facilities therein." The trial court held that this section would not bar plaintiff from proceeding on his claims in this case. Lastly, in support of their motion, defendants asserted sections 6-105 and 6-106(a) of the Act. The trial judge determined these sections were inapplicable because they are limited to causes involving medical, hospital, and public health facilities, and were "not intended to apply to jail lockups."

Finally, the trial court denied defendants' motion to strike and dismiss count VI of plaintiff's complaint, which alleged that despite the availability of any statutory immunities defendants could raise to plaintiff's negligence claims under the Tort Immunity Act, defendants may be found liable under a negligence theory pursuant to the special duty doctrine. The trial judge rejected defendants' contention that under the Illinois Constitution of 1970, the General Assembly was vested with the sole authority to define the principles governing sovereign immunity, and that the special duty doctrine, operating as an exception to the Tort Immunity Act, was therefore invalid. In its written ruling, the trial court determined that "the special duty exception still exists outside the Tort Immunity Act and that it does so without offending any provision of the Illinois Constitution."

The jury found in favor of the defendants and against plaintiff on all five counts. Subsequently, plaintiff filed a motion for a new trial, which was granted by the circuit court. Defendants, pursuant to Rule 306(a)(1) then petitioned the appellate court for leave to appeal the trial court's order granting plaintiff a new trial. In their petition, defendants raised numerous issues contending that the trial court abused its discretion in setting aside the jury verdict for defendants and granting plaintiff a new trial on all issues. Defendants thereafter filed a supplemental brief in the appellate court additionally challenging the trial court's pretrial ruling on their motion to strike and dismiss, focusing upon the trial court's allowance of plaintiff to proceed on his negligence claims under the special duty doctrine as an exception to governmental tort immunity.

The appellate court entered a summary order affirming the trial court and remanding the cause for a new trial. In its order, the appellate court not only articulated various grounds for its decision affirming the trial court's grant of a new trial, but also rejected the arguments proffered by the defendants in their supplemental brief that the operation of the special duty doctrine to negate governmental immunities provided under the Tort Immunity Act is unconstitutional. Thus, the appellate court concluded that plaintiff could properly proceed under the special duty doctrine, thereby allowing the jury to consider his negligence claims.

We granted the petition for leave to appeal from the appellate court's judgment filed by defendants Village of Skokie and certain defendant police officers. We also allowed *amicus curiae* briefs to be filed by the City of Chicago, the Du Page Mayors and Managers Conference, the Illinois Association of School Boards, the Illinois Governmental Association of Pools, the Illinois Municipal League, the Illinois Park and Recreation Association, the Municipal Insurance Cooperative Agency and High-Level Excess Liability Pool, the Northwest Municipal Conference, the Southtowns Agency for Risk Management, and the South Suburban Mayors and Managers Association in support of those defendants. In their appeal to this court, defendants state that they do "not challenge the appellate court order finding that it was not an abuse of discretion for the trial court to grant a new trial." Instead, defendants confine their appeal to the narrow question of whether the operation of the special duty doctrine as an exception to statutory governmental tort immunity violates article XIII, section 4, and article II, section 1, of the Illinois Constitution. For the reasons that follow, we hold that operation of the special duty doctrine as an exception to immunities and defenses available to a governmental entity under the Tort Immunity Act is unconstitutional.

Our grant of defendants' petition also brings before us plaintiff's requests for cross-relief in which plaintiff seeks reversal of two rulings made by the trial court in connection with defendants' motion to strike and dismiss all counts of plaintiff's complaint: (1) the trial court's rejection of plaintiff's argument that the purchase of insurance by the Village of Skokie waived defendants' right to assert provisions of the Tort Immunity Act; and (2) the trial court's dismissal of count V of plaintiff's complaint on the basis that section 4-105 of the Tort Immunity Act as it read at the time of this incident did not establish a cause of action in negligence when construed in conjunction with section 2-202 of the Act. For the reasons that follow, we affirm the trial court's ruling that the purchase of insurance by the Village of Skokie did not waive defendants' right to assert the provisions of the Tort Immunity Act. Further, we vacate with instructions the trial court's dismissal of count V of the plaintiff's complaint.

Defendants contend that when a governmental entity is immunized from liability under the Tort Immunity Act, courts may not invoke the special duty doctrine as an exception to that Act to permit the imposition of liability. Defendants argue that application of the special duty doctrine to contravene the immunities and defenses afforded to a governmental entity by the legislature under the Tort Immunity Act is an impermissible infringement not only upon the Illinois General Assembly's constitutional responsibility to be the sole determinant of governmental immunities pursuant to article XIII, section 4, of the Illinois Constitution of 1970. Plaintiff argues that the viability of the special duty doctrine as an exception to the immunities and defenses granted in the Tort Immunity Act is well established, as its existence has been consistently recognized by Illinois courts in the decades following promulgation of the Tort Immunity Act and the subsequent ratification of the Illinois Constitution of 1970. Accordingly, plaintiff urges this court not to disturb this precedent.

Under the common law doctrine of sovereign immunity, a governmental entity was afforded blanket immunity from all tort liability. In recent years, however, sovereign immunity rules have been either modified or abolished at both the state and federal level. The sovereign immunity of governmental entities in tort actions was abolished in Illinois by this court's 1959 decision in Molitor v. Kaneland Community Unit District. In response to our Molitor decision, the Illinois General Assembly in 1965 enacted the Local Governmental and Governmental Employees Tort Immunity Act. Granting only immunities and defenses, the Act adopted the general principle from Molitor "that local governmental units are liable in tort but limited this with an extensive list of immunities based on specific government functions." The immunities afforded to governmental entities under the Act work as an affirmative defense which, if properly raised and proven by the public entity, bars a plaintiff's right to recovery. However, because the Tort Immunity Act is in derogation of the common law, it must be strictly construed against the public entity involved. Five years after the legislature passed the Tort Immunity Act, the Illinois Constitution of 1970 was ratified. Article XIII, section 4, of the Illinois Constitution provides: "Except as the General Assembly may provide by law, sovereign immunity in this State is abolished." This provision "embodies the presumptive rule from Molitor that units of local government are subject to tort liability," and provides that the General Assembly possessed the exclusive power to determine whether such a governmental unit is statutorily immune from liability. Therefore, the tort liability of a governmental entity and its employees is expressly controlled by constitutional provision and legislative prerogative as embodied in the Tort Immunity Act.

The special duty doctrine which is challenged by defendants in the instant cause originated as an exception to the common law public duty rule. The rationale behind the nonliability principle of the public duty rule is that a municipality's duty is to preserve the well-being of the community and that such a duty is owed to the public at large rather than to specific members of the community. Plaintiff argues we are prevented from holding that the special duty doctrine cannot constitutionally operate to override statutory immunities because such a ruling would violate the principle of *stare decisis*. According to plaintiff, a long line of previous decisions rendered by Illinois courts, subsequent to the passage of the Tort Immunity Act and the ratification of the Illinois Constitution of 1970, recognized the viability of the special duty doctrine. Plaintiff's argument, however, misses the mark. The doctrine of *stare decisis* "expresses the policy of the courts to stand by precedents and not to disturb settled points" (Neff v. George, 364 Ill. 306, 308-09, 4 N.E.2d 388 1936). *Stare decisis*, furthermore, has "more or less force, according to the nature of the question decided." As such, plaintiff's citation to a list of decisions previously rendered by this court concerning the special duty doctrine is not persuasive on this point, as none of those rulings decided the narrow constitutional issue presented in the instant matter. Therefore, there is no "settled point" of law which is disturbed by our finding that the operation of the special duty doctrine in circumventing immunities provided under the Tort Immunity Act violates the Illinois Constitution. We conclude that because this court had not before addressed the constitutional conflict raised in the instant matter, there was no settled point of law on this precise constitutional issue, and therefore the doctrine of *stare decisis* is inapposite.

In a related argument, plaintiff urges this court to refrain from finding the operation of the special duty doctrine unconstitutional on the grounds that the Illinois General Assembly's failure to amend the Tort Immunity Act in light of court decisions which recognized the special duty doctrine as an exception to the immunities granted in the Tort Immunity Act establishes and confirms that the legislature intended the doctrine to operate in the manner pursued by the courts. Plaintiff asserts that the previous court decisions should be deemed controlling unless and until the General Assembly provides otherwise. We disagree. It is a fundamental principle that "where the legislature chooses not to amend a statute after a judicial construction, it will be presumed that it has acquiesced in the court's statement of the legislative intent" (Miller v. Lockett, 98 Ill.2d 478, 483, 75 Ill.Dec. 224, 457 N.E.2d 14 1983). However, the fact remains that this court has never ruled that operation of the special duty doctrine to negate the immunities provided to governmental entities pursuant to the Tort Immunity Act comported with the Illinois Constitution. As such, there has been no "judicial construction" concerning the validity of the operation of the special duty doctrine in which the legislature could acquiesce.

Summarizing, we hold that the imposition of the special duty exception to override the legislatively created governmental immunities in the Tort Immunity Act violates the sovereign immunity provisions of the Illinois Constitution of 1970 and also violates the separation of powers clause of the Illinois Constitution.

We now turn to the arguments raised by plaintiff in his cross-appeal pursuant to Rule 318(a) concerning two rulings made by the trial judge in connection with defendants' motion to strike and dismiss all counts of plaintiff's complaint. As an initial matter, plaintiff renews the argument made before the trial court that defendants have waived the protections of the Tort Immunity Act by purchasing policies of insurance. Based upon this contention, plaintiff urges that defendants cannot validly raise any immunities or defenses available under the Act, an issue which is of importance in light of the appellate court's remand of this cause to the circuit court for a new trial. Specifically, plaintiff asserts that under the terms of the Tort Immunity Act, as it existed at the time of this incident in 1982, a municipality waived the immunities and defenses provided by the Act if it purchased liability insurance. At the time of this incident, section 9-103(a) of the Act provided: "A local public entity may protect itself against any liability which may be imposed on it by means including, but not limited to, insurance, self-insurance, the purchase of claims services, or participation in a reciprocal insurer. Insurance shall be carried with a company authorized by the Department of Insurance to write such insurance coverage in Illinois." Furthermore, section 9-103(c) of the Act read as follows: "Every policy for insurance coverage issued to a local public entity shall provide or be endorsed to provide that the company issuing such policy waives any right to refuse payment or to deny liability thereto within the limits of said policy by reason of the non-liability of the insured public entity for the wrongful or negligent acts of itself or its employees and its immunity from suit by reason of the defenses and immunities provided in this Act."

In 1986, section 9-103 of the Act was amended by the Illinois General Assembly, eliminating the waiver provision. For purposes of the instant matter, we are concerned only with the pre-1986 amendment version of this statute. At the time of this incident, the Village of Skokie was self-insured up to $250,000, and had purchased two insurance policies: a $1 million liability policy and an excess liability policy in the additional amount of $10 million. In rejecting plaintiff's argument that by purchasing insurance Skokie waived the protections of the Tort Immunity Act, the trial court observed that Skokie had a self-insured retention and that the two insurers from whom Skokie acquired the insurance were bankrupt and defunct. The trial court held that under such circumstances, "public money is implicated, and the defendant police officers face personal responsibility. Finding a waiver under these circumstances would not be consistent with the intent and purpose of the Act." Plaintiff argues that Skokie's election to procure insurance works as a complete and irrevocable waiver of its right to invoke immunities and defenses pursuant to the Tort Immunity Act, that Skokie's self-insured retention is irrelevant, and that the trial court erred in concluding that a completed waiver may be undone based upon a subsequent fortuitous circumstance such as the liquidation of Skokie's insurers.

In situations where a judgment, or portion thereof, would be paid from public funds, Illinois courts have held in construing the pre-1986 amendment version of the statute that the immunities of the Act are not waived to the extent of the exposure of the government funds. In the instant matter, the Village of Skokie bears the primary responsibility for satisfying a damages judgment under its self-insured retention, a fact compounded by the insolvency of its excess insurance carriers. The well-established policy of the Tort Immunity Act to protect such public funds defeats plaintiff's contention that Skokie's previous procurement of insurance operated as a waiver of the immunities and defenses available under the Act. Thus, the trial court in the case at bar did not err in holding that the defendants may assert all defenses and immunities appropriately available to them under the Tort Immunity Act to the extent that public money is implicated.

Finally, in connection with the remand of this cause to the circuit court for a new trial, plaintiff asserts that the trial court erred in dismissing count V of his complaint on the basis that section 4-105 of the Tort Immunity Act, as it read at the time of this incident, did not provide a cause of action in negligence. Section 4-105 provided: "Neither a local public entity nor a public employee is liable for injury proximately caused by the failure of the employee to furnish or obtain medical care for a prisoner in his custody; but a public employee, and the local public entity where the employee is acting within the scope of his employment, is liable if the employee knows or has reason to know from his observation that the prisoner is in need of immediate medical care and fails to take reasonable action to summon medical care. Nothing in this Section requires the periodic inspection of prisoners." Plaintiff contends that the legislature's use of the phrase "knows or has reason to know" is an indication that a negligence standard was intended by the General Assembly, and that a subsequent amendment to this section in 1986 deleting the "knows or has reason to know" language and replacing it with a willful and wanton standard supports this contention.

The trial court judge ruled that section 4-105, as it read at the time of this incident, did not establish a cause of action in negligence. In arriving at this holding, the trial court judge read section 4-105 within the context of the entire statutory scheme and purpose of the Tort Immunity Act, and in his written ruling held that section "4-105 was intended to establish complete immunity for the public entity or employee who fails to furnish or obtain medical care for a prisoner in custody, but then carves out an exception to that immunity for instances where the jailer knows or has reason to know from his observation that the prisoner is in need of immediate medical care and fails to take reasonable action to summon that care. To survive, the exception must be read with section 2-202. That is, the jailer's conduct must be willful and wanton for the exception to apply. Otherwise, the exception would swallow the rule and serve no purpose." The trial judge's ruling, however, makes no findings that the conduct of defendants fell within the provisions of section 2-202.

Because the provisions of the Tort Immunity Act are to be construed in relation to every other section, it follows that under the preamended version of section 4-105, the exception to nonliability contained in that section is governed by a negligence standard unless the case falls within the parameters of section 2-202, which provides that "a public employee is not liable for his act or omission in the execution or enforcement of any law unless such act or omission constitutes willful and wanton conduct." This court has determined that section 2-202 immunity is a limited immunity, which dimensions are narrower than the scope of a police officer's employment or his performance of official functions and duties. Thus, the plain language of the preamended version of section 4-105 indicates that a negligence standard would apply to the nonliability exception contained in that section, unless a factual determination is made that the defendants' conduct fell within the parameters of the provisions of section 2-202 of the Act, thereby raising the standard to that of willful and wanton misconduct. We therefore vacate the trial court's dismissal of count V of plaintiff's complaint, and upon remand of this cause to the trial court, instruct the trial court to further consider this issue consistent with this opinion.

For the foregoing reasons, we reverse the judgment of the appellate court and the circuit court on the issue of whether the operation of the special duty doctrine in overriding immunities provided to governmental entities by the Illinois General Assembly is unconstitutional. In connection with the pretrial rulings challenged by plaintiff, we affirm the trial court's ruling that in the facts of this case, the purchase of insurance by the Village of Skokie did not waive defendants' ability to invoke the immunities and defenses available under the Tort Immunity Act. Further, we vacate the trial court's dismissal of count V of plaintiff's complaint and remand that issue to the trial court for further proceedings consistent with this opinion. Appellate court judgment reversed in part; circuit court judgment affirmed in part, reversed in part, and vacated in part; cause remanded.

Justice HARRISON, dissenting: My reason for dissenting is wholly unrelated to the constitutionality of the special duty doctrine. I dissent today because the majority has misunderstood some basic principles of appellate review and has misconstrued certain provisions of the Tort Immunity Act. In disposing of this case, the majority purports to overrule or affirm various holdings made by the circuit and appellate courts in support of the judgments those courts entered. What the majority overlooks is that our job is not to review holdings. We review judgments. It is the propriety of judgments themselves and not what else that may have been said by the lower courts that is before us on appeal. Our function as a reviewing court is simply to determine whether the lower courts reached the correct result. The reasons given by a lower court for its decision or the findings on which a decision is based are not material if the judgment is correct. A judgment may be sustained upon any ground warranted by the record.

The present case is before us on appeal from a judgment of the appellate court affirming, on interlocutory appeal under Rule 306(a)(1), an order of the circuit court granting plaintiff a new trial. The circuit court ordered a new trial based on various trial errors which had nothing to do with the viability of the special duty doctrine. The errors pertained to such matters as the admission of evidence, jury selection, and improper arguments by defense counsel. In their interlocutory appeal, defendants claimed that the trial court abused its discretion in setting aside the jury's verdict and allowing plaintiff to try his case again. The appellate court rejected this claim, noting, among other things, that defendants had failed to provide it with an adequate record. The record remains devoid of materials necessary to review the circuit court's order granting a new trial, and defendants expressly conceded in their petition for leave to appeal that the appellate court was correct in affirming the circuit court's decision to order a new trial. Under these circumstances, defendants' leave to appeal should never have been allowed, and their appeal should be summarily dismissed.

Even if I agreed that we should address the case on the merits, I still could not concur in the majority's opinion. Because this appeal challenges the propriety of the new trial order and because defendants now agree that the new trial order was proper, the only appropriate disposition at this point is to affirm the appellate court's judgment and remand to the circuit court for a new trial. Although I would affirm outright, I agree with the majority that the statutory immunity questions should be addressed. As a general rule I am reluctant to address issues that are not essential to resolution of the specific issue at hand, and I do not think that the appellate court should have addressed the special duty question given the posture of the case. If we do not step in to clarify the law now, it may only engender confusion later. In the interest of conserving judicial resources and insuring a consistent body of precedent, some discussion on our part is therefore appropriate. Unlike the majority, however, I would not alter the lower courts' judgments. I would simply affirm for different reasons.

Municipalities and their employees who seek to invoke sovereign immunity under the Tort Immunity Act must show that a particular provision of the Act shields them from liability in tort. The immunities set forth in the Act are in the nature of an affirmative defense which the public entity must plead and prove. There is no presumption in favor of statutory immunity. To the contrary, because the Tort Immunity Act is in derogation of the common law, the court has held that it must be strictly construed against the local public entity or public employee. As the majority opinion indicates, defendants initially invoked a variety of provisions under the Tort Immunity Act as a defense to plaintiff's negligence claims. By the time they reached the appellate court, defendants argued only that plaintiff's negligence claims should be barred by sections 4-103, 6-105 and 6-106(a) of the Act. In their petition for leave to appeal, which they elected to have stand as their brief, defendants winnowed their list of possible statutory immunities even further. They now rely exclusively on section 2-202, which relieves public employees from liability for acts or omissions "in the execution or enforcement of any law" unless such acts or omissions are willful and wanton.

Under the plain language of the statute, section 2-202 does not grant immunity for every act or omission of public employees while on duty. Rather, it provides immunity only where the public employee is negligent while actually engaged in the execution or enforcement of a law. Defendants tell us that they will argue on remand that they were, in fact, engaged in the execution and enforcement of a law when they abandoned Scott Zimmerman to hang himself in his cell, but this case dates back 15 years now. If defendants could make such an argument legitimately, they surely would have done so already. Accordingly, I would hold that section 2-202 does not apply to this case. Governmental units are liable in tort on the same basis as private tortfeasors unless a tort immunity statute imposes conditions upon that liability. Because section 2-202 is inapplicable and because defendants no longer claim the protection of any other provision of the Tort Immunity Act, the viability of plaintiff's negligence claims does not depend on the special duty exception. On remand, plaintiff may proceed against defendants as he would against private individuals.

In addition to any common law negligence claims he might assert, plaintiff may also proceed against defendants based on section 4-105 of the Tort Immunity Act. That statute expressly provides that "a public employee, and the local public entity where the employee is acting within the scope of his employment, is liable if the employee knows or has reason to know from his observation that the prisoner is in need of immediate medical care and fails to take reasonable action to summon medical care." This statute is broad enough to embrace all of plaintiff's negligence claims, and plaintiff has so argued. Contrary to the position taken by the majority, the applicability of section 4-105 is not limited to plaintiff's claims under count V of his third amended complaint.

The majority makes one final error. In discussing section 4-105, my colleagues assert that even if a defendant's conduct fell within the terms of the statute, that defendant still could not be held liable for negligence if the defendant's conduct involved an "act or omission in the execution or enforcement of any law." In such a case, the majority claims, the defendant could only be held liable if his conduct rose to the level of willful and wanton misconduct. Because defendants' conduct here does not fall within the terms of section 2-202, there is no need to discuss the relationship between that statute and section 4-105. Even if section 2-202 were relevant, however, the majority's analysis would be incorrect for two reasons. First, it is axiomatic that specific statutory provisions generally control over general provisions on the same subject. Section 2-202 deals generically with acts or omissions in the execution or enforcement of the law. Section 4-105, by contrast, is addressed to the specific circumstances at issue here, namely, the failure of defendants to summon medical care for Zimmerman, a prisoner in their custody, when they knew he needed it. Because the statute is more specific, it is controlling and allows recovery for ordinary negligence. Second, the practical effect of the majority's approach is to engraft a willful and wanton standard onto the version of section 4-105 governing this case. Where the legislature intends municipal liability to be governed by a willful and wanton standard, it has said so explicitly. In the case of section 4-105, what the legislature said explicitly is that liability may be premised on ordinary negligence. If that were not the legislature's intent and the majority's construction were correct, there would have been no need for the legislature's subsequent amendment to the statute to expressly include a willful and wanton standard.

In sum, I agree with the result reached by the appellate court, but for different reasons. The appellate court was correct in affirming the circuit court's judgment granting plaintiff a new trial, and plaintiff should be permitted to pursue his negligence claims on remand regardless of the viability of the special duty exception. I therefore dissent.

REVIEW SECTION

READING COMPREHENSION

Define the "special duty" doctrine and the common law "public duty" rule.

Articulate the arguments of the defense.

Elaborate the history of tort liability in Illinois.

THINKING CRITICALLY

Using opinion from the majority and dissent, discuss how you would decide this case.

CONCLUSION

We have now elaborated the exclusionary rule and the defense of entrapment which are remedies available to defendants in criminal trial cases, as well as remedies an individual may pursue against an officer that are not available at the trial stage, including prosecuting the officer through criminal law, suing a government official or entity through civil law, or administrative discipline of an officer outside of the judicial system. This chapter thoroughly reviewed these remedies for official misconduct, and discussed the issue of failure to protect by law enforcement and the conditions under which a duty to protect is assigned.

Chapter Twelve

Starting Court Proceedings

Once the police turn over a strong case to the prosecutor's office, it is the discretion of that office whether or not to charge the individual in question. Keep in mind that not all strong cases are prosecuted because it is the duty of the prosecutor's office not only to prosecute crime, but also to accomplish justice which may involve alternative criminal justice procedures such as diversion.

This chapter will review what happens after the start of court proceedings, including:

(1)   Probable cause;

(2)   First appearance and bail; and

(3)   Right to counsel.

SECTION 1: PROBABLE CAUSE

OVERVIEW

Once a defendant is arrested, the U.S. Constitution and Illinois state law require a probable cause hearing within a reasonable length of time in order to avoid the deprivation of liberty that results from imprisonment. Prosecution of an individual may involve a complaint, an information, or an indictment. According to 725 ILCS 5/113-1:

> Before any person is tried for the commission of an offense he
> shall be called into open court, informed of the charge against him,
> and called upon to plead thereto. If the defendant so requests the
> formal charge shall be read to him before he is required to plead.
> An entry of the arraignment shall be made of record.

According to 725 ILCS 5/111-2 which details the commencement of prosecutions:

> (a) All prosecutions of felonies shall be by information or by
> indictment. No prosecution may be pursued by information unless
> a preliminary hearing has been held or waived in accordance with
> Section 109-3 and at that hearing probable cause to believe the

defendant committed an offense was found, and the provisions of Section 109-3.1 of this Code have been complied with. (b) All other prosecutions may be by indictment, information or complaint.

During the preliminary exam:

> (b) If the defendant waives preliminary examination the judge shall hold him to answer and may, or on the demand of the prosecuting attorney shall, cause the witnesses for the State to be examined. After hearing the testimony if it appears that there is not probable cause to believe the defendant guilty of any offense the judge shall discharge him. (d) During preliminary hearing or examination the defendant may move for an order of suppression of evidence pursuant to Section 114-11 or 114-12 of this Act or for other reasons, and may move for dismissal of the charge pursuant to Section 114-1 of this Act or for other reasons.

The Constitution does not however, require judicial oversight of prosecutorial discretion and a conviction can not be vacated because the defendant was detained during the hearing. As well, you may note that a probable cause determination is not considered part of the critical stage of prosecution and thus does not require appointed counsel. Further, Illinois law requires either a preliminary hearing or an indictment by grand jury for all persons charged with felonies within 30 days from the date the suspect was taken into custody (725 ILCS 5/109-3.1).

CASE

The court has consolidated three cases below because they share a common issue: whether the finding of probable cause at a minor's detention hearing, required to be held within 36 hours of arrest, is deemed a finding of probable cause at a subsequent hearing to determine whether the minor ought to be transferred to the adult criminal justice system, and, if not, what recognition is to be afforded the transcript of the prior proceedings at the transfer hearing. In each case, the minor was taken into custody and within 36 hours a detention hearing was commenced pursuant to section 5-10 of the Juvenile Court Act of 1987. That section requires the juvenile court to find there is probable cause to believe that the minor is a delinquent minor and that "it is a matter of immediate and urgent necessity for the protection of the minor or of the person or property of another that the minor be detained" (705 ILCS 405/5-10(2)).

IN RE R.L.
IN RE O.U.
IN RE R.D.
668 N.E.2d 70, 282 Ill.App.3d 839 (1996)

The State believes that a finding of probable cause in the detention hearing binds the transfer hearing court on issues of probable cause for transfer out of the juvenile system under a theory of collateral *estoppel*. The minor in each case argues that the issues raised in the detention hearing are different than those of the later proceedings and that the summary nature of the detention hearing imposed by the 36-hour time limit denies the minor fundamental fairness in the administration of juvenile justice, thus requiring two independent hearings. Another approach would be that the prior determination does not bind the transfer court, but the transcript might come into evidence and the court could then make a determination that the requirement of "probable cause" for the transfer hearing was satisfied by the evidence adduced at the earlier hearing and the rebuttable presumption that the minor ought not be dealt with under the Act then arises. While this is a seductive middle road, prosecutors might find themselves more at risk in chancing that the transcript will suffice.

Overlaid upon the various sections of the Act are the stated goals of the Act, as set out in the preamble: "In all proceedings under this Act the court may direct the course thereof so as promptly to ascertain the jurisdictional facts and fully to gather information bearing upon the current condition and future welfare of persons subject to this Act. This Act shall be administered in a spirit of humane concern, not only for the rights of the parties, but also for the fears and the limits of understanding of all who appear before the court" (705 ILCS 405/1-2(2)). The first hearing is mandated by section 5-10 of the Act and is defined as a "Detention or shelter care hearing," which provides: "At the appearance of a minor before the court at the detention or shelter care hearing, all witnesses present shall be examined before the court in relation to any matter connected with the allegations made in the petition. No hearing may be held unless the minor is represented by counsel. (1) If the court finds that there is not probable cause to believe that the minor is a delinquent minor it shall release the minor and dismiss the petition. (2) If the court finds there is probable cause to believe that the minor is a delinquent minor, the minor, his or her parent, guardian, custodian and other persons able to give relevant testimony shall be examined before the court. If the court finds that it is a matter of immediate and urgent necessity for the protection of the minor or of the person or property of another that the minor be detained or placed in a shelter care facility or that he or she is likely to flee the jurisdiction of the court, the court may prescribe detention or shelter care" (705 ILCS 405/5-10(1),(2)).

"Delinquent minor" means any minor who, prior to his seventeenth birthday, has violated or attempted to violate, regardless of where the act occurred, any federal or state law or municipal ordinance. The subsequent hearing, regulated by section 5-4(3.3), is commenced upon the filing of a motion and petition by the State to determine whether the minor is not an appropriate subject to be dealt with under the Act and should be transferred to the criminal court and provides: "If the State's Attorney files a motion under subsection (3)(a) to permit prosecution under the criminal laws and the petition alleges the commission by a minor 15 years of age or older of: (i) a Class X felony other than armed violence; (ii) aggravated discharge of a firearm; (iii) armed violence with a firearm when the predicate offense is a Class 1 or Class 2 felony and the State's Attorney's motion to transfer the case alleges that the offense committed is in furtherance of the criminal activities of an organized gang and the case is not required to be prosecuted under the criminal laws of Illinois as provided by subsection (3.1) or (3.2); (iv) armed violence with a firearm when the predicate offense is a violation of Section 401, subsection (a) of Section 402 of the Illinois Controlled Substances Act; or (v) armed violence when the weapon involved was a machine gun or other weapon described in subsection (a)(7) of Section 24-1 of the Criminal Code of 1961, and, if the juvenile judge designated to hear and determine motions to transfer a case for prosecution in the criminal court determines that there is probable cause to believe that the allegations in the petition and motion are true, there is a rebuttable presumption that the minor is not a fit and proper subject to be dealt with under the Juvenile Court Act of 1987, and that, except as provided in paragraph (b), the case should be transferred to the criminal court" (705 ILCS 405/5-4(3.3)(a)).

Once the court determines that probable cause exists to believe the allegations in the State's petition and motion, a rebuttable presumption of transfer is triggered. To rebut the presumption of transfer, the minor must come forward with favorable evidence relating to the factors enumerated in paragraph (b), which are: "(i) The circumstances and gravity of the offense alleged to have been committed by the minor. (ii) The age of the minor. (iii) The degree of criminal sophistication exhibited by the minor. (iv) Whether there is a reasonable likelihood that the minor can be rehabilitated before the expiration of the juvenile court's jurisdiction. (v) The minor's previous history of delinquency. (vi) Whether the offense was committed in an aggressive, premeditated or calculated manner. (vii) Whether there are sufficient facilities available to the juvenile court for the treatment and rehabilitation of the minor" (705 ILCS 405/5-4(3.3)(b).

IN RE R.L.

After a probable cause hearing on the day of the respondent's arrest, the juvenile court made a finding of immediate and urgent necessity that the 15-year-old minor be detained. A single police officer testified that there had been two individuals who fired shots at a group of teenagers near South Shore High School, wounding one of the students. One of the group identified respondent, a student at South Shore, as one of the two shooters, although he was apparently unable to determine whether the minor was the shooter of the wounded student. No evidence was offered that the minor acknowledged his involvement. The initial petition for adjudication of wardship charged the minor with aggravated battery, aggravated battery with a firearm, attempted murder, aggravated discharge of a firearm and armed violence. At the detention hearing, the State informed the court that it intended to file a motion to permit prosecution of the minor as an adult and that it had previously so advised the minor's counsel. At the continued section 5-4(3.3) hearing, the trial court took judicial notice of the prior finding of probable cause, but declined to make a finding of probable cause for the purpose of transfer because the proceeding lacked fundamental fairness to be accorded a minor in connection with a hearing of such magnitude, so that the mere presence of a transcript of the prior hearing was insufficient.

IN RE O.U.

The 15-year-old was found to be a "delinquent minor" after a hearing, within 36 hours of his being taken into custody, which consisted of the testimony of two police officers who stated that there had been a shooting outside of Morton West High School, that the victim had identified the respondent, whom he knew from school, from an array of pictures, and that, when confronted by the officers, the minor implicated himself and provided information that led to the officers recovering the weapon used in the shooting. A written statement was prepared but not signed. On allegations that the minor was guilty of the offenses of attempted murder, aggravated battery with a firearm, armed violence and aggravated battery, the court made a finding of probable cause and ordered the minor detained. Thereafter, the State filed a petition and motion alleging that there was probable cause only on the charge of aggravated battery with a firearm and dismissed the other charges that had been considered at the detention hearing. The State maintained that the charged crime was one of those defined in section 5-4(3.3) and thus established a rebuttable presumption that the minor should not remain in the juvenile justice system. The State offered the transcript from the detention hearing, which was admitted without objection. The trial court then declined to find probable cause, ruling that the State's sole reliance on the initial finding of probable cause was insufficient evidence of probable cause at the transfer hearing, and found the State's reliance "fundamentally unfair" and at odds with the minor's rights to due process. The court therefore denied the State's motion to transfer.

IN RE R.D.

Following a detention hearing the trial court found, based on the testimony of two police officers and the victim's eye-witness identification of the minor, probable cause to believe that the minor committed attempted murder, aggravated battery with a firearm and armed violence in the shooting of William Smith and ordered the minor detained. Subsequently, the State moved to transfer the minor pursuant to section 5-4(3.3) and called the same officers, who repeated their earlier testimony. The trial court found that there was insufficient evidence to support a finding of probable cause as to the attempted murder charge, but found probable cause to believe the minor committed aggravated battery with a firearm. The trial court then denied the transfer motion, finding section 5-4(3.3) requires a finding of probable cause as to each count alleged in the State's petition and motion.

The role of an appellate court when reviewing transfer decisions is to determine whether the juvenile court has abused its discretion. As discussed below, we find no such abuse in R.L.. We are not so constrained where the trial court's error is in the application of law, and we find that in O.U. and R.D. the trial court made an error of law. In R.D., the minor was afforded a separate hearing, at which the trial court found that the State did not carry its burden in proving probable cause as to both the charged offenses. Nothing in section 5-4(3.3) requires the State to prove probable cause for all of the offenses charged. It is enough that there was probable cause on one of the offenses and that crime was one of the offenses set out in section 5-4(3.3). In O.U., the trial court based its decision to deny the State's transfer motion on its perception that "fundamental fairness" required such a ruling. While we agree that notions of fundamental fairness require additional process at the transfer hearing, we believe the trial court's decision would have benefited from substantive consideration of the allegations in the State's petition and transfer motion.

Apart from any mandate of fundamental fairness, we interpret the language of section 5-4(3.3) as requiring a probable cause determination independent of the probable cause finding made at the detention hearing. The rebuttable presumption of section 5-4(3.3) will not be invoked unless "the juvenile judge designated to hear and determine motions to transfer a case for prosecution in the criminal court determines that there is probable cause to believe that the allegations in the petition and motion are true" (705 ILCS 405/5-4(3.3)(a)). We should give enactments of our General Assembly an interpretation based upon the plain and ordinary meaning of the language employed. Moreover, reviewing courts cannot depart from the plain meaning of an unambiguous statute by creating exceptions or limitations that the legislature did not express. The State would have us add language expressing legislative intent to essentially merge the probable cause findings in the detention and transfer proceedings, when each proceeding involves different and "critically important rights" that demand independent process. We decline this invitation.

Section 5-4(3.3) mandates that the judge assigned to hear the transfer motion must "hear" and "determine" the probable cause issues. That express requirement should put to rest the State's argument that the prior determination of probable cause is binding at the transfer hearing. Although we believe that the language of section 5-4(3.3) alone mandates that the juvenile court provide two separate probable cause determinations and hearings, we also believe that the purposes of the respective hearings are so different and unique that due process and the notion of fundamental fairness require separate determinations of probable cause.

Having determined that a separate hearing is required, we next consider whether such separate hearing requirement can be satisfied by the mere filing of the transcript from the earlier hearing if those proceedings have the kind of completeness that would allow the second judge to be comfortable finding probable cause on the basis of such transcript either alone or together with additional evidence offered by the State. We need not cite authority for the proposition that probable cause can be shown by hearsay evidence. The issuance of search warrants and preliminary hearings are perhaps the most common situations that come to mind. However, probable cause has not always had the same meaning in companion cases where the objects of the proceedings have a different purpose. In two of the three cases before us, the trial court admitted the transcript without objection or took "judicial notice" of its existence. Admittedly, there are discrete differences between the several cases consolidated here. The finding in R.L. is based on the testimony of a single police officer who had a short conversation with one of the members of a crowd of youngsters at whom respondent allegedly fired a weapon. In O.U., two officers conducted the investigation and their testimony included evidence of confrontation with the minor, who implicated himself in the shooting. However, in O.U., the detention hearing court found probable cause with reference to several counts, while at the transfer hearing, the State set out only one of the charged counts. The initial finding of probable cause was not count specific so that there was no way for the transfer hearing judge to be aware of which count was found to have probable cause. Despite the differences, we believe that the State must show probable cause without resort to the prior hearing. If we allow the use of the prior transcript without additional evidence, counsel is limited to only coming forward with the responses allowed by section 5-4(3.3)(b) rather than having a real opportunity to test the State's case with real cross-examination after appropriate investigation and thoughtful interaction between counsel and the minor.

Accordingly, if objection is made to the introduction of the transcript, the court should decline to admit it into evidence. Nothing herein precludes the court from considering the transcript if there is not an objection interposed or if the minor stipulates to the admission of the transcript. In O.U., the transcript was admitted without objection but the court declined to find probable cause because of the differences in the two proceedings of the charged counts. The State raises concerns about judicial economy. If economies are to be achieved in the criminal justice system, they should be elsewhere than in the disposition of matters affecting our children. We must examine the distinct purposes for each hearing and the dynamics surrounding each. The detention hearing must be heard within 36 hours of the minor's arrest, and our courts have recently drawn a bright line with respect to the recognition of statutory deadlines when they relate to minors. More often than not, defense counsel has been advised of the proceedings only a few minutes or hours before he or she is expected to appear and cross-examine witnesses who are usually testifying to hearsay in the development of probable cause. Counsel is unlikely to have had an opportunity to conduct even the most cursory investigation of the charges facing the young client.

Even if we were not convinced that the language of the statute requires separate consideration of the proof of probable cause or that the time constraints of the detention hearing impair counsel's ability to adequately represent the client, it is the purpose of each hearing that mandates separate determination of the principal issue. The purpose of the detention hearing is to determine whether the minor is "a delinquent minor" and whether there is "immediate and urgent necessity" to detain the minor for his or her own safety or for the safety of others upon a finding of probable cause that the minor has committed a felony or misdemeanor or violation of an ordinance. But this need not be the end of the line for the minor. The court may amend or change its order upon a subsequent showing that the minor is not in need of detention. The detention order is provisional by its very nature. It addresses the concerns of the minor and society at a particular time, while the aim of the transfer hearing is one that will have a lasting and permanent effect upon the child in the event a transfer is ordered.

Illinois has an almost century-old commitment to appropriate treatment of minors; the nation's first juvenile court was established in 1899 in Chicago upon the advocacy of Jane Addams. Although Ms. Addams never envisioned children with Mac 10's, Uzis or .357 magnums, the sense of the preamble to the Act remains a strong statement of purpose. Examining the preamble, we question whether the usually abbreviated detention hearing can stand for the satisfaction of the transfer hearing and meet the test of an Act "administered in a spirit of humane concern, not only for the rights of the parties, but also for the fears and the limits of understanding of all who appear before the court" (705 ILCS 405/1-2(2)). We need not take the time to point out the obvious: that which awaits the child upon transfer to the adult criminal system. We take note that O.U. may spend a maximum of six years in the juvenile system, but in the event of transfer may be sentenced to 30 years in prison (720 ILCS 5/12-4.2). Our supreme court has acknowledged the need for fundamental fairness in the treatment of minors generally and in the procedures surrounding transfer hearings in particular. The recent amendment to the Act shifts much of the burden of coming forward with evidence that the court must consider and it is because of that shift of the burden, rather than in spite of it, that the proof of probable cause at the transfer hearing requires greater scrutiny. The mandate of fundamental fairness extends to the hearing under section 5-4(3.3) and requires that defense counsel properly represent his or her young client. It is difficult to imagine that such representation can be expected from counsel who has been in the case for a few hours at most and may not have met the client until the morning of the hearing.

In summary, we hold that (i) the finding of probable cause at the detention hearing does not bind the trial court as to probable cause at the transfer hearing and the minor is entitled to a *de novo* hearing, (ii) the transcript of the detention hearing may not be admitted at the transfer hearing unless by stipulation or if no objection is interposed by the minor, (iii) if the transcript is introduced by stipulation or by reason of the failure of the minor to object, it may be considered by the trial court together with any other evidence as proof of probable cause.

For the reasons set forth above, we affirm the trial court's finding in R.L. that section 5-4(3.3) requires its own probable cause hearing and affirm the decision to deny the State's transfer motion in the absence of such a hearing. We reverse the trial court in O.U., because, although the transcript was admitted without objection, the trial court apparently decided the transfer issue on procedural grounds. We remand to allow the trial court to conduct a new transfer hearing. We reverse the trial court in R.D., where the minor was afforded a proper transfer hearing with evidence in the proof of probable cause of a crime provided in section 5-4(3.3), but remand to afford the minor an opportunity to provide evidence of the factors established in section 5-4(3.3)(b) to rebut the presumption that arises upon the proper finding of probable cause.

REVIEW SECTION

READING COMPREHENSION

Detail the procedure for determining a delinquent minor.

What factors are considered when a transfer to adult court is an option.

Detail the purposes of the detention hearing and the transfer hearing.

THINKING CRITICALLY

Is it reasonable to require the State to show probable cause at two hearings? Should the State bear this burden to ensure minors are not transferred in haste to an adult court where the penalties are severely increased?

SECTION 2: FIRST APPEARANCE AND BAIL

OVERVIEW

There are several sections of 725 ILCS that address the issue of bail which require enumeration here. First, 725 ILCS 5/110-4 elaborates bailable offenses and will be quoted at length:

> (a) All persons shall be bailable before conviction, except the following offenses where the proff is evident or the presumption great that the defendant is guilty of the offense: capital offenses; offenses for which a sentence of life imprisonment may be imposed as a consequence of conviction; felony offenses for which a sentence of imprisonment, without conditional and revocable release, shall be imposed by law as a consequence of conviction, where the court after a hearing, determines that the release of the defendant would pose a real and present threat to the physical safety of any person or persons; stalking or aggravated stalking, where the court, after a hearing, determines that the release of the defendant would pose a real and present threat to the physical safety of the alleged victim of the offense and denial of bail is necessary to prevent fulfillment of the threat upon which the charge is based; or unlawful use of weapons in violation of item (4) of subsection (a) of Section 24-1 of the Criminal Code of 1961 when that offense occurred in a school or in any conveyance owned, leased, or contracted by a school to transport students to or from school or a school-related activity, or on any public way within 1000 feet of real property comprising any school, where the court, after a hearing, determines that the release of the defendant would pose a real and present threat to the physical safety of any person and denial of bail is necessary to prevent fulfillment of that threat. (b) A person seeking release on bail who is charged with a capital offense or an offense for which a sentence of life imprisonment may be imposed shall not be bailable until a hearing is held wherein such person has the burden of demonstrating that the proof of his guilt is not evident and the presumption is not great. (c) Where it is alleged that bail should be denied to a person

upon the grounds that the person presents a real and present threat to the physical safety of any person or persons, the burden of proof of such allegations shall be upon the State. (d) When it is alleged that bail should be denied to a person charged with stalking or aggravated stalking upon the grounds set forth in Section 110-6.3 of this Code, the burden of proof of those allegations shall be upon the State.

There are a myriad of factors considered in determining the amount of bail and the conditions of release as explicated in 725 ILCS 5/110-5. This section is extremely long, and should be referred to for reference if you are inclined. Regarding the amount of bail, 725 ILCS 5/110-5 sets forth that:

> (b) The amount of bail shall be: (1) Sufficient to assure compliance with the conditions set forth in the bail bond, which shall include the defendant's current address with a written admonishment to the defendant that he or she must comply with the provisions of Section 110-12 regarding any change in his or her address. The defendant's address shall at all times remain a matter of public record with the clerk of the court. (2) Not oppressive. (3) Considerate of the financial ability of the accused.

Thus, when deciding matters of bail, the court must weight the constitutional rights of the defendant with community security. While there is no U.S. constitutional right to bail, there is a right against excessive bail and equal protection of the law requires all defendants be provided with the same opportunity for consideration for release without discrimination. The Illinois Constitution however in Article One, Section Nine, specifically addresses the right to bail:

> All persons shall be bailable by sufficient sureties, except for the following offenses where the proof is evident or the presumption great: capital offenses; offenses for which a sentence of life imprisonment may be imposed as a consequence of conviction; and felony offenses for which a sentence of imprisonment, without conditional and revocable release, shall be imposed by law as a consequence of conviction, when the court, after a hearing, determines that release of the offender would pose a real and present threat to the physical safety of any person.

CASE

In *People v Purcell,* the defendant seeks review of the September 10, 2001 order of the circuit court denying bail. On appeal, the defendant argues that section 110--4(b) of the Code of

Criminal Procedure of 1963 is unconstitutional; and that the trial court erred in denying his request for pretrial bail.

PEOPLE V. PURCELL
Illinois Appellate Court (2001) No. 2--01--1053

On August 2001, the defendant was arrested and indicted on four counts of first-degree murder. The defendant was alleged to have killed his wife, Barbara Purcell, by striking her repeatedly in the head with a blunt object. If convicted of the charged offense, the defendant may receive a sentence of life imprisonment. Following his arrest, the defendant filed a motion requesting bail. The defendant also filed a motion seeking a determination that section 110--4 of the Code is unconstitutional. Section 110--4(a) provides that a defendant may not obtain bail where "the proof is evident or the presumption great" that the defendant committed a capital offense or an offense for which he may be sentenced to life imprisonment. Section 110--4(b) places the burden of demonstrating that the proof of guilt is not evident and the presumption of guilt not great upon the individual seeking release on bail. In his motion before the trial court, the defendant argued that subsection (b) violates the presumption of innocence accorded to criminal defendants while awaiting trial.

On August 15, 2001, the trial court denied the defendant's motion to declare section 110--4(b) of the Code unconstitutional. Then, on September 10, 2001, following a hearing, the trial court denied the defendant's motion for pretrial bail. The trial court found that the defendant did not meet his burden of demonstrating that the proof of his guilt was not evident and that the presumption of his guilt was not great. The defendant then filed the instant appeal pursuant to Supreme Court Rule 604(c). We will first address the defendant's constitutional argument. The right of an accused to obtain pretrial bail is governed by article I, section 9, of the Illinois Constitution of 1970 which provides: "All persons shall be bailable by sufficient sureties, except the following offenses where the proof is evident or the presumption great: capital offenses and offenses for which a sentence of life imprisonment may be imposed as a consequence of conviction." Section 110--4 of the Code is a codification of this constitutional provision.

As the defendant correctly notes, the due process clauses of both the United States and the Illinois Constitutions guarantee the accused that he will not be convicted on proof less than reasonable doubt of every fact necessary to constitute the crime with which he is charged. The complement to this guarantee is that the State bears the burden of proof and that the accused is presumed innocent. The presumption of innocence attaches to the accused from the onset of the proceedings and is one of the underpinnings of an accused's right to bail. The traditional right to freedom before conviction permits the unhampered preparation of a defense and serves to prevent the infliction of punishment prior to conviction. The question of whether section 110--4(b) infringes upon an accused's presumption of innocence has not previously been addressed by an Illinois court. However, Illinois' constitutional bail provision is not unique; the constitutions of most states contain similar provisions guaranteeing bail to the accused, except in cases punishable by death or life imprisonment where the proof is evident or the presumption great. As a result, there are a number of reported cases nationwide in which courts have considered the question of whether the State or the accused bears the burden during a bail hearing for an offense for which death or life imprisonment may be imposed, to show, or to disprove, that the proof is evident or the presumption great. The decisions in these cases have been conflicting, some holding that the State has the burden, and others holding that the burden falls on the accused.

In those cases placing the burden upon the State to prove that the accused's guilt is evident or that the presumption of such guilt is great, the courts have relied upon the presumption of innocence. These courts have explained that the presumption of innocence precludes any inference that the accused committed the charged offense. Finding that an indictment has no evidentiary value, these courts have held that the indictment does not raise a presumption, *prima facie* or otherwise, that the accused is guilty. Additionally, in placing the burden of proof on the State, these courts have explained that the right to bail is constitutionally guaranteed, subject only to exceptions for certain designated offenses. These courts hold that the State has the burden to show the existence of one of the exceptions and prove that the defendant is not entitled to bail.

Other jurisdictions have held that the burden to show that the proof of guilt is not evident or the presumption of guilt not great falls upon the accused seeking bail. The courts in these jurisdictions have found that the indictment raises a *prima facie* presumption of guilt that the accused must overcome by sufficient rebuttal evidence. This presumption is held to create an inference of guilt for all purposes except the actual trial. As already noted, this was the view taken by the American Law Institute in its 1930 Code of Criminal Procedure.

After careful consideration, we conclude that the correct approach is taken by those jurisdictions that place the burden upon the State to prove that the proof of the accused's guilt is evident and the presumption great. We believe that such an approach is required by the due process guarantees of both the United States and Illinois Constitutions. As noted above, the United States Supreme Court has held that the presumption of innocence applies during bail proceedings and is a primary underpinning of allowing pretrial bail. Accordingly, we must disagree with those jurisdictions that have held the presumption of innocence is not operative until the time of trial.

Because the presumption of innocence is operative during pretrial bail proceedings, we fail to see how an accused can be constitutionally required to prove that the evidence of his guilt is not great. Such a burden plainly flies in the face of the presumption of innocence and impermissibly shifts the evidentiary burden from the State to the accused. The presumption of innocence guarantees that the accused has no obligation to come forward with any evidence concerning the proof, or lack thereof, of any of the elements of the charged offense. Rather, as both the federal and state constitutions protect the right to bail, we believe that the State must have the burden of demonstrating that the defendant should be deprived of such a right.

Additionally, we note that principles of basic fairness also require that the burden of proof fall upon the State. As a practical matter, the accused is not in a good position to gather and present evidence during a bail hearing, as the criminal proceeding has been only recently initiated and the accused is in jail. The State, on the other hand, has ready access to the evidence of the alleged offense and is in a better position to present such evidence during a bail hearing. Indeed, in most cases, the State already will have presented evidence in order to secure an indictment from the grand jury. We also decline to adopt the approach of those jurisdictions holding that the indictment creates a presumption of guilt and that the burden may be shifted to the accused to present evidence rebutting this presumption in order to obtain bail. Although we acknowledge that the type of evidence introduced during a grand jury proceeding will be similar to that introduced at a bail hearing to establish that the proof of the accused's guilt is evident, we nonetheless believe that such an additional showing is constitutionally required. The presumption of innocence guarantees that the accused is not required to introduce any evidence concerning the alleged offense. We therefore do not believe that any evidentiary burden, whether it be rebuttal or otherwise, to show lack of guilt can be imposed upon the accused.

However, this is the precise burden that section 110--4(b) of the Code requires of the accused. As noted above, the statute provides that "[a] person seeking release on bail who is charged with a capital offense or an offense for which a sentence of life imprisonment may be imposed shall not be bailable until a hearing is held wherein such person has the burden of demonstrating that the proof of his guilt is not evident and the presumption is not great" (725 ILCS 5/110--4(b)). In its initial brief, the State argues that it was appropriate to place such a burden upon the defendant because the burden is imposed only after the trial court has made its own initial, independent determination that the proof of the defendant's guilt is evident and that the presumption is great. However, we find no support for this argument in section 110--4, which contains no language requiring the trial court to make such an initial determination. Even if such language did appear in the statute, we would nonetheless conclude that section 110--4(b) impermissibly violates the presumption of innocence. We hold that no burden of proof can be placed upon the defendant to establish his constitutionally guaranteed right to bail. Accordingly, we find that section 110--4(b) of the Code is unconstitutional.

We further hold that invalidity of subsection (b) is not fatal to the remainder of the statute. This court has an obligation to uphold legislative enactments whenever reasonably possible, and we may excuse an offending provision of a statute and preserve the remainder provided the remainder is complete in and of itself and is capable of being executed wholly independently of the severed portion. Offending provisions should also be severed when, even in the absence of the excised provision, the General Assembly would still have adopted the Act. We believe that the legislature would endorse the remainder of section 110--4 without subsection (b). Subsection (a) of the statute essentially codifies the bail provisions contained in article I, section 9. Subsections (c) and (d) of the statute provide that, when the State seeks to deny bail because the accused presents a threat to the physical safety of another or because the accused is charged with stalking, the burden of proof of such circumstances falls upon the State. We believe that subsections (a), (c), and (d) can stand independently of subsection (b) and that the removal of subsection (b) undermines neither the completeness of nor the ability to execute these remaining subsections. By removing section (b), this court can neutralize a constitutional infirmity without altering any of the remaining statute.

As his second contention on appeal, the defendant argues that the trial court abused its discretion in denying his request for pretrial bail. The defendant argues that he is not a danger to the community or a flight risk and requests that we direct the trial court to set his bail in the amount of $500,000. Rather than address the merits of this argument, we believe that the more appropriate course is to remand the cause for a new hearing on the defendant's motion for pretrial bail. A review of the record demonstrates that, at the hearing on the defendant's request for bond, the trial court placed the burden upon the defendant to prove that the proof of his guilt was not evident and the presumption of guilt not great. After hearing the evidence presented by the parties, the trial court found that the defendant had not satisfied his burden and denied his request for bail. In light of the foregoing discussion, we conclude that such proceedings were constitutionally infirm, as they deprived the defendant of his constitutional right to due process. We therefore believe that fundamental fairness requires that this case be remanded for a new hearing utilizing the appropriate burden of proof. Accordingly, we vacate the trial court's order denying the defendant's request for bail and remand the cause for a new hearing. At the hearing, the burden of proof shall be upon the State to show that the proof of the defendant's guilt is evident and the presumption of guilt great. For the foregoing reasons, we vacate the trial court's September 10, 2001, order, and we remand the cause for a new hearing upon the defendant's motion for pretrial bail conducted in conformity with the views expressed herein.

REVIEW SECTION

READING COMPREHENSION

Detail the facts of this case and the relevant constitutional provisions.

THINKING CRITICALLY

If the burden is on the defendant in a bail hearing, does this violate "innocent until proven guilty?"

SECTION 3: RIGHT TO COUNSEL

OVERVIEW

As mirrored in the Illinois Constitution, Article One, Section Eight, the Sixth Amendment to the U.S. Constitution states:

> In all criminal prosecution, the accused shall enjoy the right . . . to
> have the assistance of counsel for his defense.

While the court has historically recognized the right to counsel, not until the 1900s did courts recognize the right for appointed counsel in cases where the defendant was unable to avoid such assistance. Such right to counsel attaches at the accusatory stage of the trial and involves the right to counsel that passes the reasonably competent attorney standard, historically referred to as the mockery of justice standard. Should a defendant claim ineffective counsel, s/he must prove that the attorney was no reasonably competent and that this was probably responsible for the conviction.

725 ILCS 5/103-4 elaborates the right to consult with an attorney in Illinois:

> Any person committed, imprisoned or restrained of his liberty for any cause whatever and whether or not such person is charged with an offense shall, except in cases of imminent danger of escape, be allowed to consult with any licensed attorney at law of this State whom such person may desire to see or consult, alone and in private at the place of custody, as many times and for such period each time as is reasonable. When any such person is about to be moved beyond the limits of this State under any pretense whatever the person to be moved shall be entitled to a reasonable delay for the purpose of obtaining counsel and of availing himself of the laws of this State for the security of personal liberty.

Of particular note in this section is Article One, Section Eight of the Illinois Constitution which reads:

> In criminal prosecutions, the accused shall have the right to appear and defend in person and by counsel; to demand the nature and cause of the accusation and have a copy thereof; to be confronted with the witnesses against him or her and to have process to compel the attendance of witnesses in his or her behalf; and to have a speedy public trial by an impartial jury of the county in which the offense is alleged to have been committed.

CASE

In *Escobedo v Illinois,* the critical question is whether the refusal by the police to honor petitioner's request to consult with his lawyer during the course of an interrogation constitutes a denial of the Assistance of Counsel in violation of the Sixth Amendment to the Constitution as made obligatory upon the States by the Fourteenth Amendment, and thereby renders inadmissible in a state criminal trial any incriminating statement elicited by the police during the interrogation.

ESCOBEDO V. ILLINOIS
U.S. Supreme Court
378 U.S. 478, 84 S.Ct. 1758, 12 L.Ed.2d 977 (1964)

On the night of January 19, 1960, petitioner's brother-in-law was fatally shot. In the early hours of the next morning, at 2:30 a.m., petitioner was arrested without a warrant and interrogated. Petitioner made no statement to the police and was released at 5 that afternoon pursuant to a state court writ of habeas corpus obtained by Mr. Warren Wolfson, a lawyer who had been retained by petitioner. On January 30, Benedict DiGerlando, who was then in police custody and who was later indicted for the murder along with petitioner, told the police that petitioner had fired the fatal shots. Between 8 and 9 that evening, petitioner and his sister, the widow of the deceased, were arrested and taken to police headquarters. En route to the police station, the police 'had handcuffed the defendant behind his back,' and 'one of the arresting officers told defendant that DiGerlando had named him as the one who shot' the deceased. Petitioner testified, without contradiction, that the 'detective said they had us pretty well, up pretty tight, and we might as well admit to this crime,' and that he replied, 'I am sorry but I would like to have advice from my lawyer.' A police officer testified that although petitioner was not formally charged 'he was in custody' and 'couldn't walk out the door.' Shortly after petitioner reached police headquarters, his retained lawyer arrived.

The lawyer described the ensuing events in the following terms: 'On that day I received a phone call (from 'the mother of another defendant') and pursuant to that phone call I went to the Detective Bureau at 11th and State. The first person I talked to was the Sergeant on duty at the Bureau Desk, Sergeant Pidgeon. I asked Sergeant Pidgeon for permission to speak to my client, Danny Escobedo. Sergeant Pidgeon made a call to the Bureau lockup and informed me that the boy had been taken from the lockup to the Homicide Bureau. This was between 9:30 and 10:00 in the evening. Before I went anywhere, he called the Homicide Bureau and told them there was an attorney waiting to see Escobedo. He told me I could not see him. Then I went upstairs to the Homicide Bureau. There were several Homicide Detectives around and I talked to them. I identified myself as Escobedo's attorney and asked permission to see him. They said I could not. The police officer told me to see Chief Flynn who was on duty. I identified myself to Chief Flynn and asked permission to see my client. He said I could not. I think it was approximately 11:00 o'clock. He said I couldn't see him because they hadn't completed questioning. For a second or two I spotted him in an office in the Homicide Bureau. The door was open and I could see through the office. I waved to him and he waved back and then the door was closed, by one of the officers at Homicide.1 There were four or five officers milling around the Homicide Detail that night. As to whether I talked to Captain Flynn any later that day, I waited around for another hour or two and went back again and renewed my request to see my client. He again told me I could not. I filed an official complaint with Commissioner Phelan of the Chicago Police Department. I had a conversation with every police officer I could find. I was told at Homicide that I couldn't see him and I would have to get a writ of habeas corpus. I left the Homicide Bureau and from the Detective Bureau at 11th and State at approximately 1:00 A.M. (Sunday morning). I had no opportunity to talk to my client that night. I quoted to Captain Flynn the Section of the Criminal Code which allows an attorney the right to see his client.'

Petitioner testified that during the course of the interrogation he repeatedly asked to speak to his lawyer and that the police said that his lawyer 'didn't want to see' him. The testimony of the police officers confirmed these accounts in substantial detail. Notwithstanding repeated requests by each, petitioner and his retained lawyer were afforded no opportunity to consult during the course of the entire interrogation. At one point, as previously noted, petitioner and his attorney came into each other's view for a few moments but the attorney was quickly ushered away. Petitioner testified 'that he heard a detective telling the attorney the latter would not be allowed to talk to him and that he heard the attorney being refused permission to remain in the adjoining room. A police officer testified that he had told the lawyer that he could not see petitioner until 'we were through interrogating' him. There is testimony by the police that during the interrogation, petitioner, a 22-year-old of Mexican extraction with no record of previous experience with the police, 'was handcuffed' in a standing position and that he 'was nervous, he had circles under his eyes and he was upset' and was 'agitated' because 'he had not slept well in over a week.' It is undisputed that during the course of the interrogation Officer Montejano, who 'grew up' in petitioner's neighborhood, who knew his family, and who uses 'Spanish language in his police work,' conferred alone with petitioner 'for about a quarter of an hour.' Petitioner testified that the officer said to him 'in Spanish that my sister and I could go home if I pinned it on Benedict DiGerlando,' that 'he would see to it that we would go home and be held only as witnesses, if anything, if we had made a statement against DiGerlando, that we would be able to go home that night.' Petitioner testified that he made the statement in issue because of this assurance. Officer Montejano denied offering any such assurance.

A police officer testified that during the interrogation the following occurred: 'I informed him of what DiGerlando told me and when I did, he told me that DiGerlando was lying and I said, 'Would you care to tell DiGerlando that?' and he said, 'Yes, I will.' So, I brought Escobedo in and he confronted DiGerlando and he told him that he was lying and said, 'I didn't shoot Manuel, you did it." In this way, petitioner, for the first time admitted to some knowledge of the crime. After that he made additional statements further implicating himself in the murder plot. At this point an Assistant State's Attorney, Theodore J. Cooper, was summoned to take a statement. Mr. Cooper, an experienced lawyer who was assigned to the Homicide Division to take 'statements from some defendants and some prisoners that they had in custody,' 'took' petitioner's statement by asking carefully framed questions apparently designed to assure the admissibility into evidence of the resulting answers. Mr. Cooper testified that he did not advise petitioner of his constitutional rights, and it is undisputed that no one during the course of the interrogation so advised him. Petitioner moved both before and during trial to suppress the incriminating statement, but the motions were denied. Petitioner was convicted of murder and he appealed the conviction.

The Supreme Court of Illinois, in its original opinion of February 1, 1963, held the statement inadmissible and reversed the conviction. The court said: 'It seems manifest to us, from the undisputed evidence and the circumstances surrounding defendant at the time of his statement and shortly prior thereto, that the defendant understood he would be permitted to go home if he gave the statement and would be granted an immunity from prosecution.' The State petitioned for, and the court granted, rehearing. The court then affirmed the conviction. It said: 'The officer denied making the promise and the trier of fact believed him. We find no reason for disturbing the trial court's finding that the confession was voluntary.' The court also held, on the authority of this Court's decisions Crooker v. California, 357 U.S. 433, 78 S.Ct. 1287, 2 L.Ed.2d 1448, and Cicenia v. LaGay, 357 U.S. 504, 78 S.Ct. 1297, 2 L.Ed.2d 1523, that the confession was admissible even though 'it was obtained after he had requested the assistance of counsel, which request was denied.' We granted a writ of certiorari to consider whether the petitioner's statement was constitutionally admissible at his trial. We conclude, for the reasons stated below, that it was not and, accordingly, we reverse the judgment of conviction.

Massiah v. United States, 377 U.S. 201, 84 S.Ct. 1199, this Court observed that 'a Constitution which guarantees a defendant the aid of counsel at trial could surely vouchsafe no less to an indicted defendant under interrogation by the police in a completely extrajudicial proceeding. Anything less might deny a defendant 'effective representation by counsel at the only stage when legal aid and advice would help him." The interrogation here was conducted before petitioner was formally indicted. But in the context of this case, that fact should make no difference. When petitioner requested, and was denied, an opportunity to consult with his lawyer, the investigation had ceased to be a general investigation of 'an unsolved crime.' Petitioner had become the accused, and the purpose of the interrogation was to 'get him' to confess his guilt despite his constitutional right not to do so. At the time of his arrest and throughout the course of the interrogation, the police told petitioner that they had convincing evidence that he had fired the fatal shots. Without informing him of his absolute right to remain silent in the face of this accusation, the police urged him to make a statement.

Petitioner, a layman, was undoubtedly unaware that under Illinois law an admission of 'mere' complicity in the murder plot was legally as damaging as an admission of firing of the fatal shots. The 'guiding hand of counsel' was essential to advise petitioner of his rights in this delicate situation. This was the 'stage when legal aid and advice' were most critical to petitioner. It was a stage surely as critical as was the arraignment and the preliminary hearing. What happened at this interrogation could certainly 'affect the whole trial,' since rights 'may be as irretrievably lost, if not then and there asserted, as they are when an accused represented by counsel waives a right for strategic purposes.' It would exalt form over substance to make the right to counsel, under these circumstances, depend on whether at the time of the interrogation, the authorities had secured a formal indictment. Petitioner had, for all practical purposes, already been charged with murder.

Gideon v. Wainwright, 372 U.S. 335, 83 S.Ct. 792, 9 L.Ed.2d 799, we held that every person accused of a crime, whether state or federal, is entitled to a lawyer at trial. The rule sought by the State here, however, would make the trial no more than an appeal from the interrogation; and the 'right to use counsel at the formal trial would be a very hollow thing if, for all practical purposes, the conviction is already assured by pretrial examination.' It is argued that if the right to counsel is afforded prior to indictment, the number of confessions obtained by the police will diminish significantly, because most confessions are obtained during the period between arrest and indictment, and 'any lawyer worth his salt will tell the suspect in no uncertain terms to make no statement to police under any circumstances.' This argument, of course, cuts two ways. The fact that many confessions are obtained during this period points up its critical nature as a 'stage when legal aid and advice' are surely needed. The right to counsel would indeed be hollow if it began at a period when few confessions were obtained. There is necessarily a direct relationship between the importance of a stage to the police in their quest for a confession and the criticalness of that stage to the accused in his need for legal advice. Our Constitution, unlike some others, strikes the balance in favor of the right of the accused to be advised by his lawyer of his privilege against self-incrimination.

We have learned the lesson of history, ancient and modern, that a system of criminal law enforcement which comes to depend on the 'confession' will, in the long run, be less reliable and more subject to abuses than a system which depends on extrinsic evidence independently secured through skillful investigation. This Court also has recognized that history amply shows that confessions have often been extorted to save law enforcement officials the trouble and effort of obtaining valid and independent evidence. We have also learned the companion lesson of history that no system of criminal justice can, or should, survive if it comes to depend for its continued effectiveness on the citizens' abdication through unawareness of their constitutional rights. No system worth preserving should have to fear that if an accused is permitted to consult with a lawyer, he will become aware of, and exercise, these rights. If the exercise of constitutional rights will thwart the effectiveness of a system of law enforcement, then there is something very wrong with that system.

We hold, therefore, that where, as here, the investigation is no longer a general inquiry into an unsolved crime but has begun to focus on a particular suspect, the suspect has been taken into police custody, the police carry out a process of interrogations that lends itself to eliciting incriminating statements, the suspect has requested and been denied an opportunity to consult with his lawyer, and the police have not effectively warned him of his absolute constitutional right to remain silent, the accused has been denied 'The Assistance of Counsel' in violation of the Sixth Amendment to the Constitution as 'made obligatory upon the States by the Fourteenth Amendment,' and that no statement elicited by the police during the interrogation may be used against him at a criminal trial.

Nothing we have said today affects the powers of the police to investigate 'an unsolved crime,' by gathering information from witnesses and by other 'proper investigative efforts.' We hold only that when the process shifts from investigatory to accusatory—when its focus is on the accused and its purpose is to elicit a confession—our adversary system begins to operate, and, under the circumstances here, the accused must be permitted to consult with his lawyer.

The judgment of the Illinois Supreme Court is reversed and the case remanded for proceedings not inconsistent with this opinion. Reversed and remanded.

Mr. Justice STEWART, dissenting. I think this case is directly controlled by Cicenia v. La Gay, 357 U.S. 504, 78 S.Ct. 1297, 2 L.Ed.2d 1523, and I would therefore affirm the judgment. Massiah v. United States, 377 U.S. 201, 84 S.Ct. 1199, is not in point here. In that case a federal grand jury had indicted Massiah. He had retained a lawyer and entered a formal plea of not guilty. Under our system of federal justice an indictment and arraignment are followed by a trial, at which the Sixth Amendment guarantees the defendant the assistance of counsel. But Massiah was released on bail, and thereafter agents of the Federal Government deliberately elicited incriminating statements from him in the absence of his lawyer. We held that the use of these statements against him at his trial denied him the basic protections of the Sixth Amendment guarantee. Putting to one side the fact that the case now before us is not a federal case, the vital fact remains that this case does not involve the deliberate interrogation of a defendant after the initiation of judicial proceedings against him. The Court disregards this basic difference between the present case and Massiah's, with the bland assertion that 'that fact should make no difference.' It is 'that fact,' I submit, which makes all the difference. Under our system of criminal justice the institution of formal, meaningful judicial proceedings, by way of indictment, information, or arraignment, marks the point at which a criminal investigation has ended and adversary proceedings have commenced. It is at this point that the constitutional guarantees attach which pertain to a criminal trial. Among those guarantees are the right to a speedy trial, the right of confrontation, and the right to trial by jury. Another is the guarantee of the assistance of counsel.

The confession which the Court today holds inadmissible was a voluntary one. It was given during the course of a perfectly legitimate police investigation of an unsolved murder. The Court says that what happened during this investigation 'affected' the trial. I had always supposed that the whole purpose of a police investigation of a murder was to 'affect' the trial of the murderer, and that it would be only an incompetent, unsuccessful, or corrupt investigation which would not do so. The Court further says that the Illinois police officers did not advise the petitioner of his 'constitutional rights' before he confessed to the murder. This Court has never held that the Constitution requires the police to give any 'advice' under circumstances such as these. Supported by no stronger authority than its own rhetoric, the Court today converts a routine police investigation of an unsolved murder into a distorted analogue of a judicial trial. It imports into this investigation constitutional concepts historically applicable only after the onset of formal prosecutorial proceedings. By doing so, I think the Court perverts those precious constitutional guarantees, and frustrates the vital interests of society in preserving the legitimate and proper function of honest and purposeful police investigation.

Mr. Justice WHITE, with whom Mr. Justice CLARK and Mr. Justice STEWART join, dissenting. Massiah v. United States, 377 U.S. 201, 84 S.Ct. 1199, the Court held that as of the date of the indictment the prosecution is disentitled to secure admissions from the accused. The Court now moves that date back to the time when the prosecution begins to 'focus' on the accused. Although the opinion purports to be limited to the facts of this case, it would be naive to think that the new constitutional right announced will depend upon whether the accused has retained his own counsel, or has asked to consult with counsel in the course of interrogation. At the very least the Court holds that once the accused becomes a suspect and, presumably, is arrested, any admission made to the police thereafter is inadmissible in evidence unless the accused has waived his right to counsel. The decision is thus another major step in the direction of the goal which the Court seemingly has in mind—to bar from evidence all admissions obtained from an individual suspected of crime, whether involuntarily made or not. It does of course put us one step 'ahead' of the English judges who have had the good sense to leave the matter a discretionary one with the trial court. I reject this step and the invitation to go farther which the Court has now issued.

By abandoning the voluntary-involuntary test for admissibility of confessions, the Court seems driven by the notion that it is uncivilized law enforcement to use an accused's own admissions against him at his trial. It attempts to find a home for this new and nebulous rule of due process by attaching it to the right to counsel guaranteed in the federal system by the Sixth Amendment and binding upon the States by virtue of the due process guarantee of the Fourteenth Amendment. The right to counsel now not only entitles the accused to counsel's advice and aid in preparing for trial but stands as an impenetrable barrier to any interrogation once the accused has become a suspect. From that very moment apparently his right to counsel attaches, a rule wholly unworkable and impossible to administer unless police cars are equipped with public defenders and undercover agents and police informants have defense counsel at their side. I would not abandon the Court's prior cases defining with some care and analysis the circumstances requiring the presence or aid of counsel and substitute the amorphous and wholly unworkable principle that counsel is constitutionally required whenever he would or could be helpful.

It is incongruous to assume that the provision for counsel in the Sixth Amendment was meant to amend or supersede the self-incrimination provision of the Fifth Amendment, which is now applicable to the States. That amendment addresses itself to the very issue of incriminating admissions of an accused and resolves it by proscribing only compelled statements. Neither the Framers, the constitutional language, nor a century of decisions of this Court provides an iota of support for the idea that an accused has an absolute constitutional right not to answer even in the absence of compulsion—the constitutional right not to incriminate himself by making voluntary disclosures. Today's decision cannot be squared with other provisions of the Constitution which, in my view, define the system of criminal justice this Court is empowered to administer. The Fourth Amendment permits upon probable cause even compulsory searches of the suspect and his possessions and the use of the fruits of the search at trial, all in the absence of counsel. The Fifth Amendment and state constitutional provisions authorize, indeed require, inquisitorial grand jury proceedings at which a potential defendant, in the absence of counsel, is shielded against no more than compulsory incrimination. A grand jury witness, who may be a suspect, is interrogated and his answers, at least until today, are admissible in evidence at trial. And these provisions have been thought of as constitutional safeguards to persons suspected of an offense. Furthermore, until now, the Constitution has permitted the accused to be fingerprinted and to be identified in a line-up or in the courtroom itself.

The Court chooses to ignore these matters and to rely on the virtues and morality of a system of criminal law enforcement which does not depend on the 'confession.' No such judgment is to be found in the Constitution. It might be appropriate for a legislature to provide that a suspect should not be consulted during a criminal investigation; that an accused should never be called before a grand jury to answer, even if he wants to, what may well be incriminating questions; and that no person, whether he be a suspect, guilty criminal or innocent bystander, should be put to the ordeal of responding to orderly noncompulsory inquiry by the State. But this is not the system our Constitution requires. The only 'inquisitions' the Constitution forbids are those which compel incrimination. Escobedo's statements were not compelled and the Court does not hold that they were.

This new American judges' rule, which is to be applied in both federal and state courts, is perhaps thought to be a necessary safeguard against the possibility of extorted confessions. To this extent it reflects a deep-seated distrust of law enforcement officers everywhere, unsupported by relevant data or current material based upon our own experience. Obviously law enforcement officers can make mistakes and exceed their authority, as today's decision shows that even judges can do, but I have somewhat more faith than the Court evidently has in the ability and desire of prosecutors and of the power of the appellate courts to discern and correct such violations of the law. The Court may be concerned with a narrower matter: the unknowing defendant who responds to police questioning because he mistakenly believes that he must and that his admissions will not be used against him. But this worry hardly calls for the broadside the Court has now fired. The failure to inform an accused that he need not answer and that his answers may be used against him is very relevant indeed to whether the disclosures are compelled. Cases in this Court, to say the least, have never placed a premium on ignorance of constitutional rights. If an accused is told he must answer and does not know better, it would be very doubtful that the resulting admissions could be used against him. When the accused has not been informed of his rights at all the Court characteristically and properly looks very closely at the surrounding circumstances. I would continue to do so. But, in this case Danny Escobedo knew full well that he did not have to answer and knew full well that his lawyer had advised him not to answer.

I do not suggest for a moment that law enforcement will be destroyed by the rule announced today. The need for peace and order is too insistent for that. But it will be crippled and its task made a great deal more difficult, all in my opinion, for unsound, unstated reasons, which can find no home in any of the provisions of the Constitution.

REVIEW SECTION

READING COMPREHENSION

Elaborate the facts of this case.

THINKING CRITICALLY

Comment on the following by the majority: "We have learned the lesson of history, ancient and modern, that a system of criminal law enforcement which comes to depend on the 'confession' will, in the long run, be less reliable and more subject to abuses than a system which depends on extrinsic evidence independently secured through skillful investigation. This Court also has recognized that history amply shows that confessions have often been extorted to save law enforcement officials the trouble and effort of obtaining valid and independent evidence. We have also learned the companion lesson of history that no system of criminal justice can, or should, survive if it comes to depend for its continued effectiveness on the citizens' abdication through unawareness of their constitutional rights. No system worth preserving should have to fear that if an accused is permitted to consult with a lawyer, he will become aware of, and exercise, these rights. If the exercise of constitutional rights will thwart the effectiveness of a system of law enforcement, then there is something very wrong with that system."

Comment on the following by the dissent: "I do not suggest for a moment that law enforcement will be destroyed by the rule announced today. The need for peace and order is too insistent for that. But it will be crippled and its task made a great deal more difficult, all in my opinion, for unsound, unstated reasons, which can find no home in any of the provisions of the Constitution."

CONCLUSION

At the discretion of the prosecutor's office, a defendant begins his/her journey through the start of court proceedings. In this chapter we addressed probable cause, first appearance and issues of bail, as well as the intricacies of the right to counsel – when this right attaches and under what conditions counsel is required. Especially with regard to the right to counsel, issues arise regarding the taxation on the criminal justice system and how this may or may not balance with the right of an individual to a fair proceeding.

Chapter Thirteen

Pretrial, Trial, and Conviction

After a decision to charge by the prosecutor's office, what follows are adversarial proceedings as well as informal negotiation. During the pretrial, trial, and conviction stages of the process, several formal rules govern criminal cases which are the subject of this section. Article One, Section Eight of the Illinois Constitution which addresses the rights after indictment:

> In criminal prosecutions, the accused shall have the right to appear and defend in person and by counsel; to demand the nature and cause of the accusation and have a copy thereof; to be confronted with the witnesses against him or her and to have process to compel the attendance of witnesses in his or her behalf; and to have a speedy public trial by an impartial jury of the county in which the offense is alleged to have been committed.

Article One, Section 8.1 of the Illinois Constitution elaborates the rights of the crime victim:

> (a) Crime victims, as defined by law, shall have the following rights as provided by law: (1) The right to be treated with fairness and respect for their dignity and privacy throughout the criminal justice process. (2) The right to notification of court proceedings. (3) The right to communicate with the prosecution. (4) The right to make a statement to the court at sentencing. (5) The right to information about the conviction, sentence, imprisonment, and release of the accused. (6) The right to timely disposition of the case following the arrest of the accused; (7) The right to be reasonably protected from the accused throughout the criminal justice process. (8) The right to be present at the trial and all other court proceedings on the same basis as the accused, unless the victim is to testify and the court determines that the victim's testimony would be materially affected if the victim hears other testimony at the trial. (9) The right to have present at all court proceedings, subject to the rules of evidence, an advocate or other support person of the victim's choice. (10) The right to restitution.

This chapter will review:

(1)   Testing the government's case;

(2)   Pretrial motions; and

(3)   Conviction by jury trial.

SECTION 1: TESTING THE GOVERNMENT'S CASE

OVERVIEW

The government must engage in one of two procedures to test the case against a defendant. After a criminal information has been written, the case is tested in a preliminary hearing. This process is held in public and is an adversarial hearing wherein a judge presides and determines the facts of the case. If states provide a preliminary hearing, for which there is no constitutional right, the defendant does have the right to an attorney. Whether the judge decides to send the case to trial is based on either a *prima facie* case rule or a directed verdict rule, depending on the court. A *prima facie* case rule allows the judge to send the case to trial if evidence is presented that, if not rebutted by the defense, could convict the defendant. A directed verdict rule is one in which the judge views presentation of the evidence as if the hearing were a trial and makes a judgment accordingly. Should the government seek an indictment, the case is presented to a grand jury for review. The Fifth Amendment to the U.S. Constitution provides:

> . . . no person shall be held to answer for a capital, or otherwise infamous crime, unless on presentment or indictment by a Grand Jury . . .

This is mirrored in Article One, Section Seven of the Illinois Constitution which reads:

> No person shall be held to answer for a criminal offense unless on indictment of a grand jury, except in cases in which the punishment is by fine or by imprisonment other than in the penitentiary, in cases of impeachment, and in cases arising in the militia when in actual service in time of war or public danger. The General Assembly by law may abolish the grand jury or further limit its use.

A grand jury review is a private proceeding in which only the government's case is presented, but which is intended to protect citizens from unwarranted intrusion by the state. A prosecutor presides over the review and the facts are determined by grand jurors. You should keep in mind that most grand juries follow the recommendation provided by the prosecutor. In Illinois, the grand jury consists of sixteen persons, and twelve are necessary to constitute a quorum (725 ILCS 5/112-2). The oath of the grand jury is explicated in 725 ILCS 112-2(c):

> You and each of you do solemnly swear (or affirm, as the case may be), that you will diligently inquire into and true presentment make of all such matters and things as shall be given you in charge, or shall otherwise come to your knowledge, touching the present service; you shall present no person through malice, hatred or ill-will; nor shall you leave any unpresented through fear, favor, affection, or for any fee or reward, or for any hope or promise thereof; but in all of your presentments, you shall present the truth, the whole truth, and nothing but the truth, according to the best of your skill and understanding; so help you God.

In addition, 725 ILCS 5/112-4 elaborates the duties of the grand jury and the State's Attorney, and 725 ILCS 112-6 details the secrecy of the proceedings.

SECTION 2: PRETRIAL MOTIONS

OVERVIEW

Pretrial motions are requests of the court to consider issues that do not need to be ruled on during the actual trial. These include speedy trial, double jeopardy, change of venue, and suppression of evidence. While the Illinois Constitution in Article One, Section Eight guarantees defendants the right to a speedy trial, it is important to remember that according to the U.S. Supreme Court, the clock does not begin until a suspect is formally charged. Prior to this time, defendants must rely on statutes that address specifically the length of time permitted between the commission of a crime and when the charge is filed. Also note that the right to a speedy trial only prevents against undue delays and in determination the court considers the length and reason for the delay and any prejudice the delay causes to the case. Delays that result from determining the competency of the defendant, trials of the defendant that may be occurring, hearings on pretrial motions, and interlocutory appeals are not considered.

The guidelines to a speedy trial are outlined in 725 ILCS 5/103-5 and will be elaborated here in great detail:

> (a) Every person in custody in this State for an alleged offense shall be tried by the court having jurisdiction within 120 days from the date he was taken into custody unless delay is occasioned by the defendant, by an examination for fitness ordered pursuant to Section 104-13 of this Act, by a fitness hearing, by an adjudication

of unfitness to stand trial, by a continuance allowed pursuant to Section 114-4 of this Act after a court's determination of the defendant's physical incapacity for trial, or by an interlocutory appeal. Delay shall be considered to be agreed to by the defendant unless he or she objects to the delay by making a written demand for trial or an oral demand for trial on the record. The 120-day term must be one continuous period of incarceration. In computing the 120-day term, separate periods of incarceration may not be combined. If a defendant is taken into custody a second (or subsequent) time for the same offense, the term will begin again at day zero.

Another pretrial motion is double jeopardy. The Fifth Amendment to the U.S. Constitution guarantees that a person will not be tried twice for the same offense. This means that after conviction a person may not be tried for the same offense, after acquittal a person may not be tried for the same offense, and multiple punishments for the same offense may not result. Keep in mind therefore, that if a trial ends prior to either conviction or acquittal, the prosecution reserves the right to re-file charges for the same offense. Also of relevance is that it is not considered double jeopardy to both prosecute and punish a defendant for the same offense in a separate jurisdiction, or to prosecute a defendant in multiple trials for separate offenses that arose out of the same incident.

Article One, Section Eight of the Illinois Constitution guarantees a trial in the venue in which the crime was committed. Only the defense can move to change the venue of a trial, at which time the judge must consider the reasonable likelihood that the case was prejudiced in the initial venue. Change of place for the trial is elaborated in 725 ILCS 5/114-6:

> (a) A defendant may move the court for a change of place of trial
> on the ground that there exists in the county in which the charge is
> pending such prejudice against him on the part of the inhabitants
> that he cannot receive a fair trial in such county.

The final pretrial motion involves suppression of evidence using the exclusionary rule that has been discussed at length in a previous chapter.

CASE

In the consolidated appeals below, the Supreme Court of Illinois addressed whether, at resentencing, double jeopardy bars the State's second attempt to establish a defendant's eligibility for enhanced sentencing under either the Class X sentencing provision or the Habitual Criminal Act, where the appellate court has vacated the defendant's sentence for the State's failure to prove such eligibility in the first sentencing proceeding.

PEOPLE V. LEVIN
PEOPLE V. TYSON
PEOPLE V. KNOOP
PEOPLE V. JOHNS
PEOPLE V. CARTER
Supreme Court of Illinois
157 Ill.2d 138, 623 N.E.2d 317 (1993)

These several appeals are linked by the singular issue of whether double jeopardy attaches to enhanced-sentencing proceedings. Four of the appeals, People v. Levin, No. 71542, People v. Tyson, No. 71820, People v. Knoop, No. 72736, and People v. Johns, No. 72929, involve sentencing under the Class X provision of the Unified Code of Corrections. The remaining appeal, People v. Carter, No. 73108, involves sentencing under the Habitual Criminal Act. Defendants Levin, Tyson, Knoop, and Johns were convicted and sentenced as Class X offenders, while defendant Carter was convicted and sentenced as an habitual criminal. In each case the appellate court affirmed the defendant's conviction. However, the court found the State's proof of each defendant's qualifying prior convictions to be, in some manner, insufficient to support the imposition of enhanced punishment. The nature of the deficiency of proof is not important for purposes of our review. It is significant only that the court vacated the defendants' sentences and remanded those causes to the trial court for resentencing.

In Levin, the court held that, at resentencing, double jeopardy barred the State from again attempting to prove defendant's eligibility for enhanced punishment under the Class X sentencing provision. The State appealed to this court. In contrast to Levin, the court in Tyson, Knoop, Johns and Carter held that double jeopardy did not preclude the State from seeking enhanced punishment at resentencing. Defendants appealed to this court, contending, *inter alia*, the applicability of double jeopardy to resentencing. We granted the various parties' petitions for leave to appeal. On this court's motion, the appeals were consolidated and we limited review to the issue of whether double jeopardy applies to Class X and habitual-criminal sentencing procedures.

The double jeopardy clause actually embraces three separate protections, which bar (1) retrial for the same offense after an acquittal, (2) retrial for the same offense after a conviction, and (3) multiple punishment for the same offense. It is the first of these three protections upon which defendants seek to rely. Generally, double jeopardy principles have not been applied to sentencing. The imposition of a particular sentence usually is not regarded as an acquittal of any more severe sentence than could have been imposed. Thus, double jeopardy imposes no absolute prohibition against the imposition of a harsher sentence at retrial after a defendant has succeeded in having his original conviction set aside.

In Bullington v. Missouri (1981), 451 U.S. 430, 101 S.Ct. 1852, 68 L.Ed.2d 270, however, the Court carved out an exception to the general rule regarding the propriety of imposing a harsher sentence at retrial. In Bullington, the Court found that Missouri's separate capital sentencing hearing resembled the defendant's trial on the issue of guilt. The Court's analogy of the sentencing hearing to trial was supported by the presence of three specific factors at sentencing: (1) the sentencer's determination was guided by substantive standards and based on evidence introduced in a separate proceeding that formally resembled a trial; (2) the prosecution had to prove certain statutorily defined facts beyond a reasonable doubt; and (3) the discretion of the sentencer was restricted to precisely two sentencing alternatives. The formality of the separate proceeding, the standard of proof and the lack of sentencing discretion at the capital sentencing proceeding each paralleled the formality of the proceeding, the standard of proof and the lack of discretion in entering a verdict at the defendant's trial on the issue of guilt. Based upon the presence of these three trial-like factors, the Court characterized Missouri's capital sentencing proceeding as having "the hallmarks of the trial on guilt or innocence." By enacting a capital sentencing procedure that resembles a trial on the issue of guilt, Missouri requires the jury to determine whether the prosecution has proved its case. Thus, under the Missouri capital sentencing scheme, a jury sentence of life imprisonment served as an acquittal of "whatever was necessary to impose the death sentence." Accordingly, at resentencing, double jeopardy would bar the State's second attempt at obtaining the death penalty.

Bullington's determination that insufficient evidence to support the imposition of the death penalty barred any subsequent attempt to seek the death penalty flows directly from those principles announced in Burks v. United States (1977), 437 U.S. 1, 98 S.Ct. 2141, 57 L.Ed.2d 1. In Burks, the Court reasoned that reversal for insufficient evidence is tantamount to an implicit acquittal by the trial court. Thus, the Court held that the double jeopardy clause forbids retrial of a defendant whose conviction is overturned by a reviewing court because of insufficiency of the evidence at trial. Prior to Bullington, the Court had held, unequivocally, that if a defendant was convicted, sentenced to life imprisonment and then won reversal of his conviction, the State could seek the death penalty again upon retrial. The Court in Bullington also distinguished United States v. DiFrancesco (1980), 449 U.S. 117, 101 S.Ct. 426, 66 L.Ed.2d 328, the only case in which the Court had previously considered a bifurcated sentencing proceeding. DiFrancesco involved a government appeal of a sentence imposed under the Federal "dangerous special offender" statute. In Bullington, the Court compared each of the trial-like factors present under Missouri's capital sentencing procedure with those factors present under the dangerous-special-offender sentencing scheme. The Court initially focused on the nature of the resentencing proceeding. In that regard, the Court found DiFrancesco inapposite because the Federal procedures involved at resentencing included appellate review of a sentence "on the record of the sentencing court," rather than a *de novo* fact finding. Further, the Court noted that in DiFrancesco the sentencer, a Federal judge, had a large amount of discretion in imposing sentence and the prosecution's burden was merely a preponderance of the evidence.

Before proceeding with our analysis, we note that this case does not represent this court's first opportunity to consider the reaches of Bullington. In People v. Davis (1986), 112 Ill.2d 78, 96 Ill.Dec. 703, 491 N.E.2d 1163, this court acknowledged that many of the characteristics of the Missouri capital sentencing proceeding which triggered the application of double jeopardy in Bullington are present in our capital sentencing proceeding. Thus, double jeopardy may be implicated in resentencing in capital cases in Illinois. Neither the United States Supreme Court nor this court, however, has had occasion to decide whether the exception carved out in Bullington extends to noncapital sentencing procedures. Defendants assert that the sentencing procedures under the Habitual Criminal Act and the Class X sentencing provision closely resemble the sentencing procedure in Bullington. Thus, they entreat us to extend the Bullington exception to these noncapital recidivist sentencing procedures. For reasons which follow, we decline to do so.

The Court in Bullington did not address whether the presence of any one of the three trial-like factors upon which it relied would have been sufficient, alone, to support its trial analogy. Further, the Court seemingly did not place greater significance on any one factor over another. We believe, however, that it was the combined force of all three factors which supported the Court's analogy. A review of Federal decisional law in this area confirms our view. In cases where the Bullington exception has been extended to noncapital sentencing procedures, all three factors have been present. We, likewise, tailor our analysis to correspond with the analyses applied in Bullington and its progeny. Accordingly, we hold that for Bullington to apply, all three trial-like factors must be present. The absence of any one will defeat the analogy.

The Habitual Criminal Act mandates the imposition of a natural life sentence on a defendant convicted of three Class X felonies within a 20-year period. Section 33B--2 of the Act sets out the procedures that apply when the State seeks to have a court sentence a defendant as a habitual criminal. Section 33B--2(a) provides, in pertinent part: "After a plea or verdict or finding of guilty and before sentence is imposed, the prosecutor may file with the court a verified written statement signed by the State's Attorney concerning any former conviction of an offense set forth in Section 33B--1 rendered against the defendant. The court shall then cause the defendant to be brought before it; shall inform him of the allegations of the statement so filed, and of his right to a hearing before the court on the issue of such former conviction and of his right to counsel at such hearing; and unless the defendant admits such conviction, the court shall hear and determine such issue, and shall make a written finding thereon. If a sentence has previously been imposed, the court may vacate such sentence and impose a new sentence in accordance with Section 33B--1 of this Act." A defendant must be "adjudged" a Class X offender to be sentenced under the Habitual Criminal Act.

It is settled that habitual-offender legislation neither creates a separate offense nor directly involves the prior crimes. The prior-conviction evidence for purposes of sentencing enhancement is merely a matter of aggravation going solely to the punishment to be imposed; it is not an ingredient of the main offense charged. Defendants assert that the procedure for determining a defendant's habitual criminal status parallels, in all important respects, the capital sentencing procedure considered in Bullington. Defendants specifically note the following similarities between our habitual-criminal sentencing procedure and the capital sentencing procedure in Bullington: (1) a separate hearing is held on the issue of defendant's habitual-criminal status; (2) the prosecutor must prove the habitual-criminal status beyond a reasonable doubt; and (3) the trial judge is not given "unbounded discretion" to select the defendant's punishment but must, instead, impose a sentence of natural life imprisonment. These factors, defendants contend, sufficiently mark the procedure with the "hallmarks of the trial on guilt and innocence" to trigger double jeopardy protections.

We note at the outset that there is a split of authority in the Federal circuits on whether double jeopardy applies to similar habitual-offender sentencing procedures. At first glance, our habitual-criminal sentencing procedure appears to share sufficient commonalities with the sentencing procedure in Bullington to warrant extension of the exception here. However, we must be careful to avoid diminishing the value of Bullington by engaging in merely mechanical application. The focus of our inquiry, as was the Court's in Bullington, is whether our proceeding resembles a defendant's trial on the issue of guilt. We first examine the "separate hearing" factor. Under our criminal code, a sentencing hearing is required after any determination of guilt. Thus, to conclude that the sentencing hearing is trial-like simply because it is held separately from the determination of guilt would potentially subject all sentencing proceedings in Illinois to the Bullington exception. Bullington does not compel such a result. We, therefore, must consider those unique aspects of the separate sentencing proceeding which, in Bullington, rendered that factor trial-like. Under the sentencing provision considered in Bullington, the jury hears evidence in extenuation, mitigation and aggravation of punishment, subject to the laws of evidence. Only such evidence in aggravation as the prosecution has made known to the defendant prior to his trial is admissible at the hearing. In addition, the jury hears argument concerning the punishment to be imposed. The Missouri statute also expressly provides for final arguments to the jury, directing that the prosecuting attorney shall open and that the defense counsel shall conclude the argument to the jury. Further, prior to the jury's deliberations, the judge gives appropriate instructions to guide the jury in its deliberations. Additionally, a jury that imposes the death penalty must designate in writing the aggravating circumstance that it finds beyond a reasonable doubt. Finally, the Court in Bullington thought it "not without some significance that the Missouri statute spoke specifically of the capital sentencing hearing in terms of a continuing trial."

As is apparent, many of the due process protections afforded a defendant at trial on the issue of guilt are provided under Missouri's separate capital sentencing provision. These same evidentiary and procedural safeguards, however, are not present under Illinois' separate habitual-offender sentencing procedure. Except for the records certification requirement, noticeably absent is any mandate that the State comply with formalistic rules of evidence applicable at trial. Also, the State is not required, prior to trial, either to inform the defendant of its intent to seek an habitual-offender determination or to reveal what evidence it plans to present at sentencing. Further, although presumably the order of proceeding at sentencing parallels the order at trial, our Act makes no express provision concerning the order of proof or argument. Additionally, a point deemed important by the Court in Bullington, the Act refers to the sentencing proceeding as a hearing, not as a trial. Even more significant, the defendant, unlike at trial, is not entitled to a jury to decide the issue of habitual-criminal status. The absence of a jury requirement here evidences that any similar concern in habitual-criminal sentencing proceedings is not operative.

Finally, we deem it significant that the State's burden of proof for purposes of habitual-criminal sentencing may be satisfied by the presentation of certified records of the defendant's prior convictions. Notably, such proof is developed outside of the courtroom. As a result, the proceeding does not involve the same degree of adversarial testing characteristic of the evidentiary phase of trial. In contrast, the statute examined in Bullington requires the State to develop the evidence that proves an aggravating factor during the course of the proceeding, as in a trial. Under our Act, a defendant is not afforded the full panoply of due process rights which are necessarily afforded a criminal defendant at the evidentiary phase of trial. Those standards which, at trial, govern the admissibility of evidence and precisely define the manner in which the court and parties are to proceed are absent. The legislature has fashioned the habitual-criminal sentencing proceeding to be less formalized than a trial. Indeed, the paucity of due process protections at sentencing supports the conclusion that the legislature has deemed the defendant's interests at this stage of the proceeding to warrant fewer of those protections than at trial. We conclude that the separate hearing procedure under our Act bears insufficient formalities of a trial to render that factor analogous to the separate hearing procedure in Bullington and to this defendant's trial on the issue of guilt.

We recognize that the Act provides certain evidentiary and procedural safeguards, such as the requirement that the records of the defendant's prior convictions be certified, that the defendant be informed of the allegations of the prior convictions, and that the court make written findings on the issue of the defendant's habitual criminality. In this regard, the habitual-criminal sentencing proceeding is, at least, more formalistic than sentencing under our general sentencing provision. However, these limited procedural and evidentiary safeguards do not sufficiently color the separate sentencing proceeding with the shades of trial such that the two proceedings appear analogous. Defendants, proceeding on the premise that the degree of proof required in a habitual-criminal proceeding is beyond a reasonable doubt, assert this and the lack of sentencing discretion as additional commonalities with the procedure examined in Bullington and with a trial. Our finding that the separate sentencing factor lacks the formality of a trial defeats the analogy of the habitual sentencing procedure to a trial on the issue of guilt. Thus, even accepting the presence of the other two trial-like factors, we hold that the habitual-criminal sentencing proceeding does not so "approximate the ordeal of trial" to bring the proceeding within the exception of Bullington.

Defendants next contend that sentencing under the Class X provision resembles trial on the issue of guilt and, therefore, Bullington should apply. We note at the outset the disagreement in our appellate court concerning whether double jeopardy would bar the State's second attempt to sentence a defendant as a Class X offender on remand where the State failed to present sufficient proof for Class X sentencing in the original sentencing proceeding. We begin our analysis with a brief statement of the Class X offender provision. If a defendant over the age of 21 has been convicted of a Class 1 or a Class 2 felony, after having been twice convicted of any Class 2 or greater class felonies in Illinois, and such charges are separately brought and tried and arise out of a different series of acts, the defendant must be sentenced as a Class X offender. Sentencing procedures for Class X offenders are conducted pursuant to section 5--4--1 of the Unified Code of Corrections. Section 5--4--1 provides in part: "(a) At the hearing the court shall: (1) consider the evidence, if any, received upon the trial; (2) consider any presentence reports; (3) consider evidence and information offered by the parties in aggravation and mitigation; (4) hear arguments as to sentencing alternatives; (5) afford the defendant the opportunity to make a statement in his own behalf."

Noticeably absent under section 5--4--1 are those strict evidentiary and procedural rules attendant at trial. The only requirement for the admissibility of evidence in Class X sentencing under section 5--4--1 is that the evidence be relevant and reliable. Unlike sentencing under the Habitual Criminal Act, the State need not present certified records of the defendant's prior convictions for purposes of showing Class X eligibility. Presentence reports are adequate. The

State has no burden to prove a defendant's prior convictions beyond a reasonable doubt. Finally, concerning sentencing discretion, we observe that no sentencing judge has complete discretion to fashion what he or she deems an appropriate sentence. Sentencing authorities are constrained in those decisions by statute. In the case of the Class X offender, the sentencer, while required by statute to impose a sentence from an elevated sentencing range, is nonetheless permitted discretion to determine an appropriate sentence within that range. Such restriction is no different from sentencing restrictions generally. However, the sentencer's discretion under section 5--4--1 is not analogous to the lack of discretion present in Bullington. We conclude that because none of the trial-like factors present in Bullington are present under our Class X sentencing proceeding, double jeopardy does not bar a subsequent attempt to prove Class X eligibility at resentencing.

Despite the absence of these factors, defendants maintain that double jeopardy applies. They insist that the burden of proof in Class X sentencing procedures is at least by a preponderance of the evidence. They then assert the doctrine of collateral estoppel as applicable to this lesser standard and, therefore, that double jeopardy is implicated. The reasonable doubt standard applies to criminal proceedings, to which double jeopardy attaches. In contrast, the preponderance of the evidence standard is generally reserved for civil matters, to which double jeopardy does not attach. Thus, the requirement of a mere preponderance quantum of proof effectively defeats any analogy to trial on the issue of guilt and, therefore, any claim that jeopardy has attached. Further, to the extent that defendants suggest collateral estoppel as an independent basis to bar the State's second attempt to prove Class X eligibility, we reject the suggestion. The doctrine of collateral estoppel, embodied in the fifth amendment's guarantee against double jeopardy, applies to bar relitigation of a valid and final judgment. Sentencing determinations do not carry the same finality as the judgment of guilt or innocence on the merits. Thus, in the context of non-trial-like sentencing proceedings, we afford the doctrine of collateral estoppel no viability independent of the double jeopardy clause.

We note defendants' additional argument that *res judicata* or law of the case bar a second attempt to prove Class X eligibility. Defendants cite to no authority to support the conclusion that either concept, like collateral estoppel, is embodied in double jeopardy. Again, we note, however, that sentencing determinations do not carry the same finality as do final judgments. Thus, defendants' reliance on these concepts is also unavailing.

We hold that Class X sentencing, which is governed by section 5--4--1, does not bear sufficient "hallmarks of a trial" on the issue of defendants' guilt. Thus, the Bullington exception is inapplicable to bar resentencing of defendants as Class X offenders; double jeopardy is not implicated.

Defendants finally contend that if the Federal Constitution will not support application of double jeopardy principles to these noncapital recidivist sentencing procedures, then the Illinois constitution should. Defendants largely argue for our departure from the "lockstep doctrine" in construing our double jeopardy clause. Under the "lockstep doctrine" this court would apply decisions of the United States Supreme Court based on Federal constitutional provisions to the construction of comparable provisions of the State constitution. As noted earlier in this opinion, the Supreme Court has not yet spoken on the extension of double jeopardy principles to noncapital sentencing procedures. Because the Supreme Court has not interpreted the Federal double jeopardy provision in the context of noncapital sentencing proceedings, defendants' argument for departure from the lockstep approach in this regard is unavailing. The question, then, is simply whether our constitution may be interpreted to apply double jeopardy principles to noncapital sentencing procedures. In that regard, defendants assert that the wording of Illinois' double jeopardy clause supports a broader interpretation than does the wording in the Federal clause. Specifically, defendants refer to the phraseology "of life and limb" in the Federal double jeopardy clause as less expansive than the language in the Illinois clause ("no person shall be twice put in jeopardy for the same offense").

We reject defendants' attempt at a restricted construction of the Federal clause. The difference in wording offers no substantial basis to support a conclusion that Illinois' clause provides broader protections than does its Federal counterpart. Aside from the difference in language, defendants have not directed our attention to anything, either in the debates or the committee reports of the constitutional convention, which would indicate that the double jeopardy provision in our constitution is intended to be construed differently than the Federal provision. Defendants next suggest to us that to adequately safeguard the competing interests of judicial efficiency and finality, this court should interpret Illinois' double jeopardy provision to afford the defendants "protection from ordeal and risk." We have not, heretofore, recognized judicial efficiency as a value underlying double jeopardy protections. Traditionally, the interests which form the foundation of double jeopardy are principles of fairness and finality. We have already addressed the fairness issue in our discussion of defendants' policy considerations.

Double jeopardy protections represent a balancing of the defendant's interest in finality against society's interest in effective law enforcement. We regard a defendant's interest in finality with respect to sentencing as legitimate. However, we believe that a defendant's interest in the eventual length of his sentence as compared to his interest regarding a determination of guilt or innocence are not coequal. Specifically, a defendant has less of an interest in the length of his incarceration than in not being incarcerated at all. For that reason, many of the due process protections afforded a defendant at trial are not extended to sentencing proceedings. Thus, we conclude that any finality interest in sentencing is far outweighed by the State's countervailing interest to adequately protect its citizenry and to punish recidivists. We conclude that Illinois' double jeopardy clause provides no protection to the non-trial-like sentencing proceedings at issue here.

REVIEW SECTION

READING COMPREHENSION

Discuss the relevance of *Bullington v Missouri* (1981) to this case.

THINKING CRITICALLY

Should double jeopardy apply to Class X and habitual-criminal sentencing procedures? Defend you opinion.

CASE

In *People v Rievia,* the defendant appeals his conviction for aggravated possession of a stolen motor vehicle and subsequent 10-year sentence. He raises three issues on appeal: whether the stolen vehicle conviction violates (1) the Speedy Trial Act; (2) his constitutional right to a speedy trial; and (3) the prohibition against reinstating a case after the statute of limitations on the stolen vehicle charge expired.

PEOPLE V. RIEVIA
719 N.E.2d 1077 (1999)

Defendant was arrested on August 20, 1991, for possession of a stolen motor vehicle. Defendant gave his name as "Jouse Rievia" and was released on bail. Defendant did not appear at his September 18, 1991, court date. The court revoked his bail and issued a warrant for his arrest under the name "Jouse Rievia." The case was then stricken with leave to reinstate. Defendant was arrested again on January 24, 1992, this time under the name of "David Velazquez." He was charged with two armed robberies, unrelated to the 1991 stolen vehicle charge. Defendant was convicted of one armed robbery and pled guilty to the second one. His presentence investigation report listed several aliases used by him. The report also listed an outstanding warrant for the 1991 stolen vehicle charge under the name "Jouse Rievia." Defendant denied that he had been charged with that offense. Defendant completed his sentence on the armed robbery charges on January 24, 1995. He was then rearrested on the outstanding warrant issued in 1991, relating to the stolen vehicle charge. Defendant moved to dismiss the charge, claiming that the speedy trial term was broken. The court denied the motion and, after a bench trial, found defendant guilty of the 1991 offense.

Section 103-5(e) of the Speedy Trial Act (725 ILCS 5/103-5(e)) applies when a defendant is in simultaneous custody on multiple offenses. The State must try the defendant on one of the charges within 120 days. The State must then resolve all other pending charges within 160 days of the date judgment is entered on the first case. Whether defendant's actions caused or contributed to delay in bringing him to trial is always an issue in a motion to dismiss based on an alleged Speedy Trial Act violation. A defendant must establish a speedy trial violation and show that he is not responsible for the delay. The trial court's finding of responsibility for the delay is entitled to deference and will be sustained absent an abuse of discretion. Defendant's argument here is based on a claim that he was returned to custody on the 1991 stolen vehicle charge when he was arrested for the 1992 armed robbery charges. Since the first of the armed robbery charges was resolved on July 30, 1992, defendant reasons that the State then had 160 days to resolve the pending stolen vehicle charge. Defendant calculates that the time expired on January 6, 1993. He concludes that he cannot be charged with the three-year delay and that the stolen vehicle charge should have been dismissed.

Defendant relies on People v. Arnhold, 115 Ill. 2d 379, 504 N.E.2d 100 (1987). In Arnhold, our supreme court held that when a defendant is on bond and then arrested on unrelated charges, he is not "returned to custody" for the first charge until the bond on the first charge is revoked or withdrawn. Defendant reasons that since his bond on the stolen vehicle charge had been revoked well before he was arrested on the armed robbery charges in January 1992, he was automatically returned to custody on the 1991 charge. This is a novel argument, but we believe it distorts Arnhold's holding. The obvious, and we believe dispositive, difference between Arnhold and this case is the use of an alias in this case. When the Arnhold defendant was arrested on the unrelated charges, he was not posing as someone else. Defendant here was arrested on two unrelated charges, under two different names. His failure to appear in court on the 1991 charge led to a bail revocation and a warrant for his arrest as "Jouse Rievia." Defendant, under the name "Jouse Rievia," was not arrested until January 1995. To accept defendant's argument and read Arnhold to hold that defendant's 1992 arrest as "David Velasquez" returned him to custody on the 1991 stolen vehicle charge against "Jouse Rievia" charges the State with keeping track of the names felons may choose to use as they make their troubled way through life. While it is in the best interest of law enforcement to establish the true identity of those charged with crimes, we have not found a case that allows an accused to assert his constitutional right to a speedy trial under one name while he is using another. We believe that because the State never had "knowing" custody of the defendant known as "Jouse Rievia" on a 1991 stolen vehicle charge, when he was later arrested for armed robbery, his 1992 arrest did not "return him to custody" on the original charge within the meaning of the statute.

Defendant also argues that the State failed to exercise reasonable diligence in executing the stolen vehicle warrant. Defendant contends that since the State here did not make a reasonable effort to locate him, despite having alias information available in the presentence investigation report, a diligence holding supports a finding of a speedy trial violation. Defendant cites no case where the diligence required of the State was pitted against defendant's efforts to thwart it, rewarding the defendant for his efforts. We noted earlier that we could not find such a case. The absence of case law could be explained by the reluctance of defendants or their lawyers to argue that there is a beneficial (or even benign) motive for the use of aliases that would bolster a defendant's claim that his constitutional right to a speedy trial had been violated. The constitutional guarantee of a speedy trial is not (or should not be) a cat and mouse game where the mouse is rewarded for his cunning and the cat is punished for his lack of it. The use of an alias aside, our review of the record leads us to conclude that defendant's reliance on the presentence investigation report to charge the State with a lack of diligence in discovering his various identities is based on speculation.

We also agree with the State that defendant could have invoked the speedy trial protections under 730 ILCS 5/3-8-10. The section applies when a defendant is in the custody of the Illinois Department of Corrections. To invoke the speedy trial term under this section, a defendant must file a specific demand for trial. Defendant never filed such a demand. The speedy trial term in this section was never triggered. Defendant argues that the section does not apply because section 3-8-10 cannot be used to reset the speedy trial term set in section 103-5(e) of the Speedy Trial Act. This argument fails because the speedy trial term in section 103-5(e) was never triggered.

Next, defendant argues, statutory requirements aside, that his constitutional right to a speedy trial was violated. Issues not raised at trial and not presented in a posttrial motion are deemed waived. But issues relating to substantial rights may be considered by a reviewing court even if not properly preserved. We will consider defendant's speedy trial argument. It affects substantial rights. The analysis to be used in deciding whether a defendant's right to a speedy trial has been violated is set out Barker v. Wingo, 407 U.S. 514, 33 L. Ed. 2d 101, 92 S. Ct. 2182 (1972). We consider the length of the delay, the reason for the delay, defendant's assertion of his right and the prejudice caused to the defendant. These elements must be considered in light of the circumstances of each case. No one element is dispositive. Defendant contends that each of the four elements weighs in his favor. He argues that the three-year delay was presumptively prejudicial. We agree. But we do not agree with defendant's contention that the delay was caused by the State's failure to make a good-faith effort to locate him after a warrant was issued and he was rearrested in 1992 under another name. Defendant maintains that he asserted his speedy trial right on August 21, 1991. Last, defendant states that he was prejudiced by the delay in that he lost the opportunity to receive a concurrent sentence and the 180-day credit toward that sentence while he awaited trial on the robbery charges.

Defendant's argument that the State caused the delay overlooks the issuance of a warrant for his arrest in 1991 because he missed a court date and forfeited his bail. When he was arrested in 1992, he gave a different name. When the presentence report listed the 1991 stolen vehicle charge under the "Jouse Rievia" alias, defendant denied having ever been charged with that offense. This tactic succeeded since it took the State some time to unravel the doubt defendant created about his identity. We have already discussed the argument that the State was not diligent in discovering defendant's true identity. The cause of the delay was defendant's own doing. Defendant's claim that he asserted his right to a speedy trial on August 21, 1991, is incorrect. A defendant "on bond" must file a speedy trial demand to trigger the 160-day period in which he must be tried. Defendant did not file a demand while he was on bond. Defendant's speedy trial demand was filed after his arrest but before his bail was assessed. That demand was ineffective to trigger the 160-day statute. Defendant argues, nevertheless, that whether he properly asserted his right to a speedy trial is irrelevant because courts may not apply strict statutory notice requirements to a sixth amendment speedy trial analysis. We agree, but defendant's argument must be weighed against the facts that cut against him. A defendant's failure to properly assert the right makes it difficult for a defendant to prove that he was denied the right to a speedy trial.

Defendant also contends that he was prejudiced because he did not receive credit for time served or concurrent sentences. The State does not contest that defendant may have lost these opportunities. Prejudice is but one element to be considered. The prejudice defendant suffered was caused by his own conduct. This factor is also weighed against him. There was no constitutional violation of defendant's right to a speedy trial. Last, defendant argues that the three-year statute of limitations on the stolen vehicle charge expired before he was tried. Defendant reasons that since the stolen vehicle charge was stricken, with a leave to reinstate docket longer than the statute of limitations for the offense, the charge should have been dismissed. Defendant concedes that this issue was not preserved for appeal. He argues that counsel's failure to raise the issue in the trial court is ineffective assistance of counsel. Defendant alternatively asks the issue be reviewed for plain error. We will review the statute of limitations issue for plain error.

Defendant's argument assumes that the State's ability to reinstate a case is subject to the statute of limitations. The law is not as clear as defendant suggests. The State's ability to reinstate a charge is subject to the speedy trial statute. The speedy trial term continues to run even after a case is stricken with leave to reinstate. As long as the speedy trial term is not broken, the State may reinstate a case. The State's right to reinstate subject to the speedy trial statute limits the State's power to reinstate cases indefinitely. The protections of a statute of limitation are not needed. Defendant counters that the law in Illinois is the opposite: that the statute of limitations continues to run while the case is stricken with leave to reinstate. Under section 3-7(a) of the Criminal Code of 1961 (720 ILCS 5/3-7(a)), the limitation is tolled when a "defendant is not usually and publicly resident within this State." "Publicly" means "openly as opposed to private, secluded, or secret." Defendant would be hard pressed to argue that he was publicly present in the state (even in custody) if he was hiding his identity. Affirmed.

REVIEW SECTION

READING COMPREHENSION

Outline the facts of this case and the relevance of *People v Arnhold* (1987).

SECTION 3: CONVICTION BY JURY TRIAL

OVERVIEW

While only ten percent of cases are decided in trial, the U.S. Supreme Court, the U.S. Constitution, and all state constitutions guarantee the right to trial by jury, the purpose being a check on government power by transference to a community-dominated body. The only exception to the right to trial by jury is the case of 'petty offenses,' those being ones with less than six months' imprisonment as the maximum penalty. There are however, exceptions to the exception, including deception of immigration officials, driving while under the influence, and shoplifting. These offenses give a defendant the right to trial by jury regardless of the state statute indicating length of prison term. The right to trial by jury is part of Article One, Section Eight of the Illinois Constitution, as well as articulated in Article One, Section Thirteen which provides: "The right of trial by jury as heretofore enjoyed shall remain inviolate." In addition, there are limitations on who can waive a jury trial:

No person under the age of 18 years shall be permitted to plead guilty, guilty but mentally ill or waive trial by jury in any case except where the penalty is by fine only unless he is represented by counsel in open court (725 ILCS 5/113-5).

All prosecutions except on a plea of guilty or guilty but mentally ill shall be tried by the court and a jury unless the defendant waives a jury trial in writing (725 ILCS 5/115-1).

The constitution of the jury must represent a cross-section of the community in which the trial is held, including diversity of members based on race, gender, ethnicity, and religion. The Federal Jury Selection and Service Act outlines guidelines for selection of jurors and similar provisions are outlined in the *Illinois Revised Statutes*:

(a) Questions of law shall be decided by the court and questions of fact by the jury. (b) The jury shall consist of 12 members. (e) A defendant tried alone shall be allowed 20 peremptory challenges in a capital case, 10 in a case in which the punishment may be imprisonment in the penitentiary, and 5 in all other cases; except that, in a single trial of more than one defendant, each defendant shall be allowed 12 peremptory challenges in a capital case, 6 in a case in which the punishment may be imprisonment in the penitentiary, and 3 in all other cases. If several charges against a defendant or defendants are consolidated for trial, each defendant shall be allowed peremptory challenges upon one charge only, which single charge shall be the charge against the defendant authorizing the greatest maximum penalty. The State shall be allowed the same number of peremptory challenges as all of the defendants. (o) A defendant tried by the court and jury shall only be found guilty, guilty but mentally ill, not guilty or not guilty by reason of insanity, upon the unanimous verdict of the jury (725 ILCS 5/115-4).

Keep in mind that in capital cases the judge does not instruct the jury on the sentence that may be imposed. Is it fair to have the jury deliberate a defendant's guilt while remaining unaware that the potential sentence is death?

CASE

Following a bench trial, Kenneth Elders was convicted of possession of a controlled substance with intent to deliver within 1,000 feet of a public park and was sentenced to seven years' imprisonment. On appeal, defendant contends that he did not validly waive his right to a jury trial. *People v Elders* is the appeal which is reversed and remanded for a new trial.

PEOPLE V. ELDERS
Appellate Court of Illinois, First District, Second Division
No. 1-02-3298 (2004)

Defendant was arrested on November 24, 2001, at approximately 4:43 a.m., after police officers conducted a surveillance and observed him engaging in suspected narcotics transactions. On December 26, 2001, defendant was indicted on three counts of possession of a controlled substance with intent to deliver—count I alleged defendant did so within 1,000 feet of a school, count II alleged defendant did so within 1,000 feet of a public park, and count III was general. On March 11, 2002, attorney Raymond Prusak appeared on behalf of defendant at a status conference. There is no evidence defendant was present at this time. Counsel stated, "I'd like to set this down for bench trial date." The case was continued to April 4. On April 4, a different attorney, John Miraglia, appeared on behalf of defendant. The court inquired whether this was to be a bench or jury trial, but received no response. The case was continued to April 8. Again, there is no evidence defendant was present at this time. On April 8, Prusak appeared on defendant's behalf and the case was continued to April 15. On April 15, Prusak again appeared on defendant's behalf. When the court inquired whether this was to be a bench or jury trial, counsel responded it would be a bench trial. There is no evidence defendant was present. On May 15, Prusak again appeared on behalf of defendant. At this time, defendant was present. Counsel stated, "This is Kenneth Elders before the Court. He is set for a bench trial today." Counsel then requested a short status date because he was attempting to locate a witness. Counsel indicated that if he did not find the witness, defense strategy would change and there probably would not be a trial. Counsel then stated, "The State made an offer to me earlier today. If they can keep this offer open until the next court date." The case was then continued to June 13. On June 13, William Breen appeared on behalf of defendant and indicated that the case was set for status or "possible plea." He asked that the matter be reset for a trial date of August 6. The case was set for trial on the morning of August 6. Because John Morelli, counsel who was to try the case on behalf of defendant, was caught in traffic, it was continued to the afternoon. When the parties returned to the court in the afternoon, the State *nolle prossed* count I and proceeded on counts II and III. Immediately after doing so, the State began calling its witnesses.

Chicago police officer Louis Carrizal was called as a witness on behalf of the State. Carrizal testified that on November 24, 2001, at approximately 4:30 a.m., he was working with his partner, Officer Perez. The two set up a surveillance in Garfield Park to observe suspected narcotics transactions. Carrizal testified that they parked their car nearby and walked into the park. Carrizal positioned himself behind a tree and conducted surveillance. According to Carrizal, the area was well-lit by artificial lighting and he was using binoculars. Carrizal observed defendant walking, ranging from 50 to 70 feet away from Carrizal. On four occasions, Carrizal observed defendant approach the driver's side of a car, engage in a brief conversation (which Carrizal could not hear), receive an unknown amount of money, walk to the base of a tree approximately 10 feet away, retrieve something from a plastic bag lying at the base of the tree, return to the car, and hand the driver an unknown item. After observing the four transactions, Carrizal and Perez returned to their car and drove to the location where defendant was. Perez detained defendant and Carrizal went to the tree and recovered a plastic bag that contained seven Ziploc baggies inside with a white rock substance that Carrizal suspected was crack cocaine.

They also recovered $113 from defendant. On cross-examination, Carrizal stated that he and his partner observed defendant for approximately 10 minutes. He further stated that he believed defendant was receiving money from the individuals in the cars based on the color and shape of the object. Carrizal admitted that when the cars were facing westbound, defendant's back was to him and it was more difficult to observe what was occurring. However, it was still his belief that defendant received something, walked to the tree, etc.

The State then offered the stipulated testimony of Elizabeth Ilowski, a forensic chemist with the Illinois State Police Lab. According to the stipulation, Ilowski, who was qualified as a expert, "found the estimated weight to be 1.4 grams of a chunky substance and found it to be cocaine." Defense counsel stipulated to this testimony. The State then rested. Defendant moved for a directed finding, which was denied. Defendant then rested. After closing arguments, the trial court found defendant guilty on count II.

At this time the following colloquy occurred:

"THE COURT: Wait a minute. State, we have a problem. I don't have a jury waiver in the file.

MS. O'CONNOR [Assistant State's Attorney]: Did the defendant sign one?

THE COURT: I don't believe so.

MS. O'CONNOR: Was the jury waiver taken on the record?

THE COURT: I don't believe it was.

MS. O'CONNOR: Can you do it retroactively? Was it the defendant's intent to sign a jury waiver?

THE COURT: He was never asked.

MR. MORELLI [Defendant's Attorney]: The defendant indicates to me that he wanted a bench trial.

THE COURT: Pardon me?

MR. MORELLI: The defendant just indicated to me that he wanted a bench trial. That was his intention.

THE COURT: His intention was what?

MR. MORELLI: It was his intention to have a bench trial. He did not intend to have a jury trial.

THE COURT: Okay. He needs to sign a jury waiver.

The Court acknowledges the defendant signed a jury waiver in open court."

Defendant's bail was revoked, a presentence investigation report ordered, and the matter continued. On September 27, defendant's motion for a new trial was denied and the court sentenced him to seven years' imprisonment. Defendant first contends that he is entitled to a new trial because he was not admonished as to his right to have a jury trial and did not sign a jury waiver until after he was found guilty. According to defendant, a jury waiver must come before a trial, not after. Defendant also argues that his attorney's statement that defendant desired a bench trial, made after he was found guilty, and defendant's failure to object are not sufficient factors to demonstrate a valid waiver. Defendant further notes that the trial court never personally addressed him with respect to waiver of a jury trial. Defendant asks us to review this claimed error under plain error since he failed to preserve it below.

The State contends that defendant's waiver was understandingly made and done in open court, the only requirements for a valid waiver, and, therefore, no error occurred. According to the State, the fact that the waiver occurred after defendant's trial is irrelevant. The State further argues that defendant did not object when his counsel indicated his intent to have a bench trial, nor did defendant object at any point during the trial or when the court raised the issue of a lack of waiver. The State further maintains that because defendant had pled guilty four other times and was admonished at those times, he knew what he was waiving here.

A defendant validly waives his right to a jury trial only if the waiver is made "(1) understandingly, and (2) in open court." A knowing and understanding oral waiver can be found if, in the defendant's presence and without objection from him, "defense counsel expressly advised the court" that the defendant desires to proceed by way of a bench trial. This rule, however, requires "some affirmative statement by defendant's attorney, in his presence, that the defendant wishes not to exercise his right to a jury trial and, instead, chooses a bench trial." A defendant, however, "will not be deemed to have acquiesced in a jury waiver made by his counsel outside the accused's presence." Whether a jury wavier is valid does not "rest on any precise formula but depends on the facts and circumstances of each particular case." We review this claimed error under the plain error doctrine since it involves "the knowing waiver of the fundamental right to a jury trial." Since the facts are not disputed, the issue is a question of law, which we review *de novo*. Only one case appears to be directly, factually on point, i.e., where waiver came after, or was attempted after, the defendant was found guilty (People v. Collins, 9 Ill. App. 3d 185, 292 N.E.2d 115 1972), the court concluded that the defendant had not waived his right to a jury trial where the record was "devoid of any mention of a jury trial until after the evidence had been heard and a finding of guilty had been entered against defendant." However, Collins is not particularly instructive. We note that while Collins does not have any negative history, it has only been cited once. More importantly, the procedural facts, i.e., what occurred prior to trial and on the day of trial, are not detailed by the court in the opinion. Lastly, there is no evidence a written jury waiver was executed, as in the instant case. Other than Collins, the parties have not cited, nor has our independent research disclosed, any case where a jury waiver was executed after the defendant was found guilty.

The closest case we have discovered is People v. Lombardi, 305 Ill. App. 3d 33, 711 N.E.2d 426 (1999). In Lombardi, the defendant's bench trial began on September 5, 1997. On September 19, the trial court heard closing arguments and continued the matter to September 29 for a ruling. On September 29, the trial court noted that the defendant had not filed a jury waiver and wanted to correct this situation before it took the case under advisement. At this time, the trial court thoroughly admonished the defendant with respect to her right to have a jury trial and stated that, although the court had already heard the evidence, it would declare a mistrial if the defendant wanted the case heard by a jury. The court then continued the case to October 6 so that the defendant could think about her decision. On October 6, defense counsel advised the court that he had explained the defendant's rights to her and she wanted the court to render its ruling. The court again admonished the defendant, stating that it would declare a mistrial and allow the case to be heard by a jury should she so desire. The defendant signed a jury waiver and thereafter the court allowed the defendant to reopen proofs at which time defense counsel presented two additional witnesses. On October 23, the court found the defendant guilty. On appeal, the defendant argued that she was entitled to a new trial because she was not admonished with respect to the right to have a jury trial until 17 days after the bench trial had begun. The Lombardi court disagreed, noting that a defendant "will not be permitted to gamble on the outcome before the judge without a jury and then if dissatisfied make a belated demand for a jury." The court noted that, assuming there was no waiver prior to trial, "defendant knowingly waived her right before the bench trial was completed" and concluded that "the trial court gave the defendant every opportunity to demand a jury trial, and, after being completely admonished of her rights," the defendant waived them. It was the court's belief that the defendant wanted to have it both ways—"she wanted the trial court to rule and then she wanted to decide whether she wanted another bite at the apple by requesting a jury trial."

People v. Williamson, 311 Ill. App. 3d 54, 724 N.E.2d 167 (1999), relied upon by defendant here, the court again concluded that the defendant had not validly waived his right to a jury trial. On March 1, 1996, at a status hearing, defense counsel stated that the defendant would take a bench trial. On March 29, at another hearing, the assistant State's Attorney stated that, by agreement, the case was continued to April 26 for motions and a bench trial. On April 26, the assistant State's Attorney again stated the case was continued, to May 10, for motions and a bench trial. The same was true on May 10. On June 5, at another hearing, defense counsel made a similar statement. On June 27, when the matter actually proceeded to trial, no mention of a jury waiver was made. There was also no written jury waiver contained in the record. Reviewing the issue under plain error, the Williamson court noted that the State maintained that the defendant had waived a jury trial because in his presence, when a bench trial was discussed, the defendant did not object, nor did he object when his attorney proceeded to a bench trial. The Williamson court determined that mere reference to a bench trial on the day of trial did not constitute a waiver of a jury trial. The Williamson court noted that on March 1, March 29, April 26, and May 10, although "bench" was referred to, nothing was said that the defendant had a right to a jury trial or that that right had been waived. Additionally, on the day of trial, there was no discussion with respect to the defendant's right to a jury trial, nor any waiver of same. Specifically, there was no mention whether the case would proceed by jury or bench trial when the court simply proceeded to a bench trial. The Williamson court concluded that the previous references to "bench" were "insufficient to constitute a discussion of jury waiver in open court." The court also noted that the record did not demonstrate whether the defendant had been in court except for on May 10 and June 26, and that on June 26 there was no statement from the defendant or his attorney with respect to a jury waiver or proceeding by way of bench trial. The Williamson court therefore reversed the trial court's judgment and remanded the case for a new trial.

The State here relies on People v. Frey, 103 Ill. 2d 327, 469 N.E.2d 195 (1984), in support of its argument that defendant acquiesced in counsel's conduct and, therefore, validly waived his right to a jury trial. In Frey, the court reiterated that "the accused typically speaks and acts through his attorney, and we have given effect to jury waivers made by defense counsel in defendant's presence where defendant gave no indication of any objection to the court hearing the case." The court in Frey concluded that the defendant had validly waived his right to a jury trial where the record demonstrated he was aware of his right to a jury trial and had been present in court "at some point prior to trial" when the jury waiver had been discussed.

Based on the foregoing authority, we find that, at the very least, the record must disclose some evidence of some discussion in defendant's presence, prior to being found guilty, with respect to a jury waiver. There is no evidence of same here. Rather, there was one single reference to proceeding to a bench trial, in defendant's presence, some two and one-half weeks prior to trial. This does not constitute a discussion of a jury waiver or demonstrate that defendant was aware he could choose between a jury and bench trial. Accordingly, we find the evidence here is insufficient to establish a valid jury waiver by defendant. Defendant here was never admonished about his right to a jury trial, nor did the trial court, prior to a trial, confirm that defendant had waived a jury trial. On the day of trial, no mention was made whether the case would proceed to a bench or jury trial—the State simply proceeded to introduce evidence. Lastly, there was nothing stated in defendant's presence either before trial or on the day of trial that he had a choice between a jury or bench trial. The State focuses on the fact that defendant should be deemed to have acquiesced because he did not object to proceeding to a bench trial. We do not agree. The only time a bench trial was referenced in defendant's presence was on May 15, at which time defense counsel only mentioned in passing that the case was set for a bench trial. Defendant's silence when the case proceeded to a bench trial is not sufficient without some affirmative act on his or his attorney's part to waive a jury trial. There is no evidence in the instant case that defendant was even given the option of proceeding with a jury trial or a jury waiver ever being discussed. Moreover, even when the trial court here finally addressed the issue, after defendant had been found guilty, defendant was not admonished, even cursorily, that he had a right to be tried by a jury, or given an opportunity to think about his choice. In fact, the court here did not even address defendant personally. Defendant was given absolutely no opportunity to demand a jury trial, or to waive same.

Although ordering a new trial in the instant case may not be a matter of judicial economy, the trial court's error in failing to fulfill its duty to obtain a valid jury waiver in open court prior to trying defendant or, at the least, prior to rendering a finding against him, cannot be excused. Accordingly, we reverse and remand this cause for a new trial.

REVIEW SECTION

READING COMPREHENSION

What facts are at issue in this case?

Discuss the elements involved in waiving a jury trial, including an elaboration of the findings of previous courts.

CONCLUSION

After a defendant is charged, both adversarial proceedings and informal negotiation follow that are dictated by several formal rules that prevail in criminal cases. These rules are informed by Article One, Section Eight of the Illinois Constitution which addresses information of charges filed, the right to counsel, the right to a speedy and public trial, rules regarding venue, and the rights of victims in such a proceeding. This chapter explored the test of the government's case, the myriad of pretrial motions available, and rules governing trial by jury.

Chapter Fourteen

After Conviction

While offenders are entitled some rights after the conviction phase of the process, these rights are much more limited. Due process only minimally affects sentencing powers, there exists no constitutional right to appeal, and *habeus corpus* is limited. Article One, Section Eleven of the Illinois Constitution reads:

> All penalties shall be determined both according to the seriousness of the offense and with the objective of restoring the offender to useful citizenship. No conviction shall work corruption of blood or forfeiture of estate. No person shall be transported out of the State for an offense committed within the State.

This chapter will review the procedures that occur after conviction:

(1)   Sentencing;

(2)   Death sentences; and

(3)   Appeals and collateral attack.

SECTION 1: SENTENCING

OVERVIEW

From the 1600s to the late 1800s, fixed sentencing was the norm, wherein sentencing authority was in the hands of legislators. Following that a trend toward indeterminate sentencing emerged which tailored the punishment to suit the criminal with the power in the hands of judges and parole boards. Beginning in the 1970s the philosophy shifted again, this time to one of harsher penalties. While indeterminate sentencing remains, fixed sentences are beginning to gain ground in the form of sentencing guidelines and mandatory minimums. In theory, these sentences are to provide uniformity, provide certainty and truth, as well as meet the goals of retribution, deterrence, and incapacitation. From the early 1980s through the early 1990s, there was a shift to an emphasis on structured sentencing models with severe restrictions placed on 'good time credits' for offenders, a greater emphasis on a 'just deserts' model of punishment, and a reduction in judicial discretion. In the mid-1990s, Illinois received money from the government as part of a program to fund states that pursued truth-in-sentencing laws. As part of this, Illinois required violent offenders or those with a prior violent or serious drug offense to serve 85% of their sentence in prison, and instituted habitual offender laws.

In August 1995, Truth in Sentencing legislation was enacted under Public Act 89-404, however was declared unconstitutional by the Appellate Court of Illinois and the Illinois Supreme Court for violation of the single-subject rule of the State constitution. Public Act 90-593, which became effective on June 19, 1998, reenacted the original Truth in Sentencing provisions as elaborated in 730 ILCS 5/3-6-3(a)(2) and is provided here at length:

> (2) The rules and regulations on early release shall provide, with respect to offenses committed on or after June 19, 1998, the following: (i) that a prisoner who is serving a term of imprisonment for first degree murder shall receive no good conduct credit and shall serve the entire sentence imposed by the court; (ii) that a prisoner serving a sentence for attempt to commit first degree murder, solicitation of murder, solicitation of murder for hire, intentional homicide of an unborn child, predatory criminal sexual assault of a child, aggravated criminal sexual assault, criminal sexual assault, aggravated kidnapping, aggravated battery with a firearm, heinous battery, aggravated battery of a senior citizen, or aggravated battery of a child shall receive no more than 4.5 days of good conduct credit for each month of his or her sentence of imprisonment; and (iii) that a prisoner serving a sentence for home invasion, armed robbery, aggravated vehicular hijacking, aggravated discharge of a firearm, or armed violence with a category I weapon or category II weapon, when the court has made and entered a finding, pursuant to subsection (c-1) of Section 5-4-1 of this Code, that the conduct leading to conviction for the enumerated offense resulted in great bodily harm to a victim, shall receive no more than 4.5 days of good conduct credit for each month of his or her sentence of imprisonment. (2.1) For all offenses, other than those enumerated in subdivision (a)(2) committed on or after June 19, 1998, and other than the offense of reckless homicide as defined in subsection (e) of Section 9-3 of the Criminal Code of 1961 committed on or after January 1, 1999, the rules and regulations shall provide that a prisoner who is serving a term of imprisonment shall receive one day of good conduct credit for each day of his or her sentence of imprisonment or recommitment under Section 3-3-9. Each day of good conduct credit shall reduce by one day the prisoner's period of imprisonment or recommitment under Section 3-3-9. (2.3) The rules and regulations on early release shall provide that a prisoner who is serving a sentence for reckless homicide as defined in subsection (e) of Section 9-3 of the Criminal Code of 1961 committed on or after January 1, 1999 shall receive no more than 4.5 days of good conduct credit for each month of his or her sentence of imprisonment.

Partially as a result of truth-in-sentencing guidelines, Illinois (as has the rest of the nation) has dramatically increased its prison population, despite the fact that crime is dropping. Note that all numerical data provided in this chapter can be located on the website of the Illinois Criminal

290

Justice Information Authority. In Illinois since 1978, the rate at which offenders are incarcerated has almost quadrupled. This growth in prison population was both a result of sentencing reforms for violent offenders as well as the war on drugs and increased sentences for drug offenders. Determinate sentencing laws were enacted in Illinois beginning in 1978 to standardize sentencing, and the truth-in-sentencing polices of the mid-1990s increased the associated prison population boom even further. While it has already been noted that the Illinois Supreme Court struck the initial truth-in-sentencing law, this did not occur before lawmakers passed a modified version in 1998. Most students of the law and the criminal justice system are aware that the United States imprisons a larger proportion of its population than any other westernized nation. What is the state of Illinois in this regard?

In 1978, according to data from the Justice Department, 96 out of every 100,000 Illinoisans were serving a sentence of more than one year. This number rose to 211 per 100,000 in 1989, and to 368 per 100,000 in 1999. By the year 2000, 371 out of every 100,000 Illinoisans were incarcerated. This state level data puts Illinois about average for the nation. The Department of Corrections hold approximately 44,668 prisoners which is 162 percent of 'ideal capacity,' and 41.7 percent of new adult admissions during 2001 were for drug offenses. This is problematic in that many feel the $8000-$10,000 per year per inmate, would be better spent in a rehabilitation program. In addition, truth-in-sentencing laws require the most serious offenders to remain in prison for 85-100 percent of their sentences, leaving Illinois taxpayers in the next few years to fund the growing geriatric inmate population. As you read the case involving sentencing reforms and consider the implications for this policy not only at the state level, but nationally as well, consider where our priorities as a nation should lie.

CASE

After a jury trial, Brian Jones was convicted of possession of more than 100 grams, but less than 400 grams, of cocaine with intent to deliver, as well as possession of over 30 grams of cannabis. Jones was sentenced to the minimum mandatory sentence of nine years in prison on the possession with intent to deliver offense. Throughout trial and sentencing, the trial judge repeatedly expressed dissatisfaction with the mandatory sentencing requirement and noted Jones' education and work history, his lack of criminal background, and his supportive wife and family. The judge said he would sentence Jones to probation if it were available, however the State insisted on pursuing the charges as filed. Jones asks the appellate court to use its authority under Supreme Court Rule 615(b)(3) to reduce his cocaine conviction to simple possession of a controlled substance. He agrees the evidence was sufficient to support the jury's guilty verdict, but contends there was an "evidentiary weakness" in the intent to deliver element, making a reduction to the lesser included offense an available remedy for an "unduly harsh" sentence. The question for this court is whether it is empowered to reduce the degree of the offense where the State has presented enough evidence of all the essential elements of the offense to support the conviction. In *People v Jones,* the appellate court concludes they do have that power, but under limited circumstances.

PEOPLE V. JONES
286 Ill.App.3d 777, 676 N.E.2d 1335 (1997)

Jones was charged by complaint and superseding indictment with delivery of more than 1 gram but less than 15 grams of cocaine, unlawful possession of more than 100 grams but less than 400 grams of cocaine with the intent to deliver, and unlawful possession of more than 30 grams of cannabis with the intent to deliver. The events which led to Jones' arrest took place in March 1990. Trial did not begin until May 1994. At trial, Officers Anthony Bertucca and Steven Bocconcelli testified they, on March 31, 1990, learned an informant told their supervisor a drug transaction would take place that evening. The informant said the buyer would be driving a new Grand Prix automobile with license number RD9144. Based on this information, the officers took up surveillance of the apartment building at about 8:15 that evening. Between 8:30 and 9:00 p.m. the officers observed a white Grand Prix, with license number RD9144, park in front of the apartment building. A man, later identified as Timothy McCarthy, exited the car and entered the building. Officer Bertucca testified that, while standing on the sidewalk near the entrance to the building, he watched as McCarthy went up the five stairs to the front door and then through two sets of glass doors to the lobby of the building. Inside the building, McCarthy went outside the officer's line of vision for about two minutes. When McCarthy reappeared, he stood in the hallway where he was soon approached by a man later identified as Jones.

Officer Bertucca testified that he witnessed Jones hand McCarthy a briefcase. McCarthy then gave Jones some money, which Jones "rippled through." After the exchange of money, said Officer Bertucca, Jones handed McCarthy "two clear plastic bags of crushed white powder." After this transaction, McCarthy left the building and Officer Bertucca followed. When McCarthy was a short distance from the building Officer Bertucca stopped him and arrested him. Officer Bocconcelli testified that he had been standing across the street during the surveillance. He did not witness any exchange, but joined Officer Bertucca when he stopped McCarthy. Officer Bocconcelli said that he advised McCarthy of his rights as Officer Bertucca reached into McCarthy's pocket and recovered two small plastic bags of what was suspected to be cocaine, plus a larger bag of what appeared to be marijuana. After arresting McCarthy, the officers accompanied McCarthy to the fifth floor of the apartment building. As they exited the elevator on the fifth floor, the officers said, McCarthy pointed out Jones, who was in the hallway pushing a cart with cleaning products in it. Officer Bertucca said he recognized Jones as the man he had seen downstairs with McCarthy. The officers identified themselves to Jones and arrested him.

Officer Bocconcelli said he advised Jones of his rights and Jones acknowledged that he understood them. Jones, both officers said, agreed to speak with them and admitted that he sold cocaine to McCarthy. Jones also told them that he had more cocaine in his apartment. Jones then unlocked the door and directed the officers to a kitchen cabinet where, they said, he told them he kept some cocaine for "his own use." From the kitchen cabinet, Officer Bocconcelli recovered a clear plastic bag of what appeared to be cocaine. After discovering the bag of suspected cocaine in the kitchen cabinet, Officer Bertucca said he noticed some money on the kitchen table. He asked Jones about this money and, he said, Jones responded that this was the money he received from McCarthy. The officers also testified that Jones asked if he could put on some shoes before leaving the apartment building. For this reason, they accompanied him into another part of the apartment. In the living room, underneath a coffee table, the officers said they observed an open canvas gym bag. Exposed at the top of the canvas bag was a clear plastic bag containing crushed green plant matter. Officer Bocconcelli picked up the plastic bag and discovered a bag containing a larger amount of white powder underneath it. Officer Bocconcelli testified that when he asked Jones, "What's this?" Jones replied, "Okay, I've only been dealing for a few weeks." Jones then was taken to the police station. Both officers testified the apartment was in disarray and looked as if someone was moving in or out. It was suggested, during cross-examination, that Jones was moving from another apartment in the building. The officers admitted that they learned Jones was moving from another apartment and that this second apartment was never searched by the police.

The only other witness presented at trial was Grace Odibo-Harlan, a chemist for the Chicago Police Lab. She testified that on April 9, 1990, she weighed and conducted laboratory tests on the two packets of white powder recovered from McCarthy. She said these two packets contained 3.09 grams and 2.458 grams, respectively, of a substance which tested positive for cocaine. She retested the samples on December 24, 1992. On this occasion, she said, the two samples weighed 3.35 grams and 2.88 grams, respectively, and again tested positive for the presence of cocaine. Later, on January 21, 1993, she did a quantitative analysis on these samples. This analysis indicated that the samples were 71% pure cocaine and 72% pure cocaine, respectively.

The defense presented no witnesses. The jury returned a verdict finding Jones guilty of possession of more than 30 grams of cannabis and possession of more than 100 grams of cocaine with the intent to deliver; but not guilty of delivery of cocaine or cannabis. At the sentencing hearing, when hearing evidence in aggravation, the judge agreed that Jones had "a large amount of cocaine to sell." Nevertheless, he said, Jones was "salvageable." The evidence of mitigation showed that Jones had no prior criminal record, was married, had a college degree, and had nearly completed studies to be a Certified Public Accountant. Jones had been involved in several community activities. The judge expressed his belief that the mandatory nine-year minimum sentence was not "the right sentence for him." The judge said: "If I had the ability, there certainly is an appropriate sentence for Brian Jones, which includes a probationary period with community help ... There's no question in my mind that the minimum sentence required by law in this particular case is not the appropriate sentence, but I refuse to violate the law, I will follow the law." Jones was sentenced to the nine year minimum sentence required by law and placed on bond pending appeal.

The trial judge had no choice. He had to sentence the defendant to at least the minimum sentence mandated by statute. But once the case is on appeal, different rules apply. Supreme Court Rule 615(b)(3) provides: "(b) Powers of the Reviewing Court. On appeal the reviewing court may: (3) reduce the degree of the offense of which the appellant was convicted." Nothing in the rule or in the commentary to the rule guides the exercise of the power granted by Rule 615(b)(3). Nor do we find clear consistency in the decisions interpreting the rule. We have been told that other sections of Rule 615 "are to be construed according to their plain language, and should not be interpreted in a fashion that renders their terms meaningless or superfluous." Some courts have held Rule 615(b)(3) applies only where the evidence is insufficient to prove an element of the offense beyond a reasonable doubt. That is, first the court finds the State failed to prove the greater offense beyond a reasonable doubt, then it uses Rule 615(b)(3) to reduce the degree of the offense. We note that the power of an appellate court to reverse a conviction is contained in Rule 615(b)(1). Our (b)(3) power to reduce the degree of an offense is separate and apart. It is not made dependent on reversal of a conviction.

Several appellate decisions have recognized a carefully circumscribed power to reduce the degree of an offense despite the existence of enough evidence to prove the essential elements of an offense. In three of these cases, the degree of offense was reduced.

People v. Plewka, 27 Ill.App.3d 553, 327 N.E.2d 457 (1975), two defendants, age 17 and 20, were found guilty in a bench trial of indecent liberties with a 15-year-old girl. The defendants admitted sexual intercourse with the complainant, but claimed they believed she was 16, a defense to the indecent liberties charge. The court held the trial judge's finding that the defendants' beliefs were unreasonable "cannot be criticized," but used Rule 615(b)(3) to reduce the convictions to contributing to sexual delinquency because the felony penalties were "unduly harsh."

In People v. Coleman, 78 Ill.App.3d 989, 34 Ill.Dec. 510, 398 N.E.2d 185 (1979), Mary Coleman, a prostitute, was found guilty of armed robbery of one of her customers and sentenced to the mandatory minimum of six years. The trial judge expressed reluctance to impose the six-year sentence. Seizing on the customer's uncorroborated testimony about the presence of a knife, evidence characterized as "extremely weak if not fatally weak in establishing beyond a reasonable doubt that the knife was present," the court reduced the offense to robbery, saying: "The power granted by Supreme Court Rule 615(b)(3)(4) should be exercised with caution and circumspection, but the fact that such powers have been granted to a reviewing court is indicative of the fact that our supreme court recognizes that situations have arisen in the past and will arise in the future where an appellate court must in the interest of fair and uniform administration of justice exercise the powers granted by the rule."

The trial judge in People v. Jackson, 181 Ill.App.3d 1048, 130 Ill.Dec. 725, 537 N.E.2d 1054 (1989), expressed misgivings about having to sentence the defendant to four years for a residential burglary. The defendant had admitted he entered the apartment and took a small amount of money, but denied he intended to commit theft when he made his entry. His purpose, he said, was to do some work on a toilet in the apartment. He worked for the landlord and had keys to all the apartments. The court reduced the offense to criminal trespass to a residence, the only available lesser included offense. The court found the two necessary relevant factors for a "rare instance" of application of Rule 615(b)(3): "... whether an evidentiary weakness exists and whether the trial judge expressed dissatisfaction with imposing the mandatory sentence." The court found that the State's intent evidence was not "fatally weak," but "nevertheless weak."

Several appellate decisions reflect acceptance of the idea that the scope of Rule 615(b)(3) extends beyond the general principle that a conviction will not be disturbed on appeal unless the evidence is so unreasonable, improbable, or unsatisfactory as to justify a reasonable doubt of the defendant's guilt. But, for one reason or another, these courts have declined to exercise their power to reduce the degree of an offense. We join the line of cases that holds Rule 615(b)(3) authorizes us to reduce the degree of an offense despite the presence of evidence sufficient to support a guilty verdict. We understand that power is to be used with "caution and circumspection," and not "purely out of merciful benevolence" The use of Rule 615(b)(3) when the evidence is sufficient to support a conviction should be a "rare instance." We must be aware of our obligation to give deference to the trier of fact. We must bear in mind that it is the legislature's prerogative to establish sentences, not ours. It is easy to determine whether the trial judge has misgivings about imposing a mandatory minimum sentence. The trial judge in this case clearly did not want to sentence Jones to nine years in prison. Further, we have no trouble finding a lesser degree of offense in this case--simple possession. But the requirement of an "evidentiary weakness" takes us into a kind of shadow area, without clear boundaries or guidelines.

In Jackson, the evidentiary weakness was not the result of conflicts between State and defense testimony. There was no serious credibility issue. The operative fact was that the State's evidence "showed little inconsistency with the defendant's testimony that he formulated the requisite intent after he entered the apartment to perform maintenance work." In Coleman, the knife allegedly used in the robbery never was found, although the defendant was arrested soon after the event. There was little corroboration of the victim-customer's testimony about a knife. And the court found it significant that the jury first announced it could not reach a verdict, then reached one after being given the Prim instruction for deadlocked juries. In Plewka, the defendants were acquitted of rape. This meant, said the court, the trial judge did not believe the complainant's story that the intercourse was against her will. In fact, she was "sexually sophisticated" and a few months short of 16. Under these circumstances, imposition of a four-year mandatory sentence for indecent liberties was "unduly harsh."

Whatever "evidentiary weakness" means, it has to be something that causes us to have grave concern about the reliability of the guilty verdict. Something is "weak" when it is lacking or deficient in strength. There is little point in trying to frame a more precise definition of the "evidentiary weakness" standard. We have to hope we will know it when we see it. Placing the evidence in this case against that standard we do not find the kind of evidentiary weakness that would cause us to reduce the degree of the offense. The intent to deliver a controlled substance typically is proved by circumstantial evidence. Here, Jones possessed more than twice the 54.28 grams that "certainly exceeded that used for personal consumption," and far more than the 25 to 30 grams of cocaine that supported an inference of intent to deliver. The defendant's claim of evidentiary weakness rests on the lack of evidence to support an inference of intent to deliver. He did not possess the items normally associated with drug dealing, such as scales, baggies, or substances used to "cut" the cocaine. He had no weapons. No drug paraphernalia was found in his apartment. Nor did the State offer any expert testimony that would tell the jury what amount of cocaine was too great to be possessed for personal use only. Jones' admission to the police strengthened the State's case. The jury carefully picked through the charges. It did not accept the State's case concerning the delivery to McCarthy, but found the evidence sufficient to support the possession with intent to deliver charge. We do not believe the guilty verdict reflects the kind of evidentiary weakness that should trigger the exercise of our power under Rule 615(b)(3). We reserve the use of that power for that rare case where it is required by the "interest of fair and uniform administration of justice."

We decline to reduce the degree of offense because we do not find the "evidentiary weakness" that would allow us to reduce the degree of offense where the trial judge felt strong misgivings about having to impose a mandatory minimum sentence. It is not our role to question the wisdom of the legislature that established the mandatory minimum. Nor can we require the State to file charges we might believe would better serve a fair and uniform administration of justice. The defendant's conviction and sentence are affirmed.

REVIEW SECTION

READING COMPREHENSION

Explain Supreme Court Rule 615(b)(3).

Detail the facts of this case and the mitigating circumstances articulated by the trial court judge.

THINKING CRITICALLY

Should the courts use their power to challenge the 'wisdom' of the legislature under less tringent circumstances?

SECTION 2: DEATH SENTENCES

OVERVIEW

There are twelve states, in addition to the District of Columbia, that do not impose the death penalty. These states are Alaska, Maine, Minnesota, Vermont, Hawaii, Massachusetts, North Dakota, West Virginia, Iowa, Michigan, Rhode Island, and Wisconsin. In addition, there are several states which have carried out no executions since reforms in 1976. These states are New Hampshire, New Jersey, New York, South Dakota, Connecticut, and Kansas. Post-1976 reform, Illinois resumed the death penalty and has executed 12 individuals. Of interest perhaps, is that Illinois has the nation's eighth largest death row population (171). Illinois is however, notable because in January 2000, then-Governor George H. Ryan exercised his clemency and pardon power to suspend the death penalty, which resulted in the exoneration of 18 individuals.

On November 19, 2003, the state House of Representatives unanimously approved SB 472, thought by many to be a historic reform of death penalty procedures. The bill contains more than 20 measures designed to respond to Illinois' troubling history of wrongful convictions in capital cases. This action by the House means that SB 472 immediately became law. Often referred to as the Illinois Death Penalty Reform Legislation, SB 472 calls for the creation of a Capital Punishment Reform Study Committee to "study the impact of the various reforms to the capital punishment system," including issues of proportionality, quality of evidence, quality of representation, costs, and training. Members of this committee are appointed by legislative leaders of both parties in each house, the attorney general, the governor, prosecutorial, and public defender agencies, and the committee issues an annual report and a final report in five years. In addition, SB 472 modified the most used aggravating factor, "murder in the course of another felony" to very modestly reduce death-eligible crimes, added two mitigating factors ("the defendant's background includes a history of extreme emotional or physical abuse" and "the defendant suffers from a reduced mental capacity").

This bill modified the jury instruction which previously stated that: "If the jury or court determines unanimously that there are no mitigating factors sufficient to preclude the imposition of the death sentence, the court shall sentence the defendant to death." This bill changes the language to: "If the jury determines unanimously, after weighing the factors in aggravation and mitigation, that death is the appropriate sentence, the court shall sentence the defendant to death." This language removes the presumption that the defendant should be sentenced to death and places emphasis on the jury's role in determining the "appropriateness" of a death sentence. Should the trial judge disagree with the jury's imposition of a death sentence, the court is still bound by the sentencing determination, however the judge sets forth his/her reasons in writing to become part of the appeal record.

We discussed earlier the limitation of eyewitness or informant testimony, and this bill allows that if upon the close of evidence "the court finds that the only evidence supporting the defendant's conviction is the uncorroborated testimony of an informant witness. . . concerning the confession or admission of the defendant, or that the sole evidence against the defendant is a single eyewitness or single accomplice without any other corroborating evidence," the defendant or the court may motion to de-certify the case as a capital case. In addition, the state is required to provide information to the defense in discovery concerning jailhouse snitch witnesses, including criminal history, any inducements for testimony, details of the purported statements of the accused, whether the informant ever recanted, other cases in which the informant testified and whether any inducements were offered in those case(s), and any other information relevant to the credibility of the witness. As well, SB 472 empowers the Supreme Court to overturn death sentences deemed "fundamentally unjust as applied to the particular case, independent of any procedural grounds for relief."

Many states prohibit the death penalty for mentally retarded defendants, and Illinois is one such state. On June 20, 2002 in *Atkins v. Virginia* the U.S. Supreme Court held that execution of an offender who is mentally retarded is a violation of the ban on cruel and unusual punishment. Prior to this court ruling, eighteen states as well as the federal government prohibited such executions. Under Bill 472, retardation is determined by the court by a preponderance of the evidence in a pre-trial hearing, with an IQ of 75 defined as "presumptive evidence" of mental retardation. The definition of mental retardation is as follows: "In determining whether the defendant is mentally retarded, the mental retardation must have manifested itself by the age of 18. IQ tests and psychometric tests administered to the defendant must be the kind and type recognized by experts in the field of mental retardation. In order for the defendant to be considered mentally retarded, a low IQ must be accompanied by significant deficits in at least 2 of the following skill areas: communication, self-care, social or interpersonal skills, home living, self-direction, academics, health and safety, use of community resources, and work. An intelligence quotient of 75 or below is presumptive evidence of mental retardation." The issue of mental retardation can also be raised post-conviction.

Finally, Bill 472 provides that there is no time-limit on petitions for hearing in trial court claims of actual innocence, though such claims must be heard within a reasonable period of time. The criteria for a hearing is whether "there is newly discovered evidence not available to the person at the time of the proceeding that establishes a substantial basis to believe that the defendant is actually innocent by clear and convincing evidence."

After the House vote on SB 472, Governor Blagojevich asserted he would continue the moratorium on executions begun under Ryan in January 2000. While this reform is a step in the right direction, arbitrary capital sentencing practices have yet to be addressed. According to the Governor's Commission on Capital Punishment, defendants are five times more likely to be sentenced to death in downstate counties, and defendants in cases with white victims are three and a half times more likely to be sentenced to death than defendants in cases with minority victims. Such arbitrariness can be seen nationwide, and though Bill 472 attempts to reform capital punishment in Illinois, discrimination in the process remains unchanged by the new law.

CASE

This case below is an original action for a writ of *mandamus*. The Illinois Attorney General filed the complaint on behalf of the people of the state of Illinois, seeking a writ of *mandamus* ordering the Director of Corrections and the wardens of Pontiac and Menard Correctional Centers to prevent the recording of certain commutation orders entered by former Governor George H. Ryan or, in the alternative, to expunge the commutation orders where they have already been entered. The petitioners' complaint contains the following allegations: On January 10, 2003, then-Governor George H. Ryan announced that he was granting "blanket clemency" for all inmates who were then, or who had been, sentenced to death. Ryan issued orders commuting the sentences of more than 160 inmates to life imprisonment, a maximum of life imprisonment, or 40 years. The petitioners challenge the validity of the commutations with respect to two distinct groups of inmates.

THE PEOPLE *ex rel.* **LISA MADIGAN, Attorney General of Illinois,** *et al.***, Petitioners, v. DONALD N. SNYDER, JR., Director of Corrections,** *et al.***, Respondents.**
Docket No. 95663-Agenda 19-September 2003.
Opinion filed January 23, 2004.

In count I of the complaint, petitioners allege that the Governor lacked the authority to commute the sentences of inmates who failed to sign or otherwise consent to their clemency petitions. Article V, section 12, of the Illinois Constitution of 1970 provides that: "The Governor may grant reprieves, commutations and pardons, after conviction, for all offenses on such terms as he thinks proper. The manner of applying therefore may be regulated by law." Pursuant to this section, the General Assembly has exercised its authority to regulate the process of application for clemency in section 3-3-13 of the Unified Code of Corrections (730 ILCS 5/3-3-13). That section provides that petitions seeking clemency "shall be in writing and signed by the person under conviction or by a person on his behalf." A clemency application cannot be commenced on behalf of a person who has been sentenced to death, unless that person has consented. The complaint listed in an appendix a group of inmates who had not authorized the filing of clemency petitions on their behalf. The statute makes an exception for inmates who are mentally or physically incapable of deciding whether to seek clemency, but none of the inmates listed in the appendix had claimed such an infirmity. Count I alleged that the legislature had regulated the procedure for applying for executive clemency and that the section imposed a clear legal duty on the Governor not to grant a commutation to any inmate who fails to sign or consent to a commutation petition and who is not otherwise excused from doing so. Accordingly, petitioners allege that the orders granting commutations to these inmates are void.

The next three counts of the complaint deal with inmates who were allegedly not under sentence when then-Governor Ryan issued the commutations. In count II, petitioners argue that the Governor lacked the authority to issue commutations to inmates not under sentence. These inmates had been under a sentence of death at one time, but their sentences had been reversed in either direct appeals or in post-conviction proceedings and they were awaiting new sentencing hearings. The complaint alleged that then-Governor Ryan had exceeded his authority in issuing a preemptive grant of commutation and had encroached on the judiciary's sentencing powers. Accordingly, petitioner argued that these commutations were void. In count III, petitioners argue that the Governor cannot commute sentences to unspecified terms. For most of the inmates referenced in count II of the complaint, the Governor used one of the following two forms of commutation orders: "Sentence Commuted to Natural Life Imprisonment Without the Possibility of Parole or Mandatory Supervised Relief; or in the alternative, Sentence Commuted to a Sentence Other Than Death for the Crime of Murder, So that the Maximum Sentence that may be Imposed is Natural Life Imprisonment Without the Possibility of Parole or Mandatory Supervised Relief." Petitioners argue that these are void orders because the Governor cannot commute sentences to unspecified terms. Count IV alleges that the Governor may not delegate his commutation power. According to the complaint, then-Governor Ryan improperly delegated his commutation powers to the judiciary by commuting sentences of the inmates listed in count II to unspecified terms.

Mandamus is an extraordinary remedy traditionally used to compel a public official to perform a ministerial duty. Generally, a writ of mandamus will be awarded only if a plaintiff establishes a clear right to relief, a clear duty of the public official to act, and a clear authority in the public official to comply with the writ. There must also be no other adequate remedy. However, even when all of the normal requirements for the writ's award are not met initially, we may still consider a petition for a writ of *mandamus* if it presents a novel issue that is of crucial importance to the administration of justice. If, in purporting to exercise his pardon or commutation power, the Governor issues a void order, *mandamus* may be used to require the officers charged with execution of the order to disregard it.

We first consider petitioners' argument that former Governor Ryan lacked the authority to commute the sentences of inmates who did not sign or otherwise consent to the filing of petitions on their behalf. For each of the inmates listed in the appendix to count I, a petition for executive clemency was filed with former Governor Ryan. However, these inmates had not signed consent forms allowing these petitions to be filed on their behalf. Petitioners' argument is straightforward. The Illinois Constitution gives the Governor the authority to "grant reprieves, commutations and pardons, after conviction, for all offenses on such terms as he thinks proper."

However, the constitution further provides that, "the manner of applying therefore may be regulated by law." Pursuant to this section, the General Assembly has exercised its authority to regulate the process of application for clemency in section 3-3-13 of the Unified Code of Corrections (730 ILCS 5/3-3-13). Section 3-3-13(c) provides, in part, that: "Application for executive clemency under this Section may not be commenced on behalf of a person who has been sentenced to death without the written consent of the defendant, unless the defendant, because of a mental or physical condition, is incapable of asserting his or her own claim." According to petitioners, this statute limits the Governor's authority to grant reprieves, pardons, or commutations to those inmates who follow the proper application procedures. We disagree.

By its plain language, article V, section 12, of the constitution merely allows the legislature to regulate the process for applying for executive clemency. It does not purport to give the legislature the power to regulate the Governor's authority to grant clemency. Further, the 1970 Illinois Constitution does not provide that the Governor's power to grant clemency is subject to the legislature's regulation of the application process, as did the 1870 constitution. Article V, section 13, of the Constitution of 1870 provided that: "The Governor shall have power to grant reprieves, commutations and pardons, after conviction, for all offenses, subject to such regulations as may be provided by law relative to the manner of applying therefor." The notable changes between the two constitutions were the addition of the phrase "on such terms as he thinks proper" and the deletion of the "subject to" language. Although petitioners might have had at least a plausible argument under the 1870 constitution, their contention must fail under the current constitution, which allows the legislature to regulate the application process but does not in any way restrict the Governor's power to act. If petitioners' position were correct, it would mean that the legislature could nullify the Governor's clemency power through legislation, simply by enacting regulations sufficiently strict to prevent any clemency petition from ever reaching the Governor. We do not believe that was the intent of the framers of the constitution.

Further, even if we assume, *arguendo*, that the legislature could restrict the Governor's commutation powers through its power to regulate the application process, the legislature did not do so. Indeed, the legislature went out of its way to ensure that no one would read its regulation of the application process as limiting the Governor's power to act. After setting forth the procedures for the filing and consideration of clemency petitions, the statute expressly provides that: "Nothing in this Section shall be construed to limit the power of the Governor under the constitution to grant a reprieve, commutation of sentence, or pardon" (730 ILCS 5/3-3-13(e)). Petitioners contend that the relevant phrase in this section is "under the constitution." The constitution allows the legislature to regulate the application process so, according to petitioners, subsection (e) means that nothing in this section limits the Governor's power to act if this section is followed. Petitioners argue that the statute would be rendered meaningless if the Governor could grant clemency even when proper procedures were not followed. This analysis is problematic for several reasons.

First, as explained above, the Governor's power under the constitution is defined by the first sentence of article V, section 12. The second sentence, allowing the legislature to regulate the application process, is not a limitation on the Governor's power. Next, subsection (e) has no meaning except as an explanation that the statute should not be construed as a limitation on the Governor's power. If petitioners' argument were correct, section 3-3-13 would indeed be a limitation on the Governor's power-a limitation petitioners claim the legislature is entitled to enact-and subsection (e) would then have no purpose. Finally, it is simply untrue that subsection (e) renders the entire section superfluous. If an inmate fails to follow the proper procedures, then the Governor does not have to consider the petition. The Prisoner Review Board does not have to accept it, does not have to schedule a hearing, and does not have to make a recommendation to the Governor.

Thus, in the typical case, an inmate who does not follow proper procedures will not get his petition before the Governor. The failure of the inmates listed in count I to consent to their petitions would have given then-Governor Ryan a basis to refuse to consider the petitions on their merits. This, however, was not the typical case. We take judicial notice of then-Governor Ryan's public statements in issuing these commutations, and it is apparent that he intended to grant blanket clemency because he believed that Illinois' death penalty system was broken. Thus, in this instance, the failure of certain inmates to consent to their petitions was irrelevant to the Governor. That does not mean, however, that section 3-3-13 does not play an important role in the clemency process. Petitioners have not shown a clear right to relief on count I of their complaint, and we deny the request for a writ of *mandamus*.

We next address the validity of former Governor Ryan's orders commuting the sentences of inmates not currently under sentence. As stated above, the inmates listed in this count of the petition had obtained sentencing relief as part of appellate or collateral proceedings and were awaiting new sentencing hearings when former Governor Ryan purported to commute their death sentences. Before proceeding with the merits of this discussion, we address a motion that we ordered taken with the case. Respondents William Bracy and Roger Collins moved this court to dismiss them from count II. Bracy and Collins argue that they were not "unsentenced" when then-Governor Ryan commuted their sentences, and thus they should be dismissed from count II. Bracy and Collins had obtained relief in federal *habeas corpus* proceedings. The Seventh Circuit upheld a district court opinion giving the Illinois courts 90 days to hold new sentencing hearings (Bracy v. Schomig, 286 F.3d 406 7th Cir. 2002). Bracy and Collins argue that their death sentences remained intact at this point because federal courts acting under 28 U.S.C. §2254 do not issue decrees that directly affect the judgments entered in state courts. Rather, a federal court issuing a writ of *habeas corpus* essentially requires the State to retry or resentence the defendant, on pain of ordering the defendant's release if the State does not comply. We agree with Bracy and Collins that they remained under sentence. A federal court considering a state prisoner's petition for a writ of *habeas corpus* does not have the authority to revise a state court judgment.

Petitioners respond that the federal court did in fact vacate the sentences. Further, petitioners contend that, once the Supreme Court denied *certiorari* in the case, Bracy and Collins could not be said to be under a sentence of death. As set forth above, however, the federal court had no authority to revise the judgments of the Illinois courts in these cases. Thus, although the district court used the term "vacate," its order could not vacate these sentences. We also deem the denial of *certiorari* by the Supreme Court to be irrelevant. Because the federal court had no authority to revise the judgment, that judgment remained intact, even if it could never be enforced. Thus, we agree with Bracy and Collins that their state court judgment of conviction and sentence was still intact when then-Governor Ryan issued his clemency orders. The motion to dismiss is granted.

We now turn to the merits of petitioners' argument. Petitioners focus on the phrase "after conviction" in article V, section 12, of the Illinois Constitution. The constitution gives the Governor the power to grant "reprieves, commutations and pardons, after conviction, for all offenses on such terms as he thinks proper." According to petitioners, the term "conviction" sometimes refers to an adjudication of guilt and sometimes refers to both an adjudication of guilt and the imposition of a sentence, depending on the context in which it is used. Petitioners contend that the use in article V, section 12, of the term "conviction" means a finding of guilt plus a sentence. In their reply brief, however, petitioners concede that with respect to the Governor's pardoning power, article V, section 12, allows the Governor to act following an adjudication of guilt. Petitioners argue that the single term "conviction" in this section means two different things: "Accordingly, in the context of the Governor's pardon power, the term 'after conviction' means after a guilty verdict, regardless of whether there is a sentence. By contrast, in the commutation power, the term 'conviction' must include an existing sentence." We cannot agree with petitioners that "conviction" means two different things in article V, section 12. Rather, we believe that the framers intended the word to have its commonly understood meaning, which is an adjudication of guilt. Throughout the Illinois Constitution, the term "conviction" is used separately from "sentence" or other terms relating to the consequences of an adjudication of guilt.

In certain instances, we have construed the term "conviction" to be a legal term of art meaning a finding of guilt and a sentence. By contrast, nothing in the language of the constitution leads us to believe that the framers meant to use a legal term of art rather than the commonly understood meaning of the term: an adjudication of guilt. We read article V, section 12, as meaning simply that the Governor may first exercise his clemency powers after a defendant is found guilty of an offense. The majority of state courts have reached the same conclusion in interpreting the phrase "after conviction" in the clemency provisions of their state constitutions.

Nevertheless, holding that the Governor may first exercise his clemency powers after a defendant is adjudicated guilty does not end our inquiry. We believe that the relevant inquiry is not so much what the phrase "after conviction" means as whether it is within the Governor's clemency powers to do what former Governor Ryan did here. In other words, does lowering the maximum possible sentence that a defendant can receive fall within the power given the Governor to "grant reprieves, commutations and pardons for all offenses on such terms as he thinks proper"? We believe that it does. The pardon power given the Governor in article V, section 12, is extremely broad. The Governor may grant reprieves, pardons, and commutations "on such terms as he thinks proper." Even before the "on such terms as he thinks proper" language was added to the constitution, this court had recognized that the Governor's clemency powers granted by the constitution "cannot be controlled by either the courts or the legislature. His acts in the exercise of the power can be controlled only by his conscience and his sense of public duty."

A pardon is "an executive action that mitigates or sets aside punishment for a crime." Further, there are several different types of pardons: "A pardon may be full or partial, absolute or conditional. A pardon is full when it freely and unconditionally absolves the person from all the legal consequences of a crime and of the person's conviction, direct and collateral, including the punishment, whether of imprisonment, pecuniary penalty, or whatever else the law has provided; it is partial where it remits only a portion of the punishment or absolves from only a portion of the legal consequences of the crime. A pardon is absolute where it frees the criminal without any condition whatsoever; and it is conditional where it does not become operative until the grantee has performed some specified act, or where it becomes void when some specified event transpires" (67A C.J.S. Pardon & Parole §2, 2002). A commutation is the change of punishment to which a person has been condemned to a less severe one. It removes a judicially imposed sentence and replaces it with a lesser, executively imposed sentence. Finally, a reprieve is "the postponement of the execution of a sentence." The power to grant reprieves and commutations is generally viewed as a subset of the Governor's pardoning power.

The only restriction this court has heretofore found on the Governor's clemency power is that he may not change a conviction for one crime into a conviction for another. There is a dearth of authority on the issue of whether a Governor can issue a "commutation" when a defendant is not currently under sentence, but the two states to address the issue have held this to be a valid exercise of the Governor's clemency power. However, these cases contain little analysis and drew forceful dissents, arguing that a commutation can only be issued if a sentence is in place. This is a difficult question with little to guide us, but we believe that the grant of authority given the Governor under article V, section 12, is sufficiently broad to allow former Governor Ryan to do what he did.

As set forth above, the Governor's clemency powers, which attach upon an adjudication of guilt, allow him to mitigate or set aside the punishment for the crime by issuing a pardon. Pardons may be full or partial, removing some or all of the legal consequences of a crime, and may be absolute or imposed with conditions. Further, the Governor can grant a reprieve for any sentence imposed and may commute any sentence imposed to a lesser sentence. In this situation, what former Governor Ryan essentially did was to grant the inmates listed in count II a partial pardon by pardoning only the possible capital consequences of the offense. As we noted, a partial pardon exonerates a defendant from some but not all of the punishment or legal consequences of a crime. The Governor's pardon power allows him to remove or mitigate the consequences of a crime, and that is what he did here by removing the maximum sentence for these defendants in future sentencing hearings. We deem it irrelevant that the Governor used the term "commutation" in his clemency orders, because we believe that it is the substance, not the terminology, of the clemency orders that controls.

We emphasize the limited nature of our holding. We hold only that the Governor's constitutional authority to issue pardons after conviction is sufficiently broad to allow him to reduce the maximum sentence the defendant is facing. In such a situation, the Governor is exercising his power to prevent or mitigate punishment by pardoning the defendant from the full extent of the punishment allowed by law.

With respect to two of the inmates listed in the exhibit to count II, Gregory Madej and Renaldo Hudson, former Governor Ryan commuted their sentences to specific terms of life imprisonment rather than to maximum terms. However, we believe that these two inmates remained under a sentence of death and thus a commutation to a specific term was appropriate. Gregory Madej had been granted relief in a federal *habeas corpus* proceeding. Thus, Madej had an existing sentence of death that was subject to commutation. Renaldo Hudson had his sentence vacated by the circuit court in a post-conviction proceeding. The court denied relief as to Hudson's conviction, but ordered a new sentencing hearing. The State appealed, and this court remanded the cause to the circuit court for an evidentiary hearing on a jury-selection issue. However, we retained jurisdiction of the cause and ordered the circuit court to file a decision within 90 days. The circuit court decided the issue adversely to Hudson, and this court ordered additional briefing on the issue. After defendant and the State had each filed an additional brief, and while the cause was still pending before this court, former Governor Ryan issued the commutation orders. Thus, the issue of whether Hudson was entitled to a new sentencing hearing had not been finally decided. We agree with Hudson that at the time the commutation orders were entered he was not awaiting a new sentencing hearing. Rather, he was still waiting for a decision from this court as to whether his sentence should be vacated and if he should receive a new sentencing hearing. Thus, we believe that former Governor Ryan had the authority to commute Hudson's sentence to life imprisonment.

We next address counts III and IV of the complaint. Petitioners argue that the clemency orders for most of the defendants listed in the exhibit to count II were invalid because they commuted to a maximum term rather than to a specific sentence. Petitioners contend that a commutation replaces a judicially imposed sentence with an executively imposed sentence, and therefore the commutation must be to a specific term. If the sentence is for a maximum term, it leaves resentencing up to the judiciary, and petitioners claim that this is an improper delegation of the commutation power. These arguments fail because, as we explained above, then-Governor Ryan's clemency orders were more in the nature of limited pardons than sentencing commutations. The orders pardoned these inmates from the most severe potential consequences of their crimes-capital punishment. Thus, there was no problem with orders that set a maximum term, and the Governor was not delegating any of his clemency powers to the judiciary. These inmates were already going to receive new sentencing hearings ordered by the judiciary. The clemency orders merely removed the most severe possible punishment from consideration at these hearings.

Finally, petitioners claim that then-Governor Ryan's clemency orders violated separation of powers principles for two reasons. First, petitioners argue that the former Governor usurped the authority of the State's Attorneys to decide what punishment to seek in these cases. Second, petitioners argue that former Governor Ryan interfered with the judiciary's sentencing powers. We perceive no separation of powers problems. First, when the State's Attorneys perform their roles as prosecutors, they are members of the executive branch of government. The separation of powers doctrine applies only to powers assigned to separate branches of government. Further, petitioners concede that, following an adjudication of guilt, the Governor can grant a defendant a complete pardon, removing from the State's Attorneys the ability to seek any punishment against the individual. Here, the Governor exercised the much lesser power of preventing them from seeking only the maximum penalty provided by law. Similarly, there is no separation of powers problem between the Governor and the judiciary.

As set forth above, following a conviction, the Governor's constitutional clemency powers allow him to completely or partially absolve a defendant of the consequences of his crime, and to suspend or commute any sentence imposed by the judiciary. Former Governor Ryan did not exercise any powers reserved to the judiciary in entering these orders, but rather exercised the clemency powers granted him by the constitution. We deny petitioners' request for a writ of *mandamus* on counts II, III, and IV. As a final matter, we note that clemency is the historic remedy employed to prevent a miscarriage of justice where the judicial process has been exhausted. We believe that this is the purpose for which the framers gave the Governor this power in the Illinois Constitution. The grant of this essentially unreviewable power carries with it the responsibility to exercise it in the manner intended. Our hope is that Governors will use the clemency power in its intended manner-to prevent miscarriages of justice in individual cases.

For all of the above reasons, the petition for a writ of *mandamus* is denied.

REVIEW SECTION

READING COMPREHENSION

Detail the counts alleged by the petitioners and the findings by this court on each count.

Elaborate the role of the Governor in granting pardon and the applicable sections of the Constitution.

THINKING CRITICALLY

Agree or disagree with the findings of this court.

SECTION 3: APPEALS AND COLLATERAL ATTACK

OVERVIEW

It has been mentioned earlier that while there is no constitutional right to appeal, every jurisdiction in the United States has created a statutory right to appeal which applies to the intermediate appellate courts and in capital cases to the supreme courts. Other appeals to the supreme courts are discretionary. Appeals are considered direct attacks because the purpose is to attack the decision made by the trial court and/or the guilt verdict.

Conversely, *habeus corpus* proceedings are termed collateral attacks because the intent is to indirectly attack the judgment in a noncriminal forum. *Habeus corpus* is a civil action used to determine if the offender is being unlawfully detained and is extremely limited. Most *habeus corpus* proceedings begin only after all direct attacks have been exhausted, and then such a proceeding starts in the U.S. District Court, followed by the U.S. Court of Appeals, and can even reach the U.S. Supreme Court for a final review.

CASE

The Circuit Court granted prisoner's *habeas corpus* petition, and ordered his release and the warden appealed. The Appellate Court held that: (1) only original sentencing court had authority to modify its sentence on underlying charge that defendant was serving at time of his escape so that it could be served in federal prison; (2) escape sentence was to be served consecutively to sentence being served at time of escape; (3) prisoner was not entitled to "good time" credit against his remaining original sentence and his escape sentence for time served in federal prison under convictions for unrelated crimes; and (4) issue of whether defendant was entitled to post-conviction relief allowing him to withdraw certain pleas was not properly before court.

THOMAS V. GREER
543 N.E.2d 340, 135 (1989)

Warden Jim Greer of Menard Correctional Center appeals from an order of the circuit court of Peoria County granting a petition by Melvin Thomas for *habeas corpus* relief and ordering that Thomas be released from custody. Thomas was originally sentenced to a term of two to six years in the Illinois Department of Corrections in 1977 by the circuit court of Knox County following his conviction for burglary and theft. In 1978, while incarcerated in the Peoria Correctional Center under the Knox County sentence, Thomas and another inmate, Roderick Choisser, kidnapped a female employee at the Center, took her car, and drove with her to Fulton County where the two men raped her in a motel. They then drove with her to Tennessee where she managed to get away from them. The two men were subsequently arrested and charged with offenses in three separate jurisdictions. It is the disposition of those several charges that gives rise to the current dispute.

Those cases were disposed of as follows: (1) Following guilty pleas, the United States District Court sentenced Thomas to 15 years imprisonment for kidnapping and five years for transportation of a stolen vehicle. Those two sentences were to be served concurrently in federal prison. (2) Defendant entered a guilty plea to a charge of rape in Fulton County circuit court and was sentenced to ten years to be served in federal prison concurrent to previous state and federal sentences. (3) Defendant pleaded guilty to aggravated kidnapping and escape in the circuit court of Peoria County, and he was sentenced to prison terms of ten years and six years, respectively, to be served in federal prison. The court provided that the kidnapping sentence was to run concurrently to all previous state and federal sentences and that the escape sentence was to run consecutively to the Knox County sentences for burglary and theft.

In January of 1987 Thomas was released from federal prison and returned to Menard where the Department of Corrections determined that his Fulton County sentence for rape and his Peoria County sentence for aggravated kidnapping had been completed in federal prison, but that he still had time to serve on the original Knox County sentence being served at the time of the escape and on the Peoria County sentence for escape. The Department of Corrections computed his earliest release date as January 25, 1990, and the latest at January 25, 1992. Thomas then filed a petition for *habeas corpus* in Peoria County which was granted, and this appeal followed.

Two provisions in section 5-8-4 of the Unified Code of Corrections applicable here, are: "(a) When multiple sentences of imprisonment are imposed on a defendant at the same time, or when a term of imprisonment is imposed on a defendant who is already subject to sentence in this State or in another state, or for a sentence imposed by any district court of the United States, the sentences shall run concurrently or consecutively as determined by the court. When a term of imprisonment is imposed on a defendant by an Illinois circuit court and the defendant is subsequently sentenced to a term of imprisonment by another state or by a district court of the United States, the Illinois circuit court which imposed the sentence may order that the Illinois sentence be made concurrent with the sentence imposed by the other state or district court of the United States. The defendant must apply to the circuit court within 30 days after the defendant's sentence imposed by the other state or district of the United States is finalized." "(g) A sentence for escape shall be served consecutive to the terms under which the offender is held by the Department of Corrections."

Another relevant provision of the Unified Code of Corrections is in section 5-8-1: "If a defendant who has a previous and unexpired sentence of imprisonment imposed by an Illinois circuit court for a crime in this State and who is subsequently sentenced to a term of imprisonment by another state or by any district court of the United States, and must return to serve the unexpired prior sentence imposed by the Illinois Circuit Court may apply to the court which imposed sentence to have his sentence reduced. The circuit court may order that any time served on the sentence imposed by the other state or district court of the United States be credited on his Illinois sentence. Such application for reduction of a sentence under this subsection (f) shall be made within 30 days after the defendant has completed the sentence imposed by the other state or district court of the United States."

The circuit court of Peoria County found that the two to six year sentence imposed by the Knox County court, which Thomas was serving at the time of his escape, was completed in federal prison and that six year sentence for escape was also served in federal prison after the completion of the Knox County sentence. Defendant Jim Greer contends on appeal that those findings were erroneous as a matter of law, and we agree.

There is no dispute that both the Fulton County sentence for rape and the Peoria County sentence for aggravated kidnapping were served in federal prison concurrently with Thomas' federal sentence for kidnapping. The sentencing courts expressly provided for such sentences to be served in federal prison, and the courts had authority to make such orders under section 5-8-4(a) of the Unified Code of Corrections quoted above. However, it is plain that the Illinois statutes provide that, where a subsequent sentence is imposed for escape, only the original sentencing court (here, Knox County) has the authority to modify its sentence on the underlying charge so that it could be served in federal prison. The offender has two 30-day periods within which he can seek to have the court where he was originally sentenced order a modification of that sentence and thereby reduce his total time in prison. First, under section 5-8-4(a) of the Unified Code of Corrections, the offender can make such application within 30 days after the United States district court sentence is finalized. Nothing in the record on appeal indicates that Thomas applied in 1978 to Knox County circuit court to have the remainder of his interrupted burglary and theft sentences ordered to be concurrent to the federal sentence as the statute permits.

Second, under section 5-8-1(f) the offender can apply to the court which imposed the original sentence to have the sentence reduced within 30 days after completing the sentence imposed by the district court of the United States. Although nothing in the record before this court indicates that Thomas made such application to Knox County circuit court, we nevertheless take judicial notice of a decision of the Illinois Supreme Court filed on January 18, 1989, indicating that in fact such application was made by Thomas after he was released from federal prison. The Knox County court denied the motion for modification of sentence on the ground that the statute was unconstitutional. Upon direct appeal, the Supreme Court held that the statute was constitutional and remanded the cause to Knox County for a consideration of the merits of the motion. No issue concerning the Knox County proceeding is presented by this appeal.

We conclude that the order of the Peoria County court purporting to modify the Knox County sentence was void as a matter of law. The statute mandates that the escape sentence must be consecutive to the sentence being served at the time of the escape. As this court has previously said: "The legislature apparently wanted to insure that inmates, by receiving consecutive sentences for offenses committed while in prison, could not, in effect, go unpunished for them" (People v. Murphy (3d Dist.1986), 147 Ill.App.3d 122, 126, 100 Ill.Dec. 693, 695-96, 497 N.E.2d 871, 873-74). Both the remainder of the Knox County sentence and the escape sentence are yet to be served.

The dissenting opinion asserts that the statutory provisions requiring defendant to apply to the original sentencing court for sentencing credit within two 30-day periods do not control here where the subsequent sentence in question was imposed by an Illinois court, not another state or federal court. This rationale is erroneous. The question on appeal is whether the Knox County sentence could be served concurrently with the federal sentence by order of the Peoria County circuit court. As between the federal district court and the Knox County circuit court, the federal court could have ordered its sentence to be served concurrent to the Knox county sentence under section 5-8-4(a) or the Knox County court could have ordered credit against its sentence for time served on the federal sentence under either section 5-8-4(a) or section 5-8-1(f). Neither of these courts entered such an order. The Peoria County circuit court had authority to order the sentences for crimes within its jurisdiction to be served concurrently with the federal and state sentences with one exception: the Peoria court was required by statute to order the escape sentence to be served consecutively to the Knox County sentence. This statutory limitation on the discretion of the sentencing court cannot be ignored. Contrary to the dissenting position, we do not believe the Peoria County court's imposition of a sentence for escape had the effect of merging the Knox County sentence into the subsequent Peoria County escape sentence for the purpose of modifying, and in effect nullifying, the Knox County sentence.

Thomas asserts as an alternative ground for upholding the ruling of the Peoria County court that he has completed all his sentences. He claims that he is entitled to a day-for-day "good time" credit for the years served in federal prison, thereby fulfilling his six year escape sentence. The statute authorizing "good time" credit provides that the offender shall be given credit on the sentence for the time spent in custody as a result of the offense for which the sentence was imposed. This provision has been interpreted by this court to mean that the offender is not entitled to statutory credit for time served under an unrelated conviction. We hold that Thomas is not entitled to statutory credit against his remaining Knox County sentences and his escape sentence for the time served in federal prison under convictions for unrelated crimes. Finally, Thomas asks that he be allowed to withdraw his 1978 guilty plea entered in the Peoria County circuit court since he entered that plea pursuant to an agreement by which he understood that he would serve the remainder of his Knox County sentence and the escape sentence in federal prison concurrently with the federal sentence. Thomas included this request for Post Conviction Relief as a part of his petition for *Habeas Corpus* Relief, but so far as we can determine, this issue was not argued or decided in the circuit court. Accordingly, the question of Post Conviction Relief is not properly before this court.

For the reasons set forth, we reverse the order of the circuit court of Peoria County releasing Melvin Thomas, and we remand with directions that Thomas be ordered to return to the Illinois Department of Corrections to complete his sentences in conformity with this opinion.

Justice STOUDER dissenting. I respectfully dissent from the decision reached by the majority in this case. The majority's misunderstanding of the application to this case of sections 5-8-1(f) and 5-8-4(a) of the Unified Code of Corrections have led to its erroneous conclusion that *habeas corpus* relief was improperly granted to the plaintiff. There is no dispute in this case that the escape sentence was mandatorily consecutive to the original Knox County sentence. Nor is there any dispute that the aggregation rule applies to the consecutive escape and original Knox County sentences to make a single sentence of 8 to 12 years imprisonment. There is, however, a question as to whether the court which rendered the escape sentence, the circuit court of Peoria County, has the authority to decide whether the aggregated sentence will be served concurrently or consecutively to the federal sentence. The majority concludes that only the original sentencing court (the circuit court of Knox County) has authority to make such a decision. The legislature, however, has concluded otherwise.

The Code provides that "when a term of imprisonment is imposed on a defendant who is already subject to sentence in this State or in another state, or for a sentence imposed by any district court of the United States, the sentences shall run concurrently or consecutively as determined by the court" (Ill.Rev.Stat.1987, ch. 38, par. 1005-8-4a). Thus, because the circuit court of Peoria County imposed a sentence on Thomas, who was subject to other Illinois and federal sentences, it, and not the original sentencing court, was authorized to determine whether the aggregated sentence would run concurrently or consecutively with the federal sentence. As the majority notes, there is a requirement in sections 5-8-1(f) and 5-8-4(a) of the Code that a defendant apply within two different 30 day periods to the original sentencing court for sentencing credit. However, that requirement applies only where the subsequent sentence is imposed on a defendant by a court of another state or a federal district court. Here, the subsequent sentence at issue was imposed by an Illinois court. Thus, the 30 day rule does not apply.

Therefore, because the circuit court of Peoria County had the authority to and did determine that the aggregated sentence would run concurrently with the federal sentence, and because the aggregated sentence expired during Thomas' sentence of imprisonment in federal court, the circuit court was correct in granting Thomas *habeas corpus* relief. Accordingly, its judgment should be affirmed.

REVIEW SECTION

READING COMPREHENSION

Detail the facts of this case and the relevant sections from the Unified Code of Corrections.

CONCLUSION

This chapter should have illustrated that after the conviction phase, rights of offenders are much more limited than prior to conviction. While states have provided the right to appeal, there is no constitutional right as such. A review of sentencing, death sentences, and appeals and collateral attack should have provided an in-depth examination of proceedings after conviction.

Chapter Fifteen

Criminal Procedure in Crisis Times

During times of emergency, such as war, there is a recalibration of the balance between government power and individual liberties with the result being an expansion of governmental power. Because this occurs at the federal level, application at the state level is weak at best, therefore analysis in this final chapter will be primarily federal in nature. Such emergency extension of power is permitted when and to the extent it is necessary and must be temporary in nature.

This chapter will review:

(1)   Balancing rights and security during emergencies; and

(2)   Terrorist trials by military courts after 9/11.

SECTION 1: BALANCING RIGHTS AND SECURITY DURING EMERGENCIES

OVERVIEW

According to the website of the Illinois Homeland Security, the purpose of the Illinois Terrorism Task Force, created May 2000, is to "implement a comprehensive coordinated strategy for domestic preparedness in the state of Illinois, bringing together agencies, organizations and associations representing all disciplines in the war against terrorism. The purpose of the Task Force was to further Illinois' disaster preparation efforts to specifically address the State's role in Weapons of Mass Destruction (WMD) preparedness and to coordinate the response to WMD events throughout the State, utilizing expertise at local, state, and federal levels and across different disciplines. The Task Force focuses on issues such as providing quick response capability in every region of the State and basic WMD first responder training statewide."

In an attempt to improve homeland security, during Governor Ryan's tenure, in concert with the General Assembly, at least 1,840 separate public safety projects totaling over $182 million were conducted. Agencies included are the Illinois Emergency Management Agency, the State Police, Department of Public Health, Illinois National Guard, the Office of the State Fire Marshal, Illinois Environmental Protection Agency, and the Department of Nuclear Safety. Most projects are in response to the recognition that regardless of where a terrorist attack or natural disaster occur, local first responders must be as prepared as possible. Illinois as a state has passed nearly 80 percent of federal terrorism funds to local governments for the improvement of firefighters, sheriffs and police, and emergency response in an attempt to accomplish this goal. In addition, the Illinois General Assembly recently overrode a veto by Governor George Ryan, enacting a new law (HB 2058) that makes terrorism a death penalty offense. The bill gives police additional power to obtain search warrants and conduct surveillance on suspected terrorists, makes it a felony to take a firearm on an airplane, and allows the attorney general to freeze the assets of terrorists.

SECTION 2: TERRORIST TRIALS BY MILITARY COURTS AFTER 9/11

OVERVIEW

Individuals who are suspected of committing terrorist acts can be tried in Article III courts or for war crimes in special military courts. Trials that occur in Article III courts follow all the same procedures discussed in chapters ten through fourteen. In military courts however, there are relaxed rules of procedure and proof, as well as diminished rights for the defendants. The President can establish a military commission, which is a panel of military officers that act under military authority to try war crimes, under three sources of authority: Article II, Section 2 of the U.S. Constitution which makes him commander in chief of the armed forces; Article II, Section 2 of the U.S. Constitution which gives the President the power to ensure laws are executed; and the joint resolution which gives the President the power to use all necessary force against persons considered terrorists. Keep in mind that the power of the military commission extends only to noncitizens who do not benefit from the same constitutional rights as American citizens, even if the individual is in the U.S. legally. Further, such individuals are removed from the jurisdiction of all courts in and outside the U.S. Finally, no constitutional provisions apply which means the defendant has no right to a speedy trial, no right to trial by jury, no right to counsel, no right to remain silent, and there exists no requirement of proof beyond a reasonable doubt. If found guilty by the military commission panel, any sentence, including that of death, may be imposed.

In November 2001, President Bush declared an emergency in response to 9/11 which empowered him to order military trials for any individual suspected of being or collaborating with a terrorist. This results in the bypass of the American criminal justice system and all the rules of evidence and constitutional guarantees that we have discussed throughout this text. There is no judicial review and the President himself decides which defendants will face such trials. While this measure is unusual, it is not unprecedented and occurred under President Franklin D. Roosevelt during World War II. Under Roosevelt, eight suspected Nazis were tried by military commission and executed while the U.S. Supreme Court maintained that the trial was unconstitutional. The rationale used to support such commissions is "the interest of national security." An important sidenote is that some scholars and activists favor creation of international tribunals under the authority of the United Nations which would not authorize the death penalty.

CASE

In *Al-Marri v Bush,* Ali Saleh Kahlah al-Marri's ("al-Marri") files a petition for writ of *habeas corpus* pursuant to 28 U.S.C. § 2241. The government files a motion to dismiss.

AL-MARRI V. BUSH
Case No. 03-1220 (C.D. Ill. 8/1/2003) (C.D. Ill., 2003)

Al-Marri is a Qatari national who legally entered the United States on September 10, 2001, with his wife and children. He had previously obtained a bachelor's degree from Bradley University in Peoria, Illinois, in the early 1990s, and was returning to the United States to obtain a master's degree from Bradley. On December 12, 2001, al-Marri was arrested by FBI agents in Peoria at the direction of the U.S. Attorney's Office for the Southern District of New York as a material witness in the investigation of the September 11, 2001, terrorist attacks. He was then transferred to New York City. Al-Marri was formally arrested on a criminal complaint charging him with credit card fraud on January 28, 2002. On February 6, 2002, he was indicted and charged with possession of 15 or more unauthorized or counterfeit access devices with intent to defraud in the United States District Court for the Southern District of New York. He pled not guilty, and the case followed the normal course of litigation. On January 22, 2003, al-Marri was charged in a second indictment with two counts of making a false statement to the FBI, three counts of making a false statement in a bank application, and one count of using a means of identification of another person for purposes of influencing the action of a federally insured financial institution. He also entered a plea of not guilty to the second indictment and succeeded in having the two indictments consolidated.

Al-Marri initially waived any objection to venue in the Southern District of New York, but later withdrew his waiver after obtaining new counsel. He then moved to dismiss the indictments on grounds of improper venue. On May 12, 2003, al-Marri's motion was granted and the indictments were dismissed for improper venue. However, a new criminal complaint had been filed under seal in this district on May 1, 2003, and al-Marri was arraigned on that complaint on May 13, 2003. He was then transferred back to Peoria, where a grand jury indicted him on the same counts that had been charged in the two indictments in the Southern District of New York. Al-Marri was arraigned and a pretrial conference was set for July 2, 2003, with a jury trial to begin on July 21, 2003.

On June 23, 2003, President Bush designated al-Marri as an enemy combatant and directed that he be transferred to the control of the Defense Department for detention. That same morning, the U.S. Attorney's Office moved to dismiss the indictment with prejudice, and the motion was granted. Al-Marri's counsel then requested that the Court stay the case to prevent any attempt to transfer him from the jurisdiction until he could file a *habeas* petition. However, the Court determined that as the case had been dismissed with prejudice, it lacked jurisdiction to issue any type of a stay. The Court did obtain the U.S. Attorney's agreement to inform counsel of the location to which al-Marri was to be moved, and counsel has been so advised. The U.S. Attorney also agreed to provide both the Court and al-Marri's counsel with advance notice if al-Marri was going to be moved to any location outside of the United States so that counsel could seek an emergency injunction in the appropriate court. Al-Marri was then immediately transferred into military custody and transported to the Naval Consolidated Brig in Charleston, South Carolina, where he continues to be held.

On July 8, 2003, al-Marri's counsel filed the present § 2241 Petition on his behalf, as it is undisputed that al-Marri is unavailable to sign it for himself. In response, the Government moved to either dismiss or transfer the Petition to the District of South Carolina, raising essentially three arguments: (1) the Petition has not been properly brought on al-Marri's behalf; (2) no proper respondent with custody over al-Marri is present within this Court's territorial jurisdiction; and (3) venue over the action appropriately lies in South Carolina, where he is detained. On July 28, 2003, the Court held oral arguments, and this Order follows.

A petition seeking *habeas corpus* relief is appropriate under 28 U.S.C. § 2241 when a defendant is challenging the fact or duration of his confinement. The writ of *habeas corpus* may be granted where the defendant is in custody in violation of the Constitution or laws or treaties of the United States. 28 U.S.C. § 2241(c)(3). Al-Marri's ability to pursue relief pursuant to § 2241 is essentially undisputed. What is disputed is the forum in which he should pursue such relief. Section 2243 provides that any writ of *habeas corpus* that shall issue "shall be directed to the person having custody of the person detained" and that person "shall be required to produce at the hearing the body of the person detained." Moreover, it is generally established that the proper respondent in a *habeas* petition is the detainee's immediate custodian. The only noted exception to this rule involved limited circumstances where the prisoner was being held abroad and there was no domestic forum where the prisoner's custodian was present or where the prisoner was being held at an undisclosed location, neither of which apply in the present case. From this, the Government argues that the Court should not entertain the Petition, as it must be brought in South Carolina, where Commander Marr, al-Marri's day-to-day custodian, is located.

Al-Marri cites <u>Braden v. 30th Judicial Circuit Court of Kentucky, 410 U.S. 484, 93 S.Ct. 1123 (1973)</u>, for the proposition that a federal district court has the power to consider a detainee's §2241 petition so long as the court's process can reach the named respondents. In Braden, the Supreme Court took a step back from <u>Ahrens v. Clark, 335 U.S. 188, 68 S.Ct. 1443 (1973)</u>, which suggested that the prisoner's presence within the territorial confines of the district was an invariable prerequisite to the exercise of a district court's *habeas* jurisdiction. Ahrens involved *habeas* petitions filed by 120 German nationals confined at Ellis Island, New York, pending deportation in which they argued that the statutory removal orders issued by the INS exceeded the President's authority under the Alien Enemy Act of 1789. The petitions were filed in the District Court for the District of Columbia, naming the Attorney General as the respondent. The Supreme Court found that the words "within their respective jurisdictions" in the *habeas corpus* statute limited district court jurisdiction to inquiries into cases brought by those confined or restrained within the territorial jurisdiction of each court.

In distancing itself from Ahrens' inflexible rule, the Supreme Court noted developments in the law since Ahrens was decided and criticized a construction that dictated the choice of an inconvenient forum even if the type of case at issue could not have been foreseen at the time of the decision. Nevertheless, while the Supreme Court did indicate that "so long as the custodian can be reached by service of process, the court can issue a writ within its jurisdiction," it later deferred to traditional principles of venue in noting "of course, in many instances the district in which petitioners are held will be the most convenient forum for the litigation of their claims" and based its finding in part on the fact that the respondent had been properly served in the district in which the petition was filed. Initially, the Court notes that this case presents a quite different procedural posture from Braden, in which a petitioner confined in Alabama was allowed to proceed with a *habeas corpus* petition in Kentucky that challenged his right to a speedy trial on a Kentucky charge after the Court found that the matter centered around a detainer lodged by the state of Kentucky and that the respondent had been properly served in the Western District of Kentucky.

Here, al-Marri is not attacking a detainer lodged by an Illinois court while he is incarcerated in South Carolina or otherwise attacking a form of legal custody that is separate and distinct from his present physical custody. In fact, the Central District of Illinois has no real relationship to his present confinement other than the fact that he was physically present in this District prior to his arrest and at the time that he was taken into military custody after having been declared an enemy combatant. His family is no longer in this District or even in the United States, and his lead counsel that have established a relationship with him through months of representation are located in Newark, New Jersey. His involvement as a criminal defendant in this Court ceased with the dismissal of all charges against him prior to his transfer into military custody, and the fact that he had been a defendant in this Court prior to the time that he was removed from the district is only tangentially related to the circumstances of his present confinement in military custody. There is likewise no indication that any respondent is physically present within or has been served in the Central District of Illinois, and neither Braden nor any Seventh Circuit case known to the Court has addressed or specifically authorized the use of a state's long-arm statute to obtain service as a means of establishing venue in a § 2241 action where the petitioner is confined in another state.

Subsequent to the Supreme Court's decision in Braden, the Seventh Circuit has held that "the only court with jurisdiction is the federal district court where the movant is imprisoned" (United States v. Mittelsteadt, 790 F.2d 39, 40 7th Cir. 1986). In fact, the Seventh Circuit even cited Braden in its subsequent finding that "if a prisoner wants out . . . the proper venue for the *habeas corpus* proceeding is the district where the movant is being held." After finding that no custodian was within the district court's territorial limits when the petition was filed, the Court of Appeals concluded that the district court lacked habeas jurisdiction.

Under Braden's expanded view of *habeas* jurisdiction, traditional venue doctrines remain fully applicable, as even in rejecting the inflexible jurisdictional rule of Ahrens, the Supreme Court nevertheless reaffirmed the result in that case as the proper product of traditional principles of venue. Here, there is no secret as to where al-Marri is being held or that he is being held in military custody in Charleston, South Carolina, which is within the continental United States. He no longer has substantial ties to the Central District of Illinois, as his family is believed to have left the country, and his lead counsel are located in New Jersey. Under these circumstances, the question then becomes whether there is anything about this case that compels the Court to depart from the general rule and allow the petition to be entertained in a district where neither the petitioner, nor his family, nor lead counsel, nor any Respondent is located. Somewhat regretfully, the Court must conclude that the answer is no.

Al-Marri resists transfer to the District of South Carolina, where he asserts that "it appears, meaningful relief will almost certainly be foreclosed." However, the fact that the Fourth Circuit has denied relief in the case of another petitioner that has been designated as an enemy combatant really has no bearing on the question of venue in this case and presumes without any appreciable basis therefore that the Fourth Circuit would not give al-Marri's petition independent consideration. Whether the law of another forum may be more or less favorable cannot be determinative of venue, or the *habeas* inquiry would be reduced to little more than forum shopping for a better outcome.

Al-Marri argues that his choice of forum "must be accorded substantial deference." While the Court would generally agree with that assertion if this were a routine civil case, this is a *habeas corpus* proceeding, and it is axiomatic that not all general principles of civil law apply, for obvious reasons. Al-Marri has not provided, and the Court is otherwise unaware of, any support for the extension of this concept to the realm of *habeas corpus* proceedings as justification for defeating well-established principles of venue in *habeas* cases compelling another result. Al-Marri attempts to persuade the Court to follow the reasoning of Padilla v. Rumsfeld, 233 F. Supp.2d 564 (S.D.N.Y. 2002), in which the district court heard the petition in New York and declined to transfer the case to South Carolina, where Padilla was being confined. However, this portion of the non-binding opinion in Padilla is extremely brief and can be readily distinguished on several bases, not the least of which is the fact that Padilla's counsel, who had been working to obtain his release prior to his transfer to South Carolina, were located in New York. It is clear from the opinion that the district judge in that case considered this to be a key fact, as he stated that "the convenience of counsel is served by keeping the case here" and reiterated that "considerations of convenience and practicality . . . are served by keeping the case here." Here, the counsel with whom al-Marri has an established relationship are located in New Jersey, and it is presumably just as convenient, if not more so, for them to travel to South Carolina.

Al-Marri also contends that the material events charged in the indictment which led to his designation by President Bush as an enemy combatant took place in this district and that records/witnesses pertinent to the claim are likely to be found here. However, this is primarily speculation. Although it appears that al-Marri resided in Peoria for a substantial part of the time that he was in this country, there was a lengthy period of time between the time he obtained his bachelor's degree and his return on September 10, 2001, when he was not in the United States. The Court has no basis for determining whether the facts upon which he has been designated an enemy combatant center upon conduct that al-Marri allegedly engaged in while inside or outside of the country, or both. Although the Court's inability to make this determination is attributable to the fact that the Government has not divulged the specific details underlying the decision to designate him as an enemy combatant, this does not entitle al-Marri to the inference he asks the Court to draw.

After careful review and scrupulous consideration, the Court concludes that there is nothing about this situation or the relief al-Marri requests that causes the Court to deviate from traditional principles of venue in *habeas* cases. This is not a situation where the petitioner's whereabouts are unknown or where he is being held outside the confines of the United States. Al-Marri is being held in the naval brig in Charleston, South Carolina. There is a district court there. His immediate custodian is there, and the Court has been assured by the Assistant Solicitor General of the United States and the U.S. Attorney for this district that Commander Marr would obey any court order directed to her for execution. Nor is there anything about al-Marri's claims or relief sought that compels venue in the Central District of Illinois. His argument that he is being held unconstitutionally centers on his confinement in South Carolina. His request for a declaration that the President's designation of him as an enemy combatant and the Military Order of

November 13, 2001, are invalid and void involves a challenge to actions taken in the District of Columbia, does nothing to tie venue to this district, and can be addressed just as easily in South Carolina. Any order directing Secretary Rumsfeld to release him from custody or prohibiting his removal from the United States would be implemented in either the District of Columbia or South Carolina, as he is not in custody in the Central District of Illinois.

Despite the fact that none of the relief sought in al-Marri's Petition is directly related to this district, he maintains that he is entitled to seek relief here because the Government's actions in removing him from this district were unseemly. With all due respect, whether his removal from this district was or was not unseemly is not an issue for this Court to resolve. While the Court fully understands why he would like to have his Petition heard in a circuit that has not yet addressed a challenge to the detention of an individual designated as an enemy combatant, al-Marri's hope for a more favorable result in the Seventh Circuit is not enough to justify an exception that *habeas* cases should be brought in the district of confinement. After applying traditional principles of venue in *habeas* cases, the Court concludes that the Central District of Illinois is not the proper venue for this action, and the merits of al-Marri's Petition should not be entertained in this district.

After announcing this conclusion during oral argument on July 28, 2003, the Court asked counsel for al-Marri whether they would prefer to have the Petition dismissed without prejudice in order to facilitate an immediate appeal or have the Petition transferred to the District of South Carolina. As counsel has now informed the Court that they prefer dismissal, the Court finds that al-Marri's petition shall be dismissed without prejudice.

REVIEW SECTION

READING COMPREHENSION

Detail the facts of this case and the relevance of a *habeas corpus* petition and the importance of venue.

CONCLUSION

This chapter elaborated the balancing of rights that may result during times of emergency, and what has resulted since 9/11. In such a period, there is a temporary recalibration between government power and individual liberties with the result being an expansion of governmental power, especially for noncitizens. Most of this occurs at the federal level, making application at the state level weak. As noted in the text, criminal procedure during crisis times has yet to be tested in the U.S. courts, and this is especially prevalent at the state level, as evidenced by the somewhat tangential case elaborated in this chapter.

CONSTITUTION OF THE STATE OF ILLINOIS

PREAMBLE

We, the People of the State of Illinois - grateful to Almighty God for the civil, political and religious liberty which He has permitted us to enjoy and seeking His blessing upon our endeavors - in order to provide for the health, safety and welfare of the people; maintain a representative and orderly government; eliminate poverty and inequality; assure legal, social and economic justice; provide opportunity for the fullest development of the individual; insure domestic tranquility; provide for the common defense; and secure the blessings of freedom and liberty to ourselves and our posterity - do ordain and establish this Constitution for the State of Illinois. (Source: Illinois Constitution.)

ARTICLE I

BILL OF RIGHTS

SECTION 1. INHERENT AND INALIENABLE RIGHTS. All men are by nature free and independent and have certain inherent and inalienable rights among which are life, liberty and the pursuit of happiness. To secure these rights and the protection of property, governments are instituted among men, deriving their just powers from the consent of the governed.
(Source: Illinois Constitution.)

SECTION 2. DUE PROCESS AND EQUAL PROTECTION. No person shall be deprived of life, liberty or property without due process of law nor be denied the equal protection of the laws.
(Source: Illinois Constitution.)

SECTION 3. RELIGIOUS FREEDOM. The free exercise and enjoyment of religious profession and worship, without discrimination, shall forever be guaranteed, and no person shall be denied any civil or political right, privilege or capacity, on account of his religious opinions; but the liberty of conscience hereby secured shall not be construed to dispense with oaths or affirmations, excuse acts of licentiousness, or justify practices inconsistent with the peace or safety of the State. No person shall be required to attend or support any ministry or place of worship against his consent, nor shall any preference be given by law to any religious denomination or mode of worship.
(Source: Illinois Constitution.)

SECTION 4. FREEDOM OF SPEECH. All persons may speak, write and publish freely, being responsible for the abuse of that liberty. In trials for libel, both civil and criminal, the truth, when published with good motives and for justifiable ends, shall be a sufficient defense.
(Source: Illinois Constitution.)

SECTION 5. RIGHT TO ASSEMBLE AND PETITION. The people have the right to assemble in a peaceable manner, to consult for the common good, to make known their opinions to their representatives and to apply for redress of grievances.
(Source: Illinois Constitution.)

SECTION 6. SEARCHES, SEIZURES, PRIVACY AND INTERCEPTIONS. The people shall have the right to be secure in their persons, houses, papers and other possessions against unreasonable searches, seizures, invasions of privacy or interceptions of communications by eavesdropping devices or other means. No warrant shall issue without probable cause, supported by affidavit particularly describing the place to be searched and the persons or things to be seized.
(Source: Illinois Constitution.)

SECTION 7. INDICTMENT AND PRELIMINARY HEARING. No person shall be held to answer for a criminal offense unless on indictment of a grand jury, except in cases in which the punishment is by fine or by imprisonment other than in the penitentiary, in cases of impeachment, and in cases arising in the militia when in actual service in time of war or public danger. The General Assembly by law may abolish the grand jury or further limit its use. No person shall be held to answer for a crime punishable by death or by imprisonment in the penitentiary unless either the initial charge has been brought by indictment of a grand jury or the person has been given a prompt preliminary hearing to establish probable cause.
(Source: Illinois Constitution.)

SECTION 8. RIGHTS AFTER INDICTMENT. In criminal prosecutions, the accused shall have the right to appear and defend in person and by counsel; to demand the nature and cause of the accusation and have a copy thereof; to be confronted with the witnesses against him or her and to have process to compel the attendance of witnesses in his or her behalf; and to have a speedy public trial by an impartial jury of the county in which the offense is alleged to have been committed.
(Source: Amendment adopted at general election November 8, 1994.)

SECTION 8.1. CRIME VICTIM'S RIGHTS. (a) Crime victims, as defined by law, shall have the following rights as provided by law: (1) The right to be treated with fairness and respect for their dignity and privacy throughout the criminal justice process. (2) The right to notification of court proceedings. (3) The right to communicate with the prosecution. (4) The right to make a statement to the court at sentencing. (5) The right to information about the conviction, sentence, imprisonment, and release of the accused. (6) The right to timely disposition of the case following the arrest of the accused. (7) The right to be reasonably protected from the accused throughout the criminal justice process. (8) The right to be present at the trial and all other court proceedings on the same basis as the accused, unless the victim is to testify and the court determines that the victim's testimony would be materially affected if the victim hears other testimony at the trial. (9) The right to have present at all court proceedings, subject to the rules of evidence, an advocate or other support person of the victim's choice. (10) The right to restitution. (b) The General Assembly may provide by law for the enforcement of this Section. (c) The General Assembly may provide for an assessment against convicted defendants to pay for crime victims' rights. (d) Nothing in this Section or in any law enacted

under this Section shall be construed as creating a basis for vacating a conviction or a ground for appellate relief in any criminal case.
(Source: Amendment adopted at general election November 3, 1992.)

SECTION 9. BAIL AND HABEAS CORPUS. All persons shall be bailable by sufficient sureties, except for the following offenses where the proof is evident or the presumption great: capital offenses; offenses for which a sentence of life imprisonment may be imposed as a consequence of conviction; and felony offenses for which a sentence of imprisonment, without conditional and revocable release, shall be imposed by law as a consequence of conviction, when the court, after a hearing, determines that release of the offender would pose a real and present threat to the physical safety of any person. The privilege of the writ of habeas corpus shall not be suspended except in cases of rebellion or invasion when the public safety may require it. Any costs accruing to a unit of local government as a result of the denial of bail pursuant to the 1986 Amendment to this Section shall be reimbursed by the State to the unit of local government.
(Source: Amendment adopted at general election November 4, 1986.)

SECTION 10. SELF-INCRIMINATION AND DOUBLE JEOPARDY. No person shall be compelled in a criminal case to give evidence against himself nor be twice put in jeopardy for the same offense.
(Source: Illinois Constitution.)

SECTION 11. LIMITATION OF PENALTIES AFTER CONVICTION. All penalties shall be determined both according to the seriousness of the offense and with the objective of restoring the offender to useful citizenship. No conviction shall work corruption of blood or forfeiture of estate. No person shall be transported out of the State for an offense committed within the State.
(Source: Illinois Constitution.)

SECTION 12. RIGHT TO REMEDY AND JUSTICE. Every person shall find a certain remedy in the laws for all injuries and wrongs which he receives to his person, privacy, property or reputation. He shall obtain justice by law, freely, completely, and promptly.
(Source: Illinois Constitution.)

SECTION 13. TRIAL BY JURY. The right of trial by jury as heretofore enjoyed shall remain inviolate.
(Source: Illinois Constitution.)

SECTION 14. IMPRISONMENT FOR DEBT. No person shall be imprisoned for debt unless he refuses to deliver up his estate for the benefit of his creditors as provided by law or unless there is a strong presumption of fraud. No person shall be imprisoned for failure to pay a fine in a criminal case unless he has been afforded adequate time to make payment, in installments if necessary, and has willfully failed to make payment.
(Source: Illinois Constitution.)

SECTION 15. RIGHT OF EMINENT DOMAIN. Private property shall not be taken or damaged for public use without just compensation as provided by law. Such compensation shall be determined by a jury as provided by law.
(Source: Illinois Constitution.)

SECTION 16. EX POST FACTO LAWS AND IMPAIRING CONTRACTS. No ex post facto law, or law impairing the obligation of contracts or making an irrevocable grant of special privileges or immunities, shall be passed.
(Source: Illinois Constitution.)

SECTION 17. NO DISCRIMINATION IN EMPLOYMENT AND THE SALE OR RENTAL OF PROPERTY. All persons shall have the right to be free from discrimination on the basis of race, color, creed, national ancestry and sex in the hiring and promotion practices of any employer or in the sale or rental of property. These rights are enforceable without action by the General Assembly, but the General Assembly by law may establish reasonable exemptions relating to these rights and provide additional remedies for their violation.
(Source: Illinois Constitution.)

SECTION 18. NO DISCRIMINATION ON THE BASIS OF SEX. The equal protection of the laws shall not be denied or abridged on account of sex by the State or its units of local government and school districts.
(Source: Illinois Constitution.)

SECTION 19. NO DISCRIMINATION AGAINST THE HANDICAPPED. All persons with a physical or mental handicap shall be free from discrimination in the sale or rental of property and shall be free from discrimination unrelated to ability in the hiring and promotion practices of any employer.
(Source: Illinois Constitution.)

SECTION 20. INDIVIDUAL DIGNITY. To promote individual dignity, communications that portray criminality, depravity or lack of virtue in, or that incite violence, hatred, abuse or hostility toward, a person or group of persons by reason of or by reference to religious, racial, ethnic, national or regional affiliation are condemned.
(Source: Illinois Constitution.)

SECTION 21. QUARTERING OF SOLDIERS. No soldier in time of peace shall be quartered in a house without the consent of the owner; nor in time of war except as provided by law.
(Source: Illinois Constitution.)

SECTION 22. RIGHT TO ARMS. Subject only to the police power, the right of the individual citizen to keep and bear arms shall not be infringed.
(Source: Illinois Constitution.)

SECTION 23. FUNDAMENTAL PRINCIPLES. A frequent recurrence to the fundamental principles of civil government is necessary to preserve the blessings of liberty. These blessings cannot endure unless the people recognize their corresponding individual obligations and responsibilities.
(Source: Illinois Constitution.)

SECTION 24. RIGHTS RETAINED. The enumeration in this Constitution of certain rights shall not be construed to deny or disparage others retained by the individual citizens of the State.
(Source: Illinois Constitution.)